"In Worcester, Massachusetts"
Essays on Elizabeth Bishop

Elizabeth Bishop's grandparents' house in Worcester, Massachusetts, where she lived 1917-1918, now the site of Our Lady of the Angels Church. Photo courtesy of Special Collections, Vassar College Libraries.

WPI Studies

Lance Schachterle
General Editor

Vol. 18

PETER LANG
New York • Washington, D.C./Baltimore • Boston • Bern
Frankfurt am Main • Berlin • Brussels • Vienna • Canterbury

"In Worcester, Massachusetts" Essays on Elizabeth Bishop

From the 1997 Elizabeth Bishop Conference at WPI

Edited by
Laura Jehn Menides
and Angela G. Dorenkamp

PETER LANG
New York • Washington, D.C./Baltimore • Boston • Bern
Frankfurt am Main • Berlin • Brussels • Vienna • Canterbury

Library of Congress Cataloging-in-Publication Data

Elizabeth Bishop Conference (1997: Worcester Polytechnic Institute)
In Worcester, Massachusetts: essays on Elizabeth Bishop
from the 1997 Elizabeth Bishop Conference at WPI /
edited by Laura Jehn Menides and Angela G. Dorenkamp.
p. cm. — (WPI studies; vol. 18)
Includes bibliographical references.
1. Bishop, Elizabeth, 1911-1979—Criticism and interpretation—Congresses.
2. Women and literature—United States—History—20th century—Congresses.
I. Menides, Laura Jehn. II. Dorenkamp, Angela G. III. Title. IV. Series.
PS3503.I785Z638   811'.54—dc21   98-46159
ISBN 0-8204-4149-X
ISSN 0897-926X

Die Deutsche Bibliothek-CIP-Einheitsaufnahme

In Worcester, Massachusetts: Essays on Elizabeth Bishop
from the 1997 Elizabeth Bishop Conference at WPI /
ed. by: Laura Jehn Menides and Angela G. Dorenkamp.
–New York; Washington, D.C./Baltimore; Boston; Bern;
Frankfurt am Main; Berlin; Brussels; Vienna; Canterbury: Lang.
(WPI studies; Vol. 18)
ISBN 0-8204-4149-X

Cover design by Jody Shyllberg
Internal book design by Dan Lewis

The paper in this book meets the guidelines for permanence and durability
of the Committee on Production Guidelines for Book Longevity
of the Council of Library Resources.

© 1999 Peter Lang Publishing, Inc., New York

Printed in the United States of America

Acknowledgments

Reprinted by permission of Farrar, Straus & Giroux, Inc.:
Excerpts from *The Collected Prose* by Elizabeth Bishop. Copyright © 1984 by Alice Helen Methfessel.
Excerpts from *The Complete Poems 1927-1979* by Elizabeth Bishop. Copyright © 1979, 1983 by Alice Helen Methfessel.
"Country Courthouse," "Gray Church," "Interior with Extension Cord," "Olivia," "Palais du Senat," "Sha-Sha," "Sleeping Figure," and "Table with Plaid Cloth" from *Exchanging Hats: Elizabeth Bishop Paintings,* edited with introduction by William Benton. Copyright © 1996 by Alice Helen Methfessel.
Excerpts from *One Art: Letters* by Elizabeth Bishop, selected and edited by Robert Giroux. Copyright © 1994 by Alice Methfessel. Introduction and compilation Copyright © 1994 by Robert Giroux.

Reproduced by permission of Farrar, Straus & Giroux, Inc., on behalf of the Estate of Elizabeth Bishop:
Excerpts from the unpublished letters of Elizabeth Bishop. Copyright © 1999 by Alice Helen Methfessel.
Excerpts from the unpublished poetry of Elizabeth Bishop. Copyright © 1999 by Alice Helen Methfessel.
Excerpts from the unpublished prose of Elizabeth Bishop. Copyright © 1999 by Alice Helen Methfessel.

Reprinted by permission of The Ecco Press:
"The Dream of the Unified Field," "Subjectivity," from *Materialism* by Jorie Graham. Copyright © 1995 by Jorie Graham.
"Fringecups" from *Streamers* by Sandra McPherson. Copyright © 1988 by Sandra McPherson.

Reprinted by permission of the University Press of New England:
"Waiting for Lesser Duckweed: On a Proposal of Issa's," from *Edge Effect* © 1996 by Sandra McPherson, Wesleyan University Press.

Reprinted by permission of Copper Beech Press:
Lines from "The Afterimage," from *The Afterimage* © 1995 by Phillis Levin.

Contents

Images and Insights: Close Readings

Kindred Spirits: Bishop and Other Writers

Lost and Found in Translation

Imperialism, Politics, Racism

List of Illustrations

Introduction

The idea was hatched back in 1994—to have an Elizabeth Bishop Conference in Worcester, where Bishop was born, where she is buried beside her parents, and where two of her most important, and compelling works—"In the Waiting Room" and "The Country Mouse"—are set.

We—Angela Dorenkamp, professor emerita of Assumption College, and I—knew about successful conferences in other places associated with Bishop (Key West, Nova Scotia, Vassar College) and thought it time for Worcester to celebrate its brilliant native daughter and to explore her short but crucial relationship with the city. We wanted to commemorate Bishop with an event that would have at its center a scholarly conference, but that would be more than a conference—that would include poetry readings, biographical and historical exhibits, art and book displays, visits to Bishop sites in the city, and a publication featuring articles about Bishop. We wanted to involve Worcester's ten colleges as well as its high schools, libraries, and cultural organizations. We decided that the event should be a week-long celebration—an Elizabeth Bishop Conference and Poetry Festival.

Fortunately, Worcester has an established, respected poetry organization, the Worcester County Poetry Association (WCPA), which has a proven track record in sponsoring and promoting poetry events and in collaborating with the area's academic and cultural institutions. The WCPA board members agreed that WCPA would be the coordinating sponsor of the Bishop event. Fortunately also, Carle Johnson, a past president of WCPA and organizer of the highly successful Stanley Kunitz Poetry Festival, agreed to become Executive Director of the Bishop event, to join us in the planning, and to give of his expertise.

Three years of planning later, Worcester opened its arms to the participants of the Elizabeth Bishop Conference and Poetry Festival. Worcester Polytechnic Institute (WPI) sponsored the scholarly conference on its campus. The other Worcester colleges hosted readings every evening by poets who knew Bishop and admire her work: Derek Walcott at Clark University, Mark Strand at Holy Cross, Sandra McPherson and Jane Shore at Worcester State, Donald Hall at Becker College, Frank Bidart and Lloyd Schwartz at Assumption. Shrewsbury Public Library hosted Kathleen Spivack's poetry reading, and Quinsigamond Community College sponsored Ann Marie Shea's dramatic presentation of Bishop's translation, *The Diary of "Helena*

Morley." In addition, the Fletcher/Priest Gallery mounted an Elizabeth Bishop art show; the Worcester Historical Museum presented an exhibit about the J.W.Bishop Company, the firm founded by Bishop's grandfather; Tatnuck Bookseller@WPI organized a book exhibit of Elizabeth Bishop-related materials; there were poetry workshops in the schools, a literary tour, a ceremony at Bishop's gravesite, and a special Elizabeth Bishop issue of *The Worcester Review.*

I mention the multitude and variety of activities during the Bishop event because they help to account for the multitude and variety of conference participants—established Bishop scholars, young scholars, independent scholars, biographers, poets, writers, editors, art critics, teachers, translators, people from all over the United States, from Canada, England, Australia, Germany, Israel, Brazil, and Japan—and for the wealth and variety of papers delivered. This volume represents a selection of those papers.

As would be expected given the location of the conference, Bishop's connections to Worcester, Massachusetts are highlighted in this volume, as contributors explore further and provide new information about the personal and poetic effects of Bishop's traumatic childhood experiences in the city. Thus Bishop's powerful poem, "In the Waiting Room," is analyzed by several of the volume's authors, who chart new territory, ask new questions, provide new responses. Their essays examine the historicity of the Worcester setting, the issues of gender identity, the concepts of race, and "otherness," and of the poem's relationship to literature of the past, for example, Lewis Carroll's *Alice in Wonderland,* William Wordsworth's *The Prelude,* and George Herbert's "Love Unknown."

Bishop's other important work about Worcester, her memoir, "The Country Mouse," is given significant scholarly attention in this volume, as are other prose pieces, such as "In the Village," that relate to Bishop's childhood and that are important in the emerging field of Childhood Studies. Bishop scholars will certainly be at the forefront of this new field.

Several authors examine unpublished drafts and letters, attempting to reconstruct Bishop's creative process and to surmise her intentions in such poems as "The End of March," and "The Riverman." Contributors also scrutinize "Love Lies Sleeping," "Insomnia," and "Crusoe in England" and discuss the connections between Bishop's writing and her sexuality; these authors take different stands, however, on the issue of whether Bishop's lesbianism is encoded in the poems or whether they defy or subvert such encoding. Other contributors inspect Bishop's attitudes towards racial issues in her poems, "Songs for a Colored Singer" and "The Imaginary Iceberg."

The volume includes fascinating new information about Bishop and Brazil—about her personal as well as literary relationships that bloomed during her long years in that country. It also investigates many questions of travel and migration in Bishop's life, charting the moves that she and her ancestors made from place to place. And it includes a section on Bishop as translator and translated, as well as on the challenges and rewards of translation.

Several participants remarked that the Worcester Conference paved the way for new directions in Bishop scholarship or opened up new fields, and the essays in this volume demonstrate those directions. In addition to those already mentioned are Bishop's anti-militarism and cold war politics, her poetic and semiotic place in the canon of American literature, and her relation to authors such as Jorie Graham, Phillis Levin, Sandra McPherson and Sylvia Plath.

The volume offers close readings of individual Bishop poems, lines, and phrases, as well as analyses of large sweeps of geography and history, of Bishop's personae and poetics, of her images both verbal and visual, her literary ancestry and her legacy. A wealth of offerings will be found in this book—this gift to Bishop's growing readership.

This gift has many givers and I wish here to express my gratitude to those who join me in the presentation. My first words of thanks go to my co-editor, Angela Dorenkamp, who combines deep wisdom with extreme practicality, whose editing experience and skills are invaluable, whose humor and *joie de vivre* made the day-to-day editing tasks pleasurable. I thank assistant editors Carle Johnson, Lynda Johnson, and Michael Hood for their close and appreciative readings and proofreadings, and Dan Lewis for the creativity and style that he's given to the layout design of this book. I'm grateful to Daniel Martinelli, Ondrej Cistecky, and Jesse Rankin for their expertise in word processing and other computer tasks.

My university, Worcester Polytechnic Institute (WPI), has provided generous support to this venture from the first, and I offer thanks to Provost John F. Carney; to Assistant Provost and Editor of the WPI Studies series, Lance E. Schachterle; to Humanities and Arts Department Head, Lee Fontanella. The Elizabeth Bishop Society has supported the project as well, and its president, Thomas Travisano, and members Gary Fountain, Camille Roman, Richard Flynn, and Barbara Page provided valuable help and advice. I thank Owen Lancer, Karla Austin, and Bernadette Alfaro, editors at Peter Lang Publishing, for their assistance throughout the project. And I thank the Worcester County Poetry Association and its board of directors for sponsoring the Bishop conference and festival and for encouraging this publication.

I thank my husband, Byron Menides, who has always supported me in my work, and who has been enthusiastic about the Elizabeth Bishop Conference and Poetry Festival, and about this volume.

Importantly, I thank the participants of the Elizabeth Bishop Conference and the contributors to this volume for the research and for the thought and the imagination that went into the writing of these essays. May their work continue the scholarly dialogue about Elizabeth Bishop. And finally, I thank Elizabeth Bishop for her rich offerings to the world of literature.

Laura Jehn Menides
Worcester Polytechnic Institute

Elizabeth Bishop and the Origins of Childhood Studies

Thomas Travisano
Hartwick College

Abstract

Elizabeth Bishop, along with such contemporaries as Lowell, Jarrell, and Berryman, constructed a new poetics of childhood in which a traumatic past, remembered in the face of repression, emerges as the imperfectly known source of adult neurosis. This paper employs the perspective of childhood studies to argue that a renewed preoccupation with the marginalized child—passing through the painful and uncertain processes of individual human development—emerges as a key feature of Bishop's work and of that branch of postmodern poetry concerning itself with the problems of selfhood in the postmodern world.

A threatened, intensely reimagined childhood was a pivotal feature in the work of Elizabeth Bishop, and of such close colleagues as Randall Jarrell, Robert Lowell and John Berryman, whom I describe, in a forthcoming book, *Exploring Lost Worlds: Lowell, Jarrell, Bishop, Berryman and the Making of a Postmodern Aesthetic* (UP of Virginia), as a mid-century quartet who shared in the creation of a specific postmodern aesthetic. They began to discover this aesthetic separately in the mid-1930s through the mid-1940s, then they created an elaborately interwoven and ongoing four-way conversation in the years that followed, involving an intensive process of mutual interaction.

Perhaps the most important of the lost worlds these poets explored both separately and in combination is the world of early childhood experience. Jarrell, in a 1957 letter noting possible echoes of his own work in Bishop's recently published "Sestina," modestly acknowledged that "I felt as if, so to speak, some of my wash-cloths were part of a Modigliani collage, or as if my cat had got into a Vuillard." Jarrell then adds, "I think too, that all people who really remember childhood and do it at all right sound alike in some ways" (Jarrell 422). Together, the poets of this quartet, along with others of their generation, were engaged in the lonely process—long before it became a focus of White House level concern—of converting the child from the status of a marginalized cultural object into a cultural subject.

Since their brilliant, pioneering efforts that spanned the mid-century era, childhood has become a common, even commonplace, poetic theme. So it is easy to overlook that, for nearly a century, few serious poets writing in English were willing to touch it. Encouraged, in part, by the pervasive influence of poets like Lowell, Jarrell, Bishop and Berryman, childhood has reemerged over the past several decades as one of the most active fields of investigation for poetry, a position it had not held since the first generations of English and American Romantics.

This powerful reemergence of childhood as subject goes unremarked in most conventional accounts of the poetry that followed modernism. Yet our leading poetry reviews remain full of poems that return memorably to scenes of childhood, often recreated as the site of formative and traumatic early experience. This recurrent preoccupation with childhood in the several generations that have followed modernism demands more considered study. I propose to read this phenomenon through the lens of childhood studies, a newly emerging, multidisciplinary field of potentially enormous scope and importance that concerns itself with the ways cultures construct and have constructed childhood. What is childhood studies in its present incompletely recognized form? And what could it become, if appropriately recognized? Childhood studies, unrecognized, remains a sleeping giant. Named and recognized, it could become a vital and important intellectual and cultural force, the limits of whose scope and influence might be hard to predetermine. Named and recognized, childhood studies could become a multidisciplinary enterprise concerned with exploring and interpreting all aspects of childhood. Named and recognized, childhood studies would concern itself with the ways cultures construct and have constructed childhood. It would explore the diverse ways that writers and other creative artists represent and have represented childhood. It would concern itself with the birth, growth, development, care, abuse, and, sometimes, death of children in diverse cultures throughout history. It would concern itself with the emotional, intellectual and spiritual life of the child. And, named and recognized, childhood studies would, of course, concern itself with the enormous wealth of texts that have been produced by, for, and about the child. Such a field would serve to coordinate and synthesize an already vast pre-existing matrix of knowledge, methodology, and theoretical insight into the life of the child and into cultural constructs of childhood. And by bringing diverse, and at times, no doubt, contradictory, methodologies together, childhood studies would attempt to advance that insight in unforeseen directions.

Childhood studies, as I and such fellow Bishop critics as Richard Flynn, Barbara Page, Camille Roman and Gary Fountain see it, aims to explore, among other things, the diverse ways that writers and other creative artists represent and have represented childhood. A diverse range of postmodern poets, including such first generation postmodernists as Bishop and her colleagues, lend themselves to readings from the perspective of childhood studies because they display an extraordinarily persistent concern with exploring the processes and anomalies of individual childhood development. Bishop, Lowell, Jarrell and John Berryman, following lines of inquiry defined by Freud and diversely redefined by later generations of psychoanalysts, including Anna Freud, Melanie Klein, Harry Stack Sullivan, John Bowlby, D. W. Winnicott and Alice Miller, combined with other contemporaries to construct a new poetics of childhood, a mode in which a traumatic past, remembered partially and with difficulty in the face of repression, emerges as the recognized but imperfectly known source of adult neurosis. They would sustain this preoccupation with childhood experience throughout their careers, developing a probing exploration of the drama of individual human development. The difference between modernist poets, who tend to elide childhood, and postmodernist poets, who richly and variously represent it, is quite marked. From the perspective of childhood studies, one feels compelled to argue that a renewed preoccupation with the marginalized child or adolescent—as he or she passes through crucial stages in the painful and uncertain processes of an individual's human development—emerges as a key feature of that branch of postmodern poetry that concerns itself with the problems of selfhood in the postmodern world. My own discussion here will sketch the cultural background out of which Bishop's particular representation of childhood emerged, looking as well at the artistic process necessary to create the new aesthetic she helped to develop.

That Bishop's work combines the representation of childhood with the exploration of loss is no coincidence, because for her the problem of recovering childhood experience was intimately intertwined with the problem of confronting and exploring lost worlds. Loss has been a subject of poetry since time immemorial, but in most earlier aesthetic frameworks, loss involves an alteration of an original, and reasonably sustained, condition of possession or wholeness. On the other hand, Bishop and several of her closest contemporaries created an extensive body of poems that begin in a state of profound and perhaps irremediable loss, loss that accompanies, or even precedes, the protagonist's first moment of conscious awareness or considered selfhood. In poem after poem by this mid-century quartet, including, memorably, Bishop's "In the Waiting Room," the first moment of rational consciousness, the earliest glimmer of mature knowledge, dawns simultaneously with an experience of traumatic loss.

I here propose to concentrate, with reference to this sense of loss, on the motif of "expulsion from paradise." Premature expulsions from the realm of childhood innocence recur repeatedly in the work of Bishop and her colleagues in obvious and subtle mutations throughout hundreds of poems. Bishop's own expulsion was quite literal. It took place in 1917, when her paternal grandparents removed her, an unwilling six-year-old child, from the home she had found with her maternal grandparents in Nova Scotia after her mother was permanently placed in a mental institution. These virtually unknown grandparents then transported her to the Bishop homestead in Worcester, Massachusetts. In a recently rediscovered juvenile poem published in a school magazine in 1927, when she was just sixteen years old, Bishop voiced a mordantly ironic, if indirect, protest against her own expulsion from paradise. The motif of expulsion from paradise reappears in many forms throughout her poetry, marking moments of profound loss that are also points of conscious entry into selfhood, into the pleasures and dangers of the social and material world, and the parallel pleasures and dangers of artistic creation. In her work, childhood itself is dramatized as the site of one's own first taste of that bittersweet, ambiguous fruit that grows on the tree of knowledge.

Elizabeth Bishop's "The Ballad of the Subway Train," the earliest poem by Bishop that is known to survive, was published in her school magazine, *The Owl*, in the spring of 1927, when Bishop was a sixteen-year-old high school freshman attending North Shore Country Day School in Swampscott, Massachusetts. Still in her mid-teens, she had already lived through a staggering, and by now oft recited, sequence of losses, losses that shaped what Lloyd Schwartz has recently called "Bishop's now virtually mythic" childhood story. Read from the perspective of childhood studies, this poem can be seen both as a product of Bishop's early childhood experience, and the early-twentieth-century Nova Scotian and New England cultures that helped to shape it, and as a precocious, penetrating, and sharply ironic analysis of that culture and that experience on the part of the sixteen-year-old Elizabeth Bishop.

In the first six years of her life, Bishop suffered a sequence of early traumas that left a permanent imprint on her art. These include the death of her father from Bright's disease in 1911, when she was eight months old, and the mental breakdowns suffered by her mother, Gertrude Bulmer Bishop, partly, it seems, as a consequence of her father's early death. These led to her mother's temporary hospitalization in 1914 and to her permanent confinement in a Dartmouth, Nova Scotia mental hospital in the summer of 1916 when Bishop was five. After 1916, she would never see her mother again. Thereafter, Bishop experienced a series of wrenching and traumatic dislocations as she passed from one relation to another in the years that followed. But at first the five-year-old Elizabeth, now a virtual orphan, continued living, as she would for more than a year, with her modestly placed but gently affectionate maternal grandparents, the Bulmers, in Great Village, Nova Scotia—a traditional rural community that Bishop vividly recalled in prose and verse from high school on.

In the fall of 1917, when Bishop was six years old, her wealthy and dutiful but emotionally distant paternal grandparents arrived in Great Village to claim Elizabeth and bring her back to Massachusetts. As Bishop recalled the event in a 1964 letter to her first biographer, Anne Stevenson, "The B[ishop]s were horrified to see the only child of their eldest son running about the village in bare feet, eating at the table with the grownups and drinking *tea*, so I was carried off (by train) to Worcester for the one awful winter that was almost the end of me. 1917-18" (Letter to Stevenson, 1964). Within months of her removal to Worcester, Bishop began to suffer a succession of illnesses. "I had already had bad bronchitis and probably attacks of asthma—in Worcester I got much worse and developed eczema that almost killed me. One awful day I was sent home from 'first grade' because of my sores—and I imagine my hopeless shyness has dated from then. —In May, 1919, 1 was taken to live with Aunt Maud; I couldn't walk and Ronald [the Bishop chauffeur] carried me up the stairs—my aunt burst into tears when she saw me." Bishop's traumatic series of losses and displacements is thus explicitly linked to a series of debilitating physical illnesses. She later felt "that stretch is still too grim to think of, almost. My grandfather had gone to see my aunt M[aud] privately and made the arrangements—he said my grandmother didn't 'know how to take care of her own children,' most of them had died" (Letter to Stevenson). Thereafter, under the care of her maternal aunt Maud, Bishop suffered recurrent bouts of asthma that limited her ability to attend school regularly. Bishop had spent much of her isolated youth "lying in bed wheezing and reading" (Letter to Stevenson).

A contemporary analyst might conclude that in the years following her removal to Worcester, Bishop was suffering from Post-traumatic Stress Disorder. Enumerating the symptoms of this disorder, Dr. Richard Famularo notes in a recent issue of *The Harvard Mental Health Letter* that, "The traumatic experience is followed by recurrent or intrusive recollections, including repetitive play, frightening dreams, reenactment of the trauma, and intense reactions to symbolic reminders of the trauma" (Famularo 8). Evidence of many of these symptoms reappear in Bishop's extensive writings about the sequence of losses that cut her off from her main sources of nurture and reassurance. In particular, the response to symbolic reminders of the world she had lost in Nova Scotia was visceral and intense. Harking back to the mysterious columns of numbers on the blackboard that she observed as a five-year-old member of a "Primer Class" in Nova Scotia just months after her mother's climactic breakdown, Bishop would write that "Every time I see long columns of numbers, handwritten in a certain way, a strange sensation or shudder, partly aesthetic, partly painful, goes through my diaphragm.... The real name of this sensation is memory. It is a memory I do not even have to try to remember, or reconstruct; it is always right there, clear and complete" (*CPr* 3, 4). Bishop's work makes pervasive use of such memory traces, and infrequently attributes long-lasting and profound emotional effects to quite specific and sometimes trivial-seeming incidents from childhood that function as symbolic reminders of trauma. These provoke such intense reactions that, as she suggests in her first mature poem, "The Map" (1935), the "emotion too far exceeds its cause" (*CP* 3).

Bishop's resentment of her removal from Great Village, from a landscape she knew and loved and an extended family and village society that she knew and found comforting, remains palpable in the posthumously published autobiographical memoir "The Country Mouse," written in 1960, more than forty years after the event. "I had been brought back unconsulted and against my wishes to the house my father had been born in, to be saved from a life of poverty and provincialism, bare feet, suet puddings, unsanitary school slates, perhaps even from the inverted *r*'s of my mother's family. With this surprising extra set of grandparents, until a few weeks ago no more than names, a new life was about to begin" (*CPr* 17). Biographer Brett C. Millier concludes correctly that her abrupt removal from Great Village "sealed little Elizabeth's sense of loss to a permanent condition"(20).Bishop's own later comment was, "I felt as if I were being kidnapped, even if I wasn't" (*CPr* 14). Of Post-traumatic Stress Disorder, Dr. Famularo adds that "The traumatic experiences of childhood often involve maltreatment by parents or other caregivers. The resulting loss of protection, sense of betrayal, daily fear, and overwhelming sense of helplessness may color all the child's later personal relations" (Famularo 8). Bishop had simply been appropriated by her paternal grandparents at a time when she was particularly vulnerable, and she never completely recovered, either physically or emotionally, from the sense of helplessness and loss that this heedless act of exile inflicted upon her. Not until she reached sixteen was Bishop finally well enough to enroll full time as a freshman at North Shore Country Day. She had slipped a year or two behind her age-mates on the academic calendar, but she was already well ahead of them in one important respect: she had molded herself into an accomplished writer of both prose and verse.

The single poem of Bishop's that appeared in that spring 1927 issue of *The Owl*, the brilliant and darkly funny "Ballad of the Subway Train," makes incisive if indirect use of her childhood losses. Only recently republished, the "Ballad" lingered undiscovered for years in the back issue of a high school literary magazine, a quiet, unrecognized literary landmark: a poem that marks the tentative re-opening, for Bishop and many other American poets of her generation, of a field of investigation that had long remained closed to serious exploration for poets writing in English—the field of early childhood experience.

Bishop's "Ballad," written when she was just sixteen, develops the motif of expulsion from "the lost paradise of the childish past" in a manner at once allegorical and strikingly direct. She evokes a vivid and comically magical scene, in fresh, simple diction.

> Long, long ago when God was young,
> > Earth hadn't found its place.
> Great dragons lived among the moons
> > And crawled and crept through space.
>
> They bunted meteors with their heads.
> > While unseen worlds dropped by;
> And scratched their bronzy backs upon
> > The ridges of the sky. ("Ballad" 25)[1]

Despite their tremendous size, the demeanor of these "great dragons" seems curiously childlike, even infantile. The primordial world they inhabit, at a time when even "God was young," is expansive and apparently free of law or restraint. Many of Bishop's later poems feature prosaic animals such as a fish, roosters or an armadillo, as well as fantastic creatures such as her Man-Moth, seen partly on their own terms as independent beings and partly in terms that are human and cultural. Here the dragons emerge partly as free inventions but partly as emblematic surrogates of the child. These dragons start their existence in a blissful, pre-moral state, and like happily-occupied children, are so absorbed in play that they remain oblivious to momentous events occurring in the background. Free of shame, innocent of time, and governed by only the most primitive layers of consciousness, these dragons

luxuriate for "ten thousand thousand years" in a state of independent pleasure, fulfilling their own narcissistic needs without effort or guidance, enjoying a quasi-mythic scope and power. Yet this state of paradise is suddenly lost, when they are abruptly caught out in a calamitous, if inadvertent,
crime.

> The aeons came and went and came,
>   And still the dragons stayed;
> Until one night they chanced to eat
>   A swarm of stars new made.
>
> And when God saw them all full gorged,
>   Their scaly bellies fed,
> His anger made the planets shake
>   And this is what he said:
>
> "You have been feeding, greedy beasts,
>   Upon the bright young stars.
> For gluttony as deep as yours,
>   *Be changed to subway cars!*"

The climactic turn in Bishop's ballad offers nothing less than a precocious remaking of an ancient myth that she perhaps first encountered in the
old family Bible she features in "Over 2,000 Illustrations and a Complete
Concordance" and that finds its most beautiful and sustained expression in
Milton's *Paradise Lost*. Certainly Bishop's ability to deploy comedy at this
critical moment is a sign of great residual strength, but if God's punishment
here is comic, it is also far more terrible and arbitrary than His judgment in
Milton's version. According to Milton, Eve and Adam deservedly suffer
"loss of Eden." The dragons' "crime," on the other hand, seems little more
than an infantile impulse. Nonetheless, God's anger is far swifter and more
final in Bishop's version.

The God of Bishop's "Ballad" strikes without warning and departs without a word of hope or consolation. Indeed, God's parting words rub salt into
the dragons' wounds:

> "No more for you infinite space,
>   But in a narrow hole
> You shall forever grope your way,
>   Blind-burrowing like the mole!"

The word "forever" turns the key on a sentence to life imprisonment and
servitude: no whisper here of hope for "paradise regained." The poem's

texture is lucid, its imagery precise and vivid, its language comic. But teleo-logically speaking, this world remains bleak and opaque. God's purposes seem arbitrary and unreadable beyond the motive of mere vengeance, and the dragons' grief over their loss is given only veiled expression, behind the shield of high spirited humor. But Bishop's ongoing preoccupation with trau-matic and unexplained loss and her disquiet regarding the nature and sources of human knowledge are vividly prefigured.

These dragons function as poignant, if covert, emblems of Bishop's child-self, their fate paralleling uncannily Bishop's recollections of her own early experiences of displacement and loss. Bishop's early life in Nova Scotia may never have been truly paradisal. She had already lost her father before she first visited Great Village, and her mother suffered an earlier "nervous breakdown" before her permanent exile to a mental institution. "In the Vil-lage" takes as its central image a scream Bishop's mother uttered at the moment of that final breakdown. This scream's echo "hangs over that Nova Scotian village.... unheard, in memory—in the past, in the present, and those years between. It was not even loud to begin with, perhaps. It just came there to live, forever—not loud, just alive forever" (*CPr* 251). But in Bishop's personal mythology, Great Village, though itself the site of painful losses and silences, represented the closest thing to home she had ever known, and it retains its force throughout her work as a kind of irrecoverable Eden: vibrant with loss, perhaps, but also radiant with moments of childlike won-der and natural freshness that make one feel that Bishop was, as usual, far too self-deprecating when she described herself, in a letter to Lowell, as a "minor female Wordsworth."

One symbolic reminder of her traumatic exile from Nova Scotia that forms the decisive image of her 1927 "Ballad," the quasi-comic descent of an angry God upon an unwitting offender, re-appears with tragi-comic force in Bishop's writing more than thirty years later, in the opening scene from the 1960 "The Country Mouse." As the memoir begins, the six-year-old Elizabeth is aboard a sleeper car on "the old Boston and Maine" railroad, being transported from Great Village to the house of her Bishop grandpar-ents in Worcester. In the dead of night the child awakens to observe a star-tling event. Abruptly, her very tall grandfather, J. W. Bishop, a wealthy and successful building contractor who in the child's mind resembled the "grandfather's clock" of the old song because he, like the clock, was "too tall for the shelf...snapped on the overhead light again.... He had been trying to sleep in the upper berth of our 'drawing room.' Now he descended, god-like and swearing, swept Grandma out of the way, and wedged himself into the lower berth. His thick silver hair and short silver beard glittered, and so did the whites of his eyes, rolled up as if in agony" (*CPr* 13). Summarily displaced from her berth, "this grandma, jiggling too, stood by helplessly, watching him writhe and grunt." Finally, her husband commands, "'Sarah! Get in the other way around!' She turned off the overhead light once more, and obeyed." Bishop recalls, "I can look back on them now, many years and train trips later, and clearly see them looking like a Bernini fountain, or a Cellini saltcellar: a powerful but aging Poseidon with a small, elderly, curly Nereid" (*CPr* 14). In this scene, Bishop's own expulsion from the "paradise" of Nova Scotia is comically mirrored in the bizarre and awkward choreography of her grandmother's displacement by a "godlike and swearing" patriarch. J. W. Bishop's startling emergence as a "powerful but aging Poseidon" who descends from on high, commands the moral high ground, and has what it takes to displace others rudely, underlines in eerily mythic terms aspects of Bishop's own displacement that she had first dealt with in the 1927 "Ballad."

Indirect treatment of grief connected with loss was apparently ingrained in Bishop from the beginning. A taboo on the discussion of her most grievous losses seems to have been maintained by her father's family. The evidence strongly suggests that the breakdowns and institutionalization of her mother were rarely, if ever, mentioned—let alone explained to her—in Worcester. When her Bishop grandfather died, Bishop came under the supervision of his son, John Warren Bishop, Jr., whom she knew as Uncle Jack. Like his father, Uncle Jack was dutifully concerned for his ward but nonetheless aloof from her emotionally. When Uncle Jack enrolled Elizabeth at Walnut Hill School, he spoke to administrator Ruby Willis about Bishop's mother's illness. In Willis's notes, he is on record as stating, "These facts are either unknown to Elizabeth or, at most, only surmised by her, since no one has ever spoken to her about her mother and she has never mentioned her." Willis's notes provide remarkable and important external confirmation of the hints in Bishop's writings that, even up to the age of sixteen, she had never been explicitly informed regarding what happened to her mother. An embargo on the topic of her mother was, apparently, quite consistently enforced by her paternal relations, either for the child's "protection" or because the topic was simply too embarrassing or distressing for the family to discuss openly. After a summary of Gertrude Bishop's case, Willis's Walnut Hill notes continue, "Elizabeth's guardian is most anxious that no mention of these facts shall be made to Elizabeth. She had been a 'lonely little girl' and he anticipates much happiness for her at Walnut Hill"

(Fountain 29–30).

By implication, Bishop's Uncle Jack expected that her new school, in the role of surrogate family, should provide a degree of nurture and concern that might compensate Bishop for the lack of emotional care her losses had received at home. At the same time, Uncle Jack insisted on maintaining the veil of silence about Bishop's mother's condition. It should not surprise one that, as a friend at Walnut Hill recalled, "There was this big gap in Elizabeth's life. Elizabeth didn't talk much about her childhood. It was too difficult." This friend, Joan Collingwood Disney, acknowledged that Bishop "felt affection for her aunts and they for her," but, she continues, "She really had to grow up all by herself. A terrible sadness would cause her to be despondent." Disney concludes, "I remember exactly how she looked one time when she was leaving our house in Plymouth, Massachusetts, after a visit. It was a very sad look and stayed with me. Maybe the right word would have kept her there" (Fountain 28).

Apparently no one in her childhood attempted, directly at least, to help her to mourn the loss of her father, her mother, or her familiar home in Great Village. Nor did they help her to comprehend and come to terms with the feelings of guilt and abandonment that haunted her as a result of these losses. Instead, she received repeated messages to deny her losses and repress her feelings. Alice Miller argues that, "It is precisely because a child's feelings are so strong that they cannot be repressed without serious consequences. The stronger a prisoner is, the thicker the prison walls have to be, which impede or completely prevent later emotional growth" (Miller 54). Bishop would appear to agree, because in many passages in her writings she claims a direct causal link between quite specific present behavior and the influence of traumatic origins. Dr. Famularo suggests that "the child's age and developmental level when the trauma occurs, the kind, duration, and severity of the trauma, the level of parental support, and the psychiatric condition of the parents or other caregivers" (Famarulo 8) may all affect the extent and severity of Post-traumatic Stress Disorder. Given Bishop's very early age, the lack of emotional support or acknowledgment she received from caregivers, particularly after her removal from Great Village, and the psychiatric condition of her one surviving parent, these criteria would suggest that Bishop faced an uphill struggle against the traumatic losses that defined her childhood.

After a series of incidents involving Bishop caused concern for her at the school, Walnut Hill administrator Harriet Farwell wrote to Uncle Jack about a consultation that Farwell had initiated, on her own responsibility, with a certain Dr. Taylor, a woman psychiatrist with offices in Boston. "[Dr. Taylor] did not seem to be worried at all about Elizabeth's heredity. The fact, however, that Elizabeth probably has repressed within her a certain amount of information about her mother, she did consider very serious." Farwell continued, "I feel very sure myself, in fact, I may say positively that Elizabeth knows some if not all of the truth about her mother. It does not make much difference whether it is some or all—either would be enough to make her very unhappy and keep her in an abnormal state of mind. Dr. Taylor feels very decidedly that submerged facts of this kind are dangerous and should be brought out into the open" (Fountain 29). Bishop's Uncle Jack finally agreed, at Dr. Taylor's insistence, that the truth should be shared with Bishop. But when Dr. Taylor finally met with her, Bishop refused to speak.

John Bowlby, the British pioneer of attachment theory, commented in 1988 that "the belief that children are unable to mourn can... be seen to derive from generalizations that had been made from the analyses of children whose mourning had followed an atypical course. In many cases this had been due either to the child never having been given adequate information about what had happened, or else to there having been no one to sympathize with him and help him gradually to come to terms with his loss, his yearning for his lost parent, his anger, and his sorrow" (Bowlby 78–79). In the above statement, Bowlby seems almost to be reciting the documentary evidence defining Bishop's specific circumstances in relation to the loss of her mother. By her Uncle Jack's own testimony, she was never given adequate information about her mother's breakdown nor did she have anyone to sympathize with her or help her come gradually to terms with her grief. Her refusal to speak to psychologists about her losses suggests that an imperative to maintain silence about central emotional issues had been most firmly ingrained from an early age, and that she had learned to direct her grief and anger and sorrow over her losses inward, upon herself.

Bishop's private feelings of enforced self-constraint and emotional displacement remain alive in an unsettling unpublished poem that exists in a single draft in the Vassar College archive, a typescript that has written above it, in Bishop's hand, "(Poem from 1935)," the year after her mother's death in the Dartmouth, N. S. sanitarium into which she had disappeared so quickly and permanently and from which she never emerged alive.

The past
at least
is polite
it keeps out of sight.

The present
is more recent.
It makes a fuss
but is unselfconscious.

These quatrains bounce along, quite cheerfully, it seems, with their short, mostly one-foot lines, and oddly slant rhymes, until the peculiar "but is unselfconscious"—a near tongue-twister of a line that sounds anything but unselfconscious, slowing the reader down and preparing one for the fall, which arrives in the third and last quatrain.

The future
sinks through water
fast as stone,
alone alone. ("The past," Vassar)

Written the year after Bishop left Vassar and never published, this well-mannered yet penetrating and ineffably sad little lyric articulates the constrained and isolated psychological position of Bishop's early life. Despite her terrible early losses, Bishop felt that her past must be expected to "keep out of sight," and her present, even when it made a fuss, as it sometimes did, should never be self-conscious, at least in public, about its feelings or behavior. In the face of these implicit demands for silence and good manners, undermined by the unhealed losses she had already experienced, the future must often have seemed to be sinking "through water / fast as a stone." In this her future resembled her own mother Gertrude's life, for Gertrude disappeared almost without a trace, becoming in effect an unperson in Bishop's world and leaving her daughter Elizabeth both haunted by her own lack of power to shape that future and with the sense that she was truly "alone alone."

It is hardly surprising in light of her upbringing that as an artist Bishop would be known for her reticence. In her life, the past might be induced to politely keep "out of sight," but in Bishop's poetry and self-exploratory prose its effects would be felt, and perhaps even be intensified, by her skillful management, in poem after poem, of the conflict between emotional constraint and the emergence of symptomatic reminders of traumatic loss and of uncomfortable, repressed truths. In a 1935 notebook, Bishop would write of herself in her tiny, pinched, steeply-slanted and nearly-illegible hand that "My friendly circumstances, my 'good fortune,' surround me so well & safely, & only I am wrong, inadequate. It is a situation like one of those solid crystal balls with little silvery objects inside: thick, clear, appropriate glass— only the little object, me, is sadly flawed and shown off as inferior to the setting" (Notebook, Vassar). In one of her Brazilian interviews, which were always franker about her emotional life than her American interviews, Bishop acknowledges that "teaching as I am now doing, I have to keep up a happy front. See, the Americans from New England are great hypocrites. It's part of tradition not to show one's feelings. But sometimes I show mine" (Schiller 76). Bishop's "reticence" has what Octavio Paz called its "enormous power" (16) because she is able to suggest—perhaps without consciously intending to—the painful depths that lurk beneath her brilliantly polished, "polite" surfaces. She suggests these depths of emotion through the deployment of carefully selected, emblematic, details set out against a culturally telling background. As Bishop's oeuvre developed, the past might be induced to keep politely out of sight, but, fortunately for her art, it never completely succeeds. Bishop once told an interviewer, "Poetry should be as unconscious as possible" (Johnson 99). The force of the past, lodged in the unconscious, keeps re-emerging just enough to electrify Bishop's poetry with an enormous sense of latent emotional, moral, and metaphysical power.

Endnote

1. Bishop's "Ballad of the Subway Train" was discovered by Gary Fountain. The present author arranged for its republication and provided an introduction: Thomas Travisano, "Heavenly Dragons: A Newly Discovered Poem by Elizabeth Bishop," *Western Humanities Review* 45 (Spring 1991): 25–33.

Works Cited

Bishop, Elizabeth. "The Ballad of the Subway Train," *Western Humanities Review* 45 (spring 1991), 25–26.

————. *The Collected Prose*. Ed. Robert Giroux. New York: Farrar, Straus Giroux, 1984.

————. *The Complete Poems 1927–1979*. New York: Farrar Straus, Giroux, 1983.

————. Letter to Robert Lowell, 11 July 1951, Houghton Library, Harvard University, quoted from Merrin.

————. Letter to Anne Stevenson. "Answers to your questions of March 6th - [1964]," quoted from Thomas Travisano, "Emerging Genius: Elizabeth Bishop, 1927–1930," *Gettysburg Review* (Winter 1992): 34.

————. Notebook. "E. Bishop, 1934, 1935, 1936, 1937". Rare Books and Manuscripts, Vassar College Library.

————. "The past" [1935]. Rare Books and Manuscripts, Vassar College Library.

Bowlby, John. *A Secure Base: Parent-Child Attachment and Healthy Human Development*. New York: Basic Books, 1988,

Famularo, Dr. Richard. "What Are the Symptoms, Causes, and Treatments of Childhood Post-traumatic Stress Disorder?" *Harvard Mental Health Letter* 13 (January 1997): 8.

Fountain, Gary and Peter Brazeau. *Remembering Elizabeth Bishop: An Oral Biography*. Amherst: U of Massachusetts P: Amherst, 1994.

Jarrell, Randall. *Randall Jarrell's Letters*. Ed. Mary Jarrell. New York: Harcourt, 1985.

Johnson, Alexandra. "Geography of Imagination." Interview with Elizabeth Bishop (1978). *Conversations with Elizabeth Bishop*. Ed. George Monteiro. Jackson: UP of Mississippi, 1996. 98–104.

Merrin, Jeredith. "Elizabeth Bishop: Gaiety, Gayness and Change." *Elizabeth Bishop: Geography of Gender*. Ed. Marilyn May Lombardi. Charlottesville: UP of Virginia, 1993, 168.

Miller, Alice. *Drama of the Gifted Child*. Trans. Ruth Ward. New York: Basic Books, 1981.

Paz, Octavio. "Elizabeth Bishop, or the Power of Reticence." *World Literature Today* (Winter 1977): 16.

Schiller, Beatriz. "Poetry Born Out of Suffering." *Conversations with Elizabeth Bishop*. Ed. George Monteiro. Jackson: UP of Mississippi, 1996. 74–81.

Schwartz, Lloyd. Bookjacket blurb. *Remembering Elizabeth Bishop*. By Gary Fountain and Peter Brazeau. Amherst: U of Massachusetts P, 1994.

Bishop as a Poet of Childhood Recollected

Barbara Page
Vassar College

Abstract

Elizabeth Bishop, like T. S. Eliot, meditated at length on how ends of lives circle back to beginnings. In contrast to Eliot's often elderly personae, however, the persona and voice in many of Bishop's poems remain appealingly childlike. But evidence of her struggle with painful memories, especially those to do with early childhood losses, is abundant in the many poems of childhood that remained unfinished. Concentrating primarily on poems in manuscript about Bishop's relatives (and figures of nurses and dolls), I examine hesitations, textual breakdowns, alternatives, and outcries never allowed publication, in order to illuminate the way childhood memories both orient and trouble her poem-making.

It was while reflecting on the persistence of childhood in Elizabeth Bishop's work, and on the frequent difficulty she encountered in bringing poems to completion, that some lines from T. S. Eliot's *Four Quartets* popped to mind. They are from "Little Gidding":

> What we call the beginning is often the end
> And to make an end is to make a beginning.
> The end is where we start from. And every phrase
> And sentence that is right (where every word is at home,
> Taking its place to support the others, ...)
> Every phrase and every sentence is an end and a beginning,
> Every poem an epitaph. (144)

We know from her own testimony that Bishop considered Eliot an important forebear, and it is of interest to note that by certain—to be sure rather external—measures the two either resemble one another or seem mirror opposites. Both produced a relatively small body of published poems and held back a good deal of material.[1] Both suffered at times from disabling collapses of morale that impeded composition; both despaired at times of finding the means to bring poems to completion. Conversely, in his lifetime Eliot enjoyed enormous public esteem, whereas Bishop remained "a writer's writer's writer," in John Ashbery's words (8). Since his death,

however, Eliot's star has fallen far, whereas Bishop's has risen phenom-
enally; his place in the canon of poets has been challenged, actively or by
neglect, whereas hers has been championed avidly, and it now seems likely
that she will gain a permanent berth.[2] Disclosures of snobbery and bias
certainly have damaged Eliot, whereas disclosures of alcoholism and lesbianism seem only to have rendered her more sympathetic, or at least more
fascinating. But perhaps it is differences in the personae inscribed in many
of their poems that turn some contemporary readers away from Eliot while
drawing them to Bishop.

Even—or especially—in poems written in youth, and persisting throughout his career, Eliot's speaker often seems elderly; even—or especially—in
poems written in age, Bishop's speaker often seems childlike. Though they
share a turn toward irony, a sense of helplessness in the face of uncontrol-
lable forces loose in the world, and moments of giddiness before those forces,
the turn of mind and heart in each finally differs decisively. For Eliot there is
a before-and-after conversion poetry, the former tinged with longing and
tending toward despair, the latter, especially in the *Four Quartets*, melancholy, tender, nostalgic, bespeaking philosophical resignation. For Bishop,
like Eliot, there are poems of wit and virtuosic formal play. But in Bishop
we come to recognize a persistent and orienting voice of childhood, bearing
the survival of candor, or what looks like it, play, unrationalized misery—
and wonder.

Bishop wrote often of her relatives, but as an orphan had to confront a
gaping absence. Her father she never knew, though her maternal grandfather
supplied a fairly sturdy stand-in. Her mother, however, lived in memory just
enough to sear it, as an uncontainable apparition. The evidence of Bishop's
inability to compose a coherent figure of her mother lies strewn throughout
her work, published and unpublished, where she is often recalled as a cos-
tume rather than a body, or a voice, never pleasant, rather than a face. In
"First Death in Nova Scotia," the voice is sinister:

> 'Come,' said my mother,
> 'Come and say good-bye
> to your little cousin Arthur.'

In "In the Village," the voice is frightful and haunting, a scream. In a
fragment from the unpublished papers, the mother appears as accouterment,
alarmingly disembodied and funereal:

> A mother made of dress goods
> white with black polk-dots,
> black and white 'Shepherd's plaid.'
> A mother is a hat
> black hat with a black gauze rose
> falling half open
>
> A long black glove
> the swan bit
> in the Public Gardens[3]

Thomas Travisano has done us the service of bringing to light several unpublished poems from Bishop's manuscripts, including "A Drunkard" and "Salem Willows" (Bishop, "Three"). In "A Drunkard" the speaker gives, then half reneges on, an explanation for her alcoholism, by recalling the night when at the age of three she witnessed a devastating fire in Salem, Massachusetts, a disaster that prevented relations from answering her need:

> I was terribly thirsty but mama didn't hear
> me calling her. Out on the lawn
> she and some neighbors were giving coffee
> or food or something to the people landing in the boats—
> once in a while I caught a glimpse of her
> and called and called—no one paid any attention—

The child's glimpse catches her mother's white dress tinged "rose-red" by the reflected fire, and the next day, among blackened ruins, when she picks up "a woman's long black cotton / stocking,"

> My mother said sharply
> *Put that down!* I remember clearly, clearly—
> But since that night, that day, that reprimand
> I have suffered from abnormal thirst—

The mother's remoteness, rebuff, and ultimate removal, engendered an unassuaged thirst in the poet—which represents, I think, a desire for nurturance and comfort—never satisfied by the extended family, however kindly or well meaning. Bishop's upbringing differs strikingly from that of T. S. Eliot, who received abundant attention, not only from parents, especially his mother, but also from older sisters and his extended New England family. Among Bishop's fictive personae from her earlier poetry (all male, curiously) are the fugitive Man-moth and self-divided Gentleman of Shalott, as well as the vagrant drinkers, Edwin Boomer, in her story "The Sea & Its

Shore," and her Prodigal, whom David Kalstone rightly regarded as pivotal in her career. Eliot's fictive repertoire from the early career—published or privately circulated—features stifled, repressed, but assuredly superior young men: the skewered Prufrock; the schoolboy scatalogist recently made public in *The Inventions of the March Hare*; the Laforguean satirist of fussy female relations. In contrast, Bishop's one gender-conscious foray into social satire on relatives, "Exchanging Hats"—which she scrupulously withheld from her collected poems—is a tour de force of verbal play that yields suddenly between the final two stanzas to one of her extraordinary shifts in emotional register, from comedy to awesome myth:

> Unfunny uncle, you who wore a
> hat too big, or one too many,
> tell us, can't you, are there any
> stars inside your black fedora?
>
> Aunt exemplary and slim,
> with avernal eyes, we wonder
> what slow changes they see under
> their vast, shady, turned-down brim.

The polish, wit, control and emotional distance of "Exchanging Hats" are those of the fully fledged adult, certainly a more mature personage than that of the minor poems in Eliot's *Prufrock* volume. But in "Salem Willows," it is the child's eye view that controls the poet's recollection. Travisano notes that the drafts of "Salem Willows" were written toward the end of Bishop's life (at a time when many critics see in Bishop an increasing directness in her recollections of childhood), and he places "Salem Willows" in an autobiographical setting, as a poem about the child's efforts to recover from the trauma and illnesses that befell her following her abrupt removal from Nova Scotia by her paternal grandparents. It was under the care of her "dear Aunt Maud," who lived north of Boston, that the child made her gradual recovery, enabling the ride on a carousel that is the subject of "Salem Willows." After two stanzas describing the golden lion, the golden camel, the high gold elephant, gold horse and gold tigers, the focus shifts:

> There were figures at the center:
> front halves, plaster people...

a group of musicians, who raise flute, drums, lyres, but never play, drowned out by "that music, / coarse, mechanical, loud," of the calliope. Then the final stanza:

> Around and around and around.
> Were we all touched by Midas?
> Were we a ring of Saturn,
> a dizzy, turning nimbus?
> Or were we one of the crowns
> the saints 'cast down' (but why?)
> 'upon the glassy sea'?
> The carrousel slows down.
> Really, beyond the willows,
> Glittered a glassy sea
> and Aunt Maud sat and knitted
> and knitted, waiting for me.

The vertigo in this verse invites comparison to that of "In the Waiting Room," which also turns on the child's precarious connection to a relative, in that poem to her "Aunt Consuelo," a more fictionalized, perhaps less satisfactory, mother substitute than Aunt Maud. But here I want to call attention to one of those moments in Bishop's manuscripts—of which there are many—in which alternative versions reveal a serious crux. The final lines of most of the twelve drafts take the form Travisano has published, but in two of them Bishop toyed with a shift in verb tense, writing instead:

> And Aunt Maud sits and knits
> and knits, waiting for me.

These variant lines draw attention to a curious shift in one line of "Salem Willows," as we have it, from the narrative past to the present tense: "The carrousel *slows* down" (italics mine). Evidently, Bishop considered moving all of the concluding lines of the poem into the present tense, a move that would have pushed the sitting, knitting figure of Aunt Maud even more decisively than it is into the timeless realm of myth: Aunt Maud as one of the Fates, the poet's present fate, not just the child's exaggerated notion of adult presence. As the carrousel *slows* down, the adult poet who has been engaged in an act of recollection disappears into the child's experience and perception. "Really, beyond the willows," she writes—or, in one version "through the willows," as *through* a screen—"glittered a glassy sea," paradoxically both real and artificial, a cited image from a Baptist children's hymn.[4] Then, juxtaposed, unlocalized, present, *sits* Aunt Maud.

Since Bishop eventually settled Aunt Maud down into the past tense, it appears that she pulled back from the vertigo of temporal displacement, instead opting to keep her aunt placed within the narrative frame and in the past. But the temptation—lingering through two drafts—to lift her into a perpetual present gives indication of the unusual degree to which the past remained present to Bishop. In biographical terms, we have plenty of evidence of the persistence of the child in Bishop's adult life—for good and ill: both in her childlike capacity for wonder and an unvarnished innocence of response, and in her painful attacks of insecurity and retreats into importunate dependency. Bishop's insecure self-orientation seems—on the evidence of "In the Waiting Room" and also of "Salem Willows"—to have been experienced, at least in childhood, as dizziness or vertigo, a visceral expression of the child's deeply insecure sense of her attachment to relations.

In her essay on Bishop and the American sublime, Joanne Feit Diehl says of the episode of vertigo in "In the Waiting Room,"

> The fall away from awareness of distinctions disrupts the assurance of a constitutive identity. And the restoration of that identity through the intervention of the external is akin to the final stage of the experiential Sublime, wherein the poet's identity, momentarily repressed by a power felt to be greater than and external to it, reemerges. (36)

In "Salem Willows," the figure of Aunt Maud steadies the mind of the speaker, whose sense of the real has been set awhirl by the carrousel. As such she has the opposite effect from that of "Aunt Consuelo," whose cry of pain sets off the child's existential crisis, her fall into the world of others. In the past tense resolution of "Salem Willows," Aunt Maud represents both what lies outside of the dizzying artifice of the carrousel, and what remains "really," beyond the scrim of the willows. But in those moments when Bishop entertained the notion that Aunt Maud not only sat but sits, "waiting for me," she articulates the possibility that the poet's adult identity never emerges wholly from those overwhelming powers, that she in short remains caught in the unfinished identity of childhood.

I want to look briefly at two attempts at poems that Bishop gave up on before they got very far. The first, about dolls, reads as a sort of *où sont les neiges d'antan*:

> Where are the dolls who loved me so
> when I was young?
> Who cared for me with hands of bisque,
> poked breadcrumbs in between my lips,

Where are the early nurses
Gertrude, Zilpha, and Nokomis?

Through their real eyes

blank crotches,
and play wrist-watches,
whose hands moved only when they wanted -
Their stoicism I never mastered
their smiling phrase for every occasion -
They went their rigid little ways
To meditate in trunks or closets
To let unforeseen emotions
glance off their glazed complexions.

Oddly, and sadly, the opening question is not, Where are the dolls I
loved so, but rather, Where are the dolls who loved me so. The dolls are
remembered as having been the child's imagined caretakers, "early nurses,"
named Gertrude (her mother's name), Zilpha, and Nokomis (Hiawatha's
grandmother and nurse), stand-ins for the absent parents, of a child forced
to invent the love and care she cannot expect in life.[5] There is intense, if
suppressed, anger in the stated and implied contrast between the dolls and
the child: they are asexual and able to play with time; they are good little
girls, stoical, smiling, rigidly self-controlled, willingly locked away, un-
troubled by "unforeseen emotions." They enact a conventional femininity
that Bishop felt she "never mastered."

The illnesses that began in Bishop's childhood lingered into her adult
years, so that she found herself often under the care of hospital nurses. On
one occasion, probably dating from Brazil, she sputtered out two drafts of
resentment against the self-occupied chatter of neglectful nurses. The
fragment's title, "Ungracious Poem," is self-chastising, even as its scarcely
coherent lines erupt in "childish" petulance, but also inscribe her knowledge
that a vulnerable child might *die* of neglect:

Ungracious Poem

Why do Nurses talk?
What do they talk about?
From what one can make out
of temple-rites,   head-gene   breast pins, sacrifices,
blood   that ran nicely
over   newly constructed gutters.

Nurses never stop.
Sometime we barely manage
perhaps in a gasp for breath   when they gasp for bre
to get born in between,   in between   say one word or cry
and some, one suposes
dies the same way, in between.   in between —

Sometimes Nurses carry
a doll-size lily-cup
(Their own doll long ago   failed to commiserate[?]
gave up the ghost; the couldn't get i word in, & even too small
with a pill in it that falls out
No one can go scrambling, after all,
for an un nown pill, so it, too
Gives up its ghost on
Nurses call them 'Pinkies' or 'Floosies,' things like that
God knows all they are—or all they'll do to the gray linoleum.

Perhaps having vented her anger in these rough lines—having got a word in, if only in the privacy of the papers she neither published nor discarded—Bishop was able to return to her "instinctive, modest, lifelong impersonations of an ordinary woman," as James Merrill put it (121). But she did at least lay down some markers on the injured child whom she carried in memory, and whose sensibility she continued to return to until the end of her life.

Thinking about the question of where one starts from, one's home base, I want to circle back to Eliot's "Little Gidding," to these lines:

> And every phrase
> And sentence that is right (where every word is at home,
> Taking its place to support the others...).

Bishop voices her inability to locate a secure home through the notebook of her traveler in "Questions of Travel," who ends the poem with the trailing question: "Should we have stayed at home, / wherever that may be?" And though Bishop's published poems were those of "someone who knows," in Marianne Moore's words (179), she suffered at times from a syntactic perplexity amounting to a dislocation from her verbal home base, where every word was not "at home / Taking its place to support the others." In 1940, Bishop complained in a letter to Moore of having written only "a half-dozen *phrases*" she could reread without embarrassment, and of having an "uncomfortable feeling of 'things' in the head, like icebergs or rocks or awkwardly placed pieces of furniture. It's as if all the nouns were there but the verbs were lacking…" (*One Art* 94). One can speculate that the metaphorical "furniture" transfers Bishop's experience of disturbing removals from childhood homes to language, to her sense of having to struggle to put her verbal house in order. The use of puns to connect her day-to-day life with that of her art was not alien to Bishop, whose "Bight," for example, was littered with "old correspondences." As she remarked in a letter to Lowell, the mess of boats in the harbor reminded her a little of her desk (*One Art* 154). In an unfinished verse letter to Lowell and Moore, written from Brazil, Bishop wraps her anxiety in humor:

> Heavens! It's raining again
> and
>
> and the 'view'
> is now two weeks overdue / and the road is impassable
> and after shaking his paws
> the cat retires in disgust
> to the highest closet shelf,
> and the dogs smell awfully like dogs,
> and I am sick of myself,
> and sometime during the night
> the poem I was trying to write
> has turned into prepositions:
> ins and aboves and upons
> ~~overs and unders and ups~~
>
> What am I trying to do?
> Change places in a canoe?
>   method of composition
>
> Marianne, loan me a noun!
> Cal, please cable a verb!
> Or simply propulse through the ether
> [to me?] more powerful meter.

The difficulty Bishop encountered in making connections, in language and in life, without doubt gave her great pain, but finally it worked its way into her poems as esthetic effects of real power—as, for instance, a capacity to look at familiar things in new ways and to make leaps that startle and refresh the reader. In "Over 2000 Illustrations and a Complete Concordance," the speaker's agnosticism in the Holy Land leads to a headshaking deflation of claims to metaphysical insight: "Everything only connected by 'and' and 'and,'" a line Bishop held in mind from the earliest inception of the poem.

This line, however, introduces the climactic stanza of "Over 2000," in which a querulous complaint about what didn't happen yields to the illusion that it did:

> Open the book. (The gilt rubs off the edges
> of the pages and pollinates the fingertips.)
> Open the heavy book. Why couldn't we have seen
> this old Nativity while we were at it?
> —the dark ajar, the rocks breaking with light,
> an undisturbed, unbreathing flame,
> colorless, sparkless, freely fed on straw,
> and, lulled within, a family with pets,
> —and looked and looked our infant sight away.

John Ashbery glosses "our infant sight" as "power of vision," which is "both our torment and our salvation" (Rev. 204). Richard Flynn's persuasive view is that the poem says, "maturity...comes by virtue of our having first looked at the world from the child's perspective" (117), and cites Travisano saying: "To see with infant sight is not to return to childhood, but, far more difficult, to see, through the eyes of experience, with a child's curiosity" (Travisano 121).

It is odd, though, that Bishop ultimately chose "infant" rather than "child's" or even "childish" here, invoking a state more pristine than that of most of her children, who are already marked by painful experience. I wonder if Ashbery is not right, after all, in regarding infant sight as something more absolute—vision, that is both torment and salvation—quite different, then, from the philosophical musing in Eliot's lines on the cyclic nature of beginnings and ends. In one draft of "Over 2,000," Bishop tried out the adjectives "simple" and even "useless" (and in another draft, "silent") as alternatives to "infant": What "infant" sight sees is "a family with pets," an image that is, as Bonnie Costello says, "presymbolic and elemental" (137). This looking is untutored and unconstrained by culture to see "by the book," suggesting, perhaps, the tabula rasa, or more likely the figure of the Wordsworthian infant, bearing the glory of its innocent origins. Though the force of her desire for such sight displaces the question mark that conventionally "should" end the poem—"Why couldn't we have seen / this old Nativity while we were at it... and looked our infant sight away?"—the gap between desire and experience hovers in the ambiguity of the preposition "away." Like those prepositions in Bishop's "Letter to Two Friends," "away" gets loose and points in opposing directions. As Bonnie Costello explains:

The antithetical pun in 'away' suggests the wish that one may forever gaze into the scene of innocence, forgetting time; yet it also reminds us that looking, observation, itself exists in time. One may in fact cause the departure of innocence, may use up one's infant sight (which after all is fresh only at first glance) in the act of looking. (137)

The looking in this poem does imply a fall, but not into the well-trodden syntax of authorities on how things "should have been." Rather it is a fall into a frightening experience of "things" stripped of order, sequence, or comforting familiarity, where "everything" is held together breathlessly, by the weakest of grammatical connectors. But it is also a fall into "light," "flame," and "sight." To look is the traveler's desire, and for Bishop, uprooted and homesick, sight represents a certain power over the torment of childhood, and the recovery of the power in childhood, a purity of imagination that for all the ill-feeling she lived with (Bishop once remarked that she had been born guilty) lay at the core of her art and was her salvation.

Returning one last time to Eliot's lines, I want to conclude with a brief mention of a poem Bishop was working on toward the end of her life that voices the anguished appeal of the child to the ever-departing grandfather— her maternal grandfather, William Bulmer, in fact, whose Bible and Concordance she "should have" modeled her travels on.

For Grandfather

How far north are you by now?
—But I'm almost close enough to see you:
under the North Star.
stocky, broadbacked & determined,
trudging on splaying snowshoes
over the snow's hard, brilliant, curdled crust...
Aurora Borealis burns in silence.
Streamers of red, of purple,
fleck and color your bald head.
Where is your sealskin cap with ear-lugs?
That old fur coat with the black frogs?
You'll catch your death again.

If I should overtake you, kiss your cheek,
its silver stubble would feel like hoar-frost
and your old-fashioned, walrus moustaches
be hung with icicles.

Creak, creak... frozen thongs and creaking snow.
These drifts are endless, I think; as far as the Pole

> they hold no shadows but their own, and ours.
> Grandfather, please stop! I haven't been this cold in years.

Struggling to catch up with the receding figure of her grandfather, the speaker is struck by the chill of encroaching age, and we recognize that this is a poem of her own age and impending return to the frozen North, her end in her beginning. Yet the voice—unmediated and anguished—of protest against abandonment, departures, death itself remains that of the child who could not be reconciled to such losses. There is perhaps something fitting in a poet who celebrated the continuance of all the untidy activity of life that the circle joining beginning and end should remain unclosed.

Endnotes

1. As study of the Elizabeth Bishop Papers at Vassar College shows. Illustrated in the facsimile *Waste Land* and in the *Inventions of the March Hare*.

2. Bishop's extraordinary rise in reputation has been analyzed by Travisano in "The Elizabeth Bishop Phenomenon."

3. All quotations from unpublished poems are from the Elizabeth Bishop Papers, Vassar College. I have edited them for continuity, preserving the apparent sense of the draft. Readers should be reminded, however, that these are by no means finished poems; many variants will be found in the manuscripts.

4. As cited in Bishop's story, "Gwendolyn," children are the jewels in the crowns cast down "(in what kind of a tantrum?) 'around the glassy sea.'" (*CP* 215)

5. Dolls figure in a number of Bishop's stories: in "The Country Mouse," for example, the child speaks of the dolls she'd had to leave behind in Canada because they were "in no condition go traveling " on the train when her paternal grandparents removed her to Massachusetts (16). Nokomis (and Hiawatha), a pair of Indian dolls, are mentioned in "Gwendolyn" (214).

Works Cited

Ashbery, John. "Second Presentation to the Jury." *World Literature Today.* 1 (Winter 1977): 8.

———. Rev. of *The Complete Poems 1927–1979,* by Elizabeth Bishop. *Elizabeth Bishop and Her Art.* Ed. Lloyd Schwartz and Sybil P. Estess. Ann Arbor: U. of Michigan P, 1983. 201–205.

Bishop, Elizabeth. *The Collected Prose.* Ed. Robert Giroux. New York: Farrar Straus Giroux, 1984.

———. *The Complete Poems 1927–1979.* New York: Farrar Straus Giroux, 1983.

———. *One Art: Letters.* Ed. Robert Giroux. New York: Farrar Straus Giroux, 1994.

———. Papers. Vassar C, Poughkeepsie, New York.

———. "Three Previously Unpublished Poems: A Drunkard, Salem Willows, Suicide of a Moderate Dictator." Afterword by Thomas Travisano. *Georgia Review* 46 (Winter 1992): 607–616.

Costello, Bonnie. *Elizabeth Bishop: Questions of Mastery.* Cambridge and London: Harvard UP, 1991.

Diehl, Joanne Feit. "Bishop's Sexual Politics." *Elizabeth Bishop: The Geography of Gender.* Ed. Marilyn May Lombardi. Charlottesville and London: UP of Virginia, 17–45.

Eliot, T. S. *The Complete Poems and Plays 1909–1950.* New York: Harcourt, Brace, 1952.

———. *Inventions of the March Hare: Poems 1909–1917.* Ed. Christopher Ricks. New York, San Diego, London: Harcourt Brace, 1996.

———. *The Waste Land: A Facsimile and Transcript of the Original Drafts Including the Annotations of Ezra Pound.* Ed. Valerie Eliot. San Diego, New York, London: Harcourt Brace, 1971.

Merrill, James. "Elizabeth Bishop (1911–1979)." *Recitative.* Ed. J. D. McClatchy. San Francisco: North Point Press, 1986.

Moore, Marianne. "A Modest Expert: *North & South.*" *Elizabeth Bishop and Her Art.* Ed. Lloyd Schwartz and Sybil P. Estess. Ann Arbor: U of Michigan P, 1983. 177–179.

Travisano, Thomas. "The Elizabeth Bishop Phenomenon." *Gendered Modernisms: American Women Poets and Their Readers.* Ed. Margaret Dickie and Thomas Travisano. Philadelphia: U of Pennsylvania P, 1996. 217–244.

Elizabeth Bishop: Child of Past, Child of Present in "The Country Mouse"

Gail H. Dayton
Middle Tennessee State University

Abstract

In "The Country Mouse," Bishop's child persona recalls her past, not just as literary discourse, but in order to feel the expansion of self. Though some of her experiences are reminiscent of Lewis Carroll's *Alice in Wonderland* and *Through the Looking-Glass*, she uses metaphorical language rather than fantasy to bring psychological dimensions of her childhood memories of an epiphany into a narrative. In this work, Bishop produces an aesthetic rendering of her autobiography, and she finds her unified self in the exploration of past memories.

In a letter to Jerome Mazzaro in 1978, Elizabeth Bishop denies his claim that her poem "Crusoe in England" was influenced by Lewis Carroll's *Alice in Wonderland* (*One Art* 621). That may or may not be true if applied to that particular work; however, a close reading of her memoir, "The Country Mouse," written probably in 1961, reveals that her child persona bears a striking resemblance to Alice, who after encountering the strangeness of Wonderland, questions her identity and asks, "Who in the world am I? Ah, that's the great puzzle" (Carroll 15). Like Alice, she struggles to form new schemata of her reality in a kind of wonderland, but Bishop's child persona communicates an in-depth exploration of self and objectifies her experience with her paternal grandparents, the Bishops.

In this autobiographical tale of a child's developing self-awareness, Bishop's persona reaches from the present into the past, where she freely explores her memories in a linear, temporal sequence. She breaks with traditional literary techniques to compose a language all her own as she manipulates time and space into segments of personal and familial history. Although it evolves from two other prose pieces, "Gwendolyn" and "In the Village," both published in 1953, "The Country Mouse" was published posthumously in 1984, and to date it remains her most provocative yet unexplored work. Written from a six-year old's perspective, the story contains fragmented episodes that reflect a small child's version of a stay in Worcester that lasted only nine months (Millier 21). However, from a child's point of view, the period of time was a "day that seemed to include months in it, or even years" ("Country Mouse" 17). Echoing the complaint of someone who has been "brought back unconsulted and against my wishes," the persona writes with dramatic flair: "I felt as if I were being kidnapped, even if I wasn't" (14). Eventually, Bishop's first person narrator emerges an introspective child, who, after vacillating between the past and present, reaches a resolution. Thus, her transient childhood manifests itself in metaphor, and using time and memory elements, the persona recalls her past, not just in literary discourse but in order to feel the expansion of self. As she travels with her Bishop grandparents, she sees her life converge at a point; her past and present intersect in the first paragraph, and the train, her construct of linear time, hurls her into a "strange, unpredictable future" (17).

Bishop begins "The Country Mouse" with a metaphor of time: "the old Boston and Maine, gritting, grinding, occasionally shrieking" moving "west and south, from Halifax to Boston, through a black, seemingly endless night" (13). Like Marcel Proust's discovery of a link between the past and present when he recalls the memory of his grandmother's touch (218), Bishop's child persona draws memories of her past life in Nova Scotia with Grandfather Bulmer into her present time. Recalling Grandpa Bulmer, she recites in child's sing-song voice, "My grandfather's clock was too tall for the shelf...." Then she shifts from past memories to the present with the mention of Grandfather Bishop, who "seemed too tall—at any rate, too tall for this train we were on" (13).

Focusing on Grandpa Bishop's overwhelming presence, Bishop's persona tries to make sense of the unfamiliar by recounting his movements as he "snapped on the overhead light again" (13). First, she examines his clothing—his boots that "stood on the floor" and his "coat and vest and necktie... hanging up on a hanger to the right" (13). Conflating the paragraph, the narrator diverts attention from his attire to her perception of power: "Now he descended, god-like and swearing, swept Grandma out of the way, and wedged himself into the lower berth" (13). Next, she dismantles Grandpa Bishop's humanness by suggesting a simulacrum of Carroll's anthropomorphized white rabbit, who, wearing a "waistcoat-pocket" and carrying "a watch to take out of it" (9), exclaims, "Oh dear! Oh dear! I shall be too late." Resembling a white rabbit, Grandpa Bishop has "thick silver hair," a "short silver beard," and the "whites of his eyes were rolled up as if in agony" (13). And like the white rabbit, he places a watch in his vest pocket and exhibits impatience: "Grandpa finally left us to get his breakfast" (15). The narrator then turns her attention to Grandma Bishop, whose controlling personality seems to parallel that of the Red Queen in Carroll's *Through the Looking-Glass*.

In a letter to Robert Lowell in 1948, Bishop alludes to the Red Queen in the Alice stories when she says that the poet Richard Eberhart, "uses up words so fast it's a wonder he has any left by this time." She maintains that his words will "come when he calls—like the Red or White Queen's remarks on time in *Through the Looking-Glass*" (*One Art* 168). Perhaps she intentionally equates the character of Grandma Bishop with that of the temperamental Red Queen, who asks Alice, "Where do you come from....Where are you going? Look up, speak nicely, and don't twiddle your fingers all the time... curtsey while you're thinking what to say. It saves time" (Carroll 94). Clearly, Bishop's persona illustrates her perception of a power struggle, and she exclaims, "Grandma and I sat opposite each other on the two green seats, nibbling soda crackers for [h]ours and studying each other in the strong dust-filled sunlight" ("Country Mouse" 15). Mrs. Bishop also comprehends the depth of power in language, for she, believing that "every little girl should carry a doll," replaces the child's doll with a new one that has "embossed yellow-brown hair that smelled like stale biscuits, bright blue eyes, and pink cheeks" (16). She then names the doll herself and asks, "Where's your doll? Where's *Drusilla*?" (16). Although reluctant to speak of the doll much less hold it, the persona admits, "I meekly dug out the horror from under a pillow and held her on my knee until we got to Boston" (16).

Mrs. Bishop's dominant characteristics are seen obliquely through the persona's observation. As if constructing an image rather than a person, she appraises: "Grandma was dressed in gray silk, with her hat on and her veil pushed up.... The neck of the dress was filled in with fine white net... stretched on little bones, around her neck, like a miniature fish weir" (15). Her only piece of jewelry was a "small round gold case that held a fine gold chain to her pince-nez coiled up tight, on a spring" (15). Perhaps the persona realizes that the pince-nez, unlike her grandfather's watch, is ineffectual and used merely for watching time, not controlling it. By now, she understands that her grandmother's limited power is embedded in male-dominated language and that she does not possess the power or the ability to be time keeper. Feeling less threatened, she begins to relax and writes, "Yes, I was beginning to enjoy myself a little" (16).

Thus, recognizing the futility of her predicament, Bishop's persona attempts to connect the known with the unknown. Always juxtaposing the past to the present, she articulates their arrival at the Bishop house: the driveway was "lined with huge maple trees.... pointed out and named to me..." even though I had been singing "'O maple leaf' ... for years?'" (17). The persona describes the house, which "looked fairly familiar, very much the same kind of white clapboards and green shutters that I was accustomed to [in Nova Scotia], only this house was on a much larger scale, twice as large" (17). Though its physical qualities are similar to those of her house in Nova Scotia, similarities end there, for the atmosphere in the Worcester "house was gloomy, there was no denying it, and everyone seemed nervous and unsettled" (17). Perhaps alluding to artifice in the Bishop household, the narrator describes Grandma Bishop's sewing room, her "sitting room on the front, with a fireplace and bay windows onto the lawn," yet she points out that she never recalls seeing her sew (25). Analogous to the narrator's forewarnings in "In the Village," in which she speaks of her mother's scream as a "slight stain in those pure blue skies" (251), Bishop's child persona senses "something ominous, threatening, lowering in the air" (17) in the farmhouse, that "Grandma said, was 'a hundred and fifty years old,'" (19).

Bishop's persona speaks of her favorite room, but in this passage, she reaches back into the history of the house: "I explored [it] like a cat. It was an old colonial pre-Revolutionary house, but wings had been added... with no regard for period style" (24). Because people rarely frequented the room, she projects that it "had been preserved by accident" (25), perhaps suggesting a metaphorical condition much like her own. When Bishop's persona details the porches of the farmhouse as having "floors set with thick green panes of glass, frosted over and scratched, I suppose to give light to the cellar underneath" (25), she brings to mind the drawing room in which Alice sees all objects behind the looking glass inverted (Carroll 86). Conceivably, the persona alludes to Alice and imagines herself leaping through the opalescent glass from life in a bleak household where things are never as they seem. Proposing that Grandma Bishop is a game player, both victim and controller, the child persona concludes that she herself is disappearing much like Alice, who becomes marginalized after she shrinks to ten inches in height (14).

In his study of palingenetic aesthetics, James G. Tedder holds that a child's view of itself becomes distorted while attempting to define a "physical and spiritual being" according to "multiple mirrors" in which he (or she) seeks the reflection (26). Tedder asserts that "multiple mirrors" exist for the child who is often unable to realize its identity; he argues that the child views itself in a "real mirror" in order to "see himself as others see him" (28). Though Tedder's research is not directly related to Bishop's narrative, in some respects her persona delineates Tedder's theory of multiple mirrors, which reflect both grandparents. On the one hand, Grandma Bishop's mirror reflects a child transformed first with the purchase of a new doll befitting a Boston image. Then, in an attempt to "save" the child "from a life of poverty and provincialism, bare feet, suet puddings... and the inverted *r*'s of my mother's family" (17), Grandma Bishop speaks to the persona in a "confusing way," always in third person of "little girls" and "fathers" and "being good" (16). On the other hand, it is finally in her grandfather's mirror that she regards her reflection. Asked to retrieve Grandpa Bishop's glasses from his bedroom, Bishop's persona recalls standing in his "white and gold" bedroom where she sees his "two large black bottles (of whiskey, I realized years later)" (29).

Bishop attributed her own alcoholism to a long line of familial history: her father, grandfather, three uncles on the Bishop side, plus her mother's brother were alcoholics (Millier 149). In view of this fact, this portion of the memoir theoretically indicates that Bishop sees a negative mirror image, for when the persona reaches "gingerly" for the eyeglasses, she sees herself in the full-length mirror: her "ugly serge dress," her "too long hair," and her "gloomy and frightened expression" ("Country Mouse" 29). Not too surprisingly, after seeing herself in the mirror, she begins to identify with the Bishop's dog, Beppo, a Boston terrier who, she says, hides in the corner to express his shame. Sick and unhappy, the child "felt myself aging, even dying" (31) and speaks her melancholy into existence using a quotation from Louise Bogan as she lies in bed playing with her flashlight: "At midnight tears / Run into your ears" (31).

Perhaps Bishop's most significant memory in "The Country Mouse" emerges when her persona says, "Three great truths came home to me during this stretch of my life, all hard to describe and equally important" (31). Here, she illuminates an awareness of her selfhood and theoretically circumscribes this prose piece as it relates to her autobiography. The first episode occurs when her friend Emma asks about her parents, and the child recalls, "I said my father was dead; I didn't ever remember seeing him" (31). But when the friend asks specifically about her mother, whose condition she explains earlier in her prose poem "In the Village," she answers, "I thought for a moment and then I said in a *sentimental* voice: She went away and left me.... She died, too'" (31). Although her friend is satisfied, the child is not:

> I loathed myself. It was the first time I had lied deliberately and consciously, and the first time I was aware of falsity and the great power of sentimentality—although I didn't know the word. My mother was not dead. She was in a sanatorium, in another prolonged "nervous breakdown." (31, 32)

She admits that her feelings are ambiguous, for she is unsure whether she lied from shame, or from a "hideous craving for sympathy.... But the feeling of self-distaste, whatever it came from, was only too real" (32). As she arranges the pieces of this picture puzzle, she is disillusioned by a "monstrous self" who "could not keep from lying" (32). Forcing her readers to examine their concepts of reality, Bishop's persona looks into another mirror—a mirror designed by her, and she perceives a second self that is capable of lying.

As if facing a "monstrous self" were not enough, she experiences the next epiphany, when, at Grandma Bishop's insistence, she brings a friend home from school. In this segment, Bishop's persona discovers that social consciousness has a two-sided mirror, for when the "ostensible playmate" asks who lives in the rest of the house, she recalls:

> Social consciousness had struck its first blow: I realized this pallid nameless child lived in a poorer world than I (at this moment, at least, for I had never felt at all secure about my status), and that she thought we were in an apartment house. (32)

She realizes that not only is she a liar, she is also a potential game player like her Bishop grandparents, for she is at this point, painfully aware that the social law that dominates them, now dominates her. Though unexplained, it is possible that the child begins to understand Grandma Bishop's complex attempts to redefine her.

The third and most important moment of self-realization comes when young Elizabeth accompanies her aunt to the dentist. She documents the time with a copy of the *National Geographic* dated February 1918, a few days before her seventh birthday. Significantly, this episode, though it is begun in "The Country Mouse," concludes in her poem "In the Waiting Room" (1971). In both works, she understands a universal link with females; she is "one of them" ("In the Waiting" 62; "Country Mouse" 33).

Although the adult Bishop is in control of her memories, the memories nonetheless control this narrative. In "The Country Mouse," with the help of her child persona, she brings to conclusion an aesthetic rendering of her maturation process. Using her insecure childhood to explicate a child's view of her selfhood, she steps back into her past to explore the pieces closest in content to her autobiography. Like Alice, who finds the "little golden key" (49), Bishop's narrator finds the key to her inner self, and by pulling the past into the present, becomes self-aware, exclaiming: "You are you.... How strange you are, inside looking out. You are not Beppo, or the chestnut tree, or Emma, you are *you* and you are going to be *you* forever" (33). Though she answers Alice's question, "Who am I?", she poses another more inexplicable one when she convolutes the ending of her story, asking: "*Why* was I a human being?" (33).

Works Cited

Bishop, Elizabeth. "The Country Mouse," *The Collected Prose*. Ed. Robert Giroux. New York: Farrar, 1984. 13–33.

———. "In the Village," *The Collected Prose*. Ed. Robert Giroux. New York: Farrar, 1984. 251–274.

———. "In the Waiting Room," *The Complete Poems 1927–1979*. New York: Noonday, 1983. 159–61.

———. *One Art: Letters*. Ed. Robert Giroux. New York: Farrar, 1994.

Blake, Kathleen. *Play, Games, and Sport: The Literary Works of Lewis Carroll*. Ithaca: Cornell UP, 1974.

Carroll, Lewis. *Alice's Adventures in Wonderland and Through the Looking-Glass*. Chicago: Wellington, 1989.

Millier, Brett C. *Elizabeth Bishop: Life and the Memory of It*. Berkeley: U of California P, 1993.

Proust, Marcel. *Cities of the Plain*. Trans. C. K. Scott Moncrieff. New York: Random, 1927.

Tedder, James D. *The French Novel of Palingenesis: The Child's Point of View as a Novelistic Technique*. Diss. U of NC at Chapel Hill, 1967. Ann Arbor: UMI, 1967. 68–69.

The Girl Whose Voice Was Her Aunt's: Heredity and Identity in Elizabeth Bishop's "In the Waiting Room"

David Thoreen
Assumption College

Abstract

This paper examines two features of Bishop's "In the Waiting Room": the poem's immediate setting, industrial Worcester; and Bishop's much discussed but as yet inadequately understood substitution of the Aunt's name, "Consuelo." Worcester's 19th and early 20th century position as "the wire capital of the world" changes the way we must read the poem's only simile, the description of the "black, naked women with necks / wound round and round with wire / like the necks of lightbulbs." Bishop's choice of the name "Consuelo" advances her theme of an identity under assault by forging intergenerational connections that simultaneously comfort and disturb.

Like the "most photographed barn in America," of which Don DeLillo writes in *White Noise*, Elizabeth Bishop's poem "In the Waiting Room" has by now so often been painted by critical brushes both wide and fine, that it has become difficult to see. Since I am writing from Worcester, the setting of this poem, I will try to help the reader see the poem in its Worcester context, focusing on two planks on the barn that seem not to have been seen at all.

The circumstances surrounding Elizabeth Bishop's removal from Worcester to Great Village, Nova Scotia, after her father's death and her mother's subsequent breakdown and institutionalization, are well known. In "The Country Mouse," Bishop writes of her return to Worcester by train at the age of six, in the hands of her proper and moneyed paternal grandparents. Here is Bishop, sketching the day of her arrival at her grandparents' Worcester home:

> I had been brought back unconsulted and against my wishes to the house my father had been born in, to be saved from a life of poverty and provincialism, bare feet, suet puddings, unsanitary school slates, perhaps even from the inverted *r*'s of my mother's family. With this surprising extra set of grandparents, until a few weeks ago no more than names, a new life was about to begin. It was a day that seemed to include months in it, or even years, a whole unknown past I was made to feel I should have known about, and a strange, unpredictable future. (*CPr* 17)

It is not difficult to imagine the psychic mechanisms that would have propelled the grandmother to school the "rescued" granddaughter in the traditions and history of the Bishop family, in that "whole unknown past [she] should have known about." Her husband, after all, was himself a successful emigrant from north of Nova Scotia; the advertisement for "J. W. Bishop Company, Builders" which appears in the 1918 *Worcester City Directory* boasts a photograph of the company's main offices in the Worcester Trust Building, an imposing four story edifice, and lists satellite offices in New Bedford, Providence, Boston, and New York. "Established 1874," notes the advertisement. "Incorporated 1899" ("J.W. Bishop" 1192).

Even had it not been for her grandmother's desire to imprint some sense of place on her, a young schoolgirl living in Worcester during the Great War would have quickly learned certain facts about her native city. Preeminent among them: Worcester was the wire capital of the world, the city that wire built.[1] The Washburn & Moen Manufacturing Company, whose North Works on Grove Street is today home to dozens of small establishments, was praised in an 1893 Board of Trade publication in the following terms: "The output of the Washburn & Moen works is sent out to every state and territory in the Union, to the republics of Central and South America, *and to the remotest countries on the face of the earth*" ("Washburn" 71, emphasis added). One can almost hear these words being recited by a first grade class, somewhere between the Pledge of Allegiance and a squeaky rendition of the "Star Spangled Banner." In 1929, thirty years after the Washburn & Moen Company was purchased by a subsidiary of U.S. Steel, and just ten years after Elizabeth Bishop lived in Worcester with her grandparents, a publication of the Industrial Museum of the American Steel & Wire Company would make the stentoriously tentative claim that "Among the industries of the world, with the single exception of farming, there is probably none other which serves mankind so widely as the wire industry" ("Worcester Units" 5).

These wiry windings of Worcester's industrial history bring us to the one simile of "In the Waiting Room." Bishop's catalogue of *National Geographic* photographs includes

> black, naked women with necks
> wound round and round with wire
> like the necks of lightbulbs. (*CP* 159)

The image is startling, and, as the poem's only simile, demands attention. Surprisingly, although nearly every discussion of the poem cites the poem's presentation of the "black, naked women" and their "horrifying" breasts, only Lloyd Schwartz has registered the simile itself, and then only briefly: "Even the similes," Schwartz writes, "suggest the homely comparisons a child might make" (135).

Not even Lee Edelman, whose 1993 deconstructionist reading of the poem offers a critical perspective long overdue, deals with the simile itself.[2] In "The Geography of Gender: Elizabeth Bishop's 'In the Waiting Room,'" Edelman, the first critic to discuss the "material that [Bishop] incorporates...into her imagined magazine" (102), persuasively locates Osa Johnson's autobiography, *I Married Adventure*, as the source for the images of the "Babies with pointed heads / wound round and round with string,"[3] but notes somewhat disappointedly that "the mother [in Johnson's account] does not wear the rings of wire that are used to stretch women's necks in some tribal cultures" (103). For Edelman, Bishop's whole-cloth invention of the wire reveals an intentionally feminist project:

> Bishop *willfully* introduces the symmetry that characterizes her images of women and children so that both here suffer physical distortion by objects "wound round and round" their bodies. This assimilation of women to the status of children takes place simultaneously with the recognition made by the young "Elizabeth" of her own destined status as a woman, of her own inevitable role, therefore, in the sexual economy of her culture. (103, emphasis added)

Keeping in mind the history of industrial Worcester, one might add that the wire wrapped around the women's necks signifies the young "Elizabeth's" recognition of her *current* status in an *international material* economy. As a resident of Worcester, in 1918 the largest locus of wire production in the world, the wire binds her to these women and implicates her in imperialist enterprise.[4] But Elizabeth is no self-deceived "Intended," eking out her days mourning an invented self. Clear eyed and far seeing, Elizabeth's Worcester connection and the wire around the women's necks complete a mental circuit, forging her recognition of their essential and "horrifying" similarity.

This similarity is all the more horrifying because, as the simile makes clear, and in strict accord with the most brutal efficiencies of mechanization, lightbulbs are mass produced, their threads universal. Thus the simile further usurps individual identity, turning the women themselves into *interchangeable* commodities for use by the developed infrastructures of the First World. As a resident of Worcester, Elizabeth appears as the First World consumer who burns out a long series of seemingly interchangeable "lightbulbs": her mother, her maternal grandmother and her aunts in Great

Village, Nova Scotia, then her paternal grandmother and her Worcester aunts. The suppressed but ultimately volcanic knowledge that these caregivers are not, finally, interchangeable, leads to a deliberate assertion of continuous identity ("But I felt: you are an I"), the only—and all too temporary—defense against the collapse of individual identity at the center of "In the Waiting Room." Says the startled Elizabeth: "I was my foolish aunt" (160).

Indeed, this aunt is the other plank on the barn that has not been sufficiently discussed, although many commentators have noted Bishop's departure from the historical (Robert Giroux, for instance, observed that "Aunt Consuelo in 'In the Waiting Room' is Aunt Jenny in 'The Country Mouse,' and in life Aunt Florence" [xx]). Accepting for the moment Bishop's choice of a three beat line for her poem, and her need of a one-beat three syllable name, why "Consuelo," why this odd, invented assertion of Latino family heritage?

Clearly, this is a name that deserves scrutiny. While in Spanish, *"Con"* means "with," in English it also means "against" or "in opposition to." *"Suelo,"* the first person conjugation of the Spanish verb *"soler,"* might best be translated as "I have the habit of" or "I (habitually) feel or do" such and such. Meanwhile, the Spanish verb *"consolar"* (derived from the Latin *"consolor"*) means "to console." Taken together, the three syllables of this aunt's name produce some extraordinary ambiguities. Let's leave the first syllable *"Con"* for the moment, and focus first on the meanings of *"suelo."* To say that "I (habitually) feel solace" is to make two statements simultaneously: even as one asserts the achievement of an emotional stasis, a middle ground between sorrow and joy, one continues to express the ongoing need to be comforted. In other words, *"suelo"* asserts one's position as *both subject and object*, not serially, as the poem's much discussed later lines present the self as both subject and predicate ("But I felt: you are an *I*, / you are an *Elizabeth*, / you are one of *them*"),[5] but simultaneously. As subject, the "I" actively feels solace. As object, the "I" is the passive recipient of solace (in English, the imperative "Comfort me," perhaps best illustrates the objective case).

The two, and in this context opposite, meanings of the first syllable of this aunt's name, *"Con,"* further destabilize the point of emotional stasis. The aunt's presence simultaneously holds out a promise of solace ("with"), *and* threatens that solace ("against"). The "Elizabeth" in the poem, then, goes to the dentist in Worcester with an aunt imbued with "the ability to comfort" as well as having herself, apparently, the "need to be comforted"; and with an aunt who is unable to provide comfort and who may even insist that no comfort is needed.

Thus the complexity and ambiguity expressed by "Consuelo" describes not only the Worcester phase of Bishop's childhood but the preceding and successive periods as well. As Thomas Travisano explains in *Expulsion from Paradise: Elizabeth Bishop, 1927–1957*, not only Bishop's paternal grandparents, but also her Bulmer grandparents "offered a familial imperative to remain silent about painful truths, to leave grief unexpressed and losses unmourned" (14). Just as the child in "Sestina," sitting in the kitchen with a reticent grandmother who "hides her tears" (*CP* 123), must manufacture her own solace by drawing a series of "inscrutable houses" (*CP* 124), so the Elizabeth of "The Country Mouse" roams the Bishops' big Worcester farmhouse "like a cat" (*CPr* 24), that most paradoxical of domestic creatures, utterly dependent and totally self-sufficient. Something similar to this appears in the later "In the Waiting Room."[6] Combining the speaker's early assertion that "I went with Aunt Consuelo" with the later "I was my foolish aunt," we arrive at a new formulation, one that enslaves even as it empowers: "I was my own consolation."

This complex of needs and counter-assertions contained in the name "Consuelo" appears, in different form, in a 1964 letter to Anne Stevenson. Discussing the aborted psychoanalysis of her high school years, Bishop would write that the sessions were an "excellent idea," but had to be discontinued because "[u]nfortunately, I clammed up and wouldn't talk at all" (Millier 39). Here we have the recognition of the need for solace, combined with the silent insistence that no comfort is needed.

Despite living in a family system which held the discussion of her mother to be off limits—indeed, perhaps because of these limits—Bishop seems to have felt haunted by her heredity. According to Frani Blough Muser, Bishop's closest friend through high school and college, "Elizabeth felt that fear of inheriting her mother's illness was a terrible thing, but she consciously did not allow it to be a part of her life" (Fountain 30). Just how one might "consciously" keep a fear from being part of one's life, Ms. Muser does not say.

Certainly that "*oh!* of pain," uttered "in the family voice" as "a cry of pain that could have / got loud and worse but hadn't" (*CP* 161), recalls the scream of Bishop's mother which "hangs over that Nova Scotian village" and over Bishop's own childhood and adult life ("In the Village" 251). That scream, Bishop wrote in 1953, had come into her memory "to live, forever—not loud, just alive forever" (251). Faced with that "forever," and the perpetual prospect of one day screaming herself, "Elizabeth," now in the

"Waiting Room," tries to halt historical process, twice tries to fix herself at a moment and place in time.

We first see this strategy fail midway through the poem, when she says to herself:

> three days
> and you'll be seven years old.
> I was saying it to stop
> the sensation of falling off
> the round, turning world.... (*CP* 160)

The moment of fixity is ironically undermined by its referential placement in time, defined here in terms of constant advance. The source of "Elizabeth's" disorientation is the earth itself, the revolutions of which will mark the passage of those three days. At the end of the poem, "Elizabeth" recovers from her fainting spell and again reaches for reassurance:

> Then I was back in it.
> The War was on. Outside,
> in Worcester, Massachusetts,
> were night and slush and cold,
> and it was still the fifth
> of February, 1918. (*CP* 161)

Again we see the reach for fixity as a means to console an identity under assault. That a World War, a war which has raged for two-thirds of this child's life, should be a source of stability and consolation is one of the most frightening features of Bishop's landscape. Likewise, the reinscription of boundaries presented by "Outside / in Worcester, Massachusetts" offers no great measure of fixity, since we can be certain that when her aunt emerges from the dentist's treatment room, Elizabeth will herself be forced out into "night and slush and cold," and into all of the existential analogues they imply. And although it may still be "the fifth / of February, 1918," "Elizabeth's" experiences "inside" belie that continuity. The girl who entered the waiting room as a mere appendage of her aunt leaves it, in awareness and sorrow, as "one of *them*" (160), a girl with an uncomfortable sense of her impending sexuality and of her family's genetic propensities.

Endnotes

1. I wish to thank my colleague, Dr. Charles Estus, Professor of Sociology and Co-Founder and Director of the Community Studies Program at Assumption College, for sharing his expertise and resources as I prepared this paper.

2. In fact, it would be truer to say that Edelman purposely *subverts* the simile when he calls the wire wound around the women's necks "an image that conjures the garrote—an instrument of strangulation" (103). Wrapping a wire around a person's neck so repeatedly that it resembled the threads of a lightbulb would make, one must think, a rather dysfunctional garrote.

3. Edelman explains that "In her autobiography Mrs. Johnson refers to the Malekulan practice of elongating the head: 'This was done by binding soft, oiled coconut fiber around the skulls of infants shortly after birth and leaving them there for something over a year. The narrower and longer the head when the basket contrivance was removed, the greater the pride of the mother. That her baby had cried almost without ceasing during this period of distortion was of no concern whatsoever'"(Johnson 151, qtd. by Edelman 103).

4. A number of critics have recognized the imperialist ethos that informs the *National Geographic*. The oxymoronic name itself implicitly establishes and maintains national borders while simultaneously thrusting them around the globe. Likening the magazine to a ship, Bonnie Costello refers to "the imperial hold of the *National Geographic*" (*Questions* 122), while Thomas Travisano writes that "The *National Geographic*'s colonialist perspective...betrays itself through that journal's peculiar failure to see 'a dead man slung on a pole' as human" (*Elizabeth Bishop* 185).

5. In "The Impersonal and the Interrogative in the Poetry of Elizabeth Bishop," Bonnie Costello observes that these later lines present the self as both subject and predicate. Despite the "sudden moment of undifferentiation" Elizabeth experiences in the waiting room, the experience gains intensity by the "sense of difference preserved." "[T]he difference between the child and her 'foolish, timid' Aunt is preserved even while it is denied by the cry of pain. This sense of differences is especially clear in the awkwardness of the child's attempts to come to

terms with the experience: 'you are an *I*, / you are an *Elizabeth*, / you are one of *them.*' Making self both subject and predicate, she still preserves the difference" (113).

6.   "Sestina" was collected in the 1965 *Questions of Travel*. While "The Country Mouse" was first published in *Collected Prose*, the Notes to that volume tentatively assign the piece a 1961 date of composition. "In the Waiting Room," written in 1967, was collected in *Geography III* (1976).

Works Cited

Bishop, Elizabeth. *Elizabeth Bishop: The Complete Poems 1927–1979*. New York: Farrar, 1983.

———. "The Country Mouse." *Elizabeth Bishop: The Collected Prose*. New York: Farrar, 1984. 13–33.

———. "In the Village." *Elizabeth Bishop: The Collected Prose*. New York: Farrar, 1984. 251–74.

Costello, Bonnie. "The Impersonal and the Interrogative in the Poetry of Elizabeth Bishop." Schwartz and Estess, 109–32.

———. *Elizabeth Bishop: Questions of Mastery*. Cambridge: Harvard UP, 1991.

Edelman, Lee. "The Geography of Gender: Elizabeth Bishop's 'In the Waiting Room.'" *Elizabeth Bishop: The Geography of Gender*. Ed. Marilyn May Lombardi. Charlottesville: UP of Virginia, 1993: 91–107.

Fountain, Gary, and Peter Brazeau. *Remembering Elizabeth Bishop: An Oral Biography*. Amherst: U of Massachusetts P, 1994.

Giroux, Robert. Introduction. *Elizabeth Bishop: The Collected Prose*. New York: Farrar, 1984. vii–xxii.

Millier, Brett C. *Elizabeth Bishop: Life and the Memory of It*. Berkeley: U of California P, 1993.

"J. W. Bishop Company, Builders." Advertisement. *Worcester City Directory*. Worcester, MA: Drew Allis, 1918. 1192.

Schwartz, Lloyd. "One Art: The Poetry of Elizabeth Bishop, 1971–1976." Schwartz and Estess, 133–53.

——— and Sybil P. Estess, eds. *Elizabeth Bishop and Her Art*. Ann Arbor: U of Michigan P, 1983.

Travisano, Thomas. *Elizabeth Bishop: Her Artistic Development*. Charlottesville: UP of Virginia, 1988.

————. *Expulsion from Paradise: Elizabeth Bishop, 1927–1957*. Jolicure, New Brunswick: Anchorage Press, 1995.

"The Washburn & Moen Mfg. Co." *Tribute to the Columbian Year by the City of Worcester*. Worcester, MA: F. S. Blanchard (for the Board of Trade), 1893. 71.

"Worcester Units: American Steel & Wire Company." Industrial Museum of the American Steel and Wire Company, 1929.

"The Country Mouse": Con-Text, Para-Text, Contra-Text

Stanley Sultan
Clark University

Abstract

The similarity between the situation and experience Bishop reports in the last paragraph of her memoir-essay "The Country Mouse," and her subsequent poem "In the Waiting Room," has been remarked by critics. But the poem departs from the essay in ways that illuminate her mastery of the poet's craft.

Although it has been called a short story (Millier 13), Bishop's editor, Robert Giroux, seems doubly justified in placing her late prose piece, "The Country Mouse" (written in 1961, but published posthumously) in the "Memory," not the "Stories," section of *The Collected Prose*. This is so despite the fact that "The Country Mouse" is predominantly a narrative, hence *fiction* in the sense Hayden White, Northrop Frye and others have used the term. Giroux seems justified, first, because "The Country Mouse" has the structure, not of a tale, but of a chronicle with interpolated commentary. His second justification is that the manifest chronicle appears to be a work precisely of "Memory"—a memoir, narrated and analyzed personal history presented as strictly veridical—whose biographical accuracy is generally accepted (*CPr* x; Millier 19-21; 27-28). Bishop's memoir of the acutely unhappy nine months she spent as a child during the winter of 1917-18 (she turned seven on February 8, 1918), begins with the Pullman train trip after her father's rich (Worcester) Massachusetts parents assumed custody of her from her mother's relatively poor Nova Scotia parents; and it ends with her accompanying her aunt to the dentist.

As readers know, "The Country Mouse" is an extended context for Bishop's subsequent poem set in Worcester, "In the Waiting Room"; and it ends in a manifest para-text of that poem (Millier 23-28). My concern here is with the neglected third relationship my title specifies between her poem and her memoir-essay. And my purpose is to consider what is revealed about Bishop as a poet by the ways in which the manifest para-text that she made the conclusion of "The Country Mouse" is not parallel with, but rather, contrary to, "In the Waiting Room."

Bishop performs closure to "The Country Mouse" in the two final of its twenty pages, beginning: "Three great truths came home to me during this stretch of my life, all hard to describe and equally important" (*CPr* 31). In a deft narrative of the occasion on which it "came home to" her, she presents her childhood experience of each of the "great truths," the first in the remainder of that paragraph, one of the others in each of the two subsequent closing paragraphs. Moreover, she presents her three realizations, concluding with the one that occurs in the dentist's waiting room, in a tight sequence: the first is largely personal (and negative); the second is social; the third is metaphysical. Her construct encourages brief attention to the two "great truths" in the sequence that precede the para-text of "In the Waiting Room."

The child's realization of the first came about when she told her playmate "in a *sentimental* [sic] voice" that her institutionalized mother was dead:

> It was the first time I had lied deliberately and consciously, and the first time I was aware of falsity and the great power of sentimentality.... (31)

She reports that she had called herself "monstrous" because she "could not keep from lying"—and that she still does not know if her motive was "shame" or "a hideous craving for sympathy" (32). Her second, social, truth invokes the rich aptness of the title she took from one of the collection of fables attributed to Aesop, "Town Mouse and Country Mouse." The town mouse declares, "Let me tell you, my friend, you live like an ant. But I have abundance of good things to eat, and if you will come home with me you shall share them all." But his "peas and beans, bread, dates, cheese, honey, and fruit" exist in a dangerous and frightening environment (of humans). Free to leave (unlike the child Elizabeth), the country mouse does so:

> "Good-bye, my friend....You may eat your fill and enjoy yourself. But your good cheer costs you dear in danger and fear. I would rather gnaw my poor meals of barley and corn without being afraid or having to watch anyone out of the corner of my eye." (Aesop 41)

Bishop makes the fable richly illustrative of her childhood situation:

> I had been brought back...to be saved from a life of poverty and provincialism, bare feet, suet puddings, unsanitary school slates, perhaps even from the inverted *r*'s of my mother's family. (*CPr* 17)

And after a few more lines, the next paragraph begins:

The house was gloomy, there was no denying it, and everyone seemed nervous and unsettled. There was something ominous, threatening, lowering in the air. (17)

The difference between the human town mice, and their country mouse grandchild and niece going on seven, is apparent from the child's arrival with her grandparents at Boston's North Station, to be met by their chauffeur and "driven to Stern's [sic] to buy me some decent clothes.... Then we met Grandpa at the Touraine for lunch and I ate creamed chicken and was given an ice cream like nothing I had ever seen on earth—*meringue glacée*, it must have been." It is because of this difference that "later" the chauffeur and she became "good friends" (16-17). The second "great truth" the child learned during those months in Worcester was the significance of class difference—"social consciousness" Bishop calls it. She learned it, she says in the second of the three closing paragraphs, "when Grandma insisted I bring another little girl home from school to play with." Her visitor heard the servants speaking and asked, "Who lives in that part of the house?"; and "I realized [she] lived in a poorer world than I...[and] thought we were in an apartment house" (32). The child Elizabeth lied "tactfully."

In the waiting room of her aunt's dentist, the child learned the metaphysical third and most fundamental "great truth" in the sequence: her identity *as* a human, *with* all other humans. And the congruencies between the final paragraph of "The Country Mouse," devoted to that truth, and the poem portraying the child's discovery of it, are augmented by the poet's naming herself in a poem for the first and only time. Bishop's gesture asserts the historical authenticity of the poem which portrays the same transcendent experience in precisely the same time and place.

But while the manifest congruencies between essay and poem enrich understanding of the poem's subject, Elizabeth the child, the discernible differences enrich understanding of its creator, Bishop the working poet. I shall draw attention to three, in order of occurrence in the poem, which also is the order of their increasing importance. They are presented in its first verse paragraph and, in the same order, utilized in the remainder of the poem.

Bishop's Aunt Florence, slightly occulted with an equivalent name ("Aunt Jenny") in "The Country Mouse," becomes, in "In the Waiting Room," the exotic "Aunt Consuelo." The exotic name given the aunt also is incongruous: the word means consolation, comfort, joy, merriment; but the poem describes "a foolish, timid woman"—"even then I knew" it.

A subsequent and more important difference concerns the other occupants of the dentist's waiting room. The memoir recalls "two men and a plump middle-aged lady, all bundled up" (32). In the poem, the room is "full of grown-up people," who are explicitly not wearing their "arctics and overcoats," so that the child can later give "a sidelong glance" at many people's specific physical personess: "knees / trousers and skirts and boots."

A third and crucial difference is between Bishop's report in the essay that at seven she "could read *most of* the words" (my emphasis) on the *cover* of the current (February 1918) *National Geographic*, and, in the poem, Elizabeth's "reading" the *National Geographic*: "(I could read)." Bishop might simply have retained in the poem, as a strikingly realistic detail, citation of the periodical itself, ubiquitous in dentists' waiting rooms of that era. But she did much more. The child of the poem, who "could read," "read it right straight through," "and carefully / studied the photographs." The ostensible photographs of that issue then are catalogued, to make it the archetypal *National Geographic*, containing images of: the periodical's favorite white explorer couple in their unofficial uniforms; African women with naked breasts; the strange customs of that radical other which is the signature of the *National Geographic* (women's necks elongated, children's heads pointed, men about to be eaten).

Bishop's much-remarked misrepresentation of the actual February 1918 *National Geographic* emphasizes the difference between her report in "The Country Mouse" of her childhood realization, and the poem she made about that realization. It emphasizes the difference because the emblematic *National Geographic* she invented for "In the Waiting Room" is precisely an invention. It is, like the three departures from her memoir (hence, also inventions), artistic working. Those sequential departures—the aunt's name, the other occupants of the room, the child's reading the *National Geographic*—are particular signifiers of a more fundamental contrast between memoir-essay and poem.

As Bishop recalls it at the end of "The Country Mouse," she experienced her third and most fundamental childhood realization (that about *"myself"* as *"one* of them") without lifting the cover of the *National Geographic*. She "looked at the magazine cover," and it just occurred: "The black letters said: FEBRUARY 1918. A feeling of absolute and utter desolation came over me. I felt...[sic] *myself"* (32-33). Moreover, the realization involves only the specified "bundled up" two men and a woman: "I felt *I, I, I,* and looked at the three strangers in panic. I was *one* of them too...." She had not looked inside the magazine. Nor had her aunt "Jenny" even been in the dentist's chair long enough to cry out (if Bishop's aunt ever did).

The occurrence in "In the Waiting Room" corresponds to what the child was doing when she experienced her "feeling of... desolation" in "The Country Mouse." Bishop causes all three departures from her memoir-essay (the aunt's name, the other people, Elizabeth's reading), and ends the first paragraph of the poem: "And then I looked at the cover: / the yellow margins, the date." The fundamental contrast with "The Country Mouse, that the departures signify, begins at this point.

What then follows—in Bishop's poem—the child's "look[ing] at the cover" is not an exposition of that which she realized, but a portrayal of Elizabeth experiencing her realization: the contrast is between Bishop's exposition of it in her essay and portrayal of it in her poem. This portrayal commences immediately after (as in the essay) "I looked at the cover," that is, at the beginning of the second paragraph, by "from inside, / ... an *oh!* of pain / —Aunt Consuelo's voice...."

The cry of the child's aunt initiates her experience:

> What took me
> completely by surprise
> was that it was *me:*
> my voice, in my mouth. (*CP* 160)

The first in sequence, and slightest, of its three departures from Bishop's memoir, the "Aunt Consuelo" who cries out in pain, begins the poem's portrayal of the child's revelatory experience: appropriately, for she is the one of "them" in "In the Waiting Room" closest to Elizabeth, a blood relative. This departure from "The Country Mouse" begins a panoply of progressively more different Others in the poem for Elizabeth to relate to, in the same sequence in which those Others have been introduced in its first paragraph.

Second in sequence, following Elizabeth's exotically named aunt, are the adult strangers who, like her aunt, are denizens of Worcester and are real, the "grown-up people" (the room has no other children). The child "gave a sidelong glance" at their clothes and body parts "to see what it was I was."

The last departure in the sequence, and most important because most extensively used, is the child's having "read," and "studied the photographs" in, Bishop's invented current *National Geographic*. This departure continues the progressive movement outward from young Elizabeth, taking it beyond her aunt and the real adults in the waiting room. First are the photographed white explorers in their Westerners' dress ("riding breeches, / laced boots, and pith helmets"). Then farther outward are the photographed explored, the truly exotic Other: a man who is the victim of cannibal men; babies with their heads bound to a point; women with wire coils stretching their necks—all of these, the poet knows the reader familiar with the *National Geographic* knows, are black and more-or-less naked.

"In the Waiting Room" provides Elizabeth, in a progression outward from herself: her aunt crying out in pain; then adult strangers waiting their turn in the dentist's chair; then the photographs she has just seen of people like herself, her aunt, and the other adults, though in strange circumstances; and finally, the photographs of people very different, yet still possessing, the child realizes:

> similarities—
> boots, hands, the family voice
> I felt in my throat, or even
> the *National Geographic*
> and those awful hanging breasts—
> [that] held us all together
> or made us all just one. (*CP* 161)

The difference between the flat declaration in "The Country Mouse" of what Elizabeth Bishop realized when a child of seven, and the invented parsimonious setting in "In the Waiting Room" that provides the reader's experience of the child Elizabeth's experience, exemplifies the difference between the person and the poet—in Eliot's famous (if gender-challenged) formulation, between "the man who suffers and the mind which creates." For rendering the person Elizabeth's wholly chance, sudden childhood experience as art, Bishop the poet crafted, good modernist that she was, a true objective correlative to her childhood experience: a name, a cry, a crowded room, a typical dentist's-waiting-room magazine with its typical photographs.

Works Cited

Aesop, *The Fables*. Trans. S. A. Handford. Baltimore: Penguin, 1973.

Bishop, Elizabeth. *The Complete Poems: 1927–1979*. New York: Farrar, Straus, Giroux, 1983.

———. *The Collected Prose*. Ed. Robert Giroux. New York: Farrar, Straus, Giroux, 1984.

Millier, Brett. *Elizabeth Bishop: Life and the Memory of It*. Berkeley: U of California P, 1993.

Invisible Threads and Individual Rubatos: Migration in Elizabeth Bishop's Life and Work

Sandra Barry

Independent Scholar, Nova Scotia

Abstract

Scholars and critics usually read Elizabeth Bishop's life-long travelling as "homelessness." However, the underlying causes of her mobility, causes which have origins in family and communal history, are highly complex and speak of more than mere "rootlessness." This essay charts the "invisible threads" and "individual rubatos" of Bishop's participation in the global phenomenon of migration, and explores the migration motif in her art.

Imagine a young Elizabeth Bishop sitting in her room at Vassar College in 1933. Picture her, as she describes herself in an undergraduate essay, "Time's Andromedas," digging "a sort of little black cave into the subject...time in novels...expecting Heaven knows what revelation" (102–03). The "revelation" came from the heavens, as slowly her concentration shifted from the expanse of the page to the expanse of the sky, and she became aware of "the birds going South":

> They spread across a wide swath of sky, each one rather alone, and at first their wings seemed all to be beating perfectly together. But by watching one bird, then another, I saw that some flew a little slower than others, some were trying to get ahead and some flew at an individual rubato; each seemed a variation, and yet altogether my eyes were deceived into thinking them perfectly precise and regular. I watched closely the spaces between the birds. It was as if there were an invisible thread joining all the outside birds and within this fragile net-work they possessed the sky; it was down among them, of a paler color, moving with them. The interspaces moved in pulsation too, catching up and continuing the motion of the wings in wakes, carrying it on, as the rest in music does—not a blankness but a space as musical as all the sound. (102–03)

Bishop realized that she was watching the creation of intricate form, "a sort of time-pattern, or rather patterns, all closely related, all minutely varied, and yet all together forming the migration, which...was as mathematically regular as the planets" (103).

In the midst of "all this motion" and variation she also realized that the spectacle she witnessed (the migration lasted several days) was "a thing so inevitable, so absolute, as to mean nothing connected with the passage of time at all—a static fact of the world, the birds here or there, always; a fact that may hurry the seasons along for us, but as far as bird migration goes, stands still and infinite" (103). For Bishop in 1933, this complex and immense process was "an *idea* of the world's time, the migration idea" (104), which existed both in and out of time as humans perceive it.

Human migration may not be as ancient as that of the birds, but it can be viewed as a similarly inevitable process, which creates "time-patterns" at once vast or collective and intimate or individual. The phenomenon of migration had a direct impact on Bishop's life and work.[1] This impact originated in what Graeme Wynn calls the "pattern or particularity of the past" (67), meaning that Bishop lived not only at particular historical moments and in particular circumstances, but also within a "time-pattern" shaped by the forces of human interaction: geography, economics, culture, etc. The sources of Bishop's complex relationship with travel, arrival and departure, are found in the general historical patterns of human migration in the Atlantic Canada and New England regions and in the particular configurations of these patterns in Bishop's family history. This essay examines the origins and effects of the migratory experience on Bishop's life and work, and explores how the relationship between pattern and particularity, which Bishop herself so clearly perceived in the act of migration, influenced her artistic development and product.

Literary critics make much of Bishop's sense of uprootedness. Travel is a persistent theme in her poetry and prose, and scholars have explored the ways in which her peripateticism affected her writing. However, these critics and scholars have said little about the complex underlying causes of Bishop's mobility, causes which have origins in family and communal history. Bishop was more than a solitary wanderer, rootless and adrift. Her literal and poetic travelling may be interpreted as evidence of dislocation (and this was certainly one of its qualities); but the origins of her experience and understanding of *journey* lay not only in a sense of what Thomas Travisano has called the "expulsion from paradise" (9)—that is, discontinuity (e.g., Bishop's removal from Nova Scotia against her wishes in 1917)— but also in the historically—and culturally-derived phenomenon of out-migration, which was a deeply-rooted pattern of behavior—that is, continuity. "Invisible threads" bound Bishop to time, place and community, and she shared the experiences of thousands of other migrants, who moved like tide between the Atlantic Provinces and New England at the turn of the century.

In the midst of this pattern she developed her own "individual rubato...a faintly rhythmic irregularity," putting the pattern to particular use in creating her distinctive voice, which does not conveniently fit into any ideology (another human pattern), except perhaps the idea of "world's time."

Rather than seeing her as a wanderer without destination, readers should regard Bishop as a seasonal migrant. She moved between points on the compass (North & South), between environments (rural and urban), between states of being (sleeping and waking) and between moments (past and present). She reconciled this condition not by creating rigid dichotomies, "life/death, right/wrong, male/female" (*CP* 185), mutually exclusive states; but by merging dualities, creating "interspace" between the wing beats of her words, creating wakes, what she called "dazzling dialectics": "waves give in to one another's waves," "Our visions coincided....two looks," "that conflux of two great rivers," "in the past, in the present, and those years between" (*CP* 4, 177, 185; *CPr* 251). She does not deny the dichotomies; rather she makes them vibrate with each other as she at once accepts, adapts and subverts them through poetic form (yet another human pattern). The migration experience contributed to "that sense of constant re-adjustment" (*CP* 10), which became such a significant component, both a positive and a negative force, in Bishop's life and work.

Travel was an ambiguous event for Bishop. As with most of her life experiences, her relationship to travel was a questioning one. Usually she succumbed to the lure of seeing "the sun the other way around" (*CP* 93), but travel also meant that she found herself frequently among strangers. She was also drawn to the idea of finding a spot on which to settle down, but she considered perpetual sedentary existence a confinement. The tragedy and triumph of Bishop's life and work is that rather than choose, she migrated between points of view, and created an art which ebbs and flows on the page. Scholars of human migration refer to the "push and pull factors" that prompt individuals, families and communities to move (Conrad 102). One of the principal dynamics of Bishop's life was the tension between staying and going, between going and returning. This tension manifested itself in many ways in her art. For example, it helped create a language of the intermediary in which choices are merged into rather than isolated from each other, in which compromise is seen as a valuable strategy or perspective. "The tide half way in or out" became the interstitial space where her creativity flourished: the Gentleman of Shalott's ironic, "Half is enough"; the monument "turned half-way round"; the fish "half out of water" (thus half in); and the "indrawn yes's" "half groan, half acceptance" (*CPr* 264; *CP* 10, 23, 42, 17).

Almost from birth Bishop began to travel. This mobility resulted from the interaction between peculiar family circumstances and general patterns of existence, which operated in the part of the world where she was born. Born in Worcester, Massachusetts, eleven years after the turn of the twentieth century, to parents of Maritime-Canadian ancestry, it was virtually inevitable that, at an early age, Bishop was drawn into the migrational movements which had existed between New England and Atlantic Canada for centuries.

Bishop's ancestors, who were all of English origin, emigrated to North America at various times during the seventeenth, eighteenth and nineteenth centuries. Her Foster ancestors emigrated from England to Massachusetts in 1635, remaining in the Thirteen Colonies and fighting on the side of the Patriots in the War of Independence (Bishop Family Genealogy). The next group of ancestors to journey across the Atlantic were the Bulmers from Yorkshire, who came to Nova Scotia during the Yorkshire emigration of 1774–1775, settling in Cumberland and Colchester Counties (Barry 22 and 204 n4).[2] Many of the Bulmers remained in Nova Scotia (those now resident in the province are descended from these immigrants), but some of them migrated to central Canada and the mid-western United States. The Bishops emigrated from Plymouth, England, in 1818, settling first in Saint John, New Brunswick; they resettled in Prince Edward Island in the 1830s; and, subsequently, emigrated to Rhode Island in the 1860s.[3] This family exhibited most comprehensively the complex migrational links existing between New England and Atlantic Canada at this point in history (Bishop Family Genealogy). The final group of migrants were the Hutchinsons. Robert and Mary Hutchinson, both of Greenwich, England, also emigrated first to Saint John, N.B., in the 1840s. In the 1850s they resettled near Great Village, N.S. Being a ship's captain, Robert was peripatetic and Bishop clearly identified the origins of her own wanderlust in this family line. She wrote to Anne Stevenson, "That line of my family seems to have been fond of wandering like myself"—though it must be noted, all her ancestors were travellers of one sort or another.

With these general migrations completed in her family, mobility did not cease. Robert Hutchinson was involved in the West Indies trade, travelling on the North-South axis, which would later so dominate Bishop's life, until his death in a shipwreck in the 1860s. Robert's sons also led peripatetic lives: George emigrated back to England where he died in the late 1930s, though he returned several times to Nova Scotia in the late nineteenth century; John spent years as a missionary in India and also eventually returned to England where he died in 1921, though, again, only after migrating back to Nova Scotia and living there for several years in the 1880s; and William emigrated to the American Mid-West and died in Iowa in 1925, though not before he returned to the Maritimes to serve as President of Acadia University in Wolfville, N.S., from 1907–1909. After having emigrated with his family from Prince Edward Island to Rhode Island in 1859, John Bishop, Elizabeth Bishop's paternal grandfather, migrated to Worcester, MA, where he established himself in business and married Sarah Foster. Bishop's maternal grandfather, William Bulmer, migrated across the Cobequid Mountains in the early 1860s, settling in Great Village, Colchester County, N.S., where he married Elizabeth Hutchinson; but before doing so he also made his own forays into the New England States (Barry 26, 31–36 and Bishop Family Genealogy).

By the late nineteenth and early twentieth centuries, all this ancestral mobility began to converge in the generation which would be most significant for Elizabeth Bishop. Again, the general patterns of history played a significant role in the particular configuration of her circumstances. A quick glance at the pattern is needed before turning to the particulars. Graeme Wynn has examined the close ties between Nova Scotia and Massachusetts in the nineteenth century. He observes, "Contact, tradition, familiarity—in sum, experience—formed a powerful bond among the people of this international region" (72). The complex economic and familial bonds, which had developed over centuries of interaction (and clearly evidenced in Bishop's own family), retained solvency in Nova Scotia and Massachusetts even in the midst of Canadian Confederation, embodied so tangibly in the transcontinental railroad, which sought to unite the new country from east to west. In spite of this new political system, the Atlantic Canada region continued to have active and direct communication with New England, in part, because sea routes were easier to traverse than land routes. Indeed, these sea links were enhanced and expanded in the late nineteenth century with increased steamship connections between Boston/New York and Yarmouth/Saint John.

One of the most important patterns linking Atlantic Canada and New England in the late nineteenth and early twentieth centuries was the phenomenon called out-migration, as Maritimers travelled to the growing cities of the northeastern United States, especially in Massachusetts and New York, in search of work and education.[4] Margaret Conrad, among others, has examined the phenomenon of out-migration, which occurred in Atlantic Canada beginning in the late nineteenth century, and which remains an important experience of Atlantic Canadian life even today. She observes, "The extent of the exodus in the period from 1880 to 1930 was genuinely impressive, claiming at least 75,000 people and as many as 122,000 people a decade, most of them young and single, more of them women than men" (101). It was this very phenomenon of exodus, of migration of Maritimers to what was commonly called the "Boston States," which had such an immediate impact on Bishop's life.

In 1903 or 1904 Gertrude Bulmer of Great Village, N.S., joined the out-migration when she travelled to Boston to train as a nurse, something hundreds of Nova Scotian women had already done (Barry 40). She remained in Massachusetts for several years, though she made frequent visits back to Nova Scotia. Sometime in 1906 or 1907 she met William Bishop of Worcester, MA (Millier 2). The rest, as they say, is history. They married in 1908 and their only child, Elizabeth, was born on 8 February 1911.[5] The impact of migration does not end here. William died on 13 October 1911, and Gertrude and Elizabeth Bishop moved between Massachusetts and Nova Scotia several times during the next few years. Then, in April 1915, Gertrude took Elizabeth to Nova Scotia where the latter remained continuously until September 1917, when she was taken back to Worcester by her paternal grandparents—Gertrude having had a breakdown in 1916, at which time she was hospitalized, permanently, as it turned out, until her death in 1934. Bishop poignantly captured the "individual rubato" of migration in "In the Village," a private rhythm which, it must be remembered, occurred within the wider current, "invisible threads," connecting Bishop and her mother to the flock:

> First, she had come home, with her child. Then she had gone away again, alone, and left the child. Then she had come home. Then she had gone away again, with her sister; and now she was home again....So many things in the village came from Boston, and even I had once come from there. But I remembered only being here, with my grandmother. (*CPr* 252, 254)

Gertrude was not the only Bulmer daughter to go to the "Boston States." She was followed by her sisters Maude, Grace and Mary. The latter two also trained and worked as nurses in Boston. Maude settled with her husband in Revere, MA, where Bishop went to live early in 1918 (and where she remained until attending Walnut Hill School and Vassar College). From the 1910s until 1930, the Bulmer family (including Bishop's grandparents) travelled regularly between Nova Scotia and Massachusetts. At the time Bishop was born, this pattern of migration had been established by her mother and by the 1920s was a deeply-entrenched routine within the family. Thus

Bishop grew up with the ever-intensifying toing and froing of her maternal relatives. Moreover, countless friends and distant relatives from Great Village and the surrounding area were also caught in this migrational current, which flowed so freely between the Maritimes and New England. Far from being a phenomenon of rootlessness, Bishop's early experience of migration was grounded in family history (ancestral and immediate). In Bishop's case, of course, this pattern occurred within the context of a tragic, private (or particular) history, adding layers of complexity (orphanhood, grief and mourning) to an already complex set of circumstances.

Though arising from the loss of her parents and her mother's mental illness, once again, the personal conditions of Bishop's childhood occurred within the framework of broader historical patterns. Another significant and grand pattern related to Bishop's private childhood world was the Great War of 1914–1918. Bishop encountered the War in both Nova Scotia and Massachusetts, writing about it most directly in the autobiographical story, "The Country Mouse," and in the poem, "In the Waiting Room," the only poem in her *oeuvre* where she names herself directly.

The United States did not enter the War until 1917, but the close transfamilial ties between Massachusetts and Nova Scotia ensured that both places shared in the shock and grief which flooded over the world as a result of the carnage in Europe. One of the most dramatic manifestations of the link between Nova Scotia and Massachusetts is located in events of December 1917. On 9 December around 9:00 a.m., the French munitions ship *Mont Blanc* and the Belgian relief ship *Imo* collided in Halifax Harbor, resulting in one of the worst man-made, non-nuclear explosions in history. The northern end of the cities of Halifax and Dartmouth were devastated, nearly 2000 people were killed and many more thousands wounded. This catastrophe had a direct impact on Bishop and her family. Gertrude Bulmer Bishop was then resident in the Nova Scotia Hospital in Dartmouth, located on the east side of Halifax Harbor. The female wards on the north side of the building felt the brunt of the explosion to such a degree that all the windows shattered and the plastered floors and ceilings crumbled. Miraculously, no one was killed at the hospital, but this event served only to traumatize patients. Indeed, the entire city was so deeply traumatized that even today the Halifax Harbor Explosion remains a force in the psychic and civic life of the people.

Massachusetts entered the picture immediately. Its residents (a significant number of whom were Nova Scotian born or had relatives in Nova Scotia) organized the largest relief effort of any single group, sending a train loaded with volunteers and supplies to the beleaguered city the very night of the disaster. Even though she was only six, Bishop, who was living in Worcester at the time, would have been aware of this massive relief effort, which went on for several months.[6] Though not an overt factor in the content of her World War I poem, "In the Waiting Room," the strange disorientation which this poem documents (triggered by the disturbing images Bishop saw in an issue of the *National Geographic*, including photographs of an erupting volcano) must surely have had a source in the spectacular disaster which had shaken her beloved Nova Scotia to its foundations. After all, 8 February 1918 was almost exactly the two month anniversary of the disaster, and the nearly seven year old Bishop was acutely aware that "The War was on" (*CP* 161).[7]

What effect did all this coming and going have on Bishop? How did the close links between Nova Scotia and Massachusetts, so manifest in her family's activities, affect her? As regards her nationality, she told Léo Gilson Ribeiro, "In origins I am half-Canadian, half-American from New England" (17). In her parents' generation she was, and it was this duality which Robert Lowell immortalized in an unfinished poem:

> Dear Elizabeth,
> Half New-Englander, half fugitive
> Nova Scotian, wholly Atlantic sea-board—
> Unable to settle anywhere, or live
> Our usual roaring sublime. (in Hamilton 135)

Stepping back to the previous generation, as she did with Anne Stevenson, Bishop wrote on 18 March 1963, "I am 3/4th Canadian, and one 4th New Englander." In both generations, however, the ties between these geographic locations ensured that neither was unfamiliar—or foreign. She felt rooted in both places. Or, if dislocation is the preferred perspective from which to approach Bishop, she felt lost to both.

Within her transnational patriotism lies perhaps a reason why she was able to live so long as an expatriate in Brazil. As her letters reveal, her views on exile and expatriatism were complex: In 1935 she averred, "I am not, never, never, an EXPATRIATE" (*One Art* 37); in 1955 she observed, "Exile seems to work for me—I have almost a new book of poems" (*One Art* 312). She came by her penchant for travel honestly, via a strong family tradition and, perhaps, even a genetic propensity. Thus her early migration experiences were in many ways inherently derived. However, migration also reinforced and expanded what might have been left dormant had she lived in another time and place. Instead, going to and returning from a place became an enduring personal pattern.

Generally speaking (and generalizations must be proffered with caution in the case of such a complex life as Bishop's), Bishop equated the Maritimes with rural life and the past and equated New England with urban life and the present. What is vital to remember is that Bishop did not set up such a duality in oppositional terms. She certainly contrasted such environments, but her preference was to take from each what she needed and liked best. Her despair over urban alienation did not prevent her from living in and writing about cities ("Love Lies Sleeping," "Quai d'Orleans," "Arrival at Santos," "View of the Capitol from the Library of Congress," "Night City," etc.). Her love of the natural world and village life did not prevent her from identifying the darker elements they contained ("Florida," "Seascape," "First Death in Nova Scotia," "Filling Station," etc.). As "From the Country to the City" reveals, Bishop preferred to migrate between these two environments (both real and imagined) in actuality and on the page:

> Flocks of short, shining wires seem to be flying sidewise.
>   Are they birds?
> They flash again. No. They are vibrations of the tuning-fork
>   you hold and strike
> against the mirror-frames, then draw for miles, your dreams,
>   out countrywards. (*CP* 13)

Here, wires of communication vibrate like migrating birds, which are drawn into the imagination of the migrant travelling from the busy city to the quiet country. The pivot is the vibrating tuning fork in the migrant's hand (head)—contingent oscillation preferred to final destination.

Rural and urban also connoted "tradition" and "modernity," terms to which Bishop related in highly complex ways. Again, she accepted and eschewed elements in both. For example, she rejected the Baptist faith of her maternal grandparents, but retained a life-long passion for its hymns, acknowledging that they influenced her writing. On 8 January 1964, she wrote to Stevenson, "I'm full of hymns, by the way...and I often catch them in my own poems." In the same letter Bishop observed, "I do usually prefer poetry with form to it," and her *oeuvre* is evidence of strong grounding in Classical and Romantic traditions. She studied Greek and Latin literature and wrote sonnets, sestinas, villanelles, etc. Yet she was influenced by the modernists (such as Eliot, Moore and Stevens) and absorbed elements of surrealism during her European sojourns. As a result, her *oeuvre* is also evidence of a strong inclination to subvert traditional form and expand content beyond classical conceits. One way she did this was by championing prodigals, freaks and the disenfranchised in both the animal and human worlds (e.g., "Summer's Dream," "The Fish," "Cootchie," "Faustina, or Rock Roses," "Squatter's Children," "The Burglar of Babylon," "The Armadillo," "Pink Dog," "House Guest"). Such individuals are usually caught between worlds. "The Prodigal" is one of Bishop's most obvious exiles; the tight sonnet form of the poem belies a deep revision of what it means to leave and return home, a re-vision of the degree of control we have over our lives:

> Carrying a bucket along a slimy board,
> he felt the bats' uncertain staggering flight,
> his shuddering insights, beyond his control,
> touching him. But it took him a long time
> finally to make his mind up to go home. (*CP* 71)

"The Burglar of Babylon" is one of her most obvious migrants:

> The poor who come to Rio
> And can't go home again. (*CP* 112)

Micuçú is another "individual rubato" amidst the "confused migration" of "a million sparrows" trying to nest in "the fair green hills of Rio." Bishop was not only intellectually interested in these (real or imagined) individuals in transition, she identified with their transience, their moving from here to there, in many ways. She realized that the need or desire to travel, to be on the move, originated both in factors beyond one's control and in forces deeply inherent within one's soul.

It is a commonplace in Bishop scholarship to view her wanderlust as indicating a perennial search for or rejection of home, a response to the paradoxical nature of home as both sanctuary and prison. Certainly, Bishop's metaphors of house and home are highly ambivalent: one has only to think of the fragility of "Jeronimo's House," the haunting silences of "Sestina," and the impossibility of the "proto-dream house" in "The End of March." But at no point does Bishop abandon the "idea of a house," and in her life she was involved in the creation of several actual homes, in Key West, Petrópolis, Ouro Prêto, and Boston. She grieved for the loss of several of these homes, but kept right on trying to create another. The regular travel which Bishop began to experience almost at birth was a migration between homes (her grandparents' in Nova Scotia and her aunt's in Massachusetts). Even if she felt not fully part of either of them, still, they provided her with "shelter from / the hurricane." Ultimately, she carried their odd assortment of treasures, "the little that we get for free / the little of our earthly trust," with her (*CP* 34, 177). Migration itself became the framework of a home. In the spirit of the interstitial and intermediary program of Bishop's life and work, perhaps migration, which had a cyclical or seasonal quality for Bishop, might be seen as a half-way house.

Bishop was a consummate neither/nor poet; she questioned every assumption, yet managed to make profound moral judgements which did not preach but rather simply observed. Her poetry presented gentle dénouement rather than ecstatic revelation, leaving room for further travels in the imagination. She was a poet of the divided: "The Weed," "The Gentleman of Shalott," "The Man-Moth," "The Riverman," "Crusoe in England," etc. And she was a poet of the migrant: "The Iceberg," "The Sandpiper," "Large Bad Picture," "Over 2,000 Illustrations and a Complete Concordance," "Questions of Travel," "Under the Window, Ouro Prêto," etc. In all, she endeavored to accept the paradox of existence, acknowledging that one can be in both places or in neither place at the same time.

One of Bishop's most celebrated poems is her most overtly migratory, "The Moose." The history of this poem is well known: Its origins in a 1946 trip to and from Nova Scotia, its completion twenty-six years later and presentation at the Phi Beta Kappa ceremony, Harvard University, in June 1972. "The Moose" begins with an evocation of the Bay of Fundy's tides, a literal description which also stands metaphorically for the tide of human migration the poem so powerfully charts:

> From narrow provinces
> of fish and bread and tea,
> home of the long tides
> where the bay leaves the sea
> twice a day and takes
> the herrings long rides. (*CP* 169)

Bishop's working title was "Back to Boston," which, if kept, would have shifted the focus of the poem considerably (Doreski 155).[8] As it is, this directional reference (a reference to the historical and cultural patterns in which Bishop grew up) was unobtrusively incorporated and modified mid-poem, put in the mouth of one of the thousands of migrants who still journeyed between Nova Scotia and Massachusetts in 1946, "A grand night. Yes sir, / all the way to Boston."

The themes, images, complex meters and rhymes of "The Moose" interconnect in as many ways as the people of Nova Scotia and Massachusetts interconnected. The ostensible linearity of the poem (the progress from point A to point B) turns in on itself, becomes self-reflective and meditative, showing that life's journey is not a straight forward narrative, just as migrating birds keep going and coming, returning to the same place over and over again with remarkable regularity. Suddenly, this regularity is interrupted (though ultimately only to highlight its continuity in our lives); everyone on the bus is jolted out of reverie by the appearance of something at once both perfectly ordinary/natural and extraordinary/preternatural. By retitling the poem, Bishop shifted focus to the "grand, otherworldly" qualities of one of the shiest creatures of the northeastern woods. Moreover, moose are also migratory, venturing over wilderness territories, occasionally coming face to face with humanity. Like the migrating birds, the moose is both mysterious and familiar, outside the human world, yet, at the same time, not unrelated to it.

Ultimately, Bishop did not choose between the dualities she presented so regularly in her poetry and prose. She accepted that the realities of past and present (her grandparents' voices talking in eternity and the voices of the passengers going to their immediate destinations) and the realities of the mundane and mysterious co-exist:

> by craning backward,
> the moose can be seen
> on the moonlit macadam;
> then there's a dim
> smell of moose, and an acrid
> smell of gasoline. (*CP* 173)

In the late twentieth century gasoline fuels migration and the moose fuels imagination; both are journeys.

In "The Moose" Bishop affirms that both the "sweet sensation of joy" and the "smell of gasoline" must exist contiguously in our lives. She chose neither and both. Moreover, each person on the bus moves "rather alone" in an "individual rubato"; but "invisible threads" also join them together, draw them into a "fragile net-work" of shared experience, "Why, why do we feel / (we all feel) this sweet / sensation of joy?" "The Moose" also affirms that these bonds are "a thing so inevitable, so absolute" as to exist outside time itself; but it accomplishes this insight so quietly that we almost miss it—we have to crane our heads backward to get the glimpse which confirms it. For all our motion and variation (to be celebrated certainly—and Bishop did), the ties which bind us—for better or worse—to what we call "the human situation"[9] "stand still and infinite" in the world.

Endnotes

1. Bishop was not unique in being affected by and writing about her migration experiences. "The Age of Migration" has spawned a literature of its own. In the introduction to *Writing Across Worlds*, White considers "geographical movement...as a crucial human experience" (1) and defines migration "from a geographical viewpoint as 'a change in the place of residence'" (5). Literature about migration is related to, yet distinct from, "travel writing" and literature about "the relationship of people with place."

2. John Bulmer arrived in Nova Scotia on 7 May 1774, with his wife, Grace, accompanied by his three brothers, James, George and Joseph. His brother, William, and sister, Mary Frieze, had emigrated in 1772 and were settled in Amherst, N.S.

3. The Bishop progenitor was William Bishop, born in Plymouth, England, in 1809. His son, John Wilson, Bishop's paternal grandfather, was born in Prince Edward Island in 1848. Descendants of this Bishop family are found in Prince Edward Island today.

4. Out-migration also took Maritimers across Canada and to the American West Coast (particularly California), but the largest concentration of migrants was in the northeastern United States. It must again be remembered that throughout this century European emigration (e.g., the Irish potato famine exodus of the 1840s) continued to be a major factor in population growth and shifts in both regions.

5. Interestingly, Bishop was born a few months before the Canadian federal election of September 1911. The principal issue of this election was Prime Minister Wilfred Laurier's and the Liberal Party's advocation of Reciprocity with the United States. Always a controversial issue, this policy was nonetheless linked for some Maritimers with the phenomenon of out-migration, which had drained away so much of the region's youth. An anonymous contributor to *The New Era* observed on 4 September 1911, "Nova Scotia has exported thousands of her sons and daughters to the United States since the abrogation of the Reciprocity treaty of 1854 to 1886. Give us the benefits of such a treaty at this time

and we will have them back again" (3). Wynn writes, "'No truck...' [was] the slogan of opposition to the American free trade agreement that Prime Minister Wilfred Laurier took to the Canadian electorate in 1911" (66 n12).

6. Even today, a tangible reminder of the aid provided by Massachusetts is seen in the yearly gift of a gigantic Christmas tree from the people of Nova Scotia to the people of Boston, a thank you for support in time of crisis and for continued links between the two regions.

7. Bishop never refers directly to the Halifax Harbor Explosion in her poetry or prose, but oblique references to this event might be located in her frequent references to explosions, fires and shattered walls, found in works such as "The Sea and Its Shore," "The Baptism," "Visits to St. Elizabeth's," "A Cold Spring," and "Armadillo." Such references are also found in unpublished works, such as "Back to Boston" and early drafts of "Cape Breton."

8. Drafts of another poem tentatively entitled "Back to Boston" or "Just North of Boston" are found in Bishop's papers at Vassar College (Series V, no. 66.10). This unfinished poem appears to be another rural/ urban (tradition/modernity) comparison, describing a trip from the countryside, through the suburbs, into the city.

9. Bishop to Stevenson, 8 January 1964. Bishop wrote, "Any of Buster Keaton's films give me the sense of the tragedy of the human situation, the weirdness of it all, besides all the fun...."

Works Cited

Barry, Sandra. *Elizabeth Bishop: An Archival Guide to Her Life In Nova Scotia.* Great Village, N.S.: The Elizabeth Bishop Society of Nova Scotia, 1996.

Bishop, Elizabeth. *The Collected Prose.* New York: Farrar, Straus, Giroux, 1984.

———. *The Complete Poems, 1927–1979.* New York: Farrar, Straus, Giroux, 1983.

———. Family Genealogy, Elizabeth Bishop Papers, Series X, no.78.5, Vassar College Library Special Collections.

———. Letters to Anne Stevenson. Olin Library, Washington U.

———. Letters to Grace Bulmer Bowers. Elizabeth Bishop Papers, Series I, no. 25.12, Vassar College Library Special Collections.

———. *One Art: Elizabeth Bishop Letters*. New York: Farrar, Straus, Giroux, 1994.

———. "Time's Andromedas." *Vassar Journal of Undergraduate Studies* 7 (1933): 102–120.

Conrad, Margaret. "Chronicles of Exodus: Myths and Realities for Maritime Canadians in the United States, 1870–1930." *The Northeastern Borderlands: Four Centuries of Interaction*. Eds. Stephen Hornsby, et. al., Fredericton, New Brunswick: Acadiensis, 1989. 97–119.

Doreski, Carole Kiler. "'Back to Boston': Elizabeth Bishop's Journeys from the Maritimes." *Colby Library Quarterly* 24: 3 (September 1988): 151–161.

Hamilton, Ian. *Robert Lowell: A Biography*. New York: Random House, 1982.

Millier, Brett. *Elizabeth Bishop: Life and the Memory of It*. Berkeley: U of California P, 1993.

The New Era. Public Archives of Nova Scotia, Halifax, N.S. mfm. 4 September 1911.

Ribeiro, Léo Gilson. "Elizabeth Bishop: The Poetess, the Cashew, and Micuçú." *Conversations with Elizabeth Bishop*. Ed. George Monteiro. Jackson: UP of Mississippi, 1996. 14–17.

Travisano, Thomas. *Expulsion from Paradise: Elizabeth Bishop, 1927–1957*. Jolicure, New Brunswick: Anchorage, 1995.

White, Paul. "Geography, Literature and Migration." *Writing Across Worlds: Literature and Migration*. Eds. Russell King, et. al. London: Routledge, 1995. 1–19.

Wynn, Graeme. "New England's Outpost in the Nineteenth Century." *The Northeastern Borderlands: Four Centuries of Interaction*. Eds. Stephen Hornsby, et. al. Fredericton, New Brunswick: Acadiensis, 1989. 64–90.

Brazil in Bishop's Eyes

Neil Besner
University of Winnipeg

Abstract

The exploration of ways of seeing that informs many of Bishop's poems is a distinctive feature of her poems set in Brazil. In these, the mode of surface description is taken up as the subject of a more complex scrutiny from a doubting interior eye as the gaze moves from allegedly objective enumeration to more subjective reflection. The apparently fabulous overabundance and extravagance of Brazilian landscape and scenery, as well as the facts of Brazilian history and geography, become occasions for Bishop to reflect on the motives for travel, for seeing through travellers' eyes, and for writing poetry.[1]

Under any North American eye, Brazil at first glance looks extravagant, fabulous, outsized. All the senses might be dazed, might drown therein landscape, in language, under the humid hand of the heat that Bishop, for one, found so oppressive in Rio, in her lover Lota's apartment in Leme. To try to measure Brazil's apparent overabundance against whatever "home" means is the tourist's and the traveller's first temptation, as Bishop knew. And to try to protect the foreigner's perspective is the second, as Bishop also knew. Both temptations are necessary, and both are mistakes. In Bishop's Brazilian poems, these inclinations inform the descriptive eye that is a point of departure in much of her poetry.

The traveller's eye in the Brazilian poems takes several preliminary recourses to make the foreign familiar. The eye can seek, first, to see through a simplifying lens. The eye can play at becoming naive–translating what it sees first, as some travellers translate, through surface description. But whatever recourse the traveller's eye seeks, in the Brazilian poems its observations become, not simply ends in themselves, but occasions for reflections from and in the doubting interior eye that is so important to Bishop. Bishop's Brazilian sojourn invited her to develop elements in her art that were always important but that flourished in Brazil, nurtured and warmed but also sharpened by that culture's rich strangeness, its fabulous amplitude. What she saw in Brazil invited her to consider, again, her perennial "Questions of Travel" amidst a landscape teeming, brimming with improbable symmetries.

In the Brazilian poems, Bishop's measuring, enumerative, naming, and doubting eye is everywhere. In "Arrival at Santos" (*CP* 89–90), Bishop signals that she knows that surface description is both necessary and a kind of primary-school translation, marvelling wryly at its thin presumption even as she practices it. But even such postcard recollections include the faint menace of native indifference—the threat, almost a portent, of the dangerous boat-hook catching Miss Breen's skirt—and enumerate the catalogues of failed recognition that mark the foreigner. The deceptions begin with the simple assertion of location—as if assertion could stand in for more genuine identification, as if generic naming could substitute for fuller modes of knowing: "Here is a coast; here is a harbor" (89): geography lesson number one. In the lens of Bishop's imagination, such tic-tac-toe mapping signals the traveller's perspective and coloration, and, characteristically, the speaker quickly acknowledges that the impatience and eagerness and bodily hunger of such an eye must be suspect: the "meager diet of horizon" (89) that makes the eye hunger for scenery also dictates the eye's perspective. Mountains "impractically shaped" become "self-pitying mountains" (89) even as the speaker reflects on what powers would allow for such knowledge, what the legitimacy of such tourist's knowledge might be, so that the speaker asks, wryly: "who knows?" (89)

After such an acknowledgement, to see the mountains as "sad" and "harsh," to understand their greenery as "frivolous" (89) becomes marked as suspect knowledge, establishing a tentative relation between the tourist's hungry gaze and its objects. If one object of the gaze is the port of Santos and its surround, the other, just as uncertain about its subject, is the tourist herself, the traveller with the impatient eye. When the speaker admonishes those like herself–"Oh, tourist" (89)–the object splits into a chastising observer looking at her chastened self, commanding, "Finish your breakfast" (89), and then turning her eye outward again to see the approaching tender. These shifts in the direction of the gaze complement the uncertain shifts in the revealed nature of what is observed, and because both waver, both conspire to undermine the apparent confidence of announcements such as "There. We are settled" (90). Everything slides off that postcard surface. The port of entry into such a country—a "necessity"—is also, like any port, indifferent to its significance to the arriving traveller. In the face of such indifference, the eye looks to confer meaning but recognizes that meanings conferred in this way, at this time and place, are necessarily thin. That recognition is what imbues the poem's final assertion, "We leave Santos at once" with a thin trace of menace accompanying its urgency, so that "driving to the interior" (90) becomes perilous.

"Arrival at Santos" poses early questions and tentative answers about the direction and the significance of the tourist's gaze. "Brazil, January 1, 1502" (*CP* 91–92) poses related questions but asks them on a larger scale. The opening of the poem enumerates the parts of a Nature that greets "our eyes" just as it greeted "theirs" (91) some four hundred and fifty years ago. But the "greeting" is not reciprocal because both sets of travellers' eyes are intent on making Nature into an "embroidered nature," a "tapestried landscape," as the epigraph from Kenneth Clark's book warns (91). After all of this poem's early, loving attention to naming the leaves, their variety and colors might have almost soothed us away from the early suggestion that this eye describes Nature as if it were a painting on a canvas—"every square inch filling in with foliage" (91). But the stanza ends with a clearer indication of these eyes' painterly renditions: the scene is "fresh as if just finished / and taken off the frame" (91). Within a Nature made into such scenes, into paintings or fabrics, under a sky rendered as "a simple web, / backing for feathery detail," birds can become "symbolic" (91) and Sin can make an entrance, along with lust, that wicked female lizard. Now the way is open for the Christian army to rip away into the denatured "hanging fabric" (92) that hides the Indians, those "maddening little women" (92) always in retreat. To come to Brazil, in 1502 or in 1951, brings an abundant Nature before hungry eyes that, in Bishop's imagination, make art a defense that, ironically, keeps these eyes hungry.

Like "Arrival at Santos" and "Brazil, January 1, 1502," "Questions of Travel" (*CP* 93–94) opens with what the poet sees. And frequently, in Bishop's Brazil, what is seen is too large, too various, too multiform to be known or real, or to inhabit time properly. Frequently in these poems, what the speaker sees leads to what the speaker doubts. The poems travel from visual experience (here is a coast, here a harbor) to a difficult interior. In this poem, it is "too many waterfalls" that the speaker watches, clouds moving in "soft slow-motion" to turn into waterfalls "under our very eyes" (93). Under these eyes, time condenses as quickly as do the travelling clouds, travelling streams; and the quick way in Brazil that "ages go here" makes for an imaginative transformation into shipwreck and loss: the mountains begin to look like "the hulls of capsized ships, / slime-hung and barnacled" (93). This is first a poetry of observation, in which natural profusion and abundance are remarked and transformed; then, of observation turned a half-glance inwards towards figures of loss; and then, a philosophical poetry, in which the observations, the figures, lead to perplexed thoughts of home.

The series of questions in the second stanza inquires into the value of the traveller's first sight. Is the rush to look at the strange and foreign enough justification for leaving home? What is this kind of sight? What might it yield? What is this "childishness," this quality of looking that so excites? If the "inexplicable old stonework" that the speaker mentions is indeed also "impenetrable," then what is the traveller, or this poem's reader, to understand about the stonework also being "at any view / instantly seen and always, always delightful"? (93) The implications here are clear enough: to "dream our dreams / and have them, too," to make room for "one more folded sunset" (93)—a sunset made, kept warm, a traveller's souvenir—is not enough to justify travel.

And yet, this speaker then sees, and shows, unfolding each item before us, that it would have indeed been a "pity" (93) not to see the asymmetries, in the next stanza, of *this* country's arrhythmic clogs, and then the baroque Jesuit birdcages and the clogs. It would have been a pity not to hear the quality of the sound of this country's rain, and the ensuing silence. The rhetoric of the closing stanzas persuades by vivid, wondering enumeration that what the traveller sees and understands enables her, as if she were preparing (*"Write it!"*) for "One Art" (*CP* 178), to frame those vexed questions of travel, the questions that close this poem, faithfully wearing away a surer sense of home as surely as they create Bishop's conditions for poetry.

Bishop knows that what she sees and describes in Brazil, or overhears and reports, is in itself worthy of attention, and worthy of wonder as well. But her poetry also shows her working through observation towards insight. That working out—the inquiry, the doubting thought, the surprised or painful exclamation—is not the prime mover of her poems, but a result, made to seem natural and inevitable, of her complex awareness of how she sees. How she hears is vital, too, as in "The Riverman" (*CP* 105–09), where she works primarily through voice to make the magical and the mystical into something more reasonable and familiar, all the while showing us that there is too much for this voice to account for, plausible as it might sound. This ambiguity is what makes the poem so compelling, both as a rendition of a "reasonable" voice recounting a long and difficult apprenticeship, and as a poem that shows us that the ventriloquistic act of making this experience accessible is a serious exercise in rendering the strange, the exotic, the world of sorcerers and river-goddesses, as an available mystery. The Riverman narrates his experience as otherworldly *and* reasonable, magical *and* domestic.

Although Bishop travelled on the Amazon and the São Francisco river systems after she wrote this poem, she puts us on notice that the origins for this poem's details—the sacaca, the goddess Luandinha, the river dolphin and its powers, the pirarucú—are bookish, from Charles Wagley's *Amazon Town*. The voice is created, but it must sound as if it were speaking familiarly to us, reasoning with us. The care with which Bishop makes river sorcery plausible permeates this poem from its opening: the speaker recalls that the Dolphin, a "man like myself," "grunted" at him (105), and the Riverman's mode of description, including the characteristically modest qualities of his first simile, serves to make the experience believable: the bright burning of the moon looks, not otherwordly, suggestive, mystical, portentous, but rather, like "the gasoline-lamp mantle / with the flame turned up too high, / just before it begins to scorch" (105). This carefully mundane figure of speech is framed by the bare utterance, "I went down to the river" (105). Late in the poem, the Riverman refers again to the confluence of bright moon and beckoning river in a related, and relatedly accessible mode: "When the moon burns white / and the river makes that sound / like a primus pumped up high— / that fast, high whispering / like a hundred people at once" (108).

When the Riverman first wades into the water and a door opens, the description, again, is muted, domestic, mundane: "suddenly a door / in the water opened inward, / groaning a little, with water / bulging at the lintel" (105). At each step in his education, the Riverman pauses to think of his wife, his house—as if to remind us, with himself, that becoming a sacaca, like becoming a poet, happens in the observed world and not beyond it. To accompany the Riverman in his progress is to be constantly reminded that what happens here for readers, for the Riverman, and, perhaps, for Bishop can most powerfully be approached through apprehension of the ordinary, and through ordinary evidence: through the river's "fine mud" (106) on the Riverman's scalp; the "river smells" (106) in his hair; his cold hands and feet; his wife's remedies, which he throws out. Always, the figures of speech are attuned to the everyday. The stream of light in the rooms at Luandinha's parties is "like at the cinema" (107); the "virgin mirror" (107) he needs is despoiled by neighbors looking over his shoulder, useful after that only for the small vanities of girls examining the way their smiles look back at them.

The language of logic and economy pervades this poem: "Look, it stands to reason / that everything we need / can be obtained from the river" (108) the Riverman tells us. Even the ending, following on the Riverman's last lyric exaltation as he describes passages underwater with his "magic cloak of fish" (108) closes with the language of reason, of parliamentary motion and procedure: "The Dolphin singled me out; / Luandinha seconded it" (109).

I began by speculating that fabulous, outsized, atemporal Brazil greeted Bishop's traveller's eye with a profusion and abundance that invited her to sharpen her various renditions and interrogations of sight, including the tourist's impatient, hungry eye, the traveller's questioning, reflective eye, the photographer's exacting eye, the painter's artful eye. Memory, too—traveller's hindsight—is called into Bishop's court, as in the poem she finally published in 1978, years after her time in Brazil, "Santarém" (*CP* 185–87). The idea for this poem was with Bishop from around 1960, when she travelled the Amazon from Manaus to Belém, and was worked through many drafts. In its final form, the poem's striking contrasts with "Arrival at Santos," the Bishop poem that most clearly draws on the tourist's first sight of Brazil, make "Santarém" a fitting place and poem to close this preliminary glance at Brazil through Bishop's eyes.

The opening of the poem is a fine example, in tone, diction, and syntax, of the apparently frank, almost hurried, often urgent admissions that arise in Bishop's poems. Here, it is an admission that memory, "of course" (105) might have it all wrong. Yet "Santarém" brims with remembered detail. And the poem insists on the importance of both detail and framing ideas for detail, even as it works through and discards ideas—particularly, the idea of interpretation. "Santarém" presents a profuse but ironic record of what Bishop saw in that town, at that time, as rendered, with its own witty and artful faith, in memory's eye. The poem is also a powerful meditation on where these memories lead, and fail to lead.

The telling language of scenes rendered as illustrations that recalls poems like "Questions of Travel" or "Brazil, January 1, 1502" remains here in the rich presentation of detail in the opening stanza, with its "gorgeous, under–lit clouds," with "everything gilded, burnished along one side," with everything "bright, cheerful, casual" (185). Quickly, as in earlier poems, we are sharply and yet casually reminded that this eye is suspect: "or so it looked" (185). What is new here, though, is the form of the bare distinction that follows: the speaker remembers, "I liked the place; I liked the idea of the place" (185). This sharp insistence on separating "place," what is seen, what is apparent, from the idea of the place—what is made, imagined, created, interpreted from place—prefaces the poem's most abstract passage. Here, the speaker raises and then dismisses any move towards interpretation, insisting that "such notions" (that is, the notions that the poet now recognizes would not have fit her past experience) would have "resolved, dissolved, straight off / in that watery, dazzling dialectic" (185). Here is a mind agonizingly aware of its inability to work at rest with the senses: even though the speaker insists that all frames of interpretation, logical, Christian, binaries like life/death or right/wrong, would dissolve, resolve, the eye and memory cannot let go of thought. The rivers, Tapajos and the Amazon, are themselves a "dazzling dialectic." There is no innocent or pre-logical eye.

After that dazzling admission comes the charged accumulation of detail, cheerily, wryly inflected with comic visual asides—a "belvedere / about to fall into the river" (185), and with surprised exclamations—the zebu (imported from India, these cattle) are a startling *blue* (185). Still, as in the opening, the local bursts of color, the blues, the buttercup yellows of the *azulejos* (tiles) are set by the speaker above the "golden" and "dark-gold" (185) currents of evening and sand that signal and embody the hope for temporary repose. The asymmetries that Bishop's eye lingered over so lovingly in "Questions of Travel" are crazier and more disjunctive here, more maudlin and perhaps more charged with meaning—the "blue eyes, English names, / and *oars*" (186) of the descendants of displaced Civil War families, the embarked nuns waving gaily, the soon-to-be-married cow, the river schooner with a bowsprit that, from the speaker's perspective, "seemed to touch the church" (186).

Complementing this parade of unresolved incongruities, and in another indication, perhaps, of the spark of energy released in the wake of the collapsed, "dissolved" dialectics, are the verbal mockeries. Twice in "Santarém" Bishop plays with vernacular, once in English, once in Portuguese, on both occasions referring to religious vocation. First, there is the baker's dozen of nuns who, waving gaily, are off to a mission "up God knows what lost tributary" (186). The colloquial register grounds the nuns' vocation in the mundane and calls attention to the play of language at war with its literal or transactional calling, and here it is the vernacular that wins out for a golden moment. The same is true of the recounting of the priest's miraculous escape, in the next stanza, from being galvanized along with his brass bed by the lightning that had struck the Cathedral. *"Graças a deus"* (186) is an idiom so often used in Brazil that it has lost its literal meaning, so that the priest's providential escape, upriver in Belém, is rendered as comical, arbitrary.

Against this lovely chaos, burnished and backlit from above and warmed underfoot by memory and its warm evocation of golden sand, so fluid that people and zebus "waded" in it, Bishop begins to close. As a momentary promise of another, more mundane resolution than any "idea of a place" that any dialectical or interpretive resolution might yield, Bishop gives us the scene in the "blue pharmacy," complete with its pharmacist, where she sees the "exquisite" wasps' nest (186), admires it, and is given the nest by the pharmacist. Momentary repose, a gift; but against memory's gold comes the narrative (and the traveller's) imperative: "Then –" (187). Once "Then" asserts itself, she can't stay, and, back in the traveller's world, the kind of question of travel that Mr. Swan, "really a very nice old man" (187) would ask gives us the poem's closing voice, back in the past present, leaving Santarém: "What's that ugly thing?" (187)

"That ugly thing" is just as much the quality of Mr. Swan's gaze, the kind of look that he, a typical tourist, bestows on the wasp's nest, as it is the object itself, the wasp's nest, as seen through Mr. Swan's eyes. That ugly thing is a way of looking, a way of seeing. What Bishop's Brazilian poems show us among other sights is that how to look is as urgent a question of travel as where to go or what to see.

Endnote

1. I would like to acknowledge the vital contributions of my colleagues in the University of Winnipeg Fall 1997 English Honors Seminar, "English Studies in Focus." As their assignment for the first four weeks of this twelve-week course, they read a selection of Bishop's poems and then critiqued, in class and in print, three successive drafts of this paper. They also attended a public colloquium at which I read the paper, and they responded to that presentation. I incorporated many of their written suggestions and benefited greatly from the discussions. My colleagues are Carissa Almeida, Laura Barrett, Gregory Gingras, Tanis MacDonald, Mark Morton, Kris Nutting, Deborah Schnitzer, David Sinclair, Kay Stone, Sophie Walker, and Laurie Watson. All responsibility for errors and omissions in this text, of course, is my own.

Work Cited

Bishop, Elizabeth. *The Complete Poems: 1927–1979*. New York: Farrar, Straus, Giroux, 1983. All references are to this text, cited as *CP*.

Luminous Lota

Carmen L. Oliveira
Writer, Brazil

Abstract

Descended from a viscount, Lota de Macedo Soares exhibited impressive erudition and elegance, part inherited, part products of a European education. Wrapped in her protection and tenderness, Bishop's art blooms. To reveal luminous Lota, the Brazilian author drew on a wealth of data unavailable to American researchers and critics, including Lota's correspondence, interviews with dozens of people who knew them both, Brazilian newspapers and magazine articles, as well as Elizabeth Bishop's complete works and her correspondence and manuscripts.

The year is 1951. Picture a woman in her forties. Make her an American poet, a brilliant Vassar graduate, the author of a praised book, acquainted with well-known artists and writers. Bad health. What would prompt this woman to live hidden in an isolated house up a faraway mountain in Brazil, where almost no one speaks English, and everybody speaks Portuguese?

Certainly it was not a case of instant attraction to the land itself. She arrived at Santos and found the harbor mean, the vegetation frivolous, the glue very inferior. She took a train to Rio de Janeiro: all those half-naked mulattos playing soccer on the streets day in, day out, the food suspicious, the heat murderous.

Yet one sunny morning someone comes to pick her up for a trip to the misty peaks of Petropolis. There, leaning on a Jaguar, is the reason for her long stay in Brazil: another woman in her forties. To that woman our poet dedicated *Questions of Travel*, in 1965, quoting from a sonnet by Portugal's Luís de Camões:

> Assim que a vida e alma e esperança,
> E tudo quanto tenho tudo é vosso;
> E o proveito disso eu só o levo.
>
> Porque é tamanha bem-aventurança
> O dar-vos quanto tenho e quanto posso,
> Que quanto mais vos pago, mais vos devo.

[So my life, my soul, my hope
Everything I have is yours;
But the profit is all mine.

For it's such a blessing
To give you as much as I have and as much as I can
That the more I pay you, the more I owe you.]
(My translation of Camões 245)

Here is the clue: if we want to find Elizabeth Bishop, we must search
for Lota de Macedo Soares. The search begins in Europe. Lota's father, a
controversial journalist, had had to flee to France, for political reasons. Maria
Carlota Costallat de Macedo Soares was born in Paris, in 1910. She was
wellborn: she descended from a viscount. She was well-bred, too. Although
she spent her childhood in Brazil, soon her belligerent father was in exile
again, and she was educated in Belgium.

This background accounts for an unlikely, seductive quality that fascinated her American partner. Lota looked like a South American Indian. But
she tempered tropical liveliness and piquancy with aristocratic manners and
a solid European upbringing.

The woman with the Jaguar looked self-assured and bold. Yet as a
child and an adolescent she experienced the sense of displacement Elizabeth knew so well. She, too, was carried away from one place to another
against her will, and had to live among strangers. And she also had a bitter
experience of family disintegration and distress. When she was in her early
twenties, her father abandoned the family to live with a young man. The
episode was quite shocking and embarrassing in itself, but an unscrupulous
journalist, her father's enemy, made it uglier by turning it into a public scan-
dal.

This was a hard blow. Lota never got along well with her mother, whom
she found dull and sanctimonious, whereas she deeply admired her father.
Moreover, the social condemnation of her father's insurrection unveiled
piercing fears, as by that time her own sexual option was already clear.

Lota did not surrender to an abject longing for compassion. She re-
belled. In time, she declared herself free and likable.

In her thirties, Lota had an intense social life. Brazilian artists and intellectuals flocked to her apartment, seduced by her intelligence and charm.
She was a great conversationalist. Her gift for prompt reply, flawless reasoning and sharp humor would be celebrated later by the American poet, in
"The Wit" (*CP* 199). Although she did not have a degree, Lota's general

culture was impressive and she was reputed to have the best library in Rio on art, botany, architecture and urbanism. When Le Corbusier came to Brazil, Lota was included in the select group of architects who met the master. She loved New York and was a regular at the MOMA. Long before meeting Elizabeth, she was a friend of Monroe Wheeler, director of the museum, and she corresponded with Alexander Calder.

Brazilian artist Augusto Rodrigues drew a provocative cartoon of Lota as an activist of Art, in 1942 (Rodrigues 23). In 1949 painter and libertine Carlos Leão, playing on Lota's love for botany, produced a series of sketches of Lota and her circle as flowers, with scientific names in Latin and all. Lota was a *Carlota impudica* [*shameless Lota*], genus *Dubiaciae* [*Dubious*] (Leão).

By that time, Lota inherited from her mother a large area in Petropolis, called Samambaia [fern, in Portuguese], but no money. She decided to divide her estate into lots and sell some to sophisticated people she would handpick. And she decided to build for herself an outright contradiction: a supermodern house way back in the woods.

When the blue poet and the brown aesthete came together and engaged in uninnocent conversations, the house was still in its bare foundation. To measure the impact of their confluence, it is enough to consider that Elizabeth arrived in November, and in December Lota bought her a ring that read inside: "Lota/20.12.51," the day Elizabeth told her she would stay in Brazil. In a few months they were camping in the third of the house that was up. Lota may have been precipitate, but look what happened: inside the precarious skeleton of a house, they made a home.

Lota directed the construction. Elizabeth began to write to friends, recounting her daily life in detail, to show how admirable and capable Lota was. Lota did organic gardening, she used non-toxic fertilizers, she was a forestry expert. Lota could plan and execute complex construction, even reservoirs and roads. She and Lota read poetry every day, taking turns as supervisor, depending on whether the poem was in English or Portuguese. She and Lota shared a robust happiness; they almost never parted from each other.

It took nine years for the house to be finished. The result was fantastic. One of Lota's friends defined her as *someone clear*, and surely the house had Lota's transparence, one could see through it.

How discordant is Elizabeth's depiction of a small shadowy life in a tarnished house, hidden in the fog. However, *there is* a large bad picture which goes with the poem: in it we can see an almost invisible Elizabeth on the inside, Lota on the outside, a private cloud holding them both and a wall for the mildew's ignorant map.

Those two were disparate. Lota was quick, assertive, commanding. Elizabeth was slow, hesitating, compliant. All Brazilian friends agree that they had one thing in common: a lavish sense of humor. They were both finished examples of how intelligence can manifest itself through humor.

Even Joana, the maid at the Rio apartment, emphasizes this. She says that Dona Lota would go to the office every morning, to work. Dona Elizabetchy would stay home, "messing around with papers." In the evening, the moment Dona Elizabetchy heard the key turn in the lock she would run to the door to welcome Dona Lota. They would greet each other fondly. Often Dona Lota would throw her briefcase on the table and curse her day. But in a second one or the other would say something funny and both would be laughing. Joana would not know what was so amusing, because, as she explains, they used to laugh in English.

Elizabeth hated to hurry. She loved to take her time. Lota hated to wait. She loved speed. When we read Lota's letters, we find two recurrent underlined expressions: at once and it took ages. She did not have the profile of a traveler. She certainly enjoyed going shopping in New York, but Elizabeth reported that Lota hated the long trip back by ship. She found no interest in moving from one place to another for the "peculiar," and did not accompany Elizabeth to the Amazon or to Bahia. She said she agreed with Brazilian poet Mario Quintana: to travel is just to change the scenery of loneliness (Quintana 57).

Yet, in 1953, when love was young, Lota drove Elizabeth to Ouro Preto. They kept a log of the trip, which is very revealing. When Lota takes notes, they are neat and well-ordered. When Elizabeth takes notes, they are well-ordered, though not so neat. But when the two write down in the same block, it is a mess. Lota invades Bishop's space and crowds it with her observations.

Elizabeth registers all arrivals and departures, time, gas, money, plus meaningful occurrences, such as "stopped and bought a wooden bowl," "changed tire." Lota only keeps record of the arrivals, and makes two comments in Portuguese: "lousy hotel." "lousy road" (Bishop, Journal).

Lota and Elizabeth stayed most of the time in that house being built in the clouds. They practiced that art of finding fun in the trifles of daily life. Their love grew. In 1958, writer Antonio Callado came to visit them in Samambaia. He was impressed: "Like other couples in the peak of their union, the two of them—without exchanging a single word, just focusing on their visitor—passed to any stranger the clear notion that everything was quite wonderful in that house" (Callado 5–8).

As years went by, two things marred their contentment: first, Elizabeth's drinking. Her fits were a torture, as she would howl like a wounded animal throughout the night and sink into dark self-deprecation the day after. Second, Lota's inertia. However talented and skilled, she did not have anything palpable to do, besides taking care of Elizabeth. Now fifty, Lota worried. She resented that Elizabeth's friends, such as Robert Lowell or Aldous Huxley, thought of her as an eccentric landlady who built a sumptuous house, drove imported cars and smoked from a tortoise-shell.

Things changed radically in 1960, the year the capital moved from Rio to Brasilia, which had just been completed. Lota had sold a lot in Samambaia to a brilliant, contentious politician, Carlos Lacerda. They became good friends and used to talk about literature and rose gardening. They admired each other. Lacerda was elected governor and invited Lota to become part of his staff. She accepted. She did not want to be a secretary, though. To his surprise, she pointed out of a window to an extensive waterfront landfill and said: Give me that. I'll turn it into Central Park.

The existing plan for the landfill was an altogether different idea. A beach had been filled in for a four-lane high-speed road connecting Southern and downtown Rio. It was meant for cars. Skyscrapers would grow alongside the road. Engineers, architects and business administrators would take care of the project.

In came Lota, elegant and poised. She told the incredulous board of directors that the four tracks for cars would be cut down to two, that there would be no building whatsoever alongside the fill, that a five kilometer garden would be grown instead, with trails for pedestrians to walk among the trees, feeling the sea breeze on their faces, as the beach would be artificially restored. There would be opportunity for leisure, recreation and contemplation of the gorgeous scenery of Guanabara Bay, for all. (Macedo Soares, "Urbanização"). And, gentlemen, she was the boss now.

That cocktail of aesthetics, ecology, democracy and leisure was unpalatable to many. A large amount of money was involved. She was confronting insidious, ravenous interests. And of course she could not expect anything but hostility from the professionals who would have to comply with her commands.

Dona Lota was the mistress of her house, and she was used to having the last say. She was altogether unprepared for the dirty game of politics. Candid and forthright, she was easy prey for those versed in deceit and trickery. They knew the science of the spider—they could wait.

She could not. At once she detected people who were unreliable partners, who should be substituted right away for admirable people she knew. She would enter Lacerda's office without knocking and tell him so. They would quarrel furiously. She would not be convinced that things were not that easy for a politician. "Don't be stupid, Carlos!"—she would tell the governor.

Eventually Lacerda refused to receive her. Lota wanted him to hear about the essential need of beauty or the natural scenery as patrimony of the citizens. And he was involved in big national matters, such as fighting socialists and conducting a presidential coup behind the scene.

She began to write letters, just like Elizabeth. She bombed Lacerda almost daily with scolding letters, most of them about public men's indifference to the fate of people and about his stupid staff. Some excerpts from her letters:

> Mr. Governor, Your Excellency. I don't have patience, I don't have time, I don't find it the least bit funny to hang on the phone, to jump from the palace to your apartment, leaving messages, trying to talk to you. (Macedo Soares, Letter to Lacerda, 1963)

> Carlos, dear. You shouldn't authorize the construction of a hotel on top of Pasmado hill. It isn't democratic to destroy the patrimony of all for the benefit of some. Don't tell me it is necessary! Necessity is the plea for every violation of human freedom, says William Pitt. It's the argument of tyrants. (Letter to Lacerda, 1964)

> Do you know why Brasilia was built so fast? A small group planned it and the large mass of robbers put it into existence. There was no contradiction at all. (Macedo Soares, "Pequeno," 1961)

As she still kept her sense of humor, she once wrote Lacerda nominating herself candidate to succeed him. Her first act as a governor would be:

> I will have all sculptures of skinny women that you have placed in public gardens replaced for statues of fat women—from Giacometti to Marino Marini phases. I think those skinny muses are an unpatriotic allusion to our underdevelopment. Besides, all fat women will resemble me. (Letter to Lacerda, 1965)

The governor's days were often embittered by a dramatic letter from Lota. However, after her death, Lacerda admitted:

> Her letters, her notes, her imprecations—all were sheer passion, the passion of someone who has given up oneself to a tangible ideal. (Lacerda, Address)

Through the years, out of one million square meters of clay and fill, a park arose. 240 different species were planted. An arena theatre, a ring for dancing and a puppet theatre were built among the trees. To ensure that nothing in the original plan would ever be changed, she got the park, still unfinished, declared a national monument. Thanks to her, Cariocans and their visitors have today a waterside park.

Envious Iagos tried to jeopardize her park project all the time, but the young architects, called "Lota's boys," loved and admired her. Now middle-aged, they recall her permanent ambiguity: she had class, but used to curse like a sailor; her mellifluous voice contrasted with her eagerness; her "office" was a wooden shack in the park, but she used monogrammed silver flatware when she lunched there. Above all, they refer to her luminosity: she radiated, they remember.

Meanwhile the sad poet was feeling alone and dejected. Armadillos, owls and excited frogs gave way to drowned beggars, childish putas and scabby dogs in her poems. She wrote a long poem to describe the persecution and assassination of a bandit by the police, a scene she viewed through her binoculars. She escaped Joana's vigilance and rushed to the botequim, the corner bar, for a cachaça . Ladies did not drink cachaça, a fiery liquor made from sugar cane. Joana would look for her, and drag her back to the apartment through the streets of Leme. She felt miserable. But, as Brazilian poet Chico Buarque says, "however wretched the poet, still his poems will have rhyme and reason" (Buarque de Hollanda).

Elizabeth could not stand Lota's tattered nerves and flew often to Ouro Preto. The baroque city, with its precipitous streets and crooked houses, was the exact opposite of Samambaia's straight lines and perfect balance. She bought a house there. It was falling to pieces, but it was hers.

Elizabeth went to Seattle to teach, and found some consolation in a young lover there. Before Elizabeth returned to Brazil, they promised to exchange letters through Lota and Elizabeth's friend, Lilli, in Ouro Preto.

No one knows how that letter ever reached Lota. Astounded, she read a handwritten message to Elizabeth: I love you, I love you, I love you, I love you—from the top to the bottom of the page. When Elizabeth admitted the truth, Lota became crazed with pain. She had just been fired from her job in the park, after many battles. She was hurt by old friends' ingratitude, especially that of Roberto Burle-Marx, who called her, in an interview, "a rotten egg" (Burle-Marx 3). Now she felt she was losing her beloved.

We all know the unhappy end. One night, in New York, Elizabeth was awakened by a thud. She went to the kitchen in time to see Lota fall to the ground, holding a bottle of pills. A scream hung over Greenwich Village, the echo of a scream that had hung over Great Village, over a terrified girl.

Brilliant, passionate, intense, Elizabeth Bishop and Lota de Macedo Soares are one of the most remarkable couples of the century. Each in her way, they personified the artist's rage for order. Lota believed the urban man should read the poetry of nature, and left him a garden by the sea. Elizabeth took pains to lift yesterdays, and entrusted us with her accomplishment: a crystal tear.

Elizabeth was not a prolific poet. Lota was the architect of one park. Refined and perfectionists, both lived up to the motto: *Non multa, sed multum*. Not quantity, but excellence.

Works Cited

Bishop, Elizabeth. *The Complete Poems*. New York: Farrar, Straus, Giroux, 1983.

———. Journal of the trip to Ouro Preto, ms. 14 Apr. 1953. Elizabeth Bishop Papers, Vassar College Library Special Collections.

Buarque de Hollanda, Chico. "Choro Bandido" ["Criminal Song"]. *Paratodos [For All]*. CD. BMG, 1993.

Burle-Marx, Roberto. "Desmandos criarão o Aterro absurdo" ["Intemperate command will bring about the Fill of absurdity"]. Interview, *Correio da Manhã* 14 Apr. 1966: 3.

Callado, Antonio. "Poeta deu trégua à angústia em Petrópolis" ["Poet made a truce with anguish in Petropolis"]. *Folha de São Paulo,* 11 June 1994: 5–8.

Camões, Luís de. "Soneto 25", *Redondilhas, Canções, Sonetos [Quatrains, Songs, Sonnets]*. Rio de Janeiro: Real Gabinete Português de Leitura, 1980. 245.

Lacerda, Carlos. Address at Lota de Macedo Soares' funeral, ms. Sept. 1967. Private archive.

Leão, Carlos. Sketches, "Dedicados à gentil Miss Lota de M.S. B.S. etc etc etc" ["Dedicated to gentle Miss Lota M.S. B.S. etc etc etc"]. Jan. 1949. Private archive.

Macedo Soares, Lota de. Letter to Carlos Lacerda, 13 Nov. 1963. In Oliveira, *Flores* 122–23.

———. Letter to Carlos Lacerda, Jan. 1964. In Oliveira, *Flores* 127.

————. Letter to Carlos Lacerda, 3 June 1965. In Oliveira, *Flores* 150–151.

————. "Pequeno ensaio sobre administração" ["Little essay on administration"]. July 1961. In Oliveira, *Flores* 90.

————. "A Urbanização do Aterrado Gloria-Flamengo" ["The Urbanization of Gloria-Flamengo Fill"]. *Revista de Engenharia* 29 (1962): 6–8.

Oliveira, Carmen L. *Flores Raras e Banalíssimas* [*Rare and Commonplace Flowers*]. Rio de Janeiro: Rocco, 1996.

Quintana, Mario. "XXX," *Diário Poético* [*Poetic Journal*]. Rio de Janeiro: Editora Globo, 1992. 57.

Rodrigues, Augusto. "Lota de Macedo Soares." Cartoon. *Diretrizes* 23 Apr. 1942: 23.

Bishop's Brazil and Vice Versa

George Monteiro
Brown University

Abstract

Carmen L. Oliveira's *Flores Raras e Banalissimas* [*Rare and Commonplace Flowers*] (1995) recounts the relationship between Elizabeth Bishop and Lota de Macedo Soares in Brazil. This is a sympathetic and responsible contribution to the study of their lives together and to the ending of their relationship.[1]

In an interview conducted in Boston toward the end of Elizabeth Bishop's life and published in the *Jornal do Brasil* in Rio de Janeiro in 1977, Beatriz Schiller tells of an exchange with the American poet on what might still have been a delicate matter, especially for the interviewer's Brazilian audience. Schiller states:

"As a child I often went to Samambaia," I tell her. "I remember entering your house, on tiptoe, and overhearing my neighborhood friends saying: 'Two strange women live here; they never leave the house.'"

Schiller then reports Bishop's response:

"That's not true. It's a child's exaggeration. We didn't go to parties every night, but neither were we hermits. We had plenty of friends. Some of them, like Carlos Lacerda, were neighbors in the same part of town." (Monteiro 79)

It is the compelling and extraordinary story of those "two strange women," living their lives privately in Petrópolis and somewhat more publicly in a Rio apartment above the beach in Leme, a version of what in the United States might have been called, in earlier times, a Boston marriage, that is told so sympathetically and responsibly in Carmen L. Oliveira's dual biography, *Flores Raras e Banalíssimas* [*Rare and Commonplace Flowers*]. Published in late 1995, this account of Bishop's mid-life Brazilian years and of Lota's stormy professional life, told a quarter of a century after Bishop's death, is to be warmly commended for its substantial, invaluable, and now indispensable contribution to our knowledge of the joyous, rich, complex, if ultimately tragic life that Elizabeth Bishop and Lota de Macedo Soares built for themselves in their forties and fifties.

Had Bishop managed to write and publish *Black Beans and Diamonds*, the much talked-about book she planned to write about Brazil, the Brazilian rediscovery of her work might have come sooner than it has.[2] One must not complain, however, for at least there are now clear signs, three decades after the death of Lota, that the American poet's literary and (perhaps) personal recuperation in Brazil has finally taken off. The year 1990 saw the publication of the poet-critic Horácio Costa's bilingual edition of Bishop's poetry, making a goodly portion of Bishop's published poetry available in Portuguese for the first time, and of Flora Sussekind's detailed study of style, theme and technique in Bishop's poetry, using as a pre-text Bishop's acquaintance with Manuel Bandeira, one of Brazil's premier poets of this century and Bishop's neighbor in Rio de Janeiro.[3] In 1993, at the Universidade Federal de Minas Gerais (located in Belo Horizonte, just a couple of hours drive from Casa Mariana in Ouro Prêto, the poet's last home in Brazil), Regina M. Przybycien defended a very useful dissertation on the subject of Brazil and matters Brazilian in Bishop's work. And in 1994, Petrópolis, where the poet spent some thirteen years with Lota at Fazenda Samambaia, commemorated Bishop's presence in that place with an exhibition of books, letters, poems, photographs and memorabilia. In 1995 there appeared *Uma Arte: as Cartas de Elizabeth Bishop*, a translation of Robert Giroux's edition of the letters, which includes, as lagniappe, an appendix of hitherto unpublished letters, to May Swenson, Robert Lowell, Ilse and Kit Barker, and to several Brazilians—the poet Carlos Drummond de Andrade, Bishop's friend Linda Nemer, and Emanuel Brasil, Bishop's co-editor of a 1972 anthology of modern Brazilian poetry.[4] Appealing to what Brazilian readers might know about Marianne Moore, the publisher Companhia Das Letras, which brought out a volume of Moore's poetry in translation in 1991,[5] published the *Collected Prose* as *Esforços de Afeto e outras histórias*, the title coming from Bishop's piece "Efforts of Affection: A Memoir of Marianne Moore."

This increase in Brazilian interest in Bishop's life and work, particularly the influence Brazil had on Bishop, is certainly welcome, though it is somewhat belated. For there can be little doubt that the poet's long Brazilian stay affected her thinking about herself and marked her work while there and later, sometimes showing itself in the smallest of particulars, the use, sometimes, of a single, decentered word or brief expression. Knowing the Portuguese language often contributes to one's fuller understanding of the way she, in her poetry, rings an inter-cultural change on a single word— "interior" ("Arrival at Santos"), "ignorant" [*ignorado*] ("The Armadillo"), and "anniversary" [*aniversário*, meaning "birthday"] ("Twelfth Morning; or What You Will")—coins a bilingual phrase (perhaps)—"Esso—so—so— so" [*és só—só—só—só*] ("Filling Station")—or incorporates a direct, literal, and slightly off-centered translation—"took advantage" [*aproveitar*, meaning "made good use of"] ("Under the Window: Ouro Prêto") or—two final examples—"Januaries" [*Janeiras*, a new year's carol or gift] and "'one leaf yes and one leaf no'" [*folha sim folha não*] (both from "Brazil, January 1, 1502"). There are also examples from her letters, say the time she complains about Dona Alice (Al-iss-y) Brant, the original (or perhaps putative) author of *The Diary of "Helena Morley."* Soon after the book's publication, Dona Alice nags anxiously, "Is it giving any results?" [*tem dado resultado*], not a question relating to reviews or critical reception, as one might have expected from the wife of a wealthy banker, but "meaning money, of course," as Bishop correctly interprets for Joseph and U. T. Summers, her American correspondents (*One Art* 342).

Bishop's long stay in Brazil—the better part of two decades, beginning in 1951—was spent with Lota. Speaking late in life, Bishop acknowledged that Lota was the great passion of her life. She planned to write a long memorial poem but did not live to compose it. According to Brett C. Millier, who quotes from the poet's notes, Bishop's "Elegy" would celebrate Lota's "'reticence and pride'; her 'heroism, brave & young'; her 'beautiful colored skin'; 'the gestures (which [you] said you didn't have)'" (538). Oliveira's *Flores Raras e Banalíssimas* is the story of that love, examining a mid-life though less than mature relationship that began when Bishop was forty and Lota forty-one. The book incorporates information regarding the lives they led before falling in love and details of Bishop's life after Lota's death in 1967, but only insofar as such matter is necessary to the main story. The consequence is that if students of Bishop's life will find rehearsed here much of what they already know, they will be amply rewarded, nevertheless, for their effort to read Carmen Oliveira's Portuguese by the detailed information given them about Lota's work, mainly in the design and execution in Rio de Janeiro of a park along the Flamengo coastline, a project undertaken at the invitation of the governor, a friend. Extensive research into personal and public correspondence, newspapers, and governmental, legislative and regulatory documents makes this the most fully realized account of what Lota was up against in the life she was forced to live increasingly apart from Bishop during those last ten years. It is a sad story of increasing frustration before political intrigue and bureaucratic red tape and just plain bad faith on the part of opponents, enemies, and even Lota's putative allies. This public and personal pressure contributed decisively to the destruction of her life with Bishop. In the 1960s Bishop simply could not help Lota with her political problems, and clearly Lota became increasingly incapable of meeting Bishop's exigencies.

This love story is told dramatically for the most part. That is to say, conversations spun out of what one assumes to be two or three documented phrases flesh out the dramatic story, and attendant thoughts as imagined appear as facts. While the book includes a bibliography and lists informants, it lacks notes, citations for quotations, and an index. Bishop's poetry is worked into the text as if it were unquestionably and self-evidently biographical. This is not to imply that Carmen Oliveira has invented facts or constructed implausible scenes. She has availed herself of devices and strategies common to historical novels and of what is still sometimes called the New Journalism.

What might have been more helpful, however, was to have a more detailed treatment of the way certain other individuals played significant roles in this inter-hemispheric, north and south, relationship. There is not enough, for instance, about Mary Stearns Morse, the friend who stayed on in Petrópolis after being displaced in Lota's heart by Bishop. And then there is the equally sketchy account of Lilli Correia de Araújo of Ouro Preto. Lilli seems to have participated in Bishop's life, almost conspiratorially, in major ways. A friend of Lota's, she nevertheless encouraged Bishop to buy a house in Ouro Preto, a decision that Lota found difficult to accept. Lilli also covered for Bishop when she was conducting an affair while teaching at the University of Washington. Perhaps Carmen Oliveira's reluctance to talk further about these players in the drama of Bishop's life reflects her regard for the rights of the living. Mary Stearns Morse and Lilli Correia de Araújo do appear under their own names, but several others, mainly Brazilians, are given fictitious names. The identity of Bishop's lover in Seattle is also protected (as she was in the Millier biography), appearing here as "Adrienne Collins."

To better advantage is the reticence practiced by Carmen Oliveira in other areas. She does not dwell on the details of Lota's death, for instance, and, refreshingly, there is no speculation, beyond stating established facts about Lota's intentions in overdosing on her first night in New York. Nor is there any biographer's moralizing finger pointing that I can see that might justify the widespread hostility and social ostracism that greeted Bishop when she returned to Brazil months after Lota's death. Without arguing a case either way, Carmen Oliveira allows the evidence to speak for itself. It shows that towards the end both Lota and Bishop were in sorry psychological shape. Yet it is clear that the poet managed to find what she needed to put herself back together, but Lota did not. As Bishop moved to reduce her dependence on Lota, an ever more desperate Lota became increasingly dependent on Bishop. So, while Bishop was still insisting as late as 1966 to Dr. Anny Baumann, her American psychiatrist, that she was going back to Lota someday—"*Of course* I am going back, and of course I mean to live there [Brazil], and with Lota, forever and ever" (*One Art* 445)—it is all but certain that even by the time Bishop had committed herself to Casa Mariana in Ouro Preto there was already little that could be done to restore their original relationship. Carmen Oliveira recognizes this all too clearly, for as writer she separates out into discrete blocks of narrative, as Bishop and Lota drift apart, what each of them is doing or thinking at any given time, foregoing the biographer's opportunity to splice her stories into one continuous narrative. Such spatial separation of this sort orchestrates the widening gulf between Bishop and Lota and the clear threat felt by each of them that the other one was about to break away completely. Audaciously, especially in a work written primarily for Brazilians, including those who might still have a strong opinion on Bishop's role in Lota's death, Carmen Oliveira extends to Bishop one last courtesy. Courageously, the biographer allows her to have a last word on the vexed matter of allocating blame for Lota's death. Bishop speaks objectively (and only partly in her own defense), when she says bluntly, in the final words of the book, "Brazil killed Lota."

Endnotes

1. This article is reprinted with permission of the editors of the *Harvard Review*.

2. MacMahon's bibliography (165), published just after the poet's death, lists only two translations into Portuguese of Bishop poems during the poet's lifetime—"The Burglar of Babylon" ["O Ladrão da Babilònia"] in *Cadernos brasileiros*, 6 (Nov.–Dec. 1964), 61–67, and "Under the Window: Ouro Prêto" ["Debaixo da Janela: Ouro Prêto"] in *Visão* 35 (Aug. 1, 1969), 51.

3. *Elizabeth Bishop: Poemas*. Trans. by Horácio Costa (São Paulo:

Companhia Das Letras, 1990); Flora Sussekind, "A geléia & o engenho: Em torno de uma carta-poema de Elizabeth Bishop a Manuel Bandeira," *Revista USP*, no. 7 (Sept./Oct./Nov. 1990)—collected in her *Papéis Colados* (Rio de Janeiro: Editora UFRJ, 1990), 297–365.

4. *An Anthology of Twentieth-Century Brazilian Poetry*, ed. Elizabeth Bishop and Emanuel Brasil (Middletown, CT: Wesleyan UP, 1972), was reissued by Wesleyan UP/UP of New England in 1997 on the twenty-fifth anniversary of its first publication.

5. Marianne Moore, *Poemas*, ed. João Moura, Jr., trans. José Antonio Arantes (São Paulo: Companhia Das Letras, 1991).

Works Cited

Bishop, Elizabeth. *One Art: Letters*. Ed. Robert Giroux. New York: Farrar, Straus, Giroux, 1994.

———. *Uma Arte: As Cartas de Elizabeth Bishop*. Ed. Carlos Eduardo Lins de Silva and João Moreira Selles. Trans. Paulo Henrique Britto. São Paulo: Companhia de Letras, 1995.

———. *Esforços do Afeto e outras histórias*. Trans. Paulo Henrique Britto. São Paulo: Companhia de Letras, 1996.

MacMahon, Candace W. *Elizabeth Bishop: A Bibliography 1927–1979*. Charlottesville: UP of Virginia for the Bibliographical Society of the University of Virginia, 1980.

Millier, Brett C. *Elizabeth Bishop: Life and the Memory of It*. Berkeley: U of California P, 1993.

Monteiro, George, ed. *Conversations with Elizabeth Bishop*. Jackson: UP of Mississippi, 1996.

Oliveira, Carmen L. *Flores Raras e Banalíssimas: A História de Lota de Macedo Soares e Elizabeth Bishop*. Rio de Janeiro: Rocco, 1995.

Przybycien, Regina M. "Feijão Preto e Diamantes: O Brasil na obra de Elizabeth Bishop." Ph.D. diss. Faculdade de Letras da Universidade Federal de Minas Gerais, 1993.

Converging Frontiers:
Elizabeth Bishop's "North" and "South"

Maria Clara Bonetti Paro
Universidade Estadual Paulista

Abstract

This paper examines Elizabeth Bishop's evolving social views, as revealed through her poetry. A selection of poems, written before and after she moved to Brazil in 1951, are compared so as to disclose changes in her personal expression and in her approaches to issues of human interaction and social organization.

Elizabeth Bishop's long residence in Brazil deeply affected her both as a poet and as a personality, and a comparative study of her early and late poems confirms John Ashbery's observation that "her years in the la-bas of Brazil brought Miss Bishop's gifts to maturity" (qtd. in Bloom 8). In light of these considerations, this essay examines how the poet's expanding social views and concerns are revealed in her poetry and how they are affected by her Brazilian experience. Poems, selected from *North and South* (1946) through *New Poems* (1979), are analyzed as converging frontiers where "Self" and "Other," private and public, childhood and adulthood, Nova Scotia and Brazil come together and flow in the "watery" and "dazzling dialectic" of Bishop's great art.

The work of Elizabeth Bishop, shaped within modern aesthetics, with surrealist and symbolist rhetoric, gradually—mainly after her arrival in Brazil in 1951—reveals an increasing social and personal expression. In fact, Bishop herself declared to Ashley Brown that Brazil had an impact on her and that "living among people of a completely different culture [had] changed a lot of [her] old stereotyped ideas" (qtd. in Schwartz and Estess 290). Changes in her poetry have been noted by several critics who have tried to discern, describe and explain the differences. This essay seeks to contribute an explanation.

Bishop's artistic achievement can be read as a development from an intended impersonal approach, characterized by a modernist "escape from personality" to a more personal approach, which involves certain social aspects. Somehow, the remoteness, complexities and contrasts of Brazil, the country of "her full maturity as a poet," to quote Ashley Brown (Schwartz and Estess 223), leads Bishop to harmonize more deeply the private and the public voice in her poems. The geographical and cultural differences between Brazil and Nova Scotia provide the shy poet with the necessary detachment to voice more distinctly and in greater detail her suppressed childhood feelings and her needs as an adult. Trying to describe foreign landscapes, she ends up revealing personal landscapes and making "north" and "south" converge; or, as Sandra Barry puts it, "Brazil opened a floodgate of memory for Bishop" (493) and allowed her to write her greatest autobiographical poems set in Great Village.

In Bishop's poetry of "deep subjectivity," a term used by Harold Bloom (1) to distinguish her poetic achievement from confessional poetry, there is plenty of room for social matters. Since her early books, one can find socially embedded in some of the poems the perspective of people marginalized by existing power relations: Miss Lula's black servant in "Cootchie" and the barefoot maid of the old lady in "Faustina, or Rock Roses" are two unforgettable outsiders in *North and South* and *A Cold Spring*, respectively. Nevertheless, if subjects relating to the oppressed and to social injustice were already a presence in Bishop's poetry before her arrival in Brazil, it was after *Questions of Travel* that their voice became audible and poignant and that humor became a recurrent device. Although Bishop disapproves of political thinking for writers, as she makes clear in her interview with Ashley Brown (Schwartz and Estess 293), she stresses the importance of the poet's social concern. In a Brazilian article reprinted by George Monteiro in *Conversations with Elizabeth Bishop*, the poet declares quite clearly that "[e]very good writer takes into account the social problems of his times… and in one way or another, all good poetry reflects those problems" (9). Without contradiction, as she becomes capable of giving voice to others, she discovers and reveals her own voice mingled with theirs. Howard Moss is right when he says that "[s]ympathy is a form of empathy and a way of entering another world by way of transference. Where other poets change coats, Bishop sheds skins" (29). Accordingly, this essay will examine some of her "skins" and address some ways in which "Elizabeth," who probably discovered her individuality in a waiting room on 507 Main Street, in Worcester, MA, moved from the private space of a dentist's waiting room to the social contexts of the places where she lived or which she visited in Brazil.

Unlike the lyric persona in Walt Whitman's surrealist poem "The Sleepers," who sleeps close to the other sleepers and who eventually "becomes the other dreamers" (426), in "Love Lies Sleeping," Bishop's "sleepers" are alone and detached from the beholder. The poet remains apart and separated by the window from which she becomes a careful world watcher. The beholder's concern and interest are evident in her criticism of the exploitation of modern urban workers, who even in their dreams are unable to get away from the "artificial and potentially poisonous figure of the city," as Betsy Erkkila emphasizes (288). Nevertheless, faithful to Eliot's principle of impersonality, Bishop's speaker remains in her room observing the "immense city" and listening to its sounds. She hears people getting up but not their voices.

In "Cape Breton," Bishop again makes use of her acute capacity for observation, and gives minute details in her descriptions of animals, of the cliff, the mist, the water, the valleys, and the road. Such details come in striking contrast to the economy with which she describes human beings. Their existence is only suggested by the sound of a motorboat, the presence of white churches on the hills and "occasional small yellow bulldozers" without their drivers because it is Sunday. It is only in the fourth stanza that people come to life. Two preachers, or rather, two "extra" preachers are riding on the bus, together with a man who gets off with a baby in his arms and heads for an invisible poor house.

Poverty, merely suggested in the poem through the simplicity of the daisies in the fields, is, on the one hand, a good example of Bishop's awareness of social issues and, on the other, of her difficulty or unwillingness to portray them more explicitly. Even though issues of human interaction and social conditions are only mentioned in passing, they underpin the atmosphere of discouragement and displacement in the poem: the cliff's edge is "grass-frayed," hills are "matted," the road seems "abandoned," the landscape is "meaningless," fish-nets are "torn" and brooks are dark. "Cape Breton" is reminiscent of Emily Dickinson's "Because I Could not Stop for Death" (J. 712), a poem Bishop probably had in mind when she wrote the lines describing the scenes from the bus in motion. Consider the passage in which Dickinson mentions cycles of life as they are contemplated from a vehicle in motion—the carriage traveling towards death:

> We passed the School, where children strove
> at recess in the Ring—
> We passed the Fields of Gazing grain—
> We passed the Setting-Sun. (350)

In "Cape Breton," Bishop's bus follows a similar itinerary but although it carries people home or to work, it seems to travel through a lifeless world as "[i]t passes the closed roadside stand, the closed schoolhouse, / where today no flag is flying" (68).

In opposition to the subtle reference to poverty and to the atmosphere of dismay that pervades "Cape Breton," Bishop's poems written in Brazil use a more direct approach to human relations and social problems.

Brazil enters Bishop's poetry in "Arrival at Santos." In her first poem about Brazil she ironically uses the perspective of a naive, prejudiced tourist with little knowledge of Brazil:

> a strange and ancient craft, flying a strange and brilliant rag.
> So that's the flag. I never saw it before.
> I somehow never thought of there *being* a flag. (89)

The scenery is "impractically shaped," the tropical flora is described as "frivolous greenery," palms are "uncertain," and the first Brazilian she depicts is presented as a funny and careless clown who catches Miss Breen's skirt with a boat hook.

From her first poem written in Brazil, Bishop establishes the basis of her critical view on questions of colonization. Making "Miss Breen" rhyme with "green coffee beans" she mocks the import-export relations between countries: "out" go raw products, "in" come tourists looking for the exotic but complaining about differences.

Bishop takes pains to place herself apart from this type of tourist because she is extremely demanding. Her interest is greater than "seeing the world the other way around" (93) as she states in "Questions of Travel." She is in search of answers:

> Oh, tourist,
> is this how this country is going to answer you
>
> and your immodest demands for a different world,
> and a better life, and complete comprehension
> of both at last...? (89)

The speaker in "Arrival at Santos" is the same who searches for the meaning of the landscape in "Cape Breton" and who concludes that it is probably the road that is "holding it back, in the interior," where it can not be seen and "where deep lakes are reputed to be." (67) The movement toward the interior in search of meaning as is stated in "Cape Breton," is attempted again in "Santos." When Bishop tries to make sense of the "strange land" she adopted as her home, she drives toward the interior of Brazil as well as toward her own interior. Goldensohn has certainly a point when she states that "in Brazil, both Brazil and Nova Scotia come fully alive as subjects" (xi) and that "Bishop's poems in the first decade in Brazil do more than enlarge her interest in people" (195). I would add that it helps her give meaning to the landscape. On leaving "Santos" and driving to the interior, she discovers that the deep lakes mentioned in "Cape Breton" are mythically connected with the river in "The Riverman," where the Dolphin speaks to the narrator of the poem. The door in the water that opens inward in the latter poem reveals the road that held the meaning in "Cape Breton" and I would argue that Bishop realizes that one of the keys to that door is the voice of the Other.

Besides the visual qualities that have been present right from Bishop's early poems and that have attracted the attention of so many critics, she develops an aural quality in her Brazilian years. Living in a foreign country whose language she never manages to master, she becomes an attentive listener who orchestrates a variety of popular voices and social claims in her work. Not only does she speak for others, but encourages them to speak for themselves. A comparison between "Under the Window: Ouro Preto," on the one hand and " Love Lies Sleeping" and " Cape Breton," on the other, unquestionably exposes changes in Bishop's approaches.

In "Ouro Preto," the poet still contemplates the scenery from a window, as in "Love Lies Sleeping," but the focus of her gaze has changed and voice becomes a crucial element in her perception of the environment. She leans out of the window to observe what lies below and to listen. Her major concern is what is close, rather than what is distant. The microcosm rather than the macrocosm is brought to the fore. No longer does she focus on the "immense city" with the eye of a political scientist; "Ouro Preto" is described or seen with the eye of an acute and sensitive anthropologist or a sociologist. The general problems created by the urban economy in a consumer society, as examined in "Love Lies Sleeping," are now replaced by individual dramas which she sees and hears as she looks out of the window.

There is a significant difference between "Cape Breton" and "Under the Window: Ouro Preto" as to the way Bishop observes human, family, and economic relations. Unlike "Cape Breton," where a baby is carried silently to an invisible house, in "Ouro Preto" children are given action and voice. In fact, they are given priority because the poem begins with their own words: "When my mother combs my hair it hurts" (153). Unlike the solitary baby in "Cape Breton" who was carried to an invisible house by a man (whether or not he is the father is by no means revealed), the babies in

"Ouro Preto" are almost invisible because they are tended by their mothers who wrap them up in all the heat out of excessive care (153). Whereas in "Cape Breton" the landscape and animals have ascendancy over people, in "Ouro Preto" it is to people that the poet turns her attention. Another important aspect is that poverty is no longer described indirectly or generically but it is dramatized. When describing poverty or social problems, Bishop deliberately refuses pathos by diluting their emotional burden with humor, as in the lines where she details the phases of man: birth, life, death:

> "She's been in labor now two days." "Transistors
> cost much too much." "For lunch we took advantage
> of the poor duck the dog decapitated." (154)

Labor, in "Cape Breton," is represented by workers on a weekend and also by two preachers shown here as workers rather than religious men. In "Ouro Preto," these workers are replaced by truck drivers, an old tramp and a little boy who carries laundry for his mother—as one of Bishop's drafts reveals. In the best understated Bishop fashion, she omits this detail in her final version, as the context makes it clear. As poor and illiterate Brazilian women have very few job opportunities, many of them make their living by washing clothes for rich families. Their children frequently help them in this chore by carrying the laundry—especially when dirty—which is tied up in a large cloth or bedsheet and carried on their heads. That is why the boy was not initially seen by the poem's narrator, who was looking out the window. This poem has several biographical details. The window mentioned in the poem is from Bishop's room in Pouso do Chico Rey—Lilli Correia de Araujo's guesthouse in Ouro Preto—and the fountain referred to in the poem is still there and its water continues attracting truck drivers as in Bishop's time.

The truck driver and "assistant driver" of the new Mercedes Benz announce the pleasures of a consumer society: "Here Am I For Whom You Have Been Waiting" (154), but the narrator points out that they leave pollution behind: "Oil has seeped into the / margins of the ditch of standing water" (154). It is worth exploring the messages on the bumpers. Some people mistakenly believe that the messages are bumper stickers. It is important to explain that they are not ready-made bumper stickers or something industrialized that one can buy in shops. Truck drivers in Brazil take great pride in having messages painted—as Bishop writes in the poem—on the bumpers of their vehicles, thus trying to convey something of their own ideas, dreams or frustrations. People collect and study such messages for what they reveal in many ways and, not surprisingly, Bishop was one of them. A newspaper article in the Elizabeth Bishop Special Collection at Vassar College (Box 91.2) reveals that many of these messages are very creative and often humorous. A good example in Bishop's "Under the Window: Ouro Preto" is the one displayed by the driver whose truck has "a syphilitic nose" and who tries his best to find room in a competitive society: "Not Much Money But It Is Amusing" (154).

In the individual drama of the old man with the "stick and sack" who also wants to drink some water from the fountain, Bishop tackles another crucial problem—the plight of the jobless or of the "Willy Lomans" in our societies, who are discarded as unproductive or redundant. The three-foot-tall black boy, who tries to balance a bundle of somebody else's dirty clothes on his head, represents child labor, that is, the children who cannot go to school because they have to do their share to increase the family's meager income. The little boy forms a contrast with one of the preachers in "Cape Breton" who sits comfortably on a bus carrying his own clothes, his frock coat, presumably clean and on a hanger.

Social problems, which are generically and indirectly presented in Bishop's poems, as we saw in "Love Lies Sleeping," are now dramatically conveyed and they show gender, age, and race differences. Bishop can confidently use a zoom lens to draw attention to the complexities of social and economic relations. She had learned to watch everything and everybody and especially to listen to "their voices talking" (109), as is mentioned in "The Riverman," a poem from which this expression is taken. Here the Amazonian villager, who wants to become a "sacaca," or a witch doctor, can understand Luandinha's language only when she blows cigar smoke into his ears and nostrils. Bishop's acute capacity for observation, highly and duly praised by all critics, is paired with another sense—she becomes an attentive listener, as has already been mentioned. And she listens to "people talking," that is, she listens to them in their daily activities, in their own environment, and certainly within their own culture.

The tourist's hungry gaze of "Arrival at Santos" has been nourished by the time Bishop writes "Santarém." If I were to give an answer to the tourist who arrived in Santos in 1951 and who wondered how Brazil was going to answer her, I would say that it taught her to "listen to people talking" and, by doing so, she could listen to her own inner voices and finally, after 26 years, finish "The Moose"—a poem that can be compared with "Under the Window: Ouro Preto" as far as inclusion of voices is concerned. Carried by "voices of people talking," Bishop could safely travel through her poems upstream to Nova Scotia and downstream to the Amazon, and make "Self" and "Other," as well as childhood and adulthood, converge and flow alongside each other.

Criticism of one's inability to see the world from different perspectives is, in my opinion, one of Bishop's themes in "Santarém," a poem in which she comes full circle in giving voice to the Other. This time, however, the Other is not a pink dog, a burglar or squatter's children; it is the exotic European—Mr. Swan, the retiring head of Philips Electric. It is impossible to disregard Bishop's irony in this detail. In Brazil, Philips is the most famous brand of light bulbs. Thus, paradoxically, the "nice" Mr. Swan, the head of a lamp manufacturing company—someone responsible for bringing light—is himself unable to see or, at least, to have an unbiased view. He cannot perceive beauty or meaning in the empty wasps' nest because he is unable to see through cultural differences. He does not hear or understand the "language" of the waters of the Tapajós and the Amazon, which are telling him that differences are not polarities or opposites and that they do not require choices. They are simply differences and they can and should be allowed to flow peacefully together.

Works Cited

Barry, Sandra. "Elizabeth Bishop: The Autobiography of a Poet." Rev. of *The Biography of a Poetry* by Lorrie Goldensohn. *Dalhousie Review* 4 (1991–92): 489–93.

Bishop, Elizabeth. *The Complete Poems 1927–1979*. New York: Farrar, Straus, Giroux, 1989.

———. Elizabeth Bishop Collection. Vassar College.

Bloom, Harold, ed. *Elizabeth Bishop*. New York: Chelsea, 1985.

Dickinson, Emily. *Complete Poems*. Ed. Thomas H. Johnson. Boston: Little, Brown, 1960.

Erkkila, Betsy. "Elizabeth Bishop, Modernism and the Left." *American Literary History* 8 (1996): 284–310.

Goldensohn, Lorrie. *Elizabeth Bishop: The Biography of a Poetry*. New York: Columbia UP, 1992.

Monteiro, George, ed. *Conversations with Elizabeth Bishop*. Jackson: UP of Mississippi, 1996.

Moss, Howard. "The Canada-Brazil Connection." *World Literature Today* 1 (1977): 29–33.

Schwartz, Lloyd, and Sybil P. Estess, eds. *Elizabeth Bishop and Her Art.* Ann Arbor: U of Michigan P, 1983.

Whitman, Walt. *Leaves of Grass.* Ed. Sculley Bradley. New York: Norton, 1973.

A Poet Between Two Worlds: A Cross-Genre Study of Exile in the Life and Works of Elizabeth Bishop

Audrey E. Hooker
Wake Forest University

Abstract

Elizabeth Bishop once said of poetry: "The only real way to understand it is to understand the life and beliefs of the poet" (qtd. in Travisano 40). This premise is both the guiding principle and justification for an analysis of Elizabeth Bishop's poetry that is complemented and enhanced by a close reading of her revealing personal correspondence. This study aims at presenting Bishop in the very terms with which she described herself—as a figure of exile in a world in which "home" is at best undefinable, and at worst, an ambiguous nether region. The study relies heavily upon biographical data, particularly Bishop's letters to Ilse and Kit Barker, two of her dearest friends. Through a comprehensive reading of these unpublished letters, along with some of her more revealing published letters, I detected a certain shift in Bishop's attitude about herself as an exile: one that begins as an attitude of resignation towards the ambiguous geographical dualities in which she finds herself and that results in her ultimate acceptance of her geographical "exile"—a state of mind whose freedom she embraces towards the end of her life.

It is December 31, 1934, in Greenwich Village, New York. A young Elizabeth Bishop is spending her New Year's Eve infirm, somewhat medicated, and alone. Despite her sickness, Bishop passes the greater part of the evening sitting on the floor of her apartment, scrutinizing a large, glass-encased map of her North Atlantic homeland, and writing the poem that would mark, both figuratively and literally, the beginning of her career as a poet (Millier 75). "The Map," which appears first in *North & South*, her first published collection of poetry, depicts a persona who experiences the delight that comes from freedom of interpretation. As Mutlu Konuk Blasing points out in her 1995 study of Bishop's composition process, the speaker responds to the map as a purely aesthetic object rather than a practical tool used for navigation. Through this imaginative play, the persona develops a decidedly domestic sort of mastery over her subject (Blasing 73). She can "stroke these lovely bays /...as if they were expected to blossom" (*CP* 3) or, like the peninsulas, "take the water between thumb and finger / like women feeling for the smoothness of yard-goods." Furthermore, while the map is an immutable representation, the persona's perspective is motile and fluid. She voluntarily misreads the map, mistaking "shallows" for "shadows," and admitting that she does not know whether the land "lies in water" or "lean[s] down to lift the sea from under." In short, Bishop grants her persona a wonderful sort of imaginative freedom with the map that results in her ultimate sovereignty over her own geographical creation. The persona is in no way intimidated by this geographical representation; rather, geography becomes for her a freely-associative, interpretive game.

I would like to be able to contend that Bishop's own relationship with geography was as unfettered as that of her persona. Unfortunately, it was not. In fact, geography was consistently one of the most controlling conditions in Bishop's life. Virtually, from the day that she was born in Worcester, Massachusetts, until the afternoon that she quietly passed away in the study of her Lewis Wharf apartment, Elizabeth Bishop was a traveler in both a voluntary and an involuntary sense.

Bishop describes her childhood and its repercussions in a 1978 interview with Elizabeth Spires. As the poet looks back upon her life, she seems to have developed a sizable distance from the painful series of events that shaped her childhood. However, she does not attempt to refute the emotional turmoil that was caused by these events. Rather, she freely admits that as a result of her constant traveling, she did not develop a true sense of consanguinity:

> My father died, my mother went crazy when I was four or five years old. My relatives, I think they all felt so sorry for this child that they tried to do their very best.... I lived with my grandparents in Nova Scotia. Then I lived with the ones in Worcester, Massachusetts, very briefly, and got terribly sick. This was when I was six and seven. Then I lived with my mother's older sister in Boston. I used to go to Nova Scotia for the summer. When I was twelve or thirteen I was improved enough to go to summer camp at Wellfleet until I went away for school when I was fifteen or sixteen.... I was always sort of a guest, and I think I've always felt like that. (Monteiro 126)

Bishop also recounts this somewhat confusing period of her childhood in "In the Village," the autobiographical story that contains one of the only images we see of Bishop's mother, Gertrude Bulmer Bishop. The narrative voice in this prose work poignantly conveys the utter disorientation and disjointedness that Bishop began to associate with traveling. In the following excerpt from the short story, Bishop recalls her mother's pattern of disappearance, appearance, and re-appearance in her life: "First, she had come home, with her child. Then she had gone away again, alone, and left the child. Then she had come home. Then she had gone away again, with her sister; and now she was home again" (*CPr* 252).

Bishop's childhood can be identified by the same pattern of perpetual mobility. She often had little to no control over where she would live, and for many years, "home" was for her more of an elusive abstraction than a definable location. "Home" would remain a tentative term for Bishop, one that she employed less frequently and with less conviction than the average individual. One year before her death, Bishop defined her sense of home as being a portable entity rather than a fixed locale; she contended that "home" was defined by emotional investment rather than geographical position. And while she continued to assert that she did not lack a sense of home, she also avowed that she did not possess one: "I've never felt particularly homeless, but, then, I've never felt particularly at home. I guess that's a pretty good description of a poet's sense of home. He carries it within him" (Monteiro 102).

This statement places Bishop in a rather ambiguous ideological position. If she never felt quite at home and also never felt entirely homeless, then where did she situate her geographical center? Was her elusiveness an attempt to abstain from claiming any sort of geographical center at all? And where did she eventually find a center from which the rest of her world radiated and took shape?

In an essay entitled, "Notes on Exile," Bishop contemporary Czeslaw Milosz posits that the imagination plays a crucial role in the development of an individual's sense of home, centeredness, and geography, but most particularly when that person resides in a different country from that in which he was born. Milosz uses the term "exile" to refer to the process by which one creates an identity based on not one, but two centers:

> Imagination, always spatial, points north, south, east, and west of some central, privileged place, which is probably a village from one's childhood or native region. As long as a writer lives in his country, the privileged place, by centrifugally enlarging itself, becomes more or less identified with his country as a whole. Exile displaces that center or rather creates two centers.... The new point which orients space in respect to itself cannot be eliminated, i.e., one cannot abstract oneself from one's physical presence in a definite spot on the Earth. That is why a curious phenomenon appears: the two centers and the two spaces arranged around them interfere with each other or—and this is a happy solution—coalesce. (Robinson 38)

Bishop's "central, privileged place," the North Atlantic, was the first, rather tentative center in her life. In 1951 she began to center herself in an entirely different region, Brazil, where she lived for almost fourteen years with the love of her life, Lota de Macedo Soares. Brazil became the second center in her life for this and other reasons: It was far-removed from the fast-moving literary circles of New York City; its remoteness offered her the societal freedom to be whom she wanted, and to be and to love whom she wanted to love; it was entirely different from any landscape that she had experienced before. As far as we can determine from her letters to loved ones and epistolary companions during this time, Bishop's first several years in Brazil were the happiest in all her life. Here is a sampling of her comments on life in Brazil from letters dated 1952 to 1955:

> I'm quite content to live in complete confusion, about seasons, fruits, languages, geography, everything. (1952; *One Art* 243)

> I like it [Brazil] so much that I keep thinking I have died and gone to heaven, completely undeservedly. (1952; *One Art* 249)

> It is just that where I am living and what I am doing seem to suit me perfectly for the first time in ages. (1953; *One Art* 282)

> I like it here better and better—not because it is Brazil at all, but just a good place to live. (1953; *One Art* 284)

> *Oh this incredible country!* (1954; *One Art* 285)

Bishop's letters certainly suggest that she was extremely content during the first five years of her stay in Brazil. However, as she spent more time in the country, her attitude began to change. What began as intimations of homesickness for the United States and feelings of foreignness in her own surroundings turned into bitter resentment toward a country that was diminishing her domestic stability. As Lota became more and more active in shaping her country's political landscape, Bishop's home life became less tranquil and her sense of geographical insecurity was exacerbated. To bolster the unstable ground upon which she found herself, she began to crave correspondence with and news from the outside world with an unprecedented voracity. Evidence of this can be found in an assortment of her published and unpublished letters dated 1956 to 1964:

> I'm feeling rather anti-Brazil this week. (23 Mar. 1956)

> [Lota] can't take my attitude of being a fairly detached foreigner here. (23 Mar. 1956)

I suppose the novelty of Brazil has worn off for me—I never would stay for a week if it weren't for Lota, of course. (24 Mar. 1956)

But oh dear—my aunt writes me long descriptions of the "fall colors" in Nova Scotia and I wonder if that's where I shouldn't be. (1958; *One Art* 366)

I am dying for the North, and if not for the North, for a Nordic letter. (1963; *One Art* 423)

I've had ten years of a backward, corrupt country, and like Lota, I yearn for civilization. (1963; *One Art* 418)

and,

I sometimes feel that we'll never survive Rio another two years. (7 Mar. 1964)

As one can see from these examples, Bishop documented her gradually changing attitude toward Brazil in her correspondence of this time. However, being the private, reserved person she was, she did not disclose this change in attitude to all within her correspondence circle. Those with whom she seemed to feel most comfortable discussing the matter were Ilse and Kit Barker. Ilse, a novelist, and Kit, a painter, met Elizabeth at Yaddo in 1949. They, like Elizabeth, were artists living and working in a country different from their native homeland. Bishop found in her relationship with the Barkers unconditional support and a shared sense of geographical displacement that she referred to as mutual "exile." In a correspondence that numbered 225 letters and that lasted over twenty-five years, Bishop developed a strong, almost familial bond with the Barkers. She contended that the strength of their relationship grew out of its beginnings. While at Yaddo in the autumn of 1949 and early winter of 1950, Bishop experienced what she called one of "the worst stretches of her life," and noted in a letter to Loren MacIver, "I have never felt so nervous and like a fish out of water" (1949; *One Art* 186). Because the Barkers supported her during this dreadful episode, she felt a sense of candor with them that she did not share with all of her correspondents. In her relationship with the Barkers, for instance, poetic rivalry was not a concern, as it was in her epistolary relationships with Marianne Moore and Robert Lowell. In short, when Bishop wrote to the Barkers, it seems that she had nothing to hide.

Bishop's letters to the Barkers document her attempted development of a second center in her life. Those letters that are particularly noteworthy are the ones in which she finds herself on less stable emotional ground because this is when her sense of geographical estrangement is at its highest. In an unpublished letter dated May 2, 1963, Bishop wrote the Barkers from her Rio apartment, where she stayed during the week when Lota had to go to the city for business. Her weekly trips to and from Rio had begun to wear on her, causing her to bemoan the repercussions of what she called "split-level living" (15 May 1961). This is also the first time in the course of their correspondence that she refers to herself as an "exile." In this excerpt, we see not only her sense of helplessness due to the current situation, but her admitted lack of control. Rather than being an agent in her own geographical placement, she is merely an observer of its consequences:

> But I want to get away badly these days—I feel like those moments I've just been watching on the beach when two waves going at angles to each other meet and an immense confusion of helpless ripples and foam and upheavings result.... Lota wonders how we keep corresponding, Ilse, and I think—besides the fact that we both like to write letters—perhaps it is partly because we are both exiles in a way, even if voluntary and cheerful ones. (2 May 1963)

Bishop's depiction of "helpless ripples," "upheavals," and "confusion" is somewhat lightened by her notion that she and Ilse are "voluntary and cheerful" in their mutual exile. The beautiful yet tragic rendering of "two waves" meeting in "immense confusion" can be likened to Bishop's dualistic sense of home at the time. If, as Milosz contends, exiles do develop a dual sense of "home" and centeredness, this passage can be read as one of the first times when Bishop truly and deeply contemplates her dual sense of geographic reality: the result is frightening. As she began to mistrust the very country in which she was living, as she started to question the relationship that beckoned her to stay, she began to hearken back to the first, central, "privileged place." Corresponding with Ilse and Kit assuaged Bishop's sense of geographical displacement. Because of the Barkers, Bishop did not feel entirely alone in the ambiguous nether region in which home is neither here nor there, and both here and there.

But was Bishop really, as she called herself, an exile? It seems a rather punitive term to apply to a self-imposed lifestyle choice. However, there were times in her life when she felt suspended between two places, with the helpless feeling that she did not belong in either location. After Lota's suicide in 1967, Bishop felt estranged from the land that had been her home for 14 years. Her deteriorating relationship with former Brazilian friends also exacerbated her sense of homelessness. In a 1968 letter, Bishop poignantly articulates the loss of home and family that she experienced as a result of Lota's death.

...Can you imagine arriving at the only home (forgive me for being corny, but it is true) I have ever really had in this world and finding it not only not mine—I had agreed to all that—but almost stripped bare? Friends had gone up from Rio—how soon after the funeral I don't know—and taken everything. Mary left me the linen on my bed, 2 towels, 2 plates, forks, knives, etc. This was my HOME.... I left Brazil with a very heavy heart and hope to never see Rio again.... I feel now as if I'd been living in a completely false world all the time—not false, but that no one ever liked me, really or not many people, and all of them totally misunderstood the strength of the bonds between Lota and me.... (1968, *One Art* 490)

The strength of the bond between her and Lota was indeed so great that once this bond was diminished, Bishop's sense of place in Brazil vanished almost immediately. She felt the need to estrange herself from the country that had caused her so much heartache. She moved to San Francisco and lived there briefly before returning to Ouro Preto to make the final arrangements for the house that she owned there. Her correspondence from this time shows evidence of a heightened sense of geographical awareness. She frequently spoke of San Francisco but never registered any comprehensive opinions about it; she never called it home and often admitted her geographical ambivalence over it. In letters from 1968, Bishop admits that though pleasant enough, San Francisco remains for her a rather nondescript landscape:

I really don't know how I feel about S.F. (1968; *One Art* 495)

I really don't know if S.F. is my SCENE or not.... (1968; *One Art* 496)

I like the city very much.... (1968; *One Art* 500)

I think I hate California, or maybe it's mostly Reagan—but it does seem to be the place where all the awful things start and happen.... (1969; *One Art* 503)

When Bishop left San Francisco for Ouro Preto, she found that though the beauty of the Brazilian town had endured, her emotional bond to it had not. She noted that despite the location being "the most beautiful in the world," it was not enough that the place was aesthetically pleasant (1969; *One Art* 510). Aesthetics, she surmised, was not reason enough to call a place "home." Once she realized that life in Ouro Preto was an impossibility, she contemplated her return to the United States. In letters from late 1969 and early 1970, Bishop again seems suspended between two realms, this time Ouro Preto and San Francisco. In January 1970, she writes, "I don't want to go back to San Francisco very much, either. I'm hard to please!"

(1970; *One Art* 512). A month later, she admits that she does not know where she wants to live: "The trouble is, I really don't know where or how I want to live anymore. I liked San Francisco, fairly well only. . . New York seems just too much to face, somehow, although I am homesick for it. . . I love this house. . . they just don't DO things here" (1970; *One Art* 513). Finally, a few weeks later, Bishop pens her ultimate rejection of Brazil: "I must get out of this country, and never come back to it" (1970; *One Art* 513). She left Ouro Preto the following September for the United States, never to see Brazil again.

❖   ❖   ❖

Bishop often presents the image of the "creature divided" (*CP* 192) in her poetry. Whether or not she applies to it the exact term, "exile," she undoubtedly highlights instances in which individuals or beings experience a sense of being both attracted to and repelled by two extremes. In "Crusoe in England," the persona expresses as much ambivalence about his former island home as his present one. Though he enumerates several important differences between the two locations, one has a difficult time discerning which is the true island of exile and which is the island of home. The alleged island of exile, upon which Crusoe's "smallest island industry" is his "miserable philosophy" (*CP* 164) is not a far cry from the island upon which he mourns the loss of experience that is envisaged in assorted relics from previous adventures. In short, one gets the sense that just because Crusoe is back in England does not mean that he is home. This argument is furthered by the biographical fact that Bishop's first title of "Crusoe in England" was "Crusoe at Home." Apparently, Bishop could not bring herself to call England Crusoe's "home" because of what she considered his marked ambivalence about it.

Exile between two realms is a theme that appears elsewhere in her poetry as well. For instance, in her earlier work "The Fish," we witness a being that is divided between his natural environment and a more foreign one: "I caught a tremendous fish / and held him beside the boat / half out of water" (*CP* 42). In "The Gentleman of Shalott" we encounter a creature who instead of being "half sick of shadows," like Tennyson's "The Lady of Shalott," is in love with "the sense of constant re-adjustment" (*CP* 10) that the mirror provides. The mirror, a specter in which the persona views other worlds, separates everything out into halves, in suspension between visual reflection and physical reality. "In the Waiting Room" depicts a young girl slipping into and out of exile to a realm of "blue-black space" (*CP* 160). Through an encounter with visual representations and aural associations, the persona begins a vacillation between two distinctly different realms, neither of which is very welcoming to this resistant traveler. But perhaps the most revealing and poignant example of Bishop's sense of suspension between two realms occurs in the last poem that she wrote before her death, "Sonnet":

> Caught—the bubble
> in the spirit-level,
> a creature divided;
> and the compass needle
> wobbling and wavering,
> undecided.
> Freed—the broken
> thermometer's mercury
> running away;
> and the rainbow-bird
> from the narrow bevel
> of the empty mirror,
> flying wherever
> it feels like, gay! (*CP* 192)

This poem provides a potentially hopeful resolution of Bishop's divided self. The bubble that was once "caught" in the spirit level becomes "freed" from its former limitations. The compass needle that wobbles and wavers in an expression of indecision does not impede the thermometer's broken mercury from "running away." The depiction of the freed mercury prefigures the next image which is often associated with freedom: a bird. This bird is not a normal bird, however, but a sublime bird, a "rainbow" bird. Just as in "The Fish" when Bishop mutters in elation, "Until everything / was rainbow, rainbow, rainbow" (*CP* 44), the bird in "Sonnet" is an expression of her ultimate sublime freedom from the limitations that characterized her life. The sublime bird does not pay any heed to the vacillating compass needle anymore, but instead, "flies wherever / it feels like, gay!"

The marked difference in Bishop's attitude toward geography and exile that is expressed in this poem signals her decision to allow both centers in her life to coalesce rather than to conflict. While Bishop's early letters are characteristic because of the predominance of geography as a subject, Bishop's late letters are characteristic because of the lack of emphasis on geography. However, one should also remember that it was during this time that she composed the most autobiographical work of her career, encapsulated in *Geography III*. At the end of her life, Bishop felt able to articulate her geographical position more directly and more clearly through her poetry. I believe that she felt like less of an "exile" at the end of her career because she was finally able to discern and articulate her geographical tensions, rather than merely presenting them as binaries or irreconcilable extremes. Ultimately, Bishop emerges at the end of her life at peace with the geographical dualities that had once dominated her life. A work like "Sonnet" articulates the point that, like her envisioned rainbow bird, Bishop too could finally fly "wherever / [she] feels like, gay!"

Works Cited

Bishop, Elizabeth. *The Collected Prose*. Ed. Robert Giroux. New York: Farrar, Straus, Giroux, 1984.

———. *The Complete Poems*. New York: Farrar, Straus, Giroux, 1979.

———. Letters to Ilse and Kit Barker, 1952–1979. Department of Rare Books and Special Collections, Princeton University Library, New Jersey.

———. *One Art: Letters*. Ed. Robert Giroux. New York: Farrar, Straus, Giroux, 1994.

Blasing, Mutlu Konuk. "Elizabeth Bishop: Repeat, Repeat, Repeat; Revise, Revise, Revise." *Politics and Form in Postmodern Poetry*. Cambridge: Cambridge UP, 1995. 67–109.

Millier, Brett C. *Elizabeth Bishop: Life and the Memory of It*. Berkeley: UP of California, 1993.

Monteiro, George, ed. *Conversations with Elizabeth Bishop*. Jackson: UP of Mississippi, 1996.

Robinson, Marc. *Altogether Elsewhere: Writers on Exile*. Boston: Faber, 1994.

Travisano, Thomas. "Emerging Genius: Elizabeth Bishop and the Blue Pencil, 1927–1930." *Gettysburg Review* 5 (Winter 1992).

Elizabeth Bishop: Longing for Home—and Paradise

Harriet Y. Cooper
New York University

Abstract

In her memoir, "In the Village," Elizabeth Bishop retrieved the painful, defining events of her childhood, her mother's madness and subsequent removal to a sanatorium. Maternal deprivation, according to Mario Jacoby's theories (*The Longing for Paradise*), leads to the wish to replicate the early feelings of closeness with the mother and a longing for home. Bishop's desire for the absent mother and her intense need for home motivated her travels and their aim, the search for place. "In the Village" also was a storehouse for future poems, their images and metaphors.

Memoir, the hot genre among contemporary writers, Elizabeth Bishop perfected in the 1950's and 60's as she recollected her childhood in Nova Scotia and Worcester, Massachusetts. For the reticent Bishop, who eschewed personal confession in poems, the memoir was an appropriate form to marshall the disjointed, often shameful, events of her early disrupted years. The memoir served her narrative voice, using her poetic gifts of language while offering an extended occasion to speak of the awkwardness and pain of her childhood as she was shuttled among relatives. These autobiographical stories became sources, storehouses in a sense, from which she drew for her poems, their images and metaphors.

Memoir, a form which seeks to retrieve memories, is an attempt to restore the early environment. It afforded Bishop a means to re-examine the chaotic occurrences from a perspective of maturity and to integrate them in a coherent—albeit elliptical—narrative. Certain details are magnified, such as the prize pink marble, which becomes emblematic of childhood loss ("Gwendolyn" *CPr* 225). More importantly, certain preoccupations which reverberate in her future writing emerge.

At the center of Bishop's endeavor is the loss of home and the condition of displacement, a condition often shared with other writers. Adrienne Rich, in one poetic sequence, "Contradictions: Tracking Poems," speaks of her state of dispossession, her "own / unhoused spirit trying to find a home." This desire for a nurturing environment is a result of the separation from the place first known and lost. "Nostalgia"—the word coming from the Greek *nostos* for the return home and *algos* for pain—originates in the loss of that first home, and broadly signifies a yearning for what is past. This primal loss creates a longing for a place that will replicate early feelings of nurture and protection, a kind of paradise, if you will. The Swiss psychologist Mario Jacoby, in his book *The Longing for Paradise*, traces the matrix of longing to a small cluster of related phenomena, beginning with the unity between mother and infant, what he calls "the unitary reality" or "the Great Round" (5, 8). The loss of the mother and that circle of closeness creates an intense longing in the child later realized as nostalgia. Early deprivation, according to Jacoby, produces a longing for a replacement of that first closeness that persists throughout life, often setting up a pattern of search. The life of Elizabeth Bishop, her characteristic restlessness and searching travel, her need for home and her ambivalence to it, her desire for special places as well as the importance of houses and her frequent references to home, all bear out Jacoby's thesis.

The early sadnesses in Bishop's life—the death of her father and the disappearance of her mother (death, as the child Elizabeth maintains in "The Country Mouse") led to an increased, strong need for nurture and stability. The abrupt removal to the Bishops' in Worcester from the home of her Bulmer grandparents in Nova Scotia, emotionally perceived as a loss of home, compounded that need. As a result of these childhood losses, a sense of homelessness continually plagued Bishop, prompting David Kalstone to say that she "was homesick all her life" (22).[1] Homesickness, like nostalgia, issues from "longing for oneness with the mother" in a state of harmony (Jacoby 7). At school the dilemma of where to spend vacations underscored her orphan plight. From temporary stays and provisional places came her sense that she was, as she expressed it, "always sort of a guest," without place (Spires 75). Images of displacement proliferate. In a prose poem, for instance, the crab that strayed out of his natural element, says: "This is not my home. How did I get so far from water?" (*CP* 140). Because of Bishop's continual shifting and lack of attachment, feelings of impermanence and transience became an integral component of her consciousness. That she sought to ameliorate her improvised situations was often reflected in her choice of subjects. Helen Vendler, one of the first critics to systematically analyse Bishop's poems, characterizes her work, in large part, as the "domestication of the unfamiliar" (36–7). One Bishop persona, Crusoe, rescued after years on "his beloved island," is sick at heart back in England, nostalgic for his rough makeshift home. His devastation at being in England questions the definition of home and Bishop's attitude toward her own place of origin. In her years of travel, a sense of home and permanence continues to evade: *"Should we have stayed at home, / wherever that may be?"* ("Questions of Travel," *CP* 94).

Bishop's most significant memoir, "In the Village," written in Brazil in 1953 after she had settled there with Lota de Macedo Soares, recovers a central catastrophe in her young life—a dress fitting that once again sets off her mother's madness and its aftermath. In the memoir, the child, wary of the mother and her unpredictable state, stays apart, uneasy, fearing identification with her, or possibly, harm from her. A remote, passive figure in the corners of the story, the mother, even though distanced by the impersonal "she" and referred to in the past tense, is, by her very dysfunction, at the crux of the narrative, controlling as she does others' behavior. The anonymous "she," recognized by her hysterical voice—not unlike the female voice of staccato demands in *The Waste Land*'s "Game of Chess"—is conjured up through her "things"—feminine, elegant, correct—now no longer of use, accessories to a role that failed to prepare her for the adult realities of death and loss. Only damaged keepsakes with their nostalgia—handkerchiefs, perfume-stained, and faraway postcards, their glitter gone—survive as talismans of her former married happiness.

The primary event of the memoir is Gertrude Bishop's scream, a personification of her illness, a sound that, intensified, forever scores the consciousness of her five-year-old child. From the very first sentence of the narrative, the scream assumes a surreal presence, that embodied, covers the landscape. For Elizabeth that sound was to signify the origin of all pain and become its metaphor, being the antecedent of her aunt's lesser, physical pain at the dentist in "In the Waiting Room." Its equivalent in nature, the calling of black birds in Labrador's harbor, renders the sound ubiquitous: "One can hear their crying, crying / the only sound there is" ("Large Bad Picture" *CP* 11).

At Mrs. Bishop's initial fitting with the dressmaker, the dress's purple color is "all wrong," jarring, and it severely disturbs the thin nervous woman, inciting her scream. In another version of the story ("Reminiscences of Great Village"), she confuses the boundaries of the cloth and her body and fears the dressmaker's scissors will cut her flesh (Lombardi 203, Millier 10). What was intended to be an end to Gertrude's long period of "mourning" black and a step to re-enter the world does precisely the opposite—it shuts her away from the world forever.

The child's anger and aggression towards the unavailable mother who abandoned her are displaced onto another representation of the female, the dressmaker Miss Gurley. (Elizabeth dare not feel the mother is bad.) In Jungian terms, the "negative transformative character" of the mother arche-type is expressed in figures who have the power to enchant, a Circe or a Medusa, or, more broadly, witches in fairy tales. In Bishop's prose, Miss Gurley approximates a magician in that she has the potential to transform—a power contained in her name "maker"—by creating through her skills a positive persona and so restoring the mother to her former self. Instead, the dressmaker, witch-like, effects a negative transformation, for the purple dress turns the mother into a raging mad woman.

In this highly condensed section, certain conventions of fables and fairy tales are used to disguise the underlying or latent content. Bishop herself referred to "In the Village" as a "fantasy" (though it contradicts her remark that it was "completely autobiographical" [*One Art* 291]). A function of fairy tales is to help the child accept disturbing feelings of aggression in himself and in others. That the tales employ elements of the supernatural—feats and characters outside realism—and figurative, allusive language ren-der their violent acts acceptable. Their frequent incantatory tone, character-istic of the genre, is especially notable in the evocative, "She sleeps in her thimble" (*CPr* 258). Invested with the supernatural, the dressmaker is able to kill with her machine—the magic instrument of transformation and death. She relentlessly pumps the treadle on which an unsuspecting kitten had once rocked, "like a baby in a cradle," until being strangled in the cords. In Bishop's act of creating, a repressed memory of being unprotected and ex-posed surfaces. In this ominous atmosphere, another cat risks being trapped in a turban Miss Gurley sews. In the child's unconscious, the dressmaker is seen as the cause of her mother's breakdown and departure—death, as she tells her playmate Emma ("The Country Mouse," *CPr* 31). Following the dictates of the irrational, Bishop characterizes the dressmaker as a mur-derer. (In Brazil her preoccupation with dressmakers continues as she and Lota attempt to cheer their visiting seamstress. Her sadness, in the poem "House Guest," becomes portentous, assuming a sinister aura similar to that of Miss Gurley: "Can it be that we nourish / one of the Fates in our bosoms?" In the last lines when Bishop, questioning the lack of fulfillment of their lives, obliquely blames the dressmaker and her "crooked" hems as the cause, we once again witness the ghost of Miss Gurley [*CP* 148–49]).

The analogy of Miss Gurley on her knees to Nebuchadnezzar, an inspi-ration Bishop likely took from William Blake's monotype in the Boston Museum of Art, was suggested by the mad king's kneeling pose as well as by the similarity of his face, contorted in rage and despair, to her mother's.

The needles the dressmaker holds in her mouth focus the child's fears of biting and devouring. Bishop's disturbed relationship with her mother gave rise to a negative view of the "terrible mother," exemplified by Miss Gurley who represents, in Jacoby's terms, "parts of a rejecting or devouring 'environment mother'" (47). Her bodice, described as "a bosom full of needles," far from an image of the nurturing breast, is, with its potential to harm, the ultimate rejecting breast.[2] That the dressmaker makes nests of needles and their threads—certainly a metaphor for the dangerous home, the nurturing place that wounds—indicates Bishop's apprehension about her unstable mother. The threatening image of the dressmaker is, I believe, the child's cover memory of the mother who harbored dangerous impulses.

Mario Jacoby contends that whether the maternal breast is perceived as good and nourishing, evil and attacking or just withholding—depends "primarily upon the behavior of the personal mother" (40). During the period of the primal relationship it is essential that positive maternal images prevail. We can establish from Mr. Bishop's boast of his wife's bountiful milk (excessive enough to make butter, he says in a letter to Elizabeth Hutchinson Boomer, 12 February 1911 [Millier 3, 551 n.3]), that being held and nursed were part of Elizabeth's bonding with her mother. We know, too, that because of Mrs. Bishop's breakdown when Elizabeth was nine months, an interruption occurred and with that loss of contact, an interference of the positive mother image, likely causing anxiety and emotional harm. Gertrude's later comings and goings—enforced by her inconsistent, irrational behavior—set up a pattern of expectation and disappointment which injured the child's sense of trust. That formation of trust is essential for self-esteem and mature relationships.

Inadequacy or interruption of nurture can lead to a child's exaggerated and continuing need of succor. In the memoir we may safely extrapolate this need from Bishop's recollection of specific incidents. The child's thumb-sucking, her instinctive putting the nickel in her mouth (alas, swallowing it), her preference for "spit-producing" candies, and the glass buttons, which are "delicious to suck," all are symptomatic of an urgent oral appetite. Such oral needs resulting from early deprivation often lead to alcoholism.

The series of enclosures in the memoir—the turban, the women's "skein of voices"—are projections of the child's fears of entrapment in or by her mother's illness. The upstairs commotion, the aunts' anxious attempts to shield the child, their desperate inadequacy and dread of another "scream" make the child panicky, claustrophobic, wanting to get away. "I am struggling to free myself," she says as the voices close in and the crisis mounts.

Her perennial escape is to the safe haven of the blacksmith shop and to Nate. Reliable, physically powerful, he acknowledges her at once with a ring of his own making. Like the man the child draws beside the house in "Sestina" (the poetic complement to "In the Village"), he is a replacement for the absent father.

Bishop's problematic relationship with her mother created an ambivalence that resulted in the splitting of her mother into two separate images. The mother in the memoir appears mostly as the "bad" withholding mother, who scolds—"Stop sucking your thumb!"—and demands—"Do you know what I want?" (*CPr* 267). Also, in an unfinished poem, she reprimands—"Put *that* down!"—when the child picks up a black stocking from the debris of the 1914 Salem fire (Kalstone 211). That reprimand, along with her mother's ignoring her thirsty calls for water on the night of the fire, Bishop in that same poem cites as the traumatic source of her "abnormal thirst" ("A Drunkard," Millier 4–6, 148).

Recollections elsewhere negatively associate her mother with pain and death—the swan biting her gloved finger in Boston's Public Gardens and her bidding Elizabeth to say goodbye to the dead little Arthur ("First Death in Nova Scotia"). The irrational demands and hysterical tone of her mother's voice so seared Bishop's young psyche that years afterward Gertrude's "high *vox humana*" haunts her still in dream.

> *The gray horse needs shoeing!*
> *It's always the same!*
> *What are you doing,*
> *there, beyond the frame?* ("Sunday, 4 A.M." *CP* 129)

The "bad" mother's disapproval imparted a sense of stricture that inhibits the child (hence her careful drawing of the "rigid house" in "Sestina"). In "In the Village" the "good" mother, briefly smiling, feeds her porridge, but her attention's therapeutic effect is undermined by hands coercing the child's head, as if to deny growth. The child's unspoken love for the "good" mother fosters a need to hold onto something tangible, so she "abscond[s]" with her mother's ivory embroidery tool, the opposite of the dressmaker's needle and the female counterpart to the blacksmith's nail. Fearing that the ivory stick (purposely not called needle) will be taken away, she buries it near a crab-apple beneath "the bleeding heart." Only in this botanical choice does the reticent artist allow a specific reference to the painful grief caused by her mother's abandonment. Symbolically, of course, the needle is never recovered. The loss of the mother is the mother of all losses.

Another cover memory resides in the episode of the fire and its disruption, this one for Mrs. Bishop's final crisis. The memoir's account fuses the fire with another middle-of-the-night disturbance of cries and panic. The qualities of fire—raging, out of control, destructive—madness metaphorically shares. The enigmatic phrase, "being in the room with me," as well as "at McLean's place"—supposedly the source of the conflagration—pointedly suggest the mother, McLean being the name of the mental hospital from which (Bishop believed) she had recently returned. The fusion of fire and madness are presented impressionistically as a phantasmogoria, attended by the alarms of church bells and flaming red glare invading the reaches of the child's room. Years later in Brazil, fire balloons falling from the night sky stir memories of those images of fire and the early feelings of fear and danger indelibly linked with them. Described in "The Armadillo," the balloons' exploding flames indiscriminately destroy the natural habitats of animals, driving them out of their shelters. The owls, who, fleeing their burning nests, "shrieked up out of sight," unmistakably locate the poem's emotional subtext.

> *Too pretty, dreamlike mimicry!*
> *O falling fire and piercing cry*
> *and panic....* (CP 104)

No longer the frightened child, Bishop, the mature artist, triumphs in the poem's concluding image against a fate in which she is no longer trapped. The armadillo's "*weak mailed fist / clenched ignorant against the sky!*" is her cry of defiance. In "In The Village," the river's "*Slp*" and the blacksmith's "*Clang,*" evoking the elements, outlast the nightmarish scream and metaphorically render Bishop's transcendence over her past.

In the memoir, the pivotal event that irrevocably changed Bishop's childhood—the removal of her mother—takes place off stage. Only its effect is noted in the understated, brief denouement: "Now the front room is empty" (*CPr* 271). Never voiced are the child's reactions nor her feelings. Only her silent gesture—covering the sanatorium's address—as she carries a package for her mother to the post office expresses her shame and embarrassment.

To balance the chaos and anguish of the Bulmer house is the blacksmith shop, along with Great Village and its countryside. The clang of the anvil answers (and wants to obliterate) the mother's scream and stands as a sane reminder of the male world of purpose and productivity. To the child its sound is "pure and angelic," for angel-like, it delivers her from a place of tension into a place thriving with warmth and possibility. In the presence of horse-flesh amid smells of hot metal and droppings, the child finds comfort and security, remarking, in another displacement, that the onlooking men are "perfectly at home" and, repeating, for emphasis, that the horse "is very much at home," too.

Out in the pasture, another respite, the child, content to be near Nelly and the brook, is tempted not to return home. Only as the cows gather away from her does she feel a wrenching aloneness, in a space without a mother. (This reluctance to return home figures dramatically in "The Prodigal," a poem in which the son prefers deprivation and filth to the return home, in his case, a concession of defeat and need.)

Bishop's intense need for home, issuing from that maternal deprivation, is expressed in both prose and poems as well as in paintings of domestic interiors. In the Worcester memoir, "The Country Mouse," the little girl, lodged in her grandparents' unfamiliar, dreary house, utterly devoid of spontaneity, discovers an old, out-of-use carriage and remarks: "It made the most beautiful little house imaginable. I wanted to stay in it forever" (*CPr* 20). It was the beginning of Bishop's affection for many such improvised shelters and her subsequent attraction to houses. In Key West, one of the natives' abodes with its spontaneous decor of oddments and leftovers, drew her as individual and authentic, expressing as it did, the universal desire to nest and adorn. In "Jerónimo's House" she recognized the home's purpose as refuge, "shelter from the hurricane," but more importantly, as the place of love: "My house, my fairy / palace is / of perishable / clapboards.... / My home, my love-nest" (*CP* 34). For Bishop, "Samambaia" on Lota's estate outside Petrópolis, and "Casa Mariana" in Ouro Prêto, decorated with art and *objets trouvés*, were two of her "three loved houses" ("One Art," *CP* 178). But the green "artichoke" house set on beach pilings, her "proto-dream-house" recalled on a blustery shore walk, resists her fantasy of inhabiting another life there and is inaccessible. Its narrator stating "of course [it] was boarded up" is a case in which the internalized voice of a withholding mother forbidding pleasure fits the actual situation ("The End of March," *CP* 180).

The obverse side of Bishop's desire for a settled home was a compulsory need to travel. After living on three continents and in many venues, Bishop came to rest in Brazil. One particular moment, occurring on a trip to the Amazonian interior, offered a sense of repose she memorialized in "Santarém."

> That golden evening I really wanted to go no farther;
> more than anything else I wanted to stay awhile
> in that conflux of two great rivers, Tapajós, Amazon,
> grandly, silently flowing, flowing east.
> . . . .
> I liked the place; I liked the idea of the place.
> Two rivers. Hadn't two rivers sprung
> from the Garden of Eden? (*CP* 185)

These lines acknowledge Bishop's unconscious wish for an ideal place, which is, if we read the passage according to Jacoby's ideas, a clear replacement for the original home briefly known and lost. The wish, her old longing for oneness with the mother, in harmony, reasserts itself in a longing for Paradise,[3] that first Eden.

Endnotes

1. A prose piece entitled, "Homesickness," written in Wiscasset, Maine (1948), was never finished; Bishop's usual solution was to dull or obliterate painful feelings with alcohol (Millier 201).

2. An early rejection may have led to Bishop's fear and revulsion of breasts, consequently her descriptions of the natives' "awful hanging breasts" in *National Geographic* ("In the Waiting Room") and of "rocky breasts" ("Cape Breton").

3. "The ultimate goal of nostalgic longing is a *condition*,... a state of being which finds symbolic expression in the image of Paradise" (Jacoby 4).

Works Cited

Bishop, Elizabeth. *The Collected Prose*. Ed. Robert Giroux. New York: Farrar, Straus, Giroux, 1984.

———. *The Complete Poems: 1927–1979*. New York: Farrar, Straus, Giroux, 1983.

———. *One Art: Letters*. Ed. Robert Giroux. New York: Farrar, Straus, Giroux, 1994.

Jacoby, Mario. *The Longing for Paradise*. Trans. Myron B. Gubitz. Boston: Sigo Press, 1985.

Kalstone, David. *Becoming A Poet: Elizabeth Bishop with Marianne Moore and Robert Lowell*. London: Hogarth Press, 1989.

Lombardi, Marilyn May. *The Body and the Song: Elizabeth Bishop's Poetics*. Carbondale: Southern Illinois UP, 1995.

Millier, Brett C. *Elizabeth Bishop: Life and the Memory of It*. Berkeley: U of California P, 1993.

Spires, Elizabeth. "The Art of Poetry, XXVII: Elizabeth Bishop." *Paris Review* 23 (Summer 1981): 56–83.

Vendler, Helen. "Domestication, Domesticity, and the Otherworldly." *Elizabeth Bishop and Her Art*. Eds. Lloyd Schwartz and Sybil P. Estess. Ann Arbor: U of Michigan P, 1983.

Revise, Revise: Elizabeth Bishop Writing "The End of March"

Joelle Biele
University of Maryland

Abstract

With poems and stories, Elizabeth Bishop continually investigated the metaphoric potential of the seashore. It was the collision of two worlds, and in "The End of March," of two seasons, that interested Bishop. Hers is a meditation on the intermediacy of experience, both physical and psychological, of being caught in two places at once, the past and the present. By bringing together much of her earlier writing and reshaping it with longer lines, detached humor, and autobiographical detail, Bishop revises John Keats' poetics and his approach to the moment.

Though it is unclear exactly when Elizabeth Bishop began drafting "The End of March," she left for John Malcolm Brinnin and Bill Read's summer home in Duxbury, Massachuesetts, on a June 1974 evening with hopes of getting work done.[1] Bishop and Alice Methfessel visited the pair's summer home regularly, and they spent time on the beach digging clams, "little ones, delicious" (letter to Muser, 7 July 1973, VC). It was a place where Bishop could get away to spend time with friends, bicycle on the beach, watch birds, and look at wild flowers, a place where she could make a strawberry shortcake "for I don't know how many" on the Fourth of July. Describing the house to her college friend, Frani Blough Muser, Bishop observed wryly, "a very pleasant house too full of distracting books, however, when one intends to work...." (letter to Muser, 8 June 1975, VC). Bishop sent a copy of the poem to Brinnin and Read as a thank-you note for letting her and Methfessel stay at the beach house. To Robert Lowell she later wrote that the poem started out as "a sort of joke thank-you-note. John B. was so appalled when I said I wanted that ugly little green shack for my summer home! (He doesn't share my taste for the awful, I'm afraid)" (3 September 1974, HRHRC). After arriving in North Haven, Maine, from Duxbury, Bishop sent the poem to Howard Moss, her editor at *The New Yorker,* dubbing the poem "my version of the Lake Isle of Innisfree" (18 July 1974, NYP).

The way Bishop went about writing her "Lake Isle of Innisfree" resembles someone making a sketch. She typed all the extant drafts and then corrected them by hand. In what appears to be her first draft, Bishop extended almost all the lines to the right hand margin as if she were writing prose. In subsequent drafts, she broke many of these lines. She first wanted to get the base image on the page, making a general outline, and then for the next several versions she expanded these lines, testing the weight and rhythm of her words. Perhaps the story of the poem came to her quickly or perhaps there are manuscripts not in existence today; but it is fair to say that Bishop did a fair amount of pre-writing off and on since she first recorded walks along the shore and bragged about her kite for Marianne Moore (notebook, VC; *One Art* 77). In at least five different poems that she drafted but did not finish or chose not to publish, she tried to shape the images that prefigured the images of the beach and kite. When Bishop sat down at her typewriter, one can imagine her thinking through "The End of March," typing and then retyping lines or phrases, writing in the margins, perhaps when the poem was still on the platen. As she made her way through the drafts, the first stanza took shape within the first drafts, then the second stanza, and finally the third, a more or less steady progression. Bishop changed the fourth stanza after she sent the poem to *The New Yorker* and then again after those changes were made. Always, Bishop chose to simplify the language and image with one and two syllable words in order to achieve the desired understatement; simplification recreates experience as embellishment cannot. By bringing together much of her earlier writing and reshaping it with longer lines, detached humor, and autobiographical detail, Bishop revises John Keats' poetics and his approach to the moment.

The crucial decision Bishop made in the first stanza of the first draft was to have the poem begin with the walk out to the house instead of having the speaker complete her journey in a couple of lines. She probably made this judgment quickly:

> It was scarcely the day to take a walk on the long beach:
> It was cold & windy; everything seemed withdrawn:
> withdrawn as far as possible
>
> the sea birds represented by two or three, the se [sic]
>
> the tide away, way out; the sea shrunken;
> sea-birds represented only in ones or twos
> Only the icy, off-shore wind unremittingly with us
> hurting our faces on one side, then the other (as we turned back)
> and blowing back the crests of the long low breakers steadily
> fine ascending steady   of mist[2]

Crossing out "then the other (as we turned back)" was imperative for the movement of the poem. Instead of having the journey end, the narrative over, Bishop extended the moment of the poem, the memory, by bringing the closure of this line down to the last stanza on the same draft. It begins: "Turning back, our faces froze on the other cheek." The choice resulted in a lyrical treatment of time, with the speaker's meditation taking place on the beach; the first choice, a more narrative mode of reflection, would have emphasized the passage of time, with the speaker positioned in the wings. When she moved the first lines down to the bottom of the draft, she opened up the poem, and thereby the reenactment of this memory becomes the impetus behind the poem and gives it its dramatic quality. The effects of this change can be found in the switch from "It was scarcely the day to take a walk on the long beach" to "that long beach" in the first line. "That" particularized the beach, gave weight to the speaker's memory by placing it farther in the distance. We're not at "the beach" anymore, or even "this beach." The choice of "that" also lends the poem a more conversational tone. Bishop's move towards understatement heightens the intensity of the poem. She employs the same paradox in the last line of the stanza: a "fine ascending steady of mist" eventually became "upright, steely mist." An upright, steely mist has a physical heft and texture that an ascending mist, for all its aspirations, cannot. Bishop creates a dual consciousness of being here in the present and there in the past at the same time.

When Bishop sorted out the second stanza of the poem, she quickly came to the first three sentences, settling on the color of the sky, "mutton-fat jade," the prints on the beach, and the kite string. She spent much more time elaborating the sentences from "Finally" on. Bishop chose these first images so quickly that she insisted on them. "In the Duxbury poem the water *was* the color of mutton-fat jade," she wrote to Jerome Mazarro. "The settings, or descriptions, of my poems are almost invariably just plain facts—or as close to the facts as I can write them" (*One Art* 621). Both the paw-prints and kite string are images that Bishop used in earlier poems. The paw-prints go back to a poem that Bishop wrote during the mid-1960s, "Suicide of a Moderate Dictator," about Julias Vargas, a poem which she later abandoned, possibly because it dissatisfied her.[3] Among the shifts Bishop made from "Suicide of a Moderate Dictator" were putting the poem into the past tense, changing the weather from "beautiful" to windy and rainy, and expanding on the images of the dog-prints and kites. The use of the past tense may have allowed Bishop to air out the text and let memory inform the poem. She kept the present in her parenthetical clauses. These asides position the speaker in two time frames at once. The change in weather also seemed to open up additional possibilities for Bishop. By using the parenthesis to compare the dog-prints to "lion-prints," Bishop instantly sharpened the metaphor's possibility by drawing attention to the image. With the parenthetical phrase as a form of understatement, Bishop went both ways, quietly commenting on the side while amplifying her voice at the same time. This decision suggests a self-conscious relationship to the poem as does her treatment of the kites.

In "The End of March" Bishop teased out the kite image over the course of several lines, playing with the rhythms, and hinting again at metaphor with "snarl," "man-size," and "sodden ghost." She made the latter image more human and more animal at the same time; there is a blending of worlds that plays with the idea of an afterlife. Bishop came to the ghost image in "The End of March" fairly quickly. Handwritten in the margin, the image of the ghost entered "The End of March" in the second draft, an image she had used in other poems like "Ungracious Poem" and "The Tin Can" (VC). By the fifth draft, the ghost image was securely in the poem. The dolls, the pill, and the tin from the other poems echo the kite and the string, not just because of the play with the ghost and religious language but because of their homeliness. Like the kite, the dolls are discarded toys; the pill, which has the power to cure, is useless; and the tin can is trash on the beach. None of these objects serve their original functions, but it is in the memory of their original functions—to play, to cure, to satisfy—that they hold their power. Bishop's world is one that is fallen and one that she nonetheless embraces.

Bishop strove to get the poem's punctuation right since she capitalized on its visual, vocal, and rhetorical effects. The crucial line in the poem, "A light to read by—perfect! But—impossible" first appears on the third draft of the middle stanza. She moves it through a series of progressions in the drafts:

> a light to read by.
>
> Quite All perfect, but impossible
>
> Oh! It's perfect! But impossible—! [written in the margin]
>
> A light to read by—perfect. But impossible!
>
> A light to read by—perfect! But, impossible...
>
> A light to read by? Perfect! But—impossible
>
> A light to read by! Perfect! But—impossible.
>
> A light to read by—perfect! But—impossible.

Like someone sorting through a puzzle or trying to break a lock, Bishop went through all the different combinations until she got the pacing of the line just right and filled the pause with a kind of ontological erasure.

The poem's fourth stanza is the one that gave Bishop the most difficulty. While she was drafting, she did not significantly revise this stanza or make as many additions as she did with the others. She arrived at the main idea in the first draft and did not stray too far from the original image in her revisions. This decision may be due to the fact that she had already handled the sun in the closing of another poem, "Apartment in Leme, Copacabana." In "Apartment in Leme," written for Robert Lowell, the speaker walks along the littered beach early one New Year's morning.[4] Atypically, it would be the first half of the stanza she would return to later and rewrite. Bishop sent a copy of "The End of March" to Lowell, and it was his response that spurred her on to rework the first six lines. Though praising the poem, Lowell also offered some tentative criticism:

> The meter I see is steadily iambic...any number of terrific seemingly though quiet details—you arrive at your castle safely. I am troubled by one thing, a sort of whimsical iambic Frost tone to the last five lines or so, though I think they are needed. New lines might make a fine poem into one of your finest. Nothing else needed, I think (6 October 1974, VC).

Bishop must have agreed with Lowell's comments since she went on to rewrite the last stanza; however, Bishop did not locate the problem in the last five lines of the stanza but in the first five. It was an issue of positioning the poem for the closing image. She sent the revised lines to Moss even though the poem was already in the process of being readied for the printer. "I'm afraid I'm being a nuisance—but I don't think I have done this kind of thing very often, have I? The last stanza of THE END OF MARCH never pleased me, so this morning I've made some changes that I think improve it a lot. I hope you'll agree" (22 October 1974, NYP). Nonetheless, Bishop was still not satisfied with the last stanza of the poem, and she rewrote the stanza again sometime after sending the second version to Moss. The stanza was published in its final form in *Geography III*.

By sweating through the last stanza, Bishop kept the movement of the poem fluid, letting it slide from association to association. Lowell apologized for the letter in which he made suggestions:

> My suggestions for the end of your poem must have been troublesome. I think I've spent more futile hours trying to perfect something satisfactory—always pressing and invisible, the unimagined perfect lines or ending, for there it usu-

ally falls. Often I've given up, and wondered why I ever found fault. There are
the experiences we haven't had, working in a spool factory etc. and can't imagine, and there are others like the end of Lycidas where all the experience is
easily ours, but we can't turn to it or find the right sound. I've just spent a week
or more on three lines which finally ended in changing the position of two words.
(I did other things). I hope you won't bother anymore, you were probably right
all along. (18 December 1974, VC)

Bishop lets a turn of phrase, a line break, and a pause create experience
instead of greeting it head on. Her self-conscious show of invention suggests
the movement of the mind, and her rhetorical substitution indicates the flux
of time. Through the organization of her images and her subsequent transformation of them, she is both in time and outside of it, the maker commenting on her makings. The twin pull of memory and desire, a story for one's
past and one's future, though Bishop would never pick such phrases, was
where she located her own religious feeling. To borrow Wordsworth's phrase,
she found religious feeling in the spontaneous overflow of powerful emotion
recollected in tranquility, albeit a tranquility that never lasted long.

Bishop's connection to the Romantics and revision of her Romantic
thinking becomes apparent when one thinks of "The End of March" in relation to Keats' "Ode to a Nightingale." Both poems play a central role in
understanding their authors' poetry. Aside from obvious similarities—the
natural setting, the unseen object of desire, the sensory images—both poems
revise readers' attitudes towards the poets' *oeuvre* by highlighting the shadows. Both speakers observe the passing of time in their poems—Keats, ail-
ing, infected with the tuberculosis that would kill him and Bishop, aging,
registering the changes taking place in her body—and both recognize the
paradox of imagination, its powers and its failures. Despite the speakers'
situations, both poems rely on hope as a path out of dissolution. Keats enforces the underlying irony with his lifting meter and dramatic punctuation.
The colon, dash, and question mark of "Fled is that music:—Do I wake or
sleep?" is not too far from "A light to read by—perfect! But—impossible."
The punctuation allows both writers to emphasize and then reverse the metrics
of the lines' first halves in order to get the sound as close to the sense as they
can.

Bishop was a great admirer of Keats and his letters. In fact she often
remarked that she thought the letters were even better than the poems. "He
makes almost every other poet seem stupid, don't you think his letters do,
that is" (letter to Moss, 14 December [n.d.], NYP). Following T.S. Eliot's
cue, many writers of Bishop's generation held a similar view. She first reported reading his letters in 1959 and found him to be "very entertaining"

(*One Art* 371–372; letter to Florence Bishop, 30 March 1959, VC). During her 1964 trip to England, she saw the Keats house in Hampstead, "so cleaned up there's not much to say except the outside is rather pretty" (letter to Summers, 26 July 1964, VC). Bishop even joked about a comparison, made by Frani Muser, between herself and Keats. After seeing the manuscript for one of Bishop's poems at the Institute of Arts and Letters in New York, Muser told Bishop that she felt she were "writing to Keats." Bishop told her Aunt Florence, "I'm glad to say I'm alive and have already lived twice as long as Keats, even if I have so much less to show for it" (letter to Florence Bishop, [n.d.], VC).

It is likely that Bishop knew the story of "Nightingale's" composition. As Charles Brown liked to tell it, one morning soon after writing "Ode to Psyche," Keats took his chair from the breakfast table, sat under the plum tree, which we can assume was blossoming, and composed the poem in a flurry (Rollins, II.65). Though the story is too good to be true, there is something to be said about the image of the writer away from his or her desk. Bishop reflected to James Merrill a few months before she died:

> Alice & I are staying in John's house for a week or ten days. I find it much easier to work away from home than "at home" for some reason. In fact, when I think about it, it seems to me I've rarely written anything of value at the desk or in the room where I was supposed to be doing it—it's always in someone else's house, or in a bar, or standing up in the kitchen in the middle of the night. (letter to Merrill, 23 January 1979, VC)

Their situations are not unlike one another; both Keats and Bishop were at home when they were imagining such a venue in their poems. On May 1, 1819, Keats wrote his sister Fanny from the Browns' home a letter that sounds something like Bishop's wish list for her artichoke of a house:

> O there is nothing like fine weather, and health, and Books, and a fine country, and a contented Mind, and Diligent-habit of reading and thinking, and an amulet against the ennui—and please heaven, a little claret-wine cool out of a cellar a mile deep—with a few or a good many ratiafia cakes—a rocky basin to bathe in, a strawberry bed to say your prayer to Flora in, a pad nag to go your ten miles or so; two or three sensible people to chat with; two or th[r]ee spiteful folkes to spar with; two or three odd fishes to laugh at and two or three numskulls to argue with—instead of using dumb bells on a rainy day— (*Letters* 208–210)

He goes on to write a poem in a bouncing trimeter that concludes: "Two or three pegs / For two or three bonnets / Two or three dove's eggs / To hatch into sonnets—."[5] The play in Keats' letter is irresistible and, as Bishop might say, delightful. What is striking about this letter as compared to his poem, both of which were written at approximately the same time, is the difference in tone.[6] The sense of loss that pervades "Nightingale" is nowhere to be found in the letter. Bishop had written her own wish-list letter years before. She said she "always had a daydream of being a lighthouse keeper, absolutely alone, with no one to interrupt my reading or just sitting—and although such dreams are sternly dismissed at 16 or so, they always haunt one a bit, I suppose." She imagined "a cold rocky shore in the Falklands, or a house in Nova Scotia on the bay, *exactly* like my grandmother's—idiotic as it is, and unbearable as the reality would be.... perhaps it is a recurrent need" (*One Art* 388). Yet Bishop did not compose the same way Keats did. Her letter prefigured the poem instead of the letter pushing against the despair. Bishop needed the distillation of experience. Bishop revised Keats' poem and letter-poem by bringing the sense of loss and play into one piece.

In her playfulness, however, Bishop refutes many of Keats' assumptions. Though one can say that "The End of March" is an exercise in negative capability, Bishop's willing suspense is much more self-conscious than that of Keats. Where they differ is in their experience of the moment. Keats' attitude toward the moment has a feeling of sincerity, fresh yet mature, the sparrow at the windowsill. While Bishop understands the movement these feelings make, she undercuts them with her parenthetical remarks, the voice joking to one side, and her steps outside the narrative frame. Whereas earlier poems like "At the Fishhouses" and "A Cold Spring" embraced the movement of romantic poems—from meditation to crisis to resolution, "The End of March" offers a reassessment of her earlier poetics.[7] Though these Bishop poems are playful in their portrayals of animals and their personified landscapes, they begin on serious notes and end with grand proclamations. In "The End of March," the play is in motion straightaway, when she informs us that it was "scarcely the day" for a walk on the beach. The language is marked by the conversational, understated tone of a letter. She eschews any epiphany in the later poem; the poem ends because the walk is over. Her romanticism is informed by irony, the consciousness that she is writing poetry, and the idea that achieving the spontaneous moment recollected in tranquility is impossible. Keats' sincerity is found in the artful richness of his images, the lushness of his language, and the melody of his rhymes. Bishop's sincerity is found in the artfulness of the random objects she finds tossed up on shore, the exposure expressed in everyday speech, and the working of the mind. Abstract ideas become familiar, even homely, through her humor. In "The End of March" it was the collision between two worlds, and in this case two seasons, that interested Bishop and offered the most promise for her work. Hers is a meditation on the intermediacy of experience, both physical and psychological, of being caught in two places at once, the past and the present, north and south, here and there.

Endnotes

1. I would like to thank Alice Methfessel, Elizabeth Bishop's literary executor, and Elizabeth Hardwick, Robert Lowell's literary executor, for permisson to reproduce unpublished materials. I would also like to thank the following libraries for their assistance: Vassar College Library; The Houghton Library, Harvard University; The Henry W. and Albert A. Berg Collection, New York Public Library, Astor, Lenox, and Tilden Foundations; The Harry Ransom Humanities Research Center, University of Texas, Austin. They will be referred to as VC, HL, NYP, and HRHRC.

2. Bishop made many hand corrections to this sheet. They are as follows. In line 1, the second "the" is changed to "that" and a colon is placed at the end of the line. In line 2 "It was" and "seemed" are crossed out. All of line 4 is crossed out, and a marginal line is drawn to line 6. In line 6, "only in" is crossed out and "by" is written in. In line 7, "the" is crossed out. In line 8, "numbing" is typed in the left hand gutter and "hurting" and "then the other side (as we turned back)" are crossed out. In line 9, "steady" is written in hand in the left hand gutter; "and," "long" and "steadily" are crossed out.

3. In a discussion of "Suicide of a Moderate Dictator," Lorrie Goldensohn points to one of the stanzas' connections to "The End of March." *Elizabeth Bishop: The Biography of a Poetry* (New York: Columbia UP, 1992) 237.

4. Bishop to Lowell, 2 August 1965. Houghton Library, Harvard University. "I have a longer, grimmer one about Copacabana beach, too, that is to be dedicated to you—but didn't get it done in time [to be included in *Questions of Travel*]."

5. It is likely that Bishop taught this letter in her class on letter writing at Harvard University. In Bishop's collection of books stored at the Houghton, a slip of yellow paper was placed between the pages of this letter. On the slip, the number of the letter was written along with others in Bishop's handwriting (*The Letters of John Keats*, Houghton Library,

Harvard University, 87EB–233).

6. Bate thinks it possible that Keats wrote "Nightingale" sometime soon after April 30, 1819, since that was the day he referred to writing "Psyche" as his "last" poem. *John Keats* (London: Oxford UP, 1963) 501.

7. Many scholars have looked at this movement. Jerredith Merrin's study is particularly useful in this regard. *An Enabling Humility:Marianne Moore, Elizabeth Bishop, and the Uses of Tradition* (New Brunswick: Rutgers UP, 1990).

Works Cited

Bate, W. J. *John Keats.* London: Oxford UP, 1963.

Bishop, Elizabeth. Notebooks. Elizabeth Bishop Collection. Vassar College Library, Poughkeepsie, N.Y. (VC).

———. Letters to Florence Bishop. Elizabeth Bishop Collection. Vassar College Library, Poughkeepsie, N.Y. (VC).

———. Letters to Robert Lowell. Robert Lowell Papers. The Houghton Library, Harvard University, Cambridge, MA (HL).

———. Letters to Robert Lowell. Robert Lowell Papers. The Harry Ransom Humanities Research Center, University of Texas. Austin, TX (HRHRC).

———. Letters to James Merrill. Elizabeth Bishop Collection. Vassar College Library, Poughkeepsie, N.Y. (VC).

———. Letters to Howard Moss. Elizabeth Bishop Papers. The Henry W. and Albert A. Berg Collection, New York Public Library, Astor, Lenox, and Tilden Foundations (NYP).

———. Letters to Frani Blough Muser. Elizabeth Bishop Collection. Vassar College Library, Poughkeepsie, N.Y. (VC).

———. Letters to Joseph and U. T. Summers. Elizabeth Bishop Collection. Vassar College Library, Poughkeepsie, N.Y. (VC).

———. *One Art: Letters.* Ed. Robert Giroux. New York: Farrar, Straus, Giroux, 1994.

Keats, John. *Letters of John Keats.* Ed. Robert Gittings. London: Oxford UP, 1970.

Lowell, Robert. Letters to Elizabeth Bishop. Elizabeth Bishop Collection. Vassar College Library, Poughkeepsie, N.Y. (VC).

Rollins, Hyder E., Ed. *The Keats Circle.* 2 vols. Cambridge: Harvard UP, 1948.

"That World Inverted" : Encoded Lesbian Identity in Elizabeth Bishop's "Insomnia" and "Love Lies Sleeping"

Crystal Bacon
Gloucester County College

Abstract

"I don't think she ever believed in talking about the emotions much," Elizabeth Bishop said of Marianne Moore's response to Bishop's poem, "Insomnia." The same is clearly true of Bishop herself. Behind the mask of an "ordinary woman," was a poet of surprising passions. She often relied on inverted images as mirrors through which to reflect subjects too painful to talk about. This paper explores poems of inversion—mirrors through which this important poet attempted to reconcile her numerous dual worlds: "Love Lies Sleeping" and "Insomnia."

After much close reading in Elizabeth Bishop's *Complete Poems*, as well as a variety of biographies, interviews and critical articles, one gains a kind of convex mirror through which to view this enigmatic writer of mid-twentieth century poetry. The titles of her volumes themselves yield a view of her work: geographical opposition, paradoxical nature, interrogation of itinerary and implication of replication. She is and is not a poet's poet, having told Elizabeth Spires in the *Paris Review* that being a writer "just happens without your thinking about it" (381). She didn't believe in creative writing classes, and she often disagreed with what her critics attributed to her work (373). Yet across the span of over fifty years of writing, she returned again and again to familiar devices through which to throw her poetic voice. More than many of us, Elizabeth Bishop was often an inhabitant of two worlds, and her poems frequently use images of inverted perspective to distance herself, or at least her voice, from the territory which the poems cover. This is true of many of her poems, including "Love Lies Sleeping" and "Insomnia."

Much has been written about Bishop's engagement with language to find a code within which she could express herself in ways more palatable to her mentors, readers and critics. Victoria Harrison suggests that Bishop conceived of "an 'inverted' vision," writing "to discover a language for sameness that does not invoke fear as it dissolves boundaries" (44). In the case of "Love Lies Sleeping," the conclusion is generally considered to reflect one of Bishop's earliest and most profound inversions, a kind of "equation between the inverted and the revealed" (Harrison 61). Because the endings of poems must be consistent exits from the established poetics within the poem, there is an argument to be made for the existence of preliminary inversions which establish the context in which the remarkable vision of the ending occurs. There is, I would argue, a resolute topsy-turvyness throughout the poem which encodes Bishop's frustrations, fears and ironic response to her experiences with love: roundly agreed upon as being lesbian and, for the sake of this argument, inverted.

Like many of her early poems, "Love Lies Sleeping" is "set on the edge of waking" (Kalstone 12). This poem, however, is significantly different from the other sleep-related poems in the collection. It is the only poem which is clearly labeled a "love" poem. It is a grotesque love poem, to be sure, with its much-debated death at the end, but the poem demonstrates Bishop's early wrangling for the language of sameness. The first stanza's lines, "Earliest morning, switching all the tracks / that cross the sky from cinder star to star / coupling the ends of streets / to trains of light," create an eerie image in which earth and sky are merged. The perspective is distant, detached, linking electric wires and lights to stars, to trains, as though the speaker, herself, is out in the sky. The description is of morning's slipping down out of the night, rather than up from the earth, and although it is vividly drawn in a sleeper's confused and dozy state, there is no one to claim the vision until the third stanza. The technological dawn (in which street lights, a kind of cinder star, go out along the avenues, and daybreak reveals the wires which seem to link one street to another, like trains, the newly visible criss–crossing of the wires) "draw[s] us into daylight in our beds," and moves the poem into actual day and a first person plural voice.

The "us" in the poem is typically confusing: does it refer to all who wake in the city, or to two awakening in their separate beds inside the same or a similar window? The speaker is hung over, which allows for a reading of a night's drunken "coupling" like "the ends of streets / to trains of light" and who are now in separate beds under the same day.

"Love Lies Sleeping" is a marvelously balanced poem falling into 15 similar stanzas of four lines each, two long and two short, spread evenly across two pages of text, almost like a Rorschach print. There is a balance, too, in the poem's distribution of imagery. From the first stanza's outside the poem stance, subsequent stanzas continue to pan the distance outside the room in which, presumably, "Love Lies." Momentarily the second stanza situates an "us...in our beds," yet it then moves out again. This distancing, an eye somewhere outside the room, inverts the sense of location in the poem. The lights go out "down the gray avenue between the eyes," as if the speaker and the changing day are one.

There is a cinematic movement to the poem. The speaker begins by describing the outside world, moves briefly into the setting in first person plural and then resumes seeing the city rise up. The first two and a half stanzas occur in a kind of dream–state until, at the end of stanza 3, the awakened I looks out the window and literally sees the city in which everything is artificial, not what it seems to be. Daylight reveals the second and more developed image of inversion as the city

> reaching so languidly up into
> a weak white sky...seems to waver there.
> (Where it has grown
> in skies of water-glass....

The speaker is at once in "the little chemical 'garden' in a jar" and looking down into the water–glass in which it grows. These loveliest of images, "detail upon detail," lift the hung–over speaker up out of the room and perhaps even the city where love lies sleeping. It is a brief respite, the shimmering, trembling sense of the city. Even the sparrows must hurry to their play.

From the West, where day will eventually die, comes the "Boom!...Boom!" of the "exploding ball." She describes sounds of destruction, hypothesizes the reactions of other sleepers to the noises, then back to description, a shirt being taken from a clothesline, the water truck. All the while, there is no identified pair of eyes and ears which is recording this, no narrative connection between what is heard and the I who, at stanza 3, saw morning through the window. Not until the eleventh stanza does the I return to hear the "day springs of morning strike." There is a kind of dissociation between the speaker and the events spoken of. And from this accretion of dissociated details the poem shifts into its supreme oddness: the "alarms for the expected: / queer cupids of all persons getting up."

Why is what is expected "queer cupids"? It's worth noting the choice of pejorative adjective used to describe the cupids. As an adjective, it fails as adjectives do in poems: it tells rather than shows what is meant. Literally queer means peculiar, marked by oddity. If we are to envision cupids, generally naked baby boys with wings and slings of arrows, what else would they be, but "queer" in the denotative sense; hence, the adjective is in that usage redundant. Furthermore, the syntax intentionally obscures or blurs meaning: are the cupids getting up, are they the cupids of the persons who are themselves getting up, or are the wakers, themselves, the cupids? "[W]hose evening meal they will prepare all day" is further complicated in terms of pronoun referent depending on your reading of the cupids and persons, although "whose" must refer to the antecedent noun, cupids, rather than the object, persons. Within this same stanza a "you" is introduced who "will dine well / on his heart, on his, and his." It's the turn of address to the you which intrigues in this poem.

The poem includes, then, the two parties necessary in dyadic communication: a speaker and a spoken to. Typical of most of Bishop's poems, this speaker is identified by the genderless or masculine pronouns whenever he is not an I. It seems clear that it is the speaker "himself" who awakens, and "whose head has fallen over the edge of his bed, / whose face is turned" while "Love Lies Sleeping."

The poem's title presents a pun on to be prone or to prevaricate. Does Love lie in sleep, and in truth awake? Who is the you whose business the cupids do? Who is admonished to "scourge lightly," the cupids or "Love" itself? The cupids will prepare a meal on which the you will dine, a meal of hearts. Love kills, Bishop seems to say. The spoken to is Love, a personification for the one in another bed whose lie or lying in sleep leaves the speaker, and often others, to meet the morning where "the city grows down into his open eyes / inverted and distorted." The I lies alone, head dangling over the edge of her solitary bed, looking upside down out the window past the hung–over dawn and sees the city-of-love "distorted and revealed." Miss Bishop of "the natural unforced ending," as Miss Moore said of her in "Archaically New" (Schwartz and Estess 175–76) cheats this ending by first granting the hard truth about her inverted, distorted revelation, then undercutting it with a moment of doubt. For "it" is only revealed "if he sees it at all." And after 59 lines of "over-workmanship," it is clear that he, and the she he represents, have seen it indeed.

"[A]s if the subject were too painful to bear more than the briefest mention" (Williamson 30), Elizabeth Bishop drops it. The subject in the poem, "Insomnia," the eighth poem in *A Cold Spring*, published in 1955, is also an unidentified "you," the beloved to whom this brief lyric apostrophe is addressed. Since her death in 1979, Bishop's life has come under inevitable scrutiny. And the outpouring of biography reveals many difficult truths. She did not allow her poems to be anthologized in a collection of women poets, and in what Bishop knew as a world of staid "morals *as* manners" (Bishop qtd. in Kalstone 4), a world before the liberation of "the love that dare not speak its name," she did not openly embrace her sexual identity. Of course, no one's life is that simple. Bishop's poetry is everywhere marked by restraint. But her individuation and her privacy, compounded, and seemingly were compounded by, her closeted lesbianism.

It seems indisputable that Elizabeth Bishop was a master of clarity and observation. The ends to which she put that clarity vary among her poems. But one thing that is clear is that Bishop's poetry is concerned with perception: how the world is seen and what that seeing says. It may be for this reason that Bishop's poems *are* remarkably devoid of the first person singular pronoun. There are numerous theories about this selflessness in her poems, and they seem to stem from divergent roots. In *Elizabeth Bishop*, Anne Stevenson writes,

> The question of reality is one...that she tries to resolve through art,...a means of making life bearable...comprehensible and more meaningful than it normally seems...a way of reconciling the two worlds of reality...bringing together rationality and irrationality into a sustained and even mystical but never unbelievable whole. (66)

Alan Williamson, writing about Bishop as a "Poet of Feeling," says that she "characteristically distanced emotion...partly because emotion for her...tended to become immense and categorical, insusceptible to rational or...structural counterargument" (30). These two observations, a bringing together of rationality and irrationality, and the insusceptibility of emotion to rational counterargument, inform a reading of "Insomnia" as a poem of encoded lesbian identity.

Initially, the poem reads as a clearly luminous description of a haunting interior. "The moon in the bureau mirror / looks out a million miles," situating the poem squarely in a landscape recognizable to insomniacs. Further, its cool beauty evokes an emblematic female figure, the moon, the virginal lamp associated with Artemis or Diana, a myth favored in much lesbian writing. After all, this goddess shuns men to the extent of transforming them into stags, a transformation which asserts woman's purity and superiority over man. The moon's reflection in the mirror thus mirrors the myth of Narcissus, itself tinged by homo-eroticism: a beautiful boy who falls in love with his own reflection in a pool and so is turned into a flower. Writing on narcissism, Freud says, "The condition of sleep...implies a narcissistic withdrawal of the libido away from its attachments back to the subject's own person, or, more precisely, to the single desire for sleep" (109). Here, Bishop's selection of this particular image for sleeplessness reflects, unwittingly, Freud's implication that insomnia is a type of what might be called *narcissismus-interruptus.*

That the moon is narcissistic is clear in that she "looks out...perhaps with pride, at herself, / but she never, never smiles." This line suggests the moon as a symbol for the speaker, also awake, who sees the moon's display and creates the context of the extended metaphor which becomes the poem. Writing about Bishop's "treatment of personal themes," Alan Williamson suggests a "jauntiness which insists on representing defeat as triumph...a peculiar exercise of pride" (31).

The presence of the moon as the central image of the poem, an image extended for two of three stanzas, demonstrates what Ruskin called the "pathetic fallacy." Stevenson says it is "a stylistic device...for expressing human emotions—in most cases, emotional reactions *about* nature...to make images or symbols of what [poets] feel" (97). This seems an apt description of Bishop's moon imagery in this poem because it establishes a counter-point to the speaker. This counter–point doesn't become clear until the second stanza, but its underpinnings are established in stanza one.

The first line's "The Moon in the bureau mirror," features moon as a proper noun. Within the first two lines, the initial act of personification occurs, transferring the moon's simple reflection in a mirror into the act of looking. It is a complex piece of imagery because of the lack of an I, or eye, in the poem's perspective. The moon enters a room through an unmentioned window and reflects out of a bureau mirror. To be thus described, the scene must be seen, but the speaker resists entering the poem until the last stanza. It can be argued that this is the first of two conflated images in the poem. The moon simply reflects from the mirror without the mention of moonlight, darkness or window, all of which are necessary to the image.

Through the extended personification of the moon, it becomes clear that it is a symbol for the sleepless speaker. One can argue that this personification justifies the existence of the first stanza which appears to be no more than simple description. As Stevenson says, "personification is generally accepted as normal in the language of description...a conventional method, even in everyday speech, of saying that one thing is like another" (97). In this respect, Bishop's initiating image does little more than reclaim a cliché, that of the man in the moon, turning him into her and investing her with a certain narcissism, and an elevation beyond Man's limitations: "far and away beyond sleep." The necessity for the extended description becomes clearer in stanza two.

The second stanza demonstrates Bishop's emotion as "insusceptible to rational counterargument." Within the extended pathetic fallacy of the moon as prideful and inscrutable, the speaker asserts a hypothetical situation which requires the fallacy in order to exist. "By the Universe deserted / *she'd* tell it to go to hell." There is a marvelous "insouciance" (Williamson 30) in these lines which is, to my mind, illustrative of what Williamson must mean by emotion tending to become immense. It is clear that the moon is symbolic of the speaker because of the emphasis put on the italicized "she'd" in line two. This representation serves to suggest that the reader has been similarly told by the Universe—her universe—to go to hell. This scenario creates another type of fallacy, a logical fallacy, which the "irritable voice of reason" (Williamson 30) wants to argue against in the poem. Further, as Stevenson says, "a tension must be maintained between the precision of the image and the resonance of the associations...the objective situation must be clear, accurate and true" (84). Clearly, Bishop intends hyperbole in her analogy between the speaker and the moon, but precisely because the poem is so short, something—too much—seems to be missing. One is asked simply to accept as an objective situation, an image, that the universe could desert the moon. This is, of course, impossible, as is the more easily accepted act of personification on the part of the moon telling the universe to go to hell. Without sounding miserly or plain stupid, I must say that her evasion of the poem's subject until the final stanza, her distancing of emotion, for me, fails to allow the images of the moon's desertion and reaction to "resemble a third unstated something...the poem's subject" (Stevenson 82).

The moon is removed and cool in the night, reflecting herself in a bureau mirror, not an actual presence but a virtual, reflected presence. She is alone, "[b]y the Universe deserted"—an overstatement and a paradox, as the moon is part of the universe. But the sense of detachment, of aloneness, is typical of much lesbian writing from the late nineteenth to the early twentieth century. Radclyffe Hall's novel, *The Well of Loneliness*, became a talisman for lesbian readers, signifying the depth of their aloneness in a hostile, man-centered world. It is not surprising, and seems hardly accidental in keeping with my reading, that the moon seeks out a "body of water, or a mirror, on which to dwell." Finding no sleep, no mate in the universe, she is left to her own devices. Freud says the narcissist "[has] withdrawn...interest from the external world... but has by no means broken off...erotic relations to persons and things...[but] has substituted for actual objects imaginary objects founded on memories" (105). The body of water and the mirror are symbols for memory, one replicating the other in an archetypal reconstitution of human-kind's earliest reflection.

It is a short leap from this image to the actual well which constitutes the poem's closing gesture. It is at this gesture that the dropped subject of the poem is first implied with the conjunction "So" joined with the verb "wrap" which implies a you to whom the poem is spoken. "So wrap up care in a cobweb / and drop it down the well." This defeat-as-triumph keeps with the moon's telling the Universe "to go to hell." If a love poem tells the beloved to drop care—the love between them—"down a well," it may *appear* to be rejecting that human love. The care is characterized as something which could be wrapped in a "cobweb." Alan Williamson sees this image as an indication that "reciprocal love is, almost metaphysically, impossible," a point with which I agree both in the particulars of this poem and in life itself. I would also suggest that, taken with the sense the speaker has of being shunned by the universe, and living by night, "she's a daytime sleeper," the image of the smallness and delicacy of the love, which the lover is instructed to cast into the well, suggests the secrecy of the love which can only survive in "that world inverted" which the well water suggests.

The term "inverted" has deep connotations for lesbian sexuality dating back to Havelock Ellis' *Studies in the Psychology of Sex* and Julien Chevalier's *Inversion sexuelle* (Faderman 46). It is not unlikely that, given her distancing from feminism and certainly from outward identification with lesbianism, Bishop would have known the term inversion as code for lesbian sexuality. And so the poem comes to a conclusion not, as Williamson suggests, on "two readings, neither very cheery" (30), but rather to a place of wonder,

> where left is always right,
> where the shadows are really the body,
> where we stay awake all night,
> where the heavens are shallow as the sea
> is now deep, and you love me.

The idea of what's wrong or left, being "always right" sets up the sexual and celebrated world of inversion. They stay awake all night—not quite the same as insomnia, since now the speaker entertains the beloved, and in that night, the "shadows are really the body." I read that "really" to mean that where the love is dropped, where the love is right, in that night, the shadows more than appear to be the body of the beloved, they really are the body of the beloved.

This is the underworld of secret sexual love. What is above, the heavens, is not nearly as deep as the sea of love, the reflection place where "you love me." Images of female sexuality here elide the poem's surface meaning: the paradox suggested by Williamson's reading, that love, reciprocated love, is "one of a series of impossible propositions conceivable only in the narcissist's mirror world" (30). Instead, it is a love which is possible only in the upside down world of the wishing well, a measure of the depth of longing.

The poem revolves in its last stanza to the location of the second and final conflated image, that of the well, "that world inverted" where the type of catalogue common to much of Bishop's later work occurs in a string of four descriptive images leading to the poem's emotional context. It is, apparently, only in this inverted, imagined world that "you love me." More has been said of the description of the well as "inverted," yet for this reading of the poem, it is sufficient to point out here that Stevenson says, "Miss Bishop often attempts to reconcile psychic and physical experiences by treating them as if they were inversions or even correctives of each other" (67). Seen this way, the poem further illustrates the distance which emotion required in Bishop's poems. It would be twenty years before she would write one of her most famous loss of love poems, "One Art," with its understatement, its mastery of form over both content and emotion. The argument between the two worlds of "rationality and irrationality" (Stevenson 66) in "Insomnia" does what Stevenson says Bishop's art strives for: To make reality "more comprehensible and more meaningful than it normally seems." I would add, to the poems' speakers, if not to Bishop herself. Reality, in this poem, is clearly secondary to the psychic world of night, and if that is where love is found, then so be it.

Elizabeth Bishop was as private a citizen as one would ever expect to find. And yet, she was a public figure by virtue of her vocation and her art. Reading her, one is reminded of Martin Heidegger's assertion that "what is spoken is never, and in no language, what is said." Despite various modes of criticism operating often at cross purposes with each other, it seems impossible for me as a poet to believe that any poet can write poems without any references, however veiled, to his or her life. Knowing what we know of Bishop's struggles with her sense of her self, with being herself, what she wrote seems never to be what she really said. It was a code, as poetry always is, which rewards the persistent interpreter.

Works Cited

Bishop, Elizabeth. "Insomnia." *The Complete Poems, 1927–1979.* New York: Farrar, Straus, Giroux, 1992. 70.

———. "Love Lies Sleeping." *The Complete Poems, 1927–1979.* New York: Farrar, Straus, Giroux, 1992. 16.

———. "Sunday: 4 a.m." *The Complete Poems, 1927–1979.* New York: Farrar, Straus, Giroux, 1992. 129.

Faderman, Lillian. *Odd Girls and Twilight Lovers: A History of Lesbianism in Twentieth Century America.* New York: Penguin Books, 1992.

Freud, Sigmund. "On Narcissism: An Introduction." *A General Selection From the Works of Sigmund Freud.* Ed. John Rickman, M.D. New York: Doubleday 1957. 104–05.

Kalstone, David. *Becoming a Poet.* New York: Farrar, Straus, Giroux, 1989.

Moore, Marianne. "Archaically New." *Elizabeth Bishop and Her Art.* Eds. Lloyd Schwartz and Sybil P. Estess. Ann Arbor: U of Michigan P, 1983. 175–76.

Spires, Elizabeth. "Elizabeth Bishop." *Poets at Work: The Paris Review Interviews.* Ed. George Plimpton. New York: Penguin, 1989. 363–86.

Stevenson, Anne. *Elizabeth Bishop.* New York: Twayne, 1966.

Williamson, Alan. "A Cold Spring: Elizabeth Bishop as Poet of Feeling." *Eloquence and Mere Life: Essays on the Art of Poetry.* Ann Arbor: U of Michigan P, 1994. 30–31.

Elizabeth Bishop's Aural Imagery: Her Male Personae

Joan L. Fields
University of Southwestern Louisiana

Abstract

Elizabeth Bishop's personae often mask, veil, and reveal the poet herself according to her special manipulation of tonalities with her sensitive images of sight, movement, and touch. A discernible pattern in her choices of male personae in relation to the setting and focus of each poem proves a valuable consideration in learning to understand the complexity of her work.

Central to Elizabeth Bishop's poetics is her fascinating weave of sonic elements which creates a braid of intonations. Her poet's "directing tone" deftly combines cheerful and awful tonal strands into dramatized experiential events. Thus, she constructs a dynamic aurality that sounds out her visual, tactile, and kinetic images. We hear her lyrical tones as dichotomic—vibrant and meditative, exotic and familiar, sublime and comic, subjective and objective.

Bishop manages to modulate her braid of voice so that these paradoxical tonal impressions simultaneously mask and reveal her autobiographical self. Taking note of Seamus Heaney's reminder that "*persona* derives from *personare*, meaning 'to sound out through,'"[1] I argue that her choices of personae who sound out these tones are crucial to the delicacy of her purpose, and the gender of the speaker often has everything to do with the communication she longs to achieve.

Among these crucial choices are male personae who characterize the poet's tensions and uncertainties, her discoveries and delights, and her reflections and realizations at progressive stages in her writing life. We can discern a pattern in Elizabeth Bishop's uses of male personae: each one appears to dramatize a turn in her life. It is this special significance of the male persona in Bishop's work that I want to outline and verify.

Technically, she makes use of the several devices for masking the autobiographical voice, working with the mask of an identifiable male voice who speaks as "I," as well as with the masculine pronoun, he, in the fictive third person, restricted to his singular perspective. Bishop utilizes a first person speaker when she directs a distinctly dramatic voice that embodies a character different from herself in place and time.

For example, we see Bishop trying out the male voice early, in 1930, when she chose a male persona to tell her short story, "The Thumb," in which the speaker describes his sensational discovery of one flaw in Sabrina, a strikingly beautiful woman he loves; the flaw is a "horrible" rough man's thumb on her right hand, suggestive of Bishop's growing awareness of a double-sex nature (*Gettysburg Review* 30–31).

Again, in notebooks of 1934–35, where she is working toward scenes for a novel about her mother, who had died insane in May 1934, Bishop's narrator-protagonist is a boy, Lucius. He describes an apparently common experience in the night; his tones are at first hesitant and shadowed but soon become purposeful because he knows he will be needed to help. Of his mother, Lucius relates: "in the night she began to cry very gently and complainingly.... I sat up & pulled my boots on & took the stick from under the window & shut that, then I sat on the edge of the bed waiting for Aunt Grace" (Millier 7). The sonic design of his two sentences—quiet tones of gradual awakening, followed by rhythmic, active response, and then a space of waiting—shows that Bishop was early interweaving active tones with effective hesitations and silences, at the same time she was seeking voices through which she could speak her stories of longing and loss. However, she had not yet been ready to write the story of her childhood relationship with her mother, even through the distancing mask of a boy's voice.

Nevertheless, poems and prose that Bishop did complete and publish from 1936 through 1971 display her explorations of ways to dramatize male personae who mask, veil, and finally blend with her own tonalities. In three early poems, "The Gentleman of Shalott" (1936), "The Man-Moth" (1936), and "The Unbeliever" (1938), as well as in the short story, "In Prison" (1938), she chooses to subsume her own intonations beneath male voices who reveal their own special situations.

"The Gentleman of Shalott" and "The Man-Moth" are both spoken through the ambivalent third person restrictive "he"; each dramatizes in a witty, yet darkly comic voice, characters in opposite predicaments—one, enforced inaction; the other, forced, ritualistic action. Questioning his selfhood, the "Gentleman of Shalott" is trapped in a more precarious situation than Tennyson's Lady: "He felt in modesty / his person was / half looking-glass, for why should he / be doubled?...But he's in doubt / as to which side's in or out." In contrast, "The Man-Moth" periodically must "scale the faces of buildings.... / He trembles, but must investigate as high as he can climb.... / what the Man-Moth fears most he must do, although / he fails, of course...." He must repeat, "each night" his "recurrent dreams.... He regards it as a disease / he has inherited the susceptibility to." Clearly, the poet recognizes the additional intrigue for readers who hear a persona speaking as though of someone other than him/herself with an authenticity that forces us to recognize we are experiencing a personal, even probing, characterization of the poet, whose directing voice is subtle beneath the play of "he."

By the end of August 1938, Bishop again offers an observer who characterizes a "he" in astutely familiar tones, so that we soon realize this masculine pronoun is "The Unbeliever": "He sleeps on the top of a mast / with his eyes fast closed..... / Asleep he was transported there." He observes himself inside his world of dream where he hears two other male voices—a cloud and a gull; both intone security and power as founded on what they perceive as pillars and wings of marble. Ludicrous as *three* stooges, each speaks as a deluded "I" in a preponderance of *e* sounds that reverberate as an eerie fear that becomes palpable, undercutting satirical ridicule. Lorrie Goldensohn notes "the clear strain of interrogation" in this poem (117), while Thomas Travisano reads it as a "fable...which dramatizes the necessity of waking up" out of "self-absorption" and into action (48). Clearly, the poet both masks and dramatizes her uncertainty through the male voices of "The Unbeliever."

By 1940, Bishop has widened her experience of people unlike herself and expresses to Marianne Moore her desire to voice in serio-comic rhythms the plight of Cuban transients who are temporarily housed in Key West, Florida, where she is living (*One Art* 88). Her characterization of "Jerónimo's House" (1971) is spoken by the Cuban himself; but he sounds out his longing and loneliness in Bishop's tones. Jerónimo speaks of his lifestyle and identifies his values as he points out his possessions that change a building into his home, albeit briefly. Although the house is neither substantial nor enduring, his voice convinces us that it is endearing to him. His tone in the final stanza signifies that he takes the transient nature of this "home" for granted; he moves the things he values with him from house to house. Only lightly does Jerónimo's male voice veil Elizabeth Bishop's own as he speaks with pride about what he knows is incomplete and only temporarily his:

> My house, my fairy
>   palace, is
> of perishable
>   clapboards with
> three rooms in all,
>   my gray wasps' nest
> of chewed-up paper
>   glued with spit. (*CP* 34)

Jerónimo implies that he has a family—a wife and at least two small children; and his tone changes as he talks about attributes that turn this transitory house into an illusory home. It is "endowed / with a veranda / of wooden lace / [and] adorned with ferns." He points out family images: left-over Christmas decorations, a "little / center table... painted blue, / and four blue chairs / and an affair / for the *smallest* (ital mine) baby... / On the table [is] one fried fish / spattered with burning scarlet sauce," and "a little dish / of hominy grits"—the friction in the sounds of words in these lines alerts us to notice the food that is *not* on the table. Only silence fills the space where there could be some mention of the wife and babies. Instead, Jerónimo tells about his meaningful possessions: "an old French horn / ...I play each year / in the parade"—and his radio; both open a way to companionship. His final revelation: "I take these things, / not much more, from / my shelter from / the hurricane" conveys an elusive emptiness and quiet that hovers throughout the poem; words ending the lines of the final stanza—"move," "from," "from"—speak isolation and loneliness. The feeling is so deep that it will not be spoken—except when veiled by a voice from a different culture and the other gender, as Elizabeth Bishop has directed in this poem. Thomas Travisano believes her persona "was based on a real person"; and he claims that she would have liked to be friends with the Cuban cigar makers. He imagines Bishop "leaning in, straining to pursue her acquaintance with Jerónimo, a man who answers poverty with bitterness *and* love" (82–83; see also Millier 144). Evidence in two of Bishop's letters to Moore, written at this time, could support his claim (*One Art* 68, 73–74).

Near the end of the decade, she is working on a markedly different pre-sentation of a male protagonist's voicing of his predicament as "The Prodi-gal." Returning to "he" as signifier of the speaker, Bishop's observant per-sona here thinly veils herself: his self-imposed exile to the pig sty "plastered halfway up with glass-smooth dung," his guilty alcoholism "(he hid the pints behind a two-by-four)," and his difficult decision to return home, "his shud-dering insights, beyond his control, / touching him."

After her year as Poetry Consultant at the Library of Congress (Sept. '49-Sept. '50)—an experience which was anathema to her—and some time at Yaddo, Bishop boarded a freighter for South America. She decided to move to Brazil in 1952, where she encountered a culture and people she found intriguing and exciting, as well as a home life which she had never before experienced. In April 1960, she had finished a long poem in which she directed the dynamic voice of "The Riverman." It had been almost twenty years since she had dramatized Jerónimo's loneliness and longing—and through his voice, her similar feelings. In her present, very different setting, Bishop tells the story of fantasy and desire that drive a man to risk his home and marriage for the magic he longs to learn.

Through tones of delight and anticipation, Elizabeth Bishop dramatizes the voice of the "The Riverman" as he tells of being awakened in the night by an invitation to become a *sacaca* and learn the mysteries of the water spirits. Without hesitation, he removes his clothes and follows the grunting voice of the Dolphin who "is hid by the river mist, / but I glimpsed him—a man like myself." The rhythms of the opening lines recall the rhythms of Bishop's boy-narrator, Lucius, when he was awakened by the quiet weeping of his mother and responds in quick-paced phrasing, preparing himself for action in tonalities akin to this quickly responsive, risk-taking man, who reports, "I threw off my blanket, sweating; / I even tore off my shirt. / I got out of my hammock / and went through the window naked."

> I heard the Dolphin sigh
> as he slid into the water.
> I stood there listening
> till he called from far outstream.
> I waded into the river
> and suddenly a door
> in the water opened inward,
> groaning a little, with water
> bulging above the lintel.
> I looked back at my house,
> white as a piece of washing
> forgotten on the bank,
> and I thought once of my wife,
> but I knew what I was doing. (*CP* 105–06)

Just as the opening line of the poem begins with "*I*" framing the action ("*I* got up in the *night*"), in this second section, "*I*" frames the "Dolphin" ("*I* heard the Dolphin *sigh*"). Such word sounds as "sigh," "slid," "stood," "outstream"—pause—then "suddenly" again display Bishop knitting sounds into conveyers of suggestive anticipation.

The emphasis in this poem, from the beginning, is on the speaker's tonalities; his vitality and certainty are sustained throughout. Nevertheless, the rhythmic underpinning, which is the third strand of Bishop's aural braid, implies that this "Riverman" inhabits a world of fantasy, or dream, just as does the "Unbeliever," and Jerónimo.

Reflecting the risk she has taken in choosing to live in Brazil as well as her fascination with the exotic Amazon River, which she had not yet seen, the poet creates her protagonist through his own voice. He becomes enthralled by the elusive and gorgeous Luandinha—of the moon and magic.[2]

> a tall, beautiful serpent
> in elegant white satin,
> ....
> entered and greeted me.
> She complimented me
> in a language I didn't know... (*CP* 106)

"[But]... I understood, like a dog, / although I can't speak it yet." Here, the emphasis is on the sound of Luandinha's voice, which he can understand only by the aid of her magic, yet familiar, smoke that carries it into his head; although dumbly comprehending the *sounds* of her language, he is unable to voice those sounds himself. Luandinha is the gorgeous presence of the magic tones he longs to speak. He must learn to pronounce the sounds himself before he can acquire a language for the magic of a water spirit.

His final analogy is voiced as an aural image indicating that the Riverman is learning to listen as well as to observe surfaces. His working the magic in that world below the river is dependent on his acute awareness of the magic of sound, both that of the river and that of his own voice to persuade others to listen.

> When the moon burns white
> and the river makes that sound
> like a primus pumped up high—
> that fast, high whispering
> like a hundred people at once—
> I'll be there below. (*CP* 108)

Finally, in her last decade, Elizabeth Bishop dramatizes, through the monologue of a man, a microcosm of her own life. Crusoe, well-known as a lonely castaway, whose feelings of estrangement and loneliness are balanced by his wit and resourcefulness, provides a character with whom she can identify.

However, Crusoe's tale is historical, and his descriptions contain no magical excitement; unlike the Riverman, he conveys no sense of immediacy. Whereas we hear in the final lines of the Riverman his promise of future actions as a *sacaca*, we listen to Crusoe after he has finished his adventure on the "un-rediscovered, un-renamable" island of "fifty-two / miserable, small volcanoes I could climb / with a few slithery slides—." There, the sounds of rain, of hot lava meeting water, of the sea turtles, "high-domed, / hissing like teakettles," had reminded him of home and hissing teakettles that signal time for tea and companionship. Bishop's directing tonal strand blends with Crusoe's words to shape the poet's dark/bright memories of her grandmother's kitchen where the teakettle promised teatime warmth, security, and loving companionship; and the space where the mother might have been was voiced through the image of tears that ran down the side of the teakettle ("Sestina" *CP* 123).

After years of loneliness among now-dead volcanoes and goats, and guilt because his survival had meant killing the baby goats with his knife, a companion, Friday, had appeared. "He'd pet the baby goats sometimes, / Pretty to watch"; but after too brief a time of companionship, Crusoe's one sentence sounds out, understating his grief: "And then one day they came and took us off." Now Friday is gone and suddenly Crusoe is "here": "Now [on] another island...I'm old." Bishop's own tonalities are barely submerged here; her director's tonal strand is clearly the third in the braid of voices that continues from her male persona. He points to the "things" that had been with him on the island and that had both saved and sacrificed him:

> The knife there on the shelf—
> it reeked of meaning, like a crucifix.
> It lived. How many years did I
> beg it, implore it, not to break?
> I knew each nick and scratch by heart.... (*CP* 166)

He knew the knife "by heart" as he knew the loved person; but "Now it won't look at me at all." He had chosen to use the knife to kill and eat the baby goats, thus to prolong his own life—only the speaker is guilty. Yet the tonalities sound more lively in the final stanza in spite of a querulous, though still quizzical older Crusoe: "The local museum's asked me to / leave everything to them.... / How can anyone want such things?"

The question hangs there, waiting—for Crusoe has fulfilled the dramatic role assigned to him by the directing poetic tone of the poet, Elizabeth Bishop. His voice has convincingly sounded out memories of her life because his dual tones of delight and depression are interwoven with her own tone that suffers life's demands and lonely estrangements.

Through Crusoe as persona, Bishop mythologizes her life-long adventures, together with her sense of estrangement and dread of eruptions in personal relationships, which occurred over and over in her life. She speaks through the voice of Crusoe her own characteristics of resourcefulness and ability to meet the challenges of uncertainty, as well as her delight and joy in the companionships and everyday activities she had lived.

The voice who speaks "Crusoe in England" (1971) is the culmination of Elizabeth Bishop's experiments with a male persona. The aural imagery she manages through the masculine voice effectively represents her continuous sonic play of "awful but cheerful" tones which display a perception of those dark/bright polarities ever present in life.

Endnotes

1. Heaney understands persona and mask to be identical, for he continues: the "animation of verb lives in the mask's noun-like impassiveness" (149). I believe we hear Bishop's male personae *actively* characterizing each role she creates for them.

2. Lorrie Goldensohn writes, in a penetrating discussion of "The Riverman," that her style here "allowed Bishop the articulation of a fairly unique experiment in a point of view intimately both hers and not hers." She finds richness in this poem's "exploration of the ironic gap between the pretended speaker...and the voice of the poet herself, exploring her own disconnections and powers" (208–11).

Works Cited

Bishop, Elizabeth. *Complete Poems 1927–1979*. New York: Farrar, Straus, Giroux, 1983.

———. *One Art: Letters*. Ed. Robert Giroux. New York: Farrar, Straus, Giroux, 1994.

The Gettysburg Review. "A Special Feature on Elizabeth Bishop," (Winter 1992): 11–72.

Goldensohn, Lorrie. *Elizabeth Bishop: The Biography of a Poetry*. New York: Columbia UP, 1992.

Heaney, Seamus. *The Government of the Tongue: Selected Prose, 1978–1987*. New York: Farrar, Straus, Giroux, 1988.

Millier, Brett C. *Elizabeth Bishop: Life and the Memory of It*. Berkeley: U of California P, 1993.

Travisano, Thomas. *Elizabeth Bishop: Her Artistic Development*. Charlottesville: UP of Virginia, 1988.

Elizabeth Bishop and the Pastoral World

Don Adams
Florida Atlantic University

Abstract

I begin with pastoral theorist Andrew Ettin's assertion that being "at home...is the dominant impression of the pastoral environment," and then proceed to consider Bishop's concerns in her poetry with being at home, and being without one. I then draw upon Martin Heidegger's writings concerning the "plight of dwelling," in which he claims that we are made homeless by our refusal to relate in a non-consumerist fashion to the world around us. I contend that Bishop opposes the modern tendency toward consumerism by placing the human subject always in relation to her environs, as a dweller among dwellers.

In his elegant and useful book on the pastoral, Andrew Ettin writes that being "at home...is the dominant impression of the pastoral environment. The author creates a temporal or spatial setting that will satisfy, or at least have the potential to satisfy, the desire to be at home" (135). Elizabeth Bishop's concern in her poetry with at-home-ness, homeliness, homemade-ness, and homelessness is well known, but her relationship to the pastoral has not been as widely acknowledged. And yet her poems are full of pastoral figures amid pastoral settings, all of which are concerned, finally, with one's desire to be at home in the world, and to feel that the world is at home with oneself. Part of the attraction of the pastoral for so many homosexual writers of our century surely has to do, at least partially, with this desire to feel at home and to feel certain of one's acceptance there. Bishop's poems continually remind us that the task of being at home is never finished; if one is not careful, one may find oneself estranged from the world one thought to be a part of, like Crusoe in England.

Contemporary philosophy also has concerned itself with the problems of at-home-ness in this most itinerant of centuries. Writing just after the Second World War, in a Germany plagued by housing shortages, Martin Heidegger sought to turn his reader's attention to a more fundamental form of homelessness:

> The *real plight of dwelling* does not lie merely in a lack of houses.... The real dwelling plight lies in this, that mortals ever search anew for the nature of dwell-

ing, that they *must ever learn to dwell.* What if man's homelessness consisted in
this, that man still does not even think of the *real* plight of dwelling as *the*
plight? Yet as soon as man *gives thought* to his homelessness, it is a misery no
longer. Rightly considered and kept well in mind, it is the sole summons that
calls mortals into their dwelling. (Heidigger, *Poetry* 161 [italics mine])

Throughout her poetry, Bishop is concerned with the "plight of dwelling," and it is her particular achievement, in response to this plight, to portray the human figure always in relation to the place in which he lives. By
doing so, she "summons" us into a consideration of our own dwelling, which
Heidegger defines variously as the "relationship between man and space,"
and as our "stay among things and locations" (*Poetry* 157). Like Heidegger,
Bishop seems to have known intuitively that there is no such thing as an
autonomous "I." Her poems illustrate that "to be" at all is to "be with," and
that the self alienated from its environment is estranged from its own being.
The homesickness of the world-weary traveler in "2,000 Illustrations and a
Complete Concordance" is the intermittent condition of our existence, to
which we respond by relying upon our innate potential for astonishment at
the fact of mere being, our undying capacity for infant-sightedness, for seeing the world in all of its surprising otherness—"awful but cheerful"—thereby
reminding ourselves that we are not alone, or, rather, that we are *together* in
our alone-ness.

In her early work, Bishop portrayed figures who are endangered by
their propensity to turn in upon themselves when confronted by difficulties,
as is illustrated by the self-defeating rant of the love-sick hermit in "Chemin
de Fer," the paralyzing fear of the Unbeliever, and the helpless paranoia of
the Man-Moth. But we also find pastoral figures whose at-home-ness amid
difficulties and impoverishment serves as an implicit upbraiding of such
ego-maniacs. And it is these figures who seem to point the way to the de-
creasing interiority of Bishop's maturing work, as she, together with her
pastoral subjects, learns to celebrate the capacity of humans (and of life
itself) to thrive amid all types of environments, and through all sorts of
difficulties.

In the early poem, "Jerónimo's House" (*CP* 34), the pastoral speaker
seems eager to demonstrate that he is not defeated by his impoverished circumstances.

>   My house, my fairy
>   palace, is
>   of perishable
>   clapboards with
>   three rooms in all,

> my gray wasps' nest
> of chewed up paper
>   glued with spit.
>
> My home, my love-nest,
>   is endowed
> with a veranda
>   of wooden lace,
> adorned with ferns
>   planted in sponges...

The speaker's metaphorical inventiveness is proof of his delight in his surroundings. The scene is typical of the pastoral in its combining of the homely with the extravagant: the shanty-ish clapboard house is "endowed" with a veranda of wooden lace. The poverty of the scene is unmistakable, if unapologetic, and its implicit accusal of the world at large is present in the bitterly humorous metaphor of the house as a wasps' nest "glued with spit." And yet, like any good pastoral figure, Jerónimo has learned the art of singing in sadness, as well as joy, the proof of which is the poem itself, and the surprising liveliness of the seemingly dead house:

> At night you'd think
>   my house abandoned.
> Come closer. You
>   can see and hear
> the writing-paper
>   lines of light
> and the voices of
>   my radio
>
> singing flamencos
>   in between
> the lottery numbers.
>   When I move
> I take these things,
>   not much more, from
> my shelter from
>   the hurricane.

The pastoral is always supplicating the reader to "come closer" in order to hear the singular voice of the lyrical singer—as opposed to the organ voice of the epic poet, which keeps the reader at a distance. The song the pastoral poet sings is of boundless hope, illustrated by the lottery numbers, and of danger and defeat lurking on the horizon, but kept at bay by the song itself, as the cluster of prepositional phrases in the poem's conclusion serve to forestall the arrival of the inevitable hurricane.

The hurricane represents death and defeat, and its presence in the poem is testament to the pastoral poet's unwillingness to allow wishful thinking to permanently alienate the dangers (and pleasures) of the real world. The poem's conclusion is suspended emotionally between the recurring hurricanes and the unlikely lottery prize. As David Halperin comments in his historical study of the bucolic, "The tension in pastoral between the real and the ideal admits of no completely satisfactory resolution" (49).

Death is an ever-present part of the pastoral, what John Ashbery— another contemporary pastoral poet who is generally unrecognized as such— refers to as the "dark vine at the edge of the porch" (166). And it is death that makes of all of us "pastoral characters," as Ettin wisely notes: "Against the marmoreal chill of death, life on this bountiful earth, filled with moments of small yet important pleasures, is itself pastoral" (144–45).

Heidegger's definition of existence as a "Being-towards-death" is apposite here (*Being* 311). Such an awareness of death is not to be thought of as a wariness and a negation, but as a recognition and an affirmation of the nature of life itself: "Death is the laying-down, the Law, just as the mountain chain is the gathering of the mountains into the whole of its chain" (*Poetry* 126). It is our awareness of death that transforms us from animals into mortals, "To die means to be capable of death as death. Only man dies. The animal perishes" (*Poetry* 178). Furthermore, it is death that makes authentic existence possible, although not inevitable. "The hard thing is to accomplish existence" (*Poetry* 138). "Rational living beings must first *become* mortals" (*Poetry* 179).

The major hindrance to becoming mortal in our contemporary world, according to Heidegger, is modern man's willful self-assertion, by which he places himself into an adversarial relationship to the world around him, reducing all of creation into objects for use, and transforming himself into a mere consumer among objects to be consumed. The solution to this self-defeating self-assertion is to learn to "dwell" among beings *as* a being, which entails learning to "cherish and protect, to preserve and care for" other beings, and oneself (*Poetry* 147). Only by entering into such a non-adversarial relationship with existence do we enable ourselves to come alive as mortals, and to prepare the way for a "good death" that is not a mere perishing (*Poetry* 151).

The presence of death and the preciousness of life exhibited by the pastoral belie any notion of this literary mode as adolescent and irresponsible.

(Although, in its sophistication, it *does* seek to direct attention away from its ancient wisdom, and uncareful readers are apt to mistake the manner for the matter.) The pastoral is the most humble of literary modes, reducing all knowledge and wisdom to the circuit and circumference of an individual life lived amid ordinary sights and circumstances that are made to seem, nevertheless—through the exactitude of the pastoral lens—extraordinary.

In the poem "Song for the Rainy Season" (*CP* 101–2), Bishop gives us the pastoral dimensions of her private life with Lota de Macedo Soares in Brazil. The poem is set at their house in Petrópolis, the old Imperialist summer capital in the mountains back of Rio de Janeiro. The house is situated on the side of a mountain, adjacent a waterfall. The setting is admittedly spectacular, but in the poem, Bishop strives to portray the house as a homely place that has, like any residence, its peculiarities, such as the fog that arises from the waterfall, enveloping the house and its residents "in a private cloud."

> Hidden, oh hidden
> in the high fog
> the house we live in,
> beneath the magnetic rock,
> rain-, rainbow-ridden,
> where blood-black
> bromelias, lichens,
> owls, and the lint
> of the waterfalls cling,
> familiar, unbidden.

The repetition of "hidden" in the first line alerts us to the ambivalence of the speaker, who seems to regard this place as both a safe-house, keeping others out, and as a sort of prison, keeping oneself in. The house, like the town around it, is a retreat from the busy port city, from which it is both alienated and aloof. But its existence is inextricably tied to that of the city, where Bishop and Lota, like many other affluent citizens of Petrópolis, had a residence as well. The town itself, then, as well as the house by the waterfall, is symbolic of the pastoral mode, which naturally appears, according to Renato Poggioli, "whenever the hustle and bustle of metropolitan life grows hard to bear and man tries to evade its pressures" (4).

Although fashioned as a retreat from the city, the country house has taken on a life of its own. It is transformed by its inhabitants from a mere space into a "location," which Heidegger defines as something that "*gathers* the earth as landscape around it" (*Poetry* 152) thereby allowing us to "dwell" there among "things" that are themselves at home in this location, and not only objects for our convenience (*Poetry* 153). The poet accepts the presence of her various housemates—the rain, the rainbow, the lichens, and the lint—with mock exasperation. They are uninvited guests, "unbidden," and yet are family, the root word of "familiar," and not to be turned away, even supposing one could.

This pastoral landscape is populated by the familiar figures of the genre. There is the singing poet herself, accompanied as she writes by "the brook" singing "loud / from a rib cage / of giant fern." There is also the hopeless and hapless lover, in the form of the "fat frogs"—food for the "ordinary brown owl"—"that, / shrilling for love, / clamber and mount." True to its pastoral nature, the house on the mountain-side is accommodating to all comers:

> House, open house
> to the white dew
> and the milk-white sunrise
> kind to the eyes,
> to membership
> of silver fish, mouse,
> bookworms,
> big moths; with a wall
> for the mildew's
> ignorant map

All life is welcome here, including the "bookworms" who both eat and *read* the volumes that are also, presumably, home to the mildew, whose "ignorant map" on the wall is remindful of the casual, careless manner in which pastoral figures pursue their sedentary lives.

This boundaried world is highly compromised by its crowding inhabitants, and yet all the more precious for being so:

> darkened and tarnished
> by the warm touch
> of the warm breath,
> maculate, cherished,
> rejoice! For a later
> era will differ.
> (O difference that kills,
> or intimidates, much
> of all our small shadowy
> life!).

Although the Petrópolis house Bishop lived in is a reputed masterpiece of modern architecture, it is represented here as an "old master" that has only been improved by age and wear. The key words here, and the emotional center of the poem, are "maculate" and "cherished." "Maculate," means, of course, "spotted" or "stained"; but it is more familiar in its obverse form, "immaculate," a word that is perhaps most closely associated with the Christian story of the "immaculate conception," by which Jesus was brought into the world without the stain of original sin. When Bishop uses the word in its root form, we may well read it as implying not only stained, but sinful, and, therefore, *real* and *human*, as opposed to the God-like ideal exhibited in the Christian myth.

Pastoral poets traditionally have striven to oppose the epic order of heroic myth with a world in which the individual as common man is predominant. Bishop is following in the ancient tradition by creating a poem that cherishes the very inadequacies and complaints of our "small" lives, those things that make each life individual and, therefore, cherished. But everthreatening to such a humble scale of existence is the demand for something more ideal; this is the "difference that kills, / or intimidates, much / of all our small shadowy / life." The word "shadowy" here calls to mind another myth, that of Plato's cave in which ignorant beings pursue their lives, unaware of the bright light of the ideal just outside. Bishop seems to argue that we are never unaware for long of that longed-for ideal, and that the danger we face is not in staying in the world of shadows, but in leaving to pursue the ideal—a pursuit that leads us to abandon all that has been established as cherished in our pastoral existence.

Looking backwards, with our knowledge of Bishop's biography, we can perhaps see the inevitable unraveling of the relationship between Bishop and Lota in the stanza above. But the poet herself forecasts the end in her concluding stanza, in which she faces the death of the relationship with a stoicism akin to Jerónimo's acceptance of the hurricane—a courageous response that serves to turn our attention back to the heart of the poem and the cherished pastoral world that is being lost.

Without water

the great rock will stare
unmagnetized, bare,
no longer wearing
rainbows or rain,
the forgiving air
and the high fog gone;
the owls will move on

and the several
waterfalls shrivel
in the steady sun.

Sítio da Alcobaçinha
Fazenda Samambaia
Petrópolis

The concluding note, locating the exact place of composition of the poem, which is itself the celebration of that location, emphasizes that this poem is about a real place and a real time. The emphasis serves as consolation for the scene of desolation with which the poem concludes. The desolation is perhaps inevitable, but the pastoral is quick to remind us that—as with our own deaths—it has not happened yet.

In "Crusoe in England" (*CP* 162–66) the disaster producing desolation has already occurred, with Crusoe's removal from his island and the consequent death of Friday "seventeen years ago come March." "Crusoe in England" is not a pastoral poem, but it has a pastoral "inset"—Crusoe's life with Friday—around which the rest of the poem gathers. The few spare lines concerning Friday's arrival and the couple's life on the island are not so much the emotional center of the poem as they are the representative of an absence at that center. For the poem is not *about* pastoral happiness or sadness, but about emotional isolation, and what James Merrill calls the "young imagination that running wild sustained itself alone" (257). Friday's arrival, according to Merrill, serves to stabilize the imagination and life of Crusoe, whose story subsequently "goes underground" (257), sustaining itself on the silence that is the true heart of the pastoral.

The lines that we are given concerning Crusoe's life with Friday are poignantly simple and allusive (elusive, as well).

Just when I thought I couldn't stand it
another minute longer, Friday came.
(Accounts of that have everything all wrong.)
Friday was nice.
Friday was nice, and we were friends.
If only he had been a woman!
I wanted to propagate my kind,
and so did he, I think, poor boy.
He'd pet the baby goats sometimes,
and race with them, or carry one around.
—Pretty to watch; he had a pretty body.

And then one day they came and took us off.

The rigid iambics of the last line emphasize the finality and impersonality of the act. Friday and Crusoe do not seem to have been given the choice to stay, and although Crusoe's previous complaints would indicate to us that he would like nothing more than to get off of his island, the subsequent death of Friday is indicative of the terrible cost to one's private life that entry into the world at large may entail. Might we think of Friday's death by measles as representing the public denial of the private life lived by Crusoe and Friday on their island retreat? The island may only appear as a "retreat" in hindsight, but this simply serves to emphasize its un-rediscoverable-ness, being a region, finally, of the heart alone.

Bishop was notoriously reticent in life and art concerning her private life. Her reservations concerning the confessional mode are well-known, as was her dislike at being classified a "woman"—much less a feminist or lesbian—poet. In "Crusoe in England," the distancing mechanism of the allegorical narrative seems to have enabled the poet to address concerns previously unconsidered, such as the feeling of exile experienced by the homosexual couple in relation to the world at large, and the frustration caused by the biologically barren nature of their union. Despite the relatively revealing character of the poem, one's instinct is to want to know more about the life lived by Crusoe and Friday, as Merrill attests:

> I once idiotically asked the author, on being shown this poem before publication, if there couldn't be a bit more about Friday? She rolled her eyes and threw up her hands: Oh, there used to be—*lots* more! But then it seemed....And wasn't the poem already long enough? (257)

Helen Vendler accounts for the absence of more information concerning the couple by saying that "love escapes language" (106), which is surely true in an *essential* sense, but does not account for the millions of poems (including several beautiful ones by Bishop) that have been written in an attempt to capture the elusive emotion.

From a purely practical standpoint, it might be argued that more space allotted to Crusoe's pastoral life with Friday would alter the balance of mood in the entire poem, which is finally about the *failure* of the pastoral to sustain itself in the real world. Ettin contends that "whether it means to or not (and sometimes it does indeed mean to), [the pastoral] tells us of our poverty" (152). The role that Friday plays in Crusoe's narrative is to illustrate the poverty of his existence prior to his friend's arrival and following his untimely departure. Life with Friday is the ideal/idyll within Crusoe's story, which—like the window view of a distant landscape in the painting of a "domestic" scene—serves to add perspective, and to question it.

Works Cited

Ashbery, John. *Selected Poems*. New York: Penguin, 1985.

Bishop, Elizabeth. *The Complete Poems*. New York: Farrar, Straus, Giroux, 1979.

Ettin, Andrew V. *Literature and the Pastoral*. New Haven: Yale UP, 1984.

Halperin, David M. *Before Pastoral: Theocritus and the Ancient Tradition of Bucolic Poetry*. New Haven: Yale UP, 1983.

Heidegger, Martin. *Being and Time*. Trans. John Marcquarrie and Edward Robinson. San Francisco: Harper, 1962.

———. *Poetry, Language, Thought*. Trans. Albert Hofstadter. New York: Harper, 1971.

Merrill, James. Afterword. *Becoming a Poet*. By David Kalstone. New York: Farrar, Straus, Giroux, 1989.

Poggioli, Renato. *The Oaten Flute: Essays on Pastoral Poetry and the Pastoral Ideal*. Cambridge: Harvard UP, 1975.

Vendler, Helen. *Part of Nature, Part of Us*. Cambridge: Harvard UP, 1980.

Elizabeth Bishop's Written Pictures, Painted Poems

Lorrie Goldensohn

Vassar College

Abstract

This paper discusses three features common to Elizabeth Bishop's paintings and poetry: her preoccupation with perspective, her love of line as both form and subject, and her general omission or diminution of the human figure. These features manifest Bishop's sensitivity to place, isolation, and memory. Her expressive handling of line and perspective, quite distinctive in her painting, brings her to test a boundary-breaking paradox, the eye that "speaks" and "touches."

One of many contemporary poets—the mind springs to Sylvia Plath, Mark Strand, and Derek Walcott among others—whose working knowledge of the visual arts was intense and intimate, Elizabeth Bishop's deceptively casual pictures now collected and published in William Benton's *Exchanging Hats* invite us to ask questions about parallel strategies and recurrent images that spill over into both verbal and visual representation. Tentatively, I'd like to suggest that three things common to Bishop's practice of these arts appear interrelated: her preoccupation with odd perspectives; her fondness for line as both medium and subject; and especially in her paintings and drawings, an evident reluctance to picture the human body.

The first habit to tease the Bishop reader is her quirky framing, the frequently oblique or unexpected approach to the subject, in which we are brought to ask the question "Where is the painter standing or sitting to do this picture?" Or, in a couple of notable cases, "Why is there so much stuff between me and the ostensible subject?" The whole descriptive encounter pervasively resembles the game that in Bishop's writing Mary McCarthy called "the mind hiding in her words, like an 'I' counting up to a hundred waiting to be found"(McCarthy 267). Played in relation to maker and made, perceiver and perceived, the game is a kind of hide-and-seek familiar in both Bishop's painted and written world, and we might hazard a guess about the degree to which these traits link an habitually acute interest in position and place with both a longing for and a fear of possession and stability, culminating in this fascinated interrogation of spatial boundaries.

Elizabeth Bishop in "real" life, according to her Brazilian friend Linda

Nemer, traveled with a compass in her pocket book, and when sleeping, always oriented her head to the north (Janows). Yet her concern with position, even when a beat away from suppressed anxiety, stays playful, as space becomes either exhilarating or terrifying in its elasticity, throwing one's heart up against the loose connections possible between up here and down there, or between the size of an object close to you, and the size of a thing delightfully or maddeningly far away.

In the dreams recorded in her journals, perspective carries her underwater, like the Riverman, or sends her sledding with the moon (Unpub. Journals, Vassar). It is also Bishop who places the Man-Moth travelling swiftly backwards underground, or who, in "Insomnia," invents a speaker looking up from the bottom of a well into an inverted world. Likewise, it is Bishop who sketches a chandelier and sets the bottom of her drawing only a couple of feet below the place where ceiling meets the wall; or, who frames a leaning Palais du Senat in Paris and a hunched, wildly cornered cathedral roof in Ouro Preto so that both facades bleed off the paper before they can ever hit the ignored ground. Both "Palais du Senat" (Fig. 1)[1] and "Gray Church" (Fig. 2) have their lower edges pitched above door or threshold or gate where the eye of the viewer is helpless to climb in, as the artist delimits altogether too clearly the barrier between the space of painted and painter, between viewed and viewer. But whether frontal or side-angled, the eye's immediate access to the picture space is usually in tumbling or blocked question.

In "County Courthouse" (Fig. 3), a huge, disorderly growth of sawtooth palmetto obscures our view of a red brick courthouse in Florida—where palm trees and telephone lines and poles further hide a good bit of the building. Even a last brave move on the part of the courthouse to assert itself upward on the page through a clock tower is foiled by an undignified splay of drooping and broken cable from what appear to be electrical poles. She doesn't want us to look at this court of law; she wants to paint what's obstructing it, and in William Benton's words, the subject becomes "an image of impasse."

In a similar vein of expressivity, Bishop's view of the Palais du Senat, cropped just shortly below balcony and dome, stresses a truncated patch of the urban skyline seen in a flooding pinky-yellow dawn or sunset: it's not clear at which transitional light she's stationed. With a funny, engaging primness, she outlines in a toothy Chinese white each edged stone of the towering facade as it presumably catches the sun's rising or falling rays, powerfully suggesting the spooky way in which city structures, shrouded by the cluttered streets, move either into or out of daylight in a discordant rhythm with the sun fielded above the city pedestrian. The four blue casements of an upper storey, the only other blue in the picture, echo the coming or going blue of the sky and blink upwards like lashless eyes. The piece is crowded with elisions and distortions, to be read and reacted to as one might react to the Paris poems from that period of her life, those pieces whose titles alone, "Paris, 7 A.M.," "Sleeping on the Ceiling," and "Sleeping Standing Up," emphasize the insomniac traveller, disoriented in both time and space.

Her focus is tight and unconventional; the frisky details emphatic. One might add that the supple point of view in Bishop's poetry seems closely related to the dislike and distrust of bombast that keeps her generalizing at an ironic angle, evading at all costs an inflationary or sentimental rhetoric. Even when painting public buildings demanding awe or respect, Bishop prefers to jump into subjects indirectly, sideways, or from above, looking remotely down to the toes, as Robinson Crusoe does on his extinct volcano, or as the viewer must in the resolutely tiny sketch called "Fireplace," in which the sides of the fireplace tilt sharply forward, pushing those risky flames back at the feet of the presumed observer. In rhetoric and construction, a knowing indirection and tonal deflation, and an insistence on the taming power of the small, govern scale and emphasis in painting and drawing as well as in arrangements of word.

Bishop's pictures handle depth of space with insouciance and a careless flair. In "Table with Plaid Cloth" (Fig. 4), she crushes table and chair into a space where wall and floor meet in an edge that can be "read" only with difficulty to accommodate either piece of furniture. Pictures wobble on her walls. The tops of doorways and desks or bureaus refuse to line up obediently into a single vanishing point perspective; blank mirrors, doors, and tables fall out of the picture, halfway in, halfway out. The lean of the doorway located in "Interior with Extension Cord" (Fig. 5) follows one set of perspectival rules at the top and then shrugs them aside at the bottom. The ornamental urn on the balcony in "Merida from the Roof" sits insecurely on its ledge, somewhere between sky and street, but comically level in size and site with the flailing crowd of windmills drawn in the distance. The inked-in rotary blades mounted on their pointy derricks look like giant daisy-wheels, and the whole structure repeats and alternates on the fantastic horizon with church steeples topped by surreally large crosses. Church steeples and windmill towers are virtually the same size and conical shape, although in their magnificence the petalled tops of the windmills edge out the smaller crosses, as the practical might be said to diminish the spiritual. Bishop must have especially enjoyed making this picture.

The second point of my present inquiry, Bishop's fascination with line, brings up issues about both means and content. Wire or cable, line or filament, turn up ubiquitously in Bishop's poems. There are many more strings and lines to note than the five old pieces of fish-line running through the jaws of the veteran fish in "The Fish," or the mythic kite-string trailing in the seawash at "The End of March," or the unexpected fibre in the clouds of "The Monument" or the "lines of pink cloud" that are like "wandering lines in marble" from "Roosters." The dominant lines of Bishop's pictures are often close in effect to the electric metaphor in "the writing-paper lines of light" in "Jeronimo's House," and to the falling "wires" of "The great light cage" breaking up in the air of "Rain Towards Morning," and again in the re-working of this poem's material in a Bishop poem unpublished during her lifetime, "It is marvelous...." I've traced the connections between wire and sexual circuitry in this poem and others elsewhere (Goldensohn 27–52), but it is worth noting, within the context of Bishop's graphic art, that line figures here, too, as a charged element, as something enabling and vital, something that opens the circuits of perception.

In drawing and painting, Bishop's line is both an instrument of representation and a subject: her pictures think about line and its contradictory properties as both a limiting, as well as a ceaselessly connective element, even as she uses line directly as trace. "Olivia" (Fig. 6) sketches a small church on Olivia Street in Key West, where line registers contour in the corners of the building, the lip of the step, the curve of a paneled door, and becomes the manufacture of protruding edge: it is the artifice by which we make two dimensions register three-dimensional volume. But as Anne Diggory pointed out to me, line in this picture is also indexical, its cables forming the actual mark seen in "nature." Line in this picture—as in "Interior with Extension cord" and others that mix the pen and brush, the writer's and painter's instruments—is both representation, an abstraction contouring a plane, a device representing the thing, and also the thing itself.

Line's dual function in this and so many other pictures seems to please Bishop: as she moves without benefit of words in and out of round and flat space, letting reality bubble up in the rhythmic, hypnotic repetition of line, line, line—all adding up industriously to buckling or folded surface, to retreating or advancing planes. Or, decoratively and amusingly, to the dense pattern diamond-hatching a school or apartment window or striping a bedcover or clapboard housefront. A collective as well as a directional force, contour lines lash or bundle together the disparate articles of one's reality: they grope for "truth," or to echo Wallace Stevens in "The Man on the

Dump," line clings to "what one wants to get near," to finger "the the." Lariat or snag, Bishop's line actively knots her to the object that eyes and hand are decisively coordinating to keep in memory, and to embody in mimetic, fetishistic substance on the page.

Most of Bishop's pictures are relatively small, delicately colored gouache, water color, and pen and ink; very few are more than lap-sized. Her interiors in particular have flat, tippy surfaces, with shallow and irregular depth; in each of them Bishop's preoccupation with line, perhaps an unspoken anxiety about continuity of ownership and relation, brings up a resonance, like a chord with overtones, in which both word and picture signify together. The script or common currency of both writing and drawing, Bishop's wiry black line loops and splays through the rooms of her pictures, dangles from lamps, hangs from flagpoles, grains floorboard, and runs from telephone pole to telephone pole prominently and insistently. As its name suggests, "Interior with Extension Cord" stars, as central performer in a cluttered workroom, the cord that wraps the length of two walls and a ceiling before it ends, precariously turning on and off the yellow-shaded table lamp to which it is attached.

Black, calligraphic line spreads over bushes and palm trees, shutters, railings, and furniture, tirelessly netting both natural and domestic objects, indoors and out. The same exuberant energy coalesces with Bishop's love of color, as well as line, in her prose piece, "In Prison":

> One of the most effective scenes that I have ever seen, for color contrast, was a group of these libertine convicts, in their black and white stripes, spraying, or otherwise tending to, a large clump of tropical shrubbery on the lawn of a public building.... One bush, I remember, had long knife-like leaves, twisting as they grew into loose spirals, the upper surface of the leaf magenta, the under an ocher yellow. Another had large, flat, glossy leaves, dark green, on which were scrawled magnificent arabesques in lines of chalk-yellow. These designs, contrasting with the bold stripes of the prison uniform, made an extraordinary, if somewhat florid, picture. (*CPr* 183)

Tongue-in-cheek reduces a prisoner's life to participation in a vulgarly "florid" decorator's color scheme; but even color is described in terms of line, as Bishop also deliberately displaces all that unruly emotion onto insensate leaf or mute cloth.

In her pictures, line hesitates expressively between serving as writing or as representation, probing the continuities between letters, pictographs, and likeness in varying assemblies of coded meaning. Quite apart from caption and inscription, in fourteen of the paintings, words, in legible or illegible handwriting or numbers, go back and forth between status as writing or status as picture. Sometimes the form of a shingle, or a board or a brick or leaflet repeats across or through a painting, stacking or filing itself as carefully as a block of print. Twelve of these pictures make reference to writing in prominently displayed books or papers or signs, or labels, not excluding tombstones. Five of the paintings have paintings nested self-consciously inside their borders, most of them dangling askew on distinctive black cords, yanked into a jaunty angle by a cartoon nail. At moments the little motifs, scribbled hastily or made more slowly and singly like little o's, verge on a kind of tacit speech. In nature, we are made to remember by art historians, there are no lines; and only in the printed word does a reticent voice become visible, the lines of poetry truly seen, and not merely heard.

For someone whose gift was so strongly visual, it's intriguing to think about why some subjects remained stubbornly unpictured: is it lack of capability that banished people from her painting? That's hard to believe. Apart from washy although subtle color, Bishop's lines move boldly with comic inventiveness and spontaneity. The same intrepid hand that detailed a portable electric fan with all of its parts in loving display—not omitting the box into which the electric cord is plugged—and that did stoves and clocks, or that designed the mechanical workings of a patented slot machine, would not withdraw before the complexities of arm, leg, torso, or face. If Bishop didn't "do" people, it's because their presence wasn't to her purpose; she preferred painting their absence.

Again and again, her pictures are the just-evacuated containers of human activity; her comfy chairs have just been emptied, or are about to be filled; her tables are piled with what unseen hands have laid down on them. Even the bike parked in front of "The Harris School" signals the human being, as does the angle of entry into "Merida from the Roof," where the corner siting of the balcony from which the town of Merida is seen suggests the observer who is sitting, pad of paper, pen and brush at hand, to copy all those astonishing windmills.

Although Bishop's interest in big spaces displays itself in four notable landscapes and several brief street scenes, the bulk of her pictures focus on interiors; on domestic fixtures and flowers. What conclusions can we draw from the rhythm of her choices, from what she repeatedly chose to describe with brush or pen, and what she omitted?

To be precise, nineteen of the forty-odd pictures reproduced in William Benton's collection are festooned by flowers, or are individual studies of croton or starflower or bouquets of daisies and pansies; others do lamps,

Fig. 1: **Palais du Senat** (1938)
watercolor and gouache, 5½ x 9 inches
Collection of Dorothee Bowie

Fig. 2: **Gray Church** (undated)
watercolor

Fig. 3: **County Courthouse** (undated)
watercolor, gouache, and ink, 5½ x 6 inches
Collection of Alice Methfessel

Fig. 4: **Table with Plaid Cloth** (undated)
watercolor and gouache, 7½ x 5¾ inches
Vassar College Libraries, Special Collections

Fig. 5: **Interior with Extension Cord** (undated)
watercolor, gouache, and ink, 6⅛ x 6⅛ inches
Collection of Loren MacIver

Fig. 6: **Olivia** (undated)
watercolor and gouache, 5 x 7 inches
Collection of Alice Methfessel

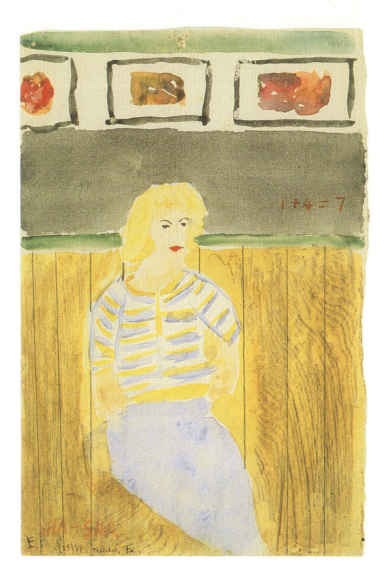

Fig. 7: **Sha-Sha** (1937)
watercolor, 9 x 6 inches
Vassar College Libraries, Special Collections

Fig. 8:. **Sleeping Figure** (undated)
watercolor and gouache, 8½ x 5½ inches
Collection of Alice Methfessel

tables, chairs, mirrors and fireplaces—but the nearest competitor to flowers as major focus are separate commemorations of buildings, of which there are nine. Like the presence-drenched domestic interiors, that hint at people by way of absenting them from what only people can use, Bishop's flowers imply the out-of-doors, the invisible gardens from which they have been plucked. As the flowers stare like guests from improvised paint bucket or pitcher or basket, their roots are elsewhere. Similarly, her metonymic buildings signal the beings they habitually contain, as well as the invisible beings responsible for their engendering.

Through the medium of Elizabeth Bishop's distinctive voice, many of her amused or disconsolate speakers are posted at a slant angle outside or above the poem, the soliloquy of their feelings audible and intelligible only by an intonation and inflection not emanating from any seen speaker. In this poetry, people's bodies have brief, walk-on parts, like the ladies at the bus-stop in "The Moose"; or they are miniaturized by distance, or become fantasized like horse and dancer in "Cirque d'Hiver." Most of Bishop's paintings are depopulated, and you are asked to read human feeling only by a signifying perspective.

In both prose and poetry, female flesh has a shy, erotic attractiveness, mostly suppressed in the published work of her lifetime; or wears a certain distastefulness, as in "Gwendolyn," the childhood friend who "stood for everything that the slightly repellent but fascinating words 'little girl' should mean." Apart from "Anjinhos," the box made in homage to Joseph Cornell, that features tiny paper cut-outs of Victorian "angel" heads with their tabs still on, there are only two paintings with people in them. What are we to make of these figures? Both are female. The seated "Sha-Sha" (Fig. 7), arms blurrily crossed at her waist, hair carefully blonde, as well as the fully clothed "Sleeping Figure" (Fig. 8) with folded arms on a huge black bed-stead blocking out the light from a nearby window are comic dolls, their middles somehow elided or foreshortened. The chair that Sha-Sha must be sitting on has vanished in the wood-paneling behind her. The faces are the merest blobs or wisps of line, the sleeping lady's face put together with what looks like a scattering of nail parings, the stripes on Sha-Sha's sweater more sharply delineated than her neck or waist. The midsections of both women are hidden as if feminine waists and bellies, as well as what joins the crowded head to the wayward body, didn't bear too close inspection. "1+4=7," announces an inscription in the portrait of Sha-Sha, as if warning us not to intrude too familiarly in this space with our logical system.

Women made up the critical mass of Bishop's emotional world, but a more intense story of loss, abandonment, or betrayal that they might tell resides strictly in the objects used by their bodies, and never by those bodies themselves. Just as line is a two-dimensional trace element that submerges the story of a three-dimensional figure, these paintings and drawings of Elizabeth Bishop's seem largely intended as symbolic keepsakes, objects that function as essence storage, or as "monuments to every moment...cages of infinity." In several cases, because signatures and dedications clearly identify paintings as gifts, or occasional presents, they testify to the ongoing and social shape of Bishop's world. In contrast to the narrative fulfillment of Bishop's late poetry, however, the deliberate omission of people from these interiors is at least one sign that Bishop herself clearly subordinated the development of her visual to her verbal art, however much delight her pictures may have afforded to either her or us, or their recipients.

In "The U.S.A School of Writing," Bishop wrote admiringly of meticulous amateur painting, valuing its innocence, its direct and earnest need to imitate what the eye beholds. Complaining about sloppy workmanship and blithe indifference to reality in amateur writers, she contrasts them with these habits:

> Where primitive painters will spend months and years, if necessary, putting in every blade of grass and building up brick walls in low relief, the primitive writer seems in a hurry to get it over with. Another thing was the almost complete lack of detail. The primitive painter loves detail and lingers over it and emphasizes it at the expense of the picture as a whole. (*CPr* 46)

This passage puts one in mind of Bishop's acquisitive embrace of that detail; of her caressive sweep following some scope of object or scene, stroking it, and scaling it down to the graspable, as eye and hand assay that looking never very far from the need to touch. As the paint dries, she—and we—explore the immovable gap between having and seeing.

Perhaps, more insistently than the poems, the painted image is to extend and communalize the arena of art's observations. Bishop's emphasis on line and contour, on the tactile element, seems the necessary balancing act: the reconciliation of the remote, imperial eye with the intimate, possessive hand, attempting to join an always hopelessly deferred desire with the objects of its pleasure. The fresh, nervous perspective of the pictures, and the occasional or commemorative nature of so many of them, vividly underscore these longings.

Endnote

1. The illustrations of Elizabeth Bishop's paintings in this article were photographed from originals or duplications in the possession of the Vassar College Library, Special Collections. The title, medium and dimensions of each picture are as given by William Benton in *Exchanging Hats: Elizabeth Bishop Paintings*, Farrar, Sraus, Giroux, New York: 1996.

Works Cited

Benton, William. *Exchanging Hats*. New York: Farrar, Straus, Giroux, 1996.

Bishop, Elizabeth. Unpublished Journals. Elizabeth Bishop Papers. Vassar College Library.

———. *Collected Prose*. Ed. Robert Giroux. New York: Farrar, Straus, Giroux, 1984.

Goldensohn, Lorrie. *Elizabeth Bishop: The Biography of a Poetry*. New York: Columbia UP, 1992.

Janows, Jill. Unpublished transcript. Interview of Linda Nemer, 1987. Vassar College Library.

McCarthy, Mary. "Symposium: I Would Like to Have Written...." *Elizabeth Bishop and Her Art*. Ed. Lloyd Schwartz and Sybil P. Estess. Ann Arbor: U of Michigan P, 1983.

"Shuddering Insights": Bishop and Surprise

Barbara Comins
City University of New York

Abstract

Elizabeth Bishop once stated that surprise is the one feature essential to a poem. Some psychologists contend that surprise might be a necessary ingredient for learning to occur because it clears the mind of preconceptions and causes it to "reset" itself. This essay explores surprise in various Bishop poems, theorizing that she valued the ability of surprise to shock us out of preconceived ways of looking at and reacting to the world.

Elizabeth Bishop once stated in an interview that surprise is the one feature necessary to a poem. "The subject and the language which conveys it should surprise you. You should be surprised at seeing something new and strangely alive" (Monteiro 104). Of course, in Bishop's poetry there is an abundance of surprising metaphor—the fish's disturbing gaze, the iris of its eyes as though "backed...with tarnished tinfoil" (*CP* 43) or the moose's uncanny otherworldliness as it emerges from the "impenetrable wood," its stature described as "Towering, antlerless, / high as a church" (*CP* 172–73). Critics have commented widely upon these and other surprising devices used by Bishop. But what exactly is surprise? And why did Bishop consider it such an essential element of a poem?

Psychologists describe it as "a short-lived phenomenon elicited by un-expected (schema-discrepant) events" (Ramachandran 353). The human response to surprise is universal: the same distinctive wide-eyed, eyebrows raised, open-mouthed facial expression. Surprised by a sudden sound, an unexpected sight, we abruptly stop our ongoing activity and veer our atten-tion toward the eliciting stimulus. That which is sudden, unexpected, un-known, unusual, improbable, or rare can surprise us into alertness, atten-tiveness, awareness.

Surprise can be both pleasurable or unpleasant (Corsini 391). Though Charles Darwin (ch. 12), whom Bishop read, categorized surprise as a nega-tive emotion, a recent theorist suggests that surprise is positive, a kind of "resetting" state in which the mind is momentarily cleared of thought (Tomkins vii, 148; Corsini 391). This brief hiatus in thought and action enables us to rapidly evaluate and respond to change and to eventually adapt to it. In fact, some studies go so far as to suggest that surprise might be a necessary ingredient to produce conditioning, adjustment to the environment, and in fact, learning itself.

One physiological response to surprise is that it momentarily takes our breath away. As an asthmatic, Bishop experienced sudden, unpleasantly surprising, losses of breath and subsequent oxygen deprivation. An asthmatic can never take life for granted. The "frightening gills" of the "caught" fish "breathing in / the terrible oxygen" in Bishop's well-known poem "The Fish" perhaps reflect those terrifying asthmatic experiences. The sudden involuntary catching of the breath during surprise momentarily enthralls us. In the subsequent freeing of the breath, the resumption of respiration, we feel the truth of our aliveness. In Bishop's poem, the fish is caught and then eventually freed by the poem's speaker. The speaker realizes the fish's previous struggles, begins to view the "five old pieces of fish-line" and the "hooks grown firmly" in the fish's mouth anthropomorphically as the "medals" a hero might wear, "ribbons frayed and wavering" or "a five-haired beard of wisdom." Critic Thomas Travisano points out that "the observations" within this poem "gain in emotional charge until they culminate in a shock of recognition" (71). Both the reader and the poem's speaker are surprised into an unselfconscious identification with the fish. Oddly enough, the fish has "caught" us, enabling a victorious transubstantiation of the oily, stagnant bilge water into a rainbow flooding the speaker's boat "until everything / was rainbow, rainbow, rainbow! / And I let the fish go" (*CP* 44). In these final lines, Bishop incorporates surprise acoustically in the astonished "oh" sounds embedded within the words "rainbow" and "go."

In Bishop's metaphysical "Sonnet" of 1979, the words "caught" and "freed" are highlighted through mirrored syntax and she again uses the rainbow as a symbol of surprising freedom:

> Caught—the bubble
> in the spirit-level,
> a creature divided;
> and the compass needle
> wobbling and wavering,
> undecided.
> Freed—the broken
> thermometer's mercury
> running away;
> and the rainbow-bird
> from the narrow bevel

> of the empty mirror,
> flying wherever
> it feels like, gay!   (*CP* 192)

There is in this and in other Bishop poems an attempt to ambush that moment when we hover between creature and spirit. Similarly, "The Man-Moth," Bishop's fictitious character based on a newspaper's typographical error, hovers between human and animal. He, too, can be "caught" and surprised. Bishop instructs us:

> If you catch him,
> hold up a flashlight to his eye. It's all dark pupil,
> an entire night itself, whose haired horizon tightens
> as he stares back, and closes up the eye. Then from the lids
> one tear, his only possession, like the bee's sting, slips.
> Slyly he palms it, and if you're not paying attention
> he'll swallow it. However, if you watch, he'll hand it over,
> cool as from underground springs and pure enough to drink. (*CP* 15)

Bishop likens the tear of the Man-Moth to the painful surprise of a "bee's sting." The poem's words highlight one important response to surprise, that of "paying attention." Psychologist Jerome Bruner points out that "the nervous system stores models of the world that, so to speak, spin a little faster than the world goes. If what impinges on us conforms to expectancy, to the predicted state of the model, we may let our attention flag a little, look elsewhere, even go to sleep. Let input violate expectancy, and the system is put on alert" (46). The abrupt change in focus elicited by surprise triggers the alert mind into "that sense of constant re-adjustment" Bishop mentions in "The Gentleman of Shalott" (*CP* 10). Interestingly enough, Bishop records the responses to surprising stimuli in a host of other poems. In "Manuelzinho," when the poem's speaker surprises her "half squatter, half tenant" by loudly yelling at him to "fetch" some potatoes, his response is comic:

> your holey hat flew off,
> you jumped out of your clogs,
> leaving three objects arranged
> in a triangle at my feet,
> as if you'd been a gardener
> in a fairy tale all this time
> and at the word "potatoes"
> had vanished to take up your work
> of fairy prince somewhere. (*CP* 97)

In some poems, Bishop anthropomorphizes the responses of various animals to surprising stimuli. In "The Armadillo," dangerous fire balloons cause owls and a "rose flecked" armadillo to flee the burning thickets. Bishop remarks:

> and then a baby rabbit jumped out,
> *short*-eared, to our surprise.
> So soft! —a handful of intangible ash
> with fixed, ignited eyes. (*CP* 104)

Bishop italicizes the word "short" in the phrase "short-eared, to our surprise," thereby displacing the shock from its rightful place.

In "Electrical Storm," the alarming thunder heard after a lightning bolt hits the house elicits the frightened reaction of the cat Tobias who jumps through the window and runs for the bed "his fur on end" (*CP* 100). Bishop vividly describes the scene, the hail the "size of artificial pearls," getting up "to find the wiring fused, / no lights, a smell of saltpetre." The pellets of hail littering the lawn are depicted as "dead-white, wax white, cold—" and later likened to "dead-eye pearls." The telephone is dead as well. This reiteration of the word "dead" conveys the impression that the speaker of the poem, like her house, "was really struck" by her narrow escape from death.

In another of Bishop's poems, "In the Waiting Room" (*CP* 159–61), a young girl is taken "completely by surprise" when she hears her aunt cry out in pain from the adjoining dentist's office. It is 1918, the war is on, and while waiting for her Aunt Consuelo, the girl reads *National Geographic* which contains a lurid photograph of "A dead man slung on a pole," bearing a caption that reads "Long Pig." Suddenly the girl hears her aunt cry out in pain, an almost animal pain with which the little girl identifies:

> What took me
> completely by surprise
> was that it was *me*:
> my voice, in my mouth.
> Without thinking at all
> I was my foolish aunt,
> I—we—were falling, falling....

To stop this scary sensation, she tries to reaffirm her sense of self and individuality by saying her name and recalling to mind the fact that in "three days" she'll be seven. Nonetheless, the feeling of eerie intersubjectivity persists and she feels that the waiting room is "sliding" beneath a series of "big black wave[s]":

> I knew that nothing stranger
> had ever happened, that nothing
> stranger could ever happen.
> Why should I be my aunt,
> or me, or anyone?
> What similarities—
> boots, hands, the family voice
> I felt in my throat, or even
> the *National Geographic*
> and those awful hanging breasts—
> held us all together
> or made us all just one?
> How—I didn't know any
> word for it—how "unlikely"...
> How had I come to be here,
> like them, and overhear
> a cry of pain that could have
> got loud and worse but hadn't?

Aunt Consuelo's sudden cry causes epistemological questioning on the part of the child. The child struggles to come up with the word "unlikely" to describe her astounding and paradoxical realization, that she is "just one" with the human family at the same time that she is an individual, "an *I*."

Some surprises are fraught with danger, shaking us out of a somnolent state, making us mindful of our mortality. In "Love Lies Sleeping," the sudden loud "Boom" of a wrecker's ball disturbs the sleep of all of those within earshot, making the "short hairs" on the "backs of necks" bristle with the threat of "Danger" or "Death" (*CP* 16–17). And in "The Weed" (*CP* 20–21), another sudden surprise occurs, this time "prodding" the poem's speaker from "desperate sleep":

> Suddenly there was a motion,
> as startling, there, to every sense
> as an explosion. (*CP* 20)

In this dream vision, the speaker of the poem imagines that she is dead and that while she is lying upon "a grave, or bed," a weed takes root in her heart. According to Travisano, "The weed connotes an unconscious suppressed wish to take the chance of life, to face the unknown consequences of love, even with a divided heart" (36). His contention is supported by the way the language shifts within the poem. Before the sudden growth of the weed, the speaker's condition is static, "unchanged for a year, a minute, an hour" and her heart is described as "the heart" or "the cold heart." The surprising "motion" of the weed wrests the speaker from a dormant state: "The rooted heart began to change." Eventually, the shift from the article in "the heart" to the possessive in "your heart" in the poem's final line signals the emotional change wrought by surprise.

Psychologists tell us that surprise is closely related to what is termed the "startle response" which is "elicited by abrupt and intense stimulation" (Ramachandran 356). In Bishop's poem "The Mountain" (*CP* 197–98), the speaker is startled and a feeling of cosmic insecurity ensues:

> At evening, something behind me.
> I start for a second, I blench,
> or staggeringly halt and burn.
> I do not know my age.

Like the little girl speaker in "In the Waiting Room" who stems her distress with the reassuring thought that in three days she'll be seven, the speaker here, too, believes there is solace in knowing one's age.

"From the Country to the City" (*CP* 13) contains an instance of startle as well. In it, the speaker of the poem and a partner travel the long roads leading cityward which are likened to "league-boots." The center lines of the roads become "satin-stripes on harlequin's / trousers" giving the impression of the city, and perhaps an urban frame of mind too, as essentially gaudy. Bishop amplifies the harlequin motif, painting the city as a "wickedest clown" who is "dressed in tatters, scribbled over with / nonsensical signs." There is the sense that the lines of the roads are poetic lines as well and that Bishop is referring to a pre-creative state, a chaos of "nonsensical signs" every bit as overwhelming as the urban landscape with its myriad lights and motley assortment of buildings. Then the glittering tops of lit skyscrapers metamorphose into a mind at work:

> his brain appears, throned in "fantastic triumph,"
>   and shines through his hat
> with jeweled works at work at intermeshing crowns,
>   lamé with lights.

Closer to the city now, the poem's speaker finds its glinting allure and the influx of creative ideas disturbing, like the mythological sirens' beckoning call to self-destruction.

> As we approach, wickedest clown, your heart and head,
> > we can see that
> glittering arrangement of your brain consists, now,
> > of mermaid-like,
> seated, ravishing sirens, each waving her hand-mirror....

Suddenly, the speaker of the poem and her companion are startled.

> > ...we start at
> series of slight disturbances up in the telephone wires
> > on the turnpike.
> Flocks of short, shining wires seem to be flying sidewise.
> > Are they birds?
> They flash again. No. They are vibrations of the tuning-fork
> > you hold and strike.... (*CP* 13)

The poet, then, is like a musician tuning an instrument at the beginning of practice. Bishop melds the idea of music with the creative stimulus.

Because the creative impetus changes and rearranges the world, it is unsettling. This explains why, though the title and its prepositions in "From the Country to the City" indicate a movement cityward, the poem contains a contrary motion drawing "your dreams, / out countrywards." There is a sense that the creative start of a poem, while exhilarating, also causes confusion and annoyance, leaving the speaker desiring tranquillity. Lastly, the poem's speaker interprets the message of the phone wires as a supplication for the overwhelming stimuli to cease: "We bring a message from the long black length of body: / 'Subside,' it begs and begs."

In "Poem (*CP* 176–77)," which constitutes a kind of *ars poetica* for Bishop, she again looks at the creative process as she examines a small painting by her great-uncle. "About the size of an old-style dollar bill," the painting:

> has never earned any money in its life.
> Useless and free, it has spent seventy years
> as a minor family relic
> handed along collaterally to owners
> who looked at it sometimes, or didn't bother to. (*CP* 176)

Bishop's choice of the word "collaterally" in referring to the inheritance of the painting is intriguing from a number of standpoints. Painting is a parallel or collateral art to that of poetry. After all, the title of "Poem" could equally have been "Painting." The poem's first stanza contains words from the financial world, thereby emphasizing the painting's value as collateral in the sense of incidental. A collateral relative is a brother or sister of a parent, grandparent or other lineal ancestor and Bishop spent a part of her life after her father's death and her mother's entry into an asylum, living with an aunt in Massachusetts. "Collateral" also means "adjacent" or "parallel" and, partway through the poem, the speaker is struck by the surprising revelation that she and her great uncle have had parallel experiences: "Heavens, I recognize the place, I know it!"(*CP* 176). This sudden recognition enables the poem's speaker to move from simply noting the painter's techniques and colors to identifying with the uncle she "never knew." The revelation dawns on her that they anachronistically:

> …both knew this place,…
> looked at it long enough to memorize it,
> our years apart. How strange. (*CP* 177)

This remark, "How strange," in "Poem" resonates with the one of "how 'unlikely'" when the child identifies with her aunt's cry of pain in "In the Waiting Room." The child's surprise in the waiting room raises epistemological questions, "How had I come to be here, / like them, and overhear / a cry of pain...?" (*CP* 161). After the surprise of collateral experience in "Poem," the speaker goes beyond a remarking upon the elements of the painting to larger issues:

> Our visions coincided—"visions" is
> too serious a word—our looks, two looks:
> art "copying from life" and life itself,
> life and the memory of it so compressed
> they've turned into each other. Which is which? (*CP* 177)

Art is a compression of "life itself"; it is handed down "collaterally" in the sense that it serves "to support or reinforce" life (Webster's). A transformation has occurred. Initially, the poet had dispassionately examined the process of making the painting's subjects, "some tiny cows, / two brushstrokes each" and "a wild iris, white and yellow, / fresh-squiggled from the tube." By the end of the poem, gerunds bring them to life and they become "munching cows" and an "iris, crisp and shivering." After the speaker's sudden revelation—"Heavens, I recognize the place, I know it!"—the elements of the painting take on greater than material value:

> Life and the memory of it cramped,
> dim, on a piece of Bristol board,

dim, but how live, how touching in detail
—the little that we get for free,
the little of our earthly trust. Not much.
About the size of our abidance....

The surprising moment of revelation in "Poem," the collateral or parallel "vision," causes the poet to understand her artistic inheritance. Like the
ordinary squiggles of paint with which her great-uncle worked, the material
of the poet is ordinary language, used in moving ways. Travisano comments
that "[t]his recognition shocks deeply submerged memories to the surface.
The place is then slowly repossessed. Such investment ... allows one to participate in the painting actively, bringing ambiguous detail (such as the steeple)
or ignored detail (such as a certain spot of white) into focus" (190). This
moment of surprise fosters an epiphanic intersubjectivity. As Wallace Stevens
expressed it, the poet's function "is to make his imagination ... [his readers']
and that he fulfills himself only as he sees his imagination become the light
in the minds of others" (29).

One of Bishop's most interesting incorporations of the phenomenon of
surprise is contained in her double sonnet, "The Prodigal," a modernization
of the Biblical story. As Brett Millier points out in her biography of Bishop,
"The poem...speaks painfully and eloquently to her own experience with
alcoholism..." (230). In self-exile, the alcoholic protagonist of Bishop's poem
lives in deplorable conditions alongside animals in a barn. Numbed by his
"drinking bouts" and inured to the pig sty's "brown enormous odor" which
is "too close ... for him to judge" his situation, he is almost thrown off
balance by a surprising stimulus which serves to help him decide eventually
to return home.

Carrying a bucket along a slimy board,
he felt the bats' uncertain staggering flight,
his shuddering insights, beyond his control,
touching him. (*CP* 71)

Eerily unsettling, as many surprises are, the sudden "staggering flight"
of the bats would seem to mimic the reeling of the drunken young man.
Moreover, this staggering mirrors his state of vacillation, the fact that, as
the poem tells us, "it took him a long time / finally to make his mind up to go
home" (*CP* 71).

William James claimed that "habit diminishes the conscious attention
with which our acts are performed" (119). Surprise can function to dislodge
us from habit or habitual patterns of thinking. The surprising "schema-dis-

crepant event" prompts us to update our "activated schema" (or world view) and subsequent actions (Ramachandran 355). Surprise can trigger the experience of joy or the realization of peril. In a sense, this sudden redirection of awareness and split-second catching of the breath focuses our attention on life itself. Good poetry must, as Bishop claimed, contain surprise because it jolts us back to life or, as the poet Paul Valéry expressed it, "It is my life itself that is surprised..." (57). In an oft-quoted letter to Anne Stevenson, Bishop wrote, "What one seems to want in art, in experiencing it, is the same thing that is necessary for its creation, a self-forgetful, perfectly useless concentration" (Stevenson 66). Perhaps the moment of surprise is that moment in which we paradoxically are most self-forgetful, yet most ourselves.

Works Cited

Bishop, Elizabeth. *The Complete Poems: 1927–1979.* New York: Farrar, Straus, Giroux, 1983.

Bruner, Jerome. *Actual Minds, Possible World.* Cambridge: Harvard UP, 1986.

Corsini, Raymond J., ed. *Encyclopedia of Psychology.* New York: Wiley, 1984.

Darwin, Charles. *The Expression of Emotions in Man and Animals.* 1872. Rpt. London: Julian Freidman, 1979.

James, William. *The Principles of Psychology.* Cambridge: Harvard UP, 1983.

Monteiro, George, ed. *Conversations with Elizabeth Bishop.* Jackson: UP of Mississippi, 1996.

Millier, Brett C. *Elizabeth Bishop: Life and the Memory of It.* Berkeley: U of California P, 1993.

Ramachandran, V. S., ed. *Encyclopedia of Human Behavior.* New York: Academic, 1994.

Stevens, Wallace. *The Necessary Angel.* New York: Random House, 1951.

Stevenson, Anne. Letter to Anne Stevenson. *Elizabeth Bishop.* New York: Twayne, 1966.

Tomkins, Silvan S. and Carroll E. Izard. *Affect, Cognition and Personality.* New York: Springer, 1965.

Travisano, Thomas J. *Elizabeth Bishop: Her Artistic Development.* Charlottesville: UP of Virginia, 1988.

Valéry, Paul. *The Art of Poetry.* New York: Random House, 1958.

Elizabeth Bishop's Productive Look

Kirstin Hotelling
Illinois State University

Abstract

This paper complicates the growing focus on Bishop as an autobiographical poet. Drawing on unpublished drafts and theoretical work by Kaja Silverman, I offer a reading of "In the Waiting Room" in which I suggest that the individuality that marks the speaker of this poem is a manifestation of the degree to which Bishop has unraveled the autonomous "I," and not an affirmation of its triumphant endurance. Not only is "Elizabeth's" "I" expressed, typically, through its association with what she is not, but what makes this other *other* is revealed in this poem more clearly than in any piece that Bishop ever wrote.

Though Elizabeth Bishop was once dismissed by feminist scholars and poets as reticent and apolitical, feminist critics in the past ten years have enriched our sense of Bishop as one of this century's most serious poets.[1] A championing of autobiography charts this reversal: as the details of Bishop's lesbianism, troubled childhood, alcoholism, and restless personal life have become common scholarly knowledge, a growing field of feminist sympathizers has emerged among Bishop scholars—a positive turn-around, to be sure, but also an ironic one, since Bishop's penchant for privacy was due in large part to her distaste for pity. Central to this critical shift is a general consensus that Bishop's later work is more personal than her earlier poems—that as Bishop's writing matured, it broke out of abstraction and fantasy to achieve a more down-to-earth, to-the-point sort of poem. And indeed, there is ample evidence for such a reading: Bishop's poems of late-life are preoccupied with her past, exploring family relations, childhood perspectives, and lost loves with an up-front openness that seems to set them apart from her earlier collections. It is tempting to read poems like "The Moose," "One Art," and "In the Waiting Room" as distinct from Bishop's previous explorations of identity—as more grounded, confident, and self-possessed than poems like "The Gentleman of Shalott," "The Weed," or "The Man-Moth." Yet, as Langdon Hammer has noted, while feminist criticism often lauds Bishop for her subversions of the "dominative ego of Romantic poetry," just as "pertinent and pressing... is Bishop's challenge to the stereotypical subject of contemporary lyric autobiography, to the expressive self, prized in American poetry since mid-century" (148–9).

I juxtapose these somewhat divergent approaches to Bishop in order to emphasize the tension that unites them: Bishop's work does become more obviously personal as she ages, while at the same time her later poems continue to question notions of selfhood that words like "personal" tend to summon. Honoring this paradoxical dimension of Bishop's poetry is central to comprehending her relevance to current discussions of feminist poetry in this country, and, in turn, the dynamic relationship between feminism and American poetry at large. While Bishop considered herself a feminist, her poetry subverts one of feminism's most time-honored goals, what Alicia Ostriker has called the quest for "autonomous self-definition" (11). But rather than read Bishop as either autobiographical (and feminist) or reticent (and not), we may fare better by examining the ways in which her writing both proffers *and* contests the possibility of an authentic, "autonomous" subjectivity. Such an approach allows that feminist poetics might be fueled at times by an ambivalent sense of self. In parallel fashion, we may read Bishop's early, more abstract explorations of difference and her gradual, later turn to autobiography as contingent, not in conflict. Along these lines, I would like to suggest that it is in Bishop's most famous and self-referential poem, "In the Waiting Room" (*CP* 159–161)—a poem laden with autobiographical details, the only poem to be spoken by an "Elizabeth" from Bishop's childhood home in Massachusetts—that Bishop offers her keenest challenge to the notion of coherent selfhood that the term "autobiography" often underscores or assumes.

While my reading picks up at the end of Bishop's career, it assumes a contiguity between her earliest poems and her last: the focus on personal history in Bishop's later poems is inextricable from her focus on otherness, a signature concern that brings her late-life poems face-to-face with her earliest pieces. Bishop's poetry insists that exploring one's self is dependent upon exploring one's notions of difference, that the pursuit of one will always come on the heels of the other. As we shall see, this double-gesture channels the pulse of Bishop's most "I"-centered poem. Consequently, I propose that the emphatic "I" of "In the Waiting Room" is named "Elizabeth" *precisely* because the mature Bishop has developed such a sophisticated understanding of the seductive though illusory promise of coherent selfhood—of the sense of autonomy that the Man-Moth and the Gentleman of Shalott struggled with years before. In this way, the singularity that marks the speaker of this poem is a manifestation of the great degree to which

Bishop has unraveled the autobiographical "I," and not an affirmation of its triumphant endurance.

Kaja Silverman's recent work helps illuminate this subtle dynamic at the heart of Bishop's poetic. In her latest book, *The Threshold of the Visible World* (1996), Silverman suggests the conditions necessary for what she calls an "ethical or non-violent relation to the other," and ultimately, for ethically loving ourselves (3–4). Towards the end of her book, Silverman, like Bishop, shifts her emphasis slightly away from the parameters of the other to the locus of the self. This transition is central to Silverman's notion of the "productive look," which she describes as follows:

> Instead of assimilating what is desirable about the other to the self, and exterior-izing what is despised in the self as the other, the subject whose look I am here describing struggles to see the otherness of the desired self, and the familiarity of the despised other. He or she attempts, that is...to recognize him- or herself precisely within those others to whom he or she would otherwise respond with revulsion and avoidance. (170)

Because the processes of identification are always in part unconscious, this sort of ethical looking can only happen in retrospect, and then only provisionally, since it is through the act of looking *again* that we might learn to restructure our ways of seeing, and thus interactions with, others and ourselves. In so doing, we must constantly admit of our desires for identify-ing with what is sanctioned as ideal, just as we remain committed to the deconstruction of those desires. The anticipated result of this investment is understanding that it is through our own psychic projections (and not be-cause of an other's "essential" character), that one body or image may ap-pear ideal and an other abject; that, as Silverman phrases it, we may finally "leap out of 'difference' and into bodily otherness" (37), to a state of aware-ness in which loving oneself does not mean either seamlessly meshing with the ideal or repudiating all that is other.

Silverman's formulation provides a perfect preamble to the seven-year old "Elizabeth" who, though horrified by the images of "black, naked women with necks / wound round and round with wire," reads the *National Geo-graphic* "right straight through" because, she says, she is "too shy to stop." While sitting in the dentist's waiting room among adult strangers, waiting for her "foolish, timid" Aunt Consuelo, the young Elizabeth is then seized by the revelation that she is "an *I*," "an *Elizabeth*," "one of *them*." "*Why*," she asks herself,

> should you be one, too?
> I scarcely dared to look
> to see what it was I was.
>
> ....
>
> I knew that nothing stranger
> had ever happened, that nothing
> stranger could ever happen.
> Why should I be my aunt,
> or me, or anyone?
> What similarities—
> boots, hands, the family voice
> I felt in my throat, or even
> the *National Geographic*
> and those awful hanging breasts—
> held us together
> or made us all just one? (*CP* 160–61)

"Elizabeth's" understanding of being an "I" is wholly dependent in this poem upon her articulation of what she despises in those around her: the foolish timidity of her aunt, and the black, naked, "awful hanging breasts" of the women in the *National Geographic*. Not only is Elizabeth's "I" expressed, typically, through its association with what she is not, but what makes those others other is revealed in this poem more clearly than in any piece that Bishop ever wrote.

Looking at the unpublished drafts of this poem, one realizes just how central the "struggle to see the otherness of the desired self, and the familiarity of the despised other" was for Bishop while writing "In the Waiting Room."[2] More worked over than any other portion of the poem, the description of the black women's breasts went through six variations before Bishop settled on the final version. While the breasts initially fill the speaker with awe, they soon terrify her as well. The penultimate version modifies the breasts as black just as it describes them as agents of horror. Working through variations of these phrases, Bishop eventually decided on the somewhat less explicit "Their breasts were horrifying" of the published version. What these drafts reveal is the degree to which the image of these black breasts both attracted *and* repelled Bishop, and the interlacing of blackness and femaleness at the core of this tension. As the recipient of such scrupulous attention, the black women's breasts clearly fascinated Bishop; like the young "Elizabeth," she can't stop looking at, or rewriting them, and according to the sequence of drafts, what the poet is initially cognizant of is the awe she feels in their presence. "Awe" is an especially revealing word in this context; according to Webster's, it is "an overwhelming feeling of reverence, admiration, fear, etc." It suggests from the outset that allure and aversion are inextricably bound, a suggestion that is borne out by the poem as a whole. These drafts also underline the contingency that exists for Bishop between race and gender and, given the focus on "I" in this poem, the central role this relationship occupies in the articulation of identity for the poet. With this understanding, it becomes all the more clear why earlier poems like "Cootchie" and "Faustina" are not only very much a part of Bishop's poetic project, but why it is that they are key in comprehending the issues at stake in her poetry at large.

The small "Elizabeth" indeed struggles with the apprehension of her self, and it is this struggle that charts the flow of the poem. While "suddenly" realizing the "similarities" that link her to Aunt Consuelo and "those awful hanging breasts," "Elizabeth" simultaneously sees such kinship as "'unlikely'"; it is just when she comprehends the connection between her self and others' that she grasps the lack that, paradoxically, fosters her identity, an insight literalized by the "sensation of falling / off the round, turning world / into cold, blue-black space" that permeates the poem. Understanding that the utterance of her "I" is enabled by her relationship to what she deems most horrific, "Elizabeth" describes the wholeness of being as, indeed, "unlikely." This understanding is what allows her to engage in Silverman's "productive look," to "recognize... herself precisely within those others to whom... she would otherwise respond with revulsion and avoidance." Both seduced and disgusted by the black women's breasts and the foolishness of her aunt, "Elizabeth's" "I" is simultaneously crystallized *and* destabilized through her interactions with them, and in turn, their images become linked; it is after the moments when "Elizabeth" spells most clearly her proximity to those she's repelled by that her "self" is most anchored ("I said to myself: three days / and you'll be seven years old....") and most uprooted ("...I was saying it to stop / the sensation of falling off / the... world"). Maintaining this tension throughout the poem, "Elizabeth's" "I" resists the comforting closure of self-sameness in favor of subtle and rigorous interrogation, never once losing sight of what it is "Outside" that keeps her safe, in the waiting room, while the wintry night and war-torn world spin ceaselessly around her.

Negotiating the passage between self and other without seeking respite in illusions of essential selfhood is what Bishop's productive look accomplishes in this poem. The horror that "Elizabeth" feels when gazing at the black women's breasts does not preempt her desire to keep looking—indeed, it fuels her desire to do so. Consequently, what began for Bishop as "awe" becomes, for "Elizabeth," a never-ending journey along the slippery path from ideality to abjection and back again. Constructing this journey around the act of "Elizabeth's" literal *looking* (at the magazine, and then at those around her) not only reminds us of the central place *perspective* always occupies in Bishop's work, but of the dynamic relationship between seeing and being that lies at the heart of Bishop's poetic. Like her ancestor, the Gentleman of Shalott, "Elizabeth" steers her course through revelation by way of her eyes: while Aunt Consuelo is "inside / what seemed like a long time," the young girl picks up the *National Geographic* and "carefully / studied the photographs." It is this act that leads her to the images of black breasts, and then, to her next look—"at the cover: / the yellow margins, the date"—in an effort, as Lee Edelman explains, "to contextualize the text so as to prevent her suffocation, her strangulation within it" (104). Throughout the poem, "Elizabeth" maneuvers her look to stop herself from "falling off / the round, turning world" or sliding into the seductions of binary opposi- tions. It is her "sidelong glance," for instance, that enables her to see "what it was I was" without looking "any higher"—allowing her, that is, to be both one of "them" and something quite separate from the "trousers and skirts and boots / and different pairs of hands / lying under the lamps." As readers, we are swept up by "Elizabeth's" eye, held aloft in the face of "blue-black space," and brought microscopically close to "awful black breasts," insides of volcanoes, and "rivulets of fire." The camera-like lens of "In the Waiting Room," with its abrupt turns and twists, its sudden zooms and cuts, con- stantly reminds us of the particular look—"Elizabeth's" look—through which we are viewing her world.

Building on Lacan, Silverman distinguishes the "look" from the "gaze" and the "screen," explaining that together, these three elements of the visual field shape the relationship between seeing and subjectivity. Like Lacan, Silverman maintains that the gaze is distinct from the look: the gaze can be thought of as the general "presence of others"—what gives us that feeling we all sometimes have of *being seen*, even when alone; it is in some senses transhistorical and unspecific. On the other hand, the look is psychic and individual, emanating from a specific human at a specific time and place. In Silverman's words, the gaze is the "inscription in the field of vision of the symbolic, of the necessity of every subject to be seen in order to 'be'"(222). The look, on the other hand, "is always finite, always embodied... although it does not necessarily acknowledge itself as such." Like "Elizabeth's" insa- tiable yet horrified eye, the look is "propelled by desire, and vulnerable to the lures of the imaginary" (134).

Of course the gaze and the look do not operate independently of one another any more than "Elizabeth" does in relation to those around her in the waiting room, and it is the screen that shapes this interdependency at any given time. The screen is where cultural and personal specificities come into play; it is akin to the ideological paradigms that permeate any viewing situation—the hovering historicity, for instance, of World War I and Worcester, Massachusetts, in "In The Waiting Room." The screen, "in other words, gives shape and significance to how we are seen by 'others as such,' how we define and interact with the agency to whom we attribute our visibility, and how we perceive the world" (Silverman 174). I side-step into these demarcations at this point because in order to comprehend the nature of "Elizabeth's" "I," I believe we need to understand the mechanisms of her vision as it manipulates that "self" into being. To look productively, one must be conscious of the distance between the gaze and the look, so that the ecstatic and illusory feeling of "wholeness" that happens when our look coincides with the gaze—that feeling of destined belonging and essential completeness—can be resisted, or at least repeatedly questioned.

Just as Bishop's speakers routinely tread the threshold between you-versus-me, frustrating the possibility of subsuming one in the other, "Elizabeth's" look remains slightly ajar from the greater gaze of those around her in the poem. Her "sidelong glance" emanates at an angle against the horizontal plane of "shadowy gray knees, / trousers and skirts and boots," so that just as it reveals the "similarities" between her "self" and the others, her look insures the distance between them as well. It is no coincidence that this kind of crooked vision brings us back to Bishop's earliest pieces, in which perspectives are skewed and subjects seem utterly fantastic.

And so we have "Elizabeth's" "I," the most self-assertive proclamation in all of Bishop's work, an "I" that does not engender a sense of jubilation, but rather, one whose very utterance begins the disorienting cycle of its own displacement. Such a gesture, however, cannot happen simply as a matter of choice; the processes of identification and idealization that shape one's subjectivity are for the most part unconscious. We cannot decide to idealize differently, then do so. Rather, we can only learn to look again, revising how we see in retrospect, with the hope that such efforts will transform the way we see in the future. Thus, Silverman claims that memory is what "implies more than anything else the possibility of effecting change at the level of representation" (190), and it is for this reason that the majority of poems from *Geography III* , Bishop's last book, are ones in which Bishop looks back to her past. As she herself observed in an essay of 1934, "We live in great whispering galleries, constantly vibrating and humming, or we walk through salons lined with mirrors where the reflections between the narrow walls are limitless, and each present moment reaches immediately and directly the past moments, changing them both" (98). Written during Bishop's senior year at Vassar, this bit of imagery bears an uncanny likeness to the world of poems Bishop had yet to produce. Acutely aware, as she once wrote, of "whatever it is one can never really see full face but that seems enormously important" (Stevenson 66), Bishop never gave up her efforts to articulate the "whispers" that urged her observant eye. From the Gentleman's mirrored world to "Elizabeth's" "sidelong glance," Bishop's look is so productive precisely because of its ability to shape what will come through what has come before.

Endnotes

1. For just a sampling of this rich body of work, see Lorrie Goldensohn, *Elizabeth Bishop: The Biography of a Poetry* (New York: Columbia UP, 1992); Victoria Harrison, *Elizabeth Bishop's Poetics of Intimacy* (Cambridge: Cambridge UP, 1993); and Mariliyn May Lombardi, ed., *Elizabeth Bishop: The Geography of Gender* (Charlottesville: UP of Virginia, 1993).

2. Vassar Special Collections, Box 58: Folder 58.14.

Works Cited

Bishop, Elizabeth. "Dimensions For a Novel." *Vassar Journal of Undergraduate Studies* 8 (May 1934): 95–103.

———. *The Complete Poems, 1927–1979*. New York: Farrar, Straus, Giroux, 1993. (Abbreviated in the text as *CP*).

Edelman, Lee. "The Geography of Gender: Elizabeth Bishop's 'In the Waiting Room.'" *Elizabeth Bishop: The Geography of Gender*. Ed. Marilyn May Lombardi. Charlottesville: UP of Virginia, 1993. 91–107.

Hammer, Langdon. "The New Elizabeth Bishop." *Yale Review* 82:1 (1994): 135–149.

Ostriker, Alicia. *Stealing the Language: The Emergence of Women's Poetry in America*. Boston: Beacon, 1986.

Silverman, Kaja. *The Threshold of the Visible World*. New York: Routledge, 1996.

Stevenson, Anne. *Elizabeth Bishop*. New York: Twayne, 1966.

Elizabeth Bishop and the Pragmatic Line in American Poetry

Helen McNeil
University of East Anglia

Abstract

Placing Elizabeth Bishop's poetry at the center of American poetics sets off a
massive cognitive shift, with Bishop becoming part of a newly visible pragmatic
line whose dominant figures are Dickinson, Stein, Moore, and Bishop herself,
while Stevens, Eliot, Frost, Ammons, Kumin, and Ashbery display some of that
line's elements. Using William James as a contributing, but not dominant, figure (and thus modifying Richard Poirier's argument in *Poetry and Pragmatism*),
this poetic pragmatism would have a strong epistemological drive, be empiri-
cally observational and skeptical, see writing as work, be metonymic, somatic
and gender-aware, accept repetition, and desire an embedding in the same sex
or known place.

This essay offers a speculation about a major epistemological drive of
American poetics: a poetics of pragmatism. I am defining this pragmatism
not only, or even mainly, as William James defined it, but rather according
to the consequences of a more immediate speculation: what happens to
American poetics if—speculatively—we place Elizabeth Bishop at its center? Amidst our awareness of ways in which Bishop did *not* seem to be part
of a poetic or cultural center—her sexuality, her long exile and involvement
in another culture, her distancing from institutions most of her life—it is
equally significant that many of the circumstances of her life do point to a
centering: the New England cultural background, the excellent education
culminating in Vassar, the creative friendships with other poets, and the ease
with which poems were published, grants gained, and prizes awarded all her
life.

Bishop at the center would open up an American poetic which would
have as its key figures Dickinson, Stein, Moore and Bishop. Indebted to
some of Emerson's thought, such as the essays "Self-Reliance" and "Experience," but not of consequence in Emerson's poetry, this poetic appears in
some aspects of Whitman (though less than one might expect), in some aspects of Stevens, in Frost, in Eliot (a striking and neglected presence), and in
Williams, though his vitalist materialism points elsewhere. It is dominant in
later Lowell, in Maxine Kumin and in A. R. Ammons. It operates in the less

discursive poems of Randall Jarrell, and in John Ashbery's poems from the 1970s onward.

Some of these writers have a direct connection with American philosophical pragmatism: Stein studied with William James in the early 1890s, the period of *Principles of Psychology* (1890), though leading toward *Pragmatism* (1907). Stevens also studied at Harvard in the era of James's dominance. Moore, brought up and educated in a tradition of duty and service, read and admired the pragmatist philosopher and educationalist, John Dewey. Charles Molesworth has even suggested that Chapter Two of Dewey's *Art as Experience* (1934) offers the best gloss on Moore's poetry (Molesworth *xx*). Bishop's intellectual friendship with Kenneth Burke linked her work with the psychological pragmatism of his earlier literary theory. When Bishop became friendly with Dewey in Key West in the late 1930s, she was strongly impressed by the similarities between his character and Moore's, particularly in their emphasis on democratic manners (Millier 146; *One Art* 365). This emphasis permits a rare nostalgic turn in Bishop's "Manners: For a Child of 1918," when the child is assured that a polite greeting is what has elicited the crow's correspondent "Caw!" (a passing automobile is less good-mannered). William James himself had argued that it is "temperament" (12), or as Stein put it in *Look at Me*, "the bottom nature in people" (86), rather than logic, which forms philosophy. For James, "strong temperamental vision" (12) served as the most potent premise for future philosophy.

The pragmatic line I am proposing is descended from the Puritan tradition (James unpleasantly uses rationalism and monism as sticks to beat Catholicism with), but it does not need concepts of original sin, elect and reprobate, and it sees nature as complex collections of objects and sensations with value in themselves, rather than as a Book of God to be read only as sign. (There are other links in Dickinson's readings of 17th century emblem books, and Moore's and Bishop's interest in 17th century descriptive prose.) Dickinson is the transitional post-Puritan figure establishing the modern pragmatic line, a line established without Romanticism. The pragmatic is not "nature poetry" as such since nature there is the object displayed in the discourse, and the effort of pragmatist poets is to emphasize the processes of discovery, which may or may not use nature as their means. Nor is it poetic realism, since that involves character and narrative, as in Crabbe's *The Borough*, Frost, and much of Browning (whom William James quoted approvingly). It overlaps with the poetry of experience traced by Roy Harvey Pearce in *The Continuity of American Poetry* and by Eric Homberger in *The Art of the Real: Poetry in England and America Since 1945.* The Bishop-centered poetics I am proposing is not the American sublime set forth by Harold Bloom, a poetics of strong transcendent idealism with Emerson as founder.

A Bishop-centered pragmatism would diverge from James's Ur-text and thus from Richard Poirier's *Poetry and Pragmatism,* a major study based on William James (and to which this and any new study of pragmatism must owe a debt). Poirier's argument, itself a riposte to Bloom and "theory," begins with Emerson, takes James as core figure, and continues through Stein, Frost and Stevens; two Dickinson poems are discussed, and Moore and Bishop do not appear. The example of Bishop, however, would make James only another example. Amid the similarities, many operating through the medium of Moore, some marked differences separate James and Bishop. Amongst them, for James the "plastic" and "malleable" (117) world in which man lives is "waiting to receive its final touches at our hands" (123). It is a passive material to be molded by the active male thinker or social reformer: "man engenders truths upon it" (213). Using etymology as philosophy, James emphasizes the derivation, and thus the assignment, of both his and C. S. Peirce's pragmatism from the Greek "pragma," meaning action (Peirce himself did not use the term "pragmatism"). The Jamesian pragmatist "turns toward concreteness and adequacy, towards facts, towards action and towards power" (51). The Jamesian conscious subject-position performs the Derridan logocentric poetics of presence. Like Emerson, James promoted his ideas through the medium of the public lecture, in which the idea is presented through the man. He defined pragmatism as "common-sense" action taken by the "tough-minded" man (13). Although Peirce's emphasis on language founded modern semiological theory, James has little to say about linguistic action, as distinct from oratory; these omissions are not accidental. When, a generation later, Stevens praised "the poem of the act of the mind" (240), he was arguably re-forming the Jamesian cognitive "act" into an aesthetic one: "the finding of a satisfaction...a man skating, a woman dancing"(240).

A Bishop-centered pragmatic poetic would be broadly empirical, have a strong investigative/epistemological drive, would locate materiality in an object-based real, and would embrace ordinary objects and the ordinariness of objects in a self-described "ordinary" language. Its conclusions would be hard-earned, partial and provisional. The refusal to assume an *a priori* or a definite logical method is shared by James and Bishop, but Bishop would differ from Dewey's version of pragmatism where it ascribes truth value to social practice. Bishop's pragmatism would see writing as work, engaged in a repetitive and gradually improving craft process. As literary text, the poem would tend towards the metonymic, emphasizing connection and contiguity. Its poetic line is prosy or eclectic; in semiological terms, it prefers the shifter to the icon; indeed icons become shifters. A Bishop-based pragmatic text would be somatic through body and corpus, using text as body even when its overt topic is not the body. Its heightened state is the moment of revelation (always only a brief moment), its lowered states those of depression, poverty, loss or mourning. Its expressive dangers are those of stylistic prosiness, flatness, and repetitiveness (though not in Bishop herself). It is generally anti-psychoanalytic, anti-confessional, a psychology of consciousness. It sees memory as ambivalently redemptive or regressive (recapitulatory), but where memory identifies or fixes the persona, it is seen as painful and threatening to self-realization: "You are one of *them*," as the horrified Elizabeth-child realizes in "In the Waiting Room" (*CP 160*). When "our knowledge is historical," as in "At the Fishhouses," even the less personal "we" must experience knowledge descended from the mother as cold, "flowing, and flown"(*CP* 66). For William James, however, continuity is necessary and new truth conservatively "marries old opinion to new fact" (35). The Bishop-based pragmatic poetic prefers the present to either future or past, and sees memory as at best an ambivalent repetition process. At worst, as for Stein, it is the crutch of externalized man: "memory is necessary to make them exist and so they cannot create masterpieces" (*Look at Me* 153).

Both in Poirier's James-based formulation and in one based more on Bishop, the pragmatic poetic is broadly empirical. It concentrates on experience, experiencing observation of the Stevensian "things as they are" (Stevens 165) as a virtue. It veers from the mimetic, however, in its characteristic questioning of conventions of what constitutes the real. It accepts a "tangled, muddy, painful and perplexed" real, as James put it in one of his darker hypotheses (17–18). In her earlier work, Bishop's wanderer must endure the stench and loneliness of the real: "carrying a bucket along a slimy board" ("The Prodigal," *CP* 71) or the "wretched, uneasy" city of "Varick Street," where "nostrils haired with spikes / give off such stenches" and "Our bed / shrinks from the soot" (75). An earlier essay of mine on Bishop emphasized ways Bishop altered "poetry of observation" (McNeil 395–426). She doesn't assume a fixed perspective and lacks the secure prospect, the possession of the landscape through perspectival security, the sense of an observing "I" who knows what it is or even knows the difference between the unknown and the repressed uncanny. In Bishop and Moore the "I" may operate through tentative renditions of tentatively described objects. (In Moore the "I" is usually absent.) In Bishop a calculated decision is sometimes made to risk inserting the looker as agent in the poem. In "Arrival at Santos," the speaker notes "So that's the flag. I never saw it before"(*CP* 89), implying that she has herself been absent from what the poem has been seeing in its first half. In "Brazil, January 1, 1502," the poem opens with "Januaries, Nature greets our eyes"(*CP* 91), subsuming the contemporary exploitative tourist into the sixteenth century conqueror, after which "we" are not mentioned again. In "Questions of Travel," the generalised "we" who ask "Should we have stayed home and thought of here?"(*CP* 93) stand in for all moderns from Pascal forward. Look does not necessarily lead to act, let alone public act, since it is a demanding and threatening process in itself. The eyes of the giant toad in "Rainy Season: Sub-Tropics" "see too much, above, below, and yet there is not much to see"(*CP* 139). In a somber take on the phenomenological turn of so much 20th century poetry, the toad-persona "sees" only what is necessary for his survival: his own skin and the poisons he secretes beneath it.

In Bishop's pragmatic poetic, the real does not have to be distinguished from the semiological tools used to pull it into meaning. Bishop's maps, geography and routes are semiologies of space. Her flags, semaphors, almanacs, encyclopedias, concordances, taxonomics are all relational systems, some with visual signing, some not. To these tools Moore had added natural history, advertising and vitrines, Dickinson had added botany, astronomy, geology, law, (also using geography), and Stein had stressed syntax, with the syntactic diagram (diagrammatic parsing) operating as a graphic re-enactment of her use of syntax as metonymic investigation. Relational systems relate to each other, and relate within, among, amidst a type or system: as figuration they are expressed through the indexical and the metonymic.

Bishop's "line" carries forward the Puritan respect for the humble object or creature (Francis Quarles's *Emblems*, Edward Taylor's "To a Wasp Chilled with Cold" or "The Spinning Wheel," Dickinson's "weed of summer" (657). The poet should be humble in the face of the object, a humility of enormous import, since endowing the gaze at the ordinary with impersonal value may offer to this century's image-dominated poetic a way to regain something of the spiritual and epistemological authority of earlier poetics. The humility should not call attention to the personal performance of private or public virtue. But the lower the object, the better? Bishop offers the "cloud-dump," the "fifty-two miserable small volcanoes"(*CP* 162) of "Crusoe in England," the eponymous "Faustina, or Rock Roses," and the miserable dog-mother of "Pink Dog." The worthlessness of the object or place can even be paraded, as in Stevens's "The Man on the Dump" and "An Ordinary Evening in New Haven," or A. R. Ammons's *Garbage*, a book-length *tour de force* calling attention to the vast, death-defying capacities of English syntax, syntax being, as Stein knew, the organizer, connector and creator of "emotional balance" (134–5) in what would otherwise be mere heaps of jumbled and repetitious words. Conglomerations of bits and bumps and dumps are often comic in Bishop, with discrepancies sweetly rather than fatally ironic. "Curious creatures.... / Look at that, would you," as the driver says in "The Moose" of the moose as big as his bus (*CP* 173*).* Looking at the mother-moose in all her reality gives the passengers "a sweet sensation of joy" (*CP* 173) and turns them into parts of a whole (a community), a delicious leap which, however, can last only a moment of time. "Dim / smell of moose" takes the perception back to the intimate sense registers of the nursling; but "acrid / smell of gasoline" (*CP* 173), immediately following, returns us sharply to the alienated darkness of the road ahead.

When objects are charged with meaning by the poet, that meaning can overflow. When an agony of desire projects all power onto the object that has stimulated it (or an object that looks like or smells like or feels like the original object of desire), then the object becomes a fetish. Ungranted, ungiven, unnourishing, the classic Kleinian part-object is fetishized by the supplicant speaker of Bishop's "O Breath": "that loved and celebrated breast / silent, bored really blindly veined"(*CP* 79). In Freudian terms these objects charged with erotic need are "cathected" objects. In "Crusoe in England" again, those clouds and volcanoes and exotic turtles are inspirations for the picturesque, but they are turned into garbage by Crusoe: unhonored by him, they become repetitiously, tediously interchangeable. This detritus is an aspect of mourning, and as the poem develops, even that is shown to be an evasion (an anaesthetizing through undervaluation, undersemiotizing as it were) of even deeper grief. Crusoe's hopeless desire for Friday erupts and attaches itself to the only surviving object, the knife that "reeked of meaning, like a crucifix" (again, smell, the key sense for fetishism). Bishop's extreme condensation assumes the phallic, the sacred, the aggressive, the sacrificial, the ritual and pushes them all into the ordinary knife-tool—until these projections are weakened by time and the fetish becomes appropriately a relic to be placed in a museum/mausoleum. Denied his beloved, denied even his projection of meaning into a fetish object, denied his perversion and his inversion, Crusoe is ready to die. Meanwhile inversion is being enacted in the male-for-female, north-for-south inversions of the poem, and the play on "invert" as a term for homosexual.

Money is perhaps the quintessential semiological system by which meaning is imposed on otherwise meaningless objects—mass-produced decorated oblongs of paper. We constantly say of objects, "How much is this worth?" meaning, how much money does it cost to possess it. William James spoke provocatively of wanting only "the cash-value of words" (32)—words as exchange, as shifters, worth what you trade them for. He saw his work as "an account of truths in the plural...having only this in common, *that they pay"* (104). Applied to marketplaces where more than words are traded, James's pragmatism has unsurprisingly become the philosophy of commonsense capitalism. Both the medium of exchange and the commodity are fetishized. Bishop, who often discusses exchanges and trade-offs, invokes money as fetishized object in poems such as "Going to the Bakery": "I give him seven cents in *my* / terrific money"(*CP* 152). Also, of course, both Bishop and Moore benefited from the long-term generosity of Louise Crane (*One Art* 372, 499, 514 and *passim*), whose family made money by making money, the Crane Paper Company, then and now, being manufacturers of U.S. currency. Wallace Stevens's comment in *Opus Posthumous* that "Money is a kind of poetry" was not entirely—I suspect not at all—tongue in cheek. In "Novices," Moore combines an attack on rigid subject-positions with an appreciation of the differing meanings of money. She criticizes "the little assumptions of the sacred ego confusing the issue" so that egotists "do not know 'whether it is the buyer or the seller who gives the money' / an abstruse idea plain to none but the artist, the only seller who buys, and holds on to the money"(60). Money is standing for poetry here. Stein, who wrote several short essays on money, felt that "the thing that differentiates man from animals is money" (333). There is an acute, and underestimated, awareness of such exchanges and valuations in Dickinson, Stein, Frost and Stevens as well as in Bishop and Moore.

If the object is ordinary, then the way it is figured in the poem should be ordinary too. In Bishop's pragmatist poetic, poetry is seen as work, as it is in William James. Dickinson, Moore and Bishop really worked at their poems, all three being inveterate revisers. Since the labor towards knowledge is always incomplete, death is when "You can't derange, or re-arrange / your poems again," as Bishop said of Lowell in "North Haven"(*CP* 189). Because poetry is a never-ending job or process, the means can be modest, even apparently inadequate, as in "Large Bad Picture." This isn't the "right" way or the "best" way to represent the Strait of Belle Isle, but it will do; looking at the "scribbled" birds, "One can hear their crying, crying" (*CP* 11). In the generic "Poem" the "little painting (a sketch for a larger one?)"

by the same great-uncle suffices to bring on Bishop's perception: "Heavens, I recognize the place, I know it!"(*CP* 176). Such redemption of an otherwise lost past is one of the roles of high art, but the amateur painting is nevertheless more than good enough. In fact, its bare adequacy is the same as what we get from all of life: "The little of our earthly trust. Not much. / About the size of our abidance"(*CP* 177). I wonder if this provisionality is why Bishop never took her own artistic talent beyond the watercolor sketch and the fragile vitrine of fetishes. The point is practice, as in the comforting clang of the blacksmith that means sanity in "In the Village."

Bishop internalized her characteristic relationships between work, duty, pleasure, poetry and love early in her career. In a long letter to Marianne Moore, Sept 1, 1943, she opens with a disquisition on kinds of mangoes and the proper manner of eating them (she has just sent Moore a gift of some mangoes). Then she discusses her single week of "war work," where she was paid, she proudly notes, $5.04 a day, although her work proved inadequate. She has been moved by the "gaiety" of the workers. "I am infinitely impressed with the patience of these men fiddling day after day with those delicate maddening little instruments"(*One Art* 115). The men are constructing binoculars, a seeing device. Then she writes of the beauty of prisms, and offers an anecdote about buying green eyeglasses with pink rims for Flossie the housekeeper, that color combination being much in fashion, she remarks condescendingly, among the Negroes. Since Moore seems to her very much part of a society, she dismisses Moore's complaint of "solitude." Yet her own poetic work, like her war work, feels not quite good enough: "I want so badly to get something good done to show you" (116). If she can't write well, she declares, perhaps she should take up "lens grinding" instead (a practice leading to disciplined sight). The letter closes with another gift to her surrogate mother, Moore, an image of "nine white herons in a group" (116) which Bishop has seen recently. It is very much a Moore image, reminiscent of "Nine Nectarines." They are reassuringly all white, and they constitute a group. Some of the phrases in this letter recall other Bishop poems, most interestingly the "maddening little women" always just out of reach in "Brazil, January 1, 1502" (*CP* 92), but the heron image occupies the climactic position in the letter that a closing revelation takes in some poems. It is the gift of "rainbow, rainbow, rainbow!" that comes in "The Fish"(*CP* 44) after the work of fishing and the ethical act of returning the fish. In this letter Bishop is fishing for the right work and giving to mother the fish she has found (the gift image of fish-eating herons).

The work of looking, feeling, and writing in this tradition is necessarily repetitive. This practice separates it from (or makes it a particular case of) the general phenomenological move of 20th century poetry. The repetition is of situation as well as of act, as in Dickinson: "How many times these low feet staggered —" (88), "There's a certain Slant of light" (118), "A Prison gets to be a friend —" (324). There are literally hundreds more. Dickinson was less committed than Bishop to enactment or repetition as a means to knowledge, preferring the leap or jolt that breaks out of the mold: "To make Routine a Stimulus / Remember it can cease.—" (529). Near the end of his credo in "Notes Toward a Supreme Fiction," Stevens accepts that possibly the "exceptional monster" of the modern is not the "man-hero," but "he that of repetition is most master" (406). Both Dickinson and Bishop, though, represent agony by a break in the solid floor of the normal and a shift into the aural register: "As all the Heavens were a Bell, / And Being, but an Ear," writes Dickinson (129) of the "Funeral, in my Brain" (128). For Bishop the "break" from earthly routine comes from above as the sky-piercing shriek of the living-dead mother in "In the Village," or Aunt Consuelo's "*oh!* of pain" assaulting the child until "I—we—were falling, falling" downward, Alice-like, into the black hole of shared femininity (*CP* 160). And while repetition is security, Bishop knows it can become obsession, as in "Sandpiper," in which the bird goes mad trying to grasp the infinite detail of every single subtly different Blakean grain of sand.

Stein's declared goal of exact representation of inner and outer reality now seems wildly improbable, but Stein embraced and enacted the pre-Freudian optimism of her age, believing that it was entirely possible to attain exact linguistic equivalents of thought. Something of that optimism survives in Moore and Bishop, even though both wrote in the era of Freudian dominance: the Saussurean separation of signifier and signified seems to operate positively for them, as linguistic instrumentality. The Poundian ideal of convergence between sign and signified has been turned down. The operative distinction here is that the pragmatist poet isn't fixed on the image, and thus with the image's heritage as the lowest rung on the metaphoric ladder. Bishop and her line are involved with the necessarily metonymic process of connecting images and lessons. The failure of language ever to convey inner or outer reality fully is less devastating if all that is being attempted is a good try, as in Stevens's characteristic titles: "Notes Toward...," "Parts...," "Anecdote...," "Thirteen Ways...," "Certain Phenomena...." At the end of her birthday poem, "The Bight," Bishop comments knowingly "All the untidy activity continues, / awful but cheerful"(*CP* 61). Those last two ordinary, repetitious words took great revisionary effort. In Bishop, even in her darkest moments, language does not betray its user. These writers are not tormented by the dread of a fragmented linguistic inheritance, as were the Pound of "Mauberley," the Eliot of "The Waste Land," and late Yeats. Do consciousness of work and consciousness of practice keep the tool in good shape?

The Bishop-centered poetic would be somatic. That is, it would see the text as being bodily, being in some way a body. When William James quotes approvingly Whitman's line "Who touches this, / touches a man" from "So Long!" in "Songs of Parting," he significantly misquotes it as "Who touches this book touches a man" (24), thereby suppressing Whitman's hint that the text is a body. From Emerson to James there has been a loss, as Emerson's eye/aye/I shrinks to the "I" of James. Although much of his argument centers on the need to find truth in the perception of the everyday, whose "contents" "simply *come* and *are*" (36), James is unvisual, indeed non-sense-orientated. Critical thinking about the Bishop-pragmatist writers has been moving towards the somatic, as in the 1970s essays by Catherine Stimpson and Elizabeth Fifer, and more recent work by Lisa Ruddick, Marilyn May Lombardi and Anne Colwell (though Colwell emphasizes personification). In Stein, as Ruddick notes, *Tender Buttons* is about objects and/as food, either male-centered, seeing food as ritual sacrifice, or female, where food is nourishment. One might add that the quintessential object/food of the "tender button," the clitoris, pleasures the suckling and the feeder almost excessively, as when Stein appears to ask her "aider" or helper Ada/Alice: "whow stop touch, aider whow, aider stop the muncher, muncher munchers" (*Look At Me* 176). A later Stein text such as *Lifting Belly* seeks to embody through its form the bodily action of lesbian sex without mimetically representing it.

In Bishop, the key somatic texts have to be "Song for a Rainy Season" and "The Shampoo," with their blissful dissolution of barriers creating a state which is definite enough, real enough, to be at ease in a loose but distinct poetic form. The great binaries of inside/outside, self/other, now/then are dealt with through the smaller binary of wet/dry, offering evidence that yes, there are times when everything is wet. Maxine Kumin's equivalent (another "wet" poem) is "Morning Swim," in which the body-beat, the poem-beat and a hymn-beat are one. The body is also thematized and formally re-enacted in less joyous Bishop poems, such as "O Breath," where the line can't catch its breath and gasps in the caesura which breaks the line into self/other, beginning/end. Yet even there in the anguished lesbian relationship which ends with the cry "within if never with"(*CP* 79), the speaker can enter (has entered) into that which she already is—a woman. She is already metonymically "within" the female and the poem, even if she can never be "with" the bad breast and the cold mistress of which it is part. The line refers partly to the sex act as the poem enacts the doomed effort of the lover to get far enough inside the beloved. It also specifically integrates its homoerotic desire with a poetic of insideness. Put another way, I think it can be argued that there is a link between a somatic poetic, its metonymic expression and the homoerotic. This is not to say that a more transcendent or transformative poetic is hostile to the homoerotic—look at Hart Crane's "Voyages" or Ovid's *Metamorphoses*. What I am speculating here is that the process of seeking knowledge through observations or situations in which the speaker is part of a group, or the objects are, or where the process of investigation itself yields connections, creates a metonymic poetic and a potentially recapitulative thematics of being one of the group, the type, the sex that you also desire.

While it may not ever be verifiable I think Bishop's renowned formal command forms part of this recapitulative process: A(1) desiring A(2) but needing the poem for that desire to become act. Even in highly artificial repetitive forms such as the sestina or villanelle, Bishop always seems natural, a naturalness achieved without a rhetoric of organic form. Because she is able to experience these artificial forms as "embodied" forms, she uses them to express some of her most painful topics: the entrapment of the child in the magic prison of maternity in "Sestina," and the terrible recognition in "One Art" that a life in art may be only a cover for a life devoted to loss. In the latter poem it seems that the reassuring shape of the repetitious rhyme is what lets her speaker force herself to "*Write* it!," knowing the poem must end (*CP* 178). Conversely, Bishop's more prosy poems always look contained, without extraneous matter. Form itself is made to work for her as a way of being inside what you are also forming, a bodily self-making—there's a meaningful pun available here on *corpus* making.

In Bishop's somatic poetic the desire is to become truly embedded in the world, the society, the sex you already are in, by knowing it through poetic inquiry. Rarely is the process smooth or complete, but Bishop uses it again and again as her epistemological tool, knowing that its conclusions are provisional and its ecstasies time-bound. A number of her poems address the uncanny recognition that one is mysteriously one of/part of. The uncanniness lies in the within-the-sameness, as in "In the Waiting Room." As Helen Vendler has noted, "the work of domestication of the unfamiliar" is constantly repeated in Bishop, even as "the guerilla attack of the alien" springs "from the very bulwarks of the familiar"(36, 37). Her female uncanny is not usually dissociative, though an alienating procedure like tourism's ocular re-enactment of political and sexual imperialism can provide alienation enough. The courageous leap Bishop took in settling in Brazil with Lota de Macedo Soares had to do with acting on her recognition that her ostensible "home" as a New England woman in New England or a poet on the scene in New York was insufficient. She realized that she could be more at home with another woman, Lota, in an everyday (though highly cultured) domesticity, itself embedded in a humid, warm-climate culture whose body rhythms are expressed by the pervasive beat of the samba (as Carmen Oliveira has reminded me, Bishop collected samba records). To my knowledge Bishop is the only major American writer to have chosen a long-term partner from another language and another culture. Cherished by Lota, Bishop nevertheless had to creatively *make* her home in Brazil. When her poetry nears sentimentality, it is because she is pushing the value of the integrated beyond what the images bear: "Filling Station," maybe, or her enthusiasm for the primitive, or her immense admiration for *The Diary of "Helena Morley."*

One of the distinctions between poetic realism and the enhanced pragmatism I have sought to outline has been pragmatism's lesser emphasis on character and narrative. The narrative movement of the Bishop persona seems the minimum needed to track the image and perception shifts, and it often came late in her compositional process. "The Moose," for example, stayed stuck as an image collection for at least sixteen years until Bishop completed the connecting narrative (*One Art* 334, 568; Millier 463–4). Bishop's narrative acts as connectivity more than as a way of showing destiny or will (it does show chance). The exception to this rule is not really an exception: the Brazilian ballad poems, in which Bishop adopts the position of impersonal narrator recounting the adventures of her protagonists, or has them speak for themselves. All indigenous, these figures operate within the magical world of Brazilian folklore. Although a foreign chronicler can never be wholly free from accusations of exploiting the exotic, I do think Bishop succeeds in writing bi-cultural folk tales. In "The Riverman," the speaker, initiated by the male river dolphin and the female serpent, Luandinha, becomes himself an oddly metonymic spirit of place, dissolving into the river he swims in. In " The Burglar of Babylon," the homeless migrants to Rio are housed by the poem, and the rhythm can be described as ballad meter (from the Anglo perspective) or samba rhythm (from the Brazilian perspective).

Crediting Bishop and Stein with a somatic pragmatism does not mean that by virtue of being women writers, or gay women writers, they have automatic access to some kind of somatic pastoral, in which mind and body are happily melded. I do think it is the case that when writers' bodies or sexualities are non-normative, they are more likely to foreground these in the investigative or formal drive of their work. When the somatic feminism of French feminist theory of the 1970s argued for a privileged relation between the female body and female authorship, Luce Irigaray proposed an analogy between the lips of the labia and the multivalent feminine text as her rebarbative response to the historic privileging of the phallus as creative analogue. The analogy between mythicized physiology and literary excellence would seem doubtful in both cases, but Irigaray's argument in *The Sex Which Is Not One* for the energy released "when the goods get together" resonates in contemporary lesbian theory of the woman-centered text for the female audience. Although the inner audience for Bishop's poems was often female, she did follow the critical orthodoxy of her generation, seeing poetry *per se,* poetry as a cultural concept, as ungendered. Within the activity of being and desire inside the Bishop poem, however, that pattern of desiring what you already are, addressing what you already are, coming to know yourself by the philosophical application of metonym, is dominant. There is no generic and cross-cultural "feminine," and the woman writer need not necessarily place being a woman at the center of her work. At the same time, though, the way in which the "I" of the poem is constructed is always, to a greater or lesser extent, reacting with the social and individual construction of gender. The epistemological push of these writers runs along lines—or in awareness of lines—of gender.

William James never claimed that his pragmatism was the result of any straightforward drive of the will, a "hard" consciousness, as it were. Truths arise from vagueness, from the mental fringes (Poirier, 41–44), a consciousness very like Bishop's "perfectly useless concentration" (Schwartz and Estess 288)—though James is distinctly less "self-forgetful" (288) than Bishop. Like everyone else of her generation, Bishop knew Freudian terminology, but even though she was attracted to surrealism, she never considered the unconscious dominant, preferring, as she wrote to Anne Stevenson, "the always more successful surrealism of everyday life" (288). After a brief experience with Freudian analysis (Millier 174), Bishop benefited from an apparent Kleinian analysis (that is, she found a feminine-orientated view of child-mother relations). She also read Klein's *Envy and Gratitude* (*One Art* 371). Bishop's work responds well to Kleinian readings, as reported in Joanne Feit Diehl's paper on "The Bight" at the 1996 Bishop-Ashbery conference in Reading, England. Because a Kleinian reading doesn't depend upon the analyst extracting latent content from the "unaware" text, it can blend almost seamlessly with a practical-criticism reading in a poet whose literary psychology involved the re-presentation through contiguity of forces other-wise liable to burst out imitatively.

If the female-informed pragmatist tradition is not dominated by the un-conscious, it is also anti-confessional. As in Bishop's now-famous remark to Frank Bidart, she wanted " closets, closets, and more closets" (Fountain and Brazeau 327), and not only because of justified fears about the profes-sional consequences of "coming out." Like Stein, she didn't want to be de-fined by an external "identity." In all these writers, male and female, a quest for self-knowledge is (relatively) non-performative and it is not necessarily associated with purging guilt. In my view, one major motive for this relative discretion is awareness of the futility of any literary striptease. Self-revela-tion inevitably calls attention to the inaccuracy and incompleteness of the information revealed to the audience, and it makes brutally obvious the limi-tations thrown up by the dramatic persona of the lyric speaker. Telling all is just another pose. We can never know all about Diana and Charles, Sylvia and Ted, Emily and Sister Sue (or was it Reverend Wadsworth or Editor Bowles)—or Elizabeth and Lota. While our present cultural appetite for intimate revelations appears to be unslakeable, stardom and celebrity are based upon a projection of the audience into the imaginary vessel of the protagonist. The more the work of the poem visibly takes place in the shap-ing of the text, however, the less available such a projection becomes. Al-though Bishop's persona is often indistinguishable from the biographical Bishop, her "I" doesn't plead for us to take its side: "The Country Mouse" was rejected by Bishop because she detected autobiographical pleading in it, and indeed it has been used as direct evidence by her biographer Brett C. Millier (19–23, 27–8). In addition, the coding of any intimate message in Bishop makes for much of the force of the message that is sent. When the way in which knowledge is gained comprises a lot of that knowledge, the literary embodiment *is* the knowledge: take it away and not much is left.

In Bishop, the past certainly yields knowledge for a generalized "us," usually revealed by working through an emotionally charged image, such as the "bad" pictures in "Large Bad Picture," "Cape Breton," and "Poem," or by a return to a known place. The past is a source of enforced group identity, as in the child entrapped in her shared femaleness in "In the Waiting Room" or the somber family groupings in "First Death in Nova Scotia." The past is also cultural inheritance: Bishop's April 4, 1962 letter to Lowell recognized just how deeply embedded both poets were in historic New England culture: "I hadn't realized just how purely the stream has run." (*One Art* 407). (Lowell had just sent her the ms. of *For the Union Dead* and Bishop had just read

Lucy Larcom's *A New England Girlhood.*) When the past is so powerful that it overleaps history into myth, the Bishop persona seems crushed rather than mythically enlarged. Myth means that the past, like a revenant, takes over the present. "Sestina" is set in the present: then, now and forever, it is:

> *Time to plant tears*, says the almanac.
> The grandmother sings to the marvellous stove
> and the child draws another inscrutable house. (*CP* 124).

The child is not going to escape from that uncanny house.

The present tense of the endlessly repeated fairy tale set outside history "once upon a time" implies a timeless wisdom in the contents, but as a fable of modern identity it also implies blockage, repression, acting-out. At the Worcester Bishop conference in 1997, Barbara Page's paper on Bishop's revisions pointed out that verb tense was a major revision issue for Bishop. As Page's paper showed, in most of the drafts of the unfinished poem, "Salem Willows," Bishop used the past tense in the poem's final lines, so that while "I" rode on the carousel, Aunt Maud "sat and knitted / and knitted, waiting for me." If, however, the poem closes in the present tense, as in two drafts, so that Aunt Maud "sits and knits / and knits, waiting for me," then its use of memory would be, as Page noted, more mythic and less historical. The "past" passage actually allows Bishop both a past-historic and a past-continuous, while the more strongly locked-in chaismus of the present-tense version (X and knits / knits and Y) knits the child into the aunt's repetitive pattern—into the fate her family is spinning for her. The passage reminded me forcefully of Sylvia Plath's decision at the end of "The Disquieting Muses" in which, after a series of classical, fairy-tale and autobiographical recastings of memory, the speaker ends the poem re-enacting the situation of the fairy-tale curse at Sleeping Beauty's cradle. The Fates or evil aunts are still looming over the child-adult's bed as the poem ends. Plath chose to recapitulate the child position so that her poetic myth re-enacts a timeless anger against the mother .

If I sought earlier to distinguish a Bishop-based pragmatism from any somatic pastoral, I must conclude with a warning about any idealizing of the pragmatic line. Returning to the William James model, James's buoyantly assertive pragmatism serves as a tonic against depression. In the less positivist usage of the poets I have been discussing, the pragmatist position offers a way forward in the basically untenable mess of life. In the pragmatic mode, the fetishizing and the rubbishing of objects are mirrored perversions to keep time and death at bay. If the high note of this pragmatist poetic is the unforced insight or the moment when work becomes play, then its low note is dullness. The everyday is not necessarily interesting. Objects are not necessarily interesting. Partial solutions smell middle-aged. An ungenerous look at much American poetry of the Fifties to Seventies would see much of such sub-pragmatism, including the almost obligatory sub-surrealist twist that ends many such poems.

Why not, then, use myth? One of the most important discoveries of poetry and fiction of the past twenty-five years has been that myth has survived the ruin of the transcendent. Economical and transformative, it even survives exploitation by dominant cultures as an instrument of their domination. Bishop does use myth, though usually bracketed by immersion in a "magical" other culture. But there is a fundamental difference of purpose. Myth is about the way things are and have always been, with each reader or writer making their own version. Bishop-pragmatist mode is about working out for oneself—never assuming a fixed self—some temporary home where some truth might be found, however partial, painful or untransformed. As Bishop notes in "North Haven":

> and the White-throated Sparrow's five-note song,
> pleading and pleading, brings tears to the eyes.
> Nature repeats herself, or almost does:
> *repeat, repeat, repeat; revise, revise, revise.* (*CP* 188)

Works Cited

Bishop, Elizabeth. *The Collected Prose.* Ed. Robert Giroux. New York: Farrar, 1991.

_____. *The Complete Poems, 1927–1979.* New York: Farrar, 1986.

_____. *One Art: Letters.* Ed. Robert Giroux. New York: Farrar, 1994.

Burke, Kenneth. *Counterstatement.* New York: Harcourt Brace, 1931.

_____. *Towards a Better Life.* New York: Harcourt Brace, 1932.

_____. *Permanence and Change.* New York: New Republic, 1932.

Colwell, Anne. *Inscrutable Houses: Metaphors of the Body in the Poems of Elizabeth Bishop.* Tuscaloosa: U of Alabama P, 1997.

Dickinson, Emily. *The Complete Poems.* Ed. Thomas H. Johnson. London: Faber, 1975.

Fifer, Elizabeth. "Is Flesh Advisable? The Interior Theater of Gertrude Stein," *Signs* 4.3 (1979): 472–83.

Fountain, Gary and Peter Brazeau. *Remembering Elizabeth Bishop: An Oral Biography*. Amherst: U of Massachusetts P, 1994.

Homberger, Eric. *The Art of the Real: Poetry in England and America Since 1945*. London: Dent, 1977.

Irigaray, Luce. "When the Goods Get Together." *The Sex Which Is Not One*. Ithaca: Cornell UP, 1985.

James, William. *The Works of William James*. Ed. Fredson Bowers. Vol I: *Pragmatism*. Cambridge: Harvard UP, 1975.

Lombardi, Marilyn May, ed. *Elizabeth Bishop: Geography of Gender*. Charlottesville: U of Virginia P, 1993.

_____. *Elizabeth Bishop's Poetics: The Body and the Song*. Carbondale: Southern Illinois UP, 1995.

McNeil, Helen. "Elizabeth Bishop." In Vendler, *Voices and Visions*, 395–426.

Millier, Brett C. *Elizabeth Bishop: Life and the Memory of It*. Berkeley: U of California P, 1995.

Molesworth, Charles. *Marianne Moore: A Literary Life*. New York: Athenaeum, 1990.

Moore, Marianne. *Complete Poems*. London: Faber, 1968.

Pearce, Roy Harvey. *The Continuity of American Poetry*. Princeton: Princeton UP, 1960.

Peirce, Charles Sanders. "How to Make Our Ideas Clear." *Collected Papers*. Cambridge: Harvard UP, 1931–58, Vol. 1, 248–271.

Poirier, Richard. *Poetry and Pragmatism*. Cambridge: Harvard UP, 1992.

Ruddick, Lisa. *Reading Gertrude Stein: Body Text Gnosis*. Ithaca: Cornell UP, 1990.

Schwartz, Lloyd and Sybil P. Estess, eds. *Elizabeth Bishop and Her Art*. Ann Arbor: U of Michigan P, 1983.

Stein, Gertrude. *Look at Me Now and Here I Am: Writings and Lectures 1909–45*. Ed. Patricia Meyrowitz. Harmondsworth: Penguin, 1978.

Stevens, Wallace. *The Collected Poems*. New York: Knopf, 1965.

Vendler, Helen. "Domestication, Domesticity and the Otherworldly." In Schwartz and Estess, 32–48.

_____, ed. *Voices and Visions: The Poet in America*. New York: Random House, 1978.

"Obstinate Questionings...Equivocal Replies": Wordsworth and Bishop as Orphans

Gary Fountain
Ithaca College

Abstract

In their writing both William Wordsworth and Elizabeth Bishop show them-selves struggling to master disorientation and fear from childhood abandonment as a means to crossing the threshold into a certain adult comfort and independence. The child is the unsettling mother and father of both poets. Wordsworth's "spots of time" from *The Prelude* demonstrate the restorative powers of childhood experiences to fortify the grieving mind. Bishop's dialogue with these various Wordsworthian consolations snakes its way through her poetry, concluding with Bishop's most sceptical, modernist examination of the Romantic poet in "Crusoe in England."

In August 1936, Elizabeth Bishop was vacationing at West Falmouth, Massachusetts, reading Wordsworth's *The Prelude* (along with St. Augustine's *Confessions* and Amiel's *Journals*), and, at the age of 25, undergoing a crisis of poetic confidence. As she wrote to Marianne Moore, "[T]his heaped-up autobiography is having extreme results, maybe fortunate. I cannot, cannot decide what to do....I feel that I have given myself more than a fair trial, and the accomplishment has been nothing at all" (August 21, 1936. *One Art* 45). Perhaps, Bishop thought, she would abandon poetry altogether, and turn to medicine or biochemistry.

Moore's encouragement helped to keep Bishop on a literary track, yet Moore could not exorcise the presence of Wordsworth, who hovered in the background throughout Bishop's career. When Bishop was preparing *North & South*, her first book of poems, for publication fifteen years later, she characterized herself to Robert Lowell as a "minor female Wordsworth—at least I don't know of anyone else who seems to be such a Nature Lover" (July 11, 1951. *One Art* 222). In *Geography III*, Bishop's final book of poems, there is a playfully provocative yet significant reference to Wordsworth, when the stranded Crusoe of "Crusoe in England" quotes from "I Wandered Lonely As a Cloud":

"They flash upon the inward eye,
which is the bliss..." The bliss of what?
One of the first things I did
when I got back was look it up. (*CP* 164)[1]

In this late poem Bishop asks, What consolation is there in memory? Is there bliss in solitude? Was Wordsworth right?

As a number of shrewd critics have already noted, Wordsworth weaves his way through Bishop's poetry in a complex dialogue over issues of personal identity, landscape, imagination, and memory. Robert Pinsky has analyzed the famous Mt. Snowdon scene from "Book Fourteenth" of *The Prelude* as a means to showing how Bishop forges a "vehemently personal identity for herself" (6–8) in "In the Waiting Room." Willard Spiegelman has argued that "Bishop's best poems show her to be an epistemological poet in the tradition of William Wordsworth and S.T. Coleridge," for whom "landscape...is a major means of human relationship and connection" ("Landscape" 203, 222). Spiegelman also feels that Bishop's "qualifying scepticism" ("'Natural Heroism'" 29) can playfully soften the impact of heroic imagery, internalize conflict, and make learning itself an heroic enterprise in her poetry:

> Where Bishop surpasses Wordsworth, however, where her egoism is simply less intense, is in her continual insistence on the need for symbiosis: mutual support, rather than epiphanies wrought by otherworldly visitors, is the key to natural polity, as well as piety. (41)

Most recently, Bonnie Costello has traced Bishop's sceptical, modernist dialogue with Wordsworth over the transcending powers of recollection. After noting references to Melville, Darwin, Genesis, and Wordsworth in "Crusoe in England," Costello writes, "This is a poem less about the poet's ability to transform personal experience to mythic and epic dimension than about the nature of memory as both personal and cultural" (208).

In addition to similar aesthetic and philosophical preoccupations, Wordsworth and Bishop share an important biographical link: both were orphaned in childhood, and the sense of dislocation resulting from these traumatic events was a source and subject of their writing. It is difficult to imagine Bishop reading *The Prelude* during that confusing summer of 1936 in West Falmouth, when she turned to Marianne Moore for maternal advice, without an eye for Wordsworth's descriptions of family loss. In contrast to Bishop, Wordsworth experienced early years of family security before his mother died when he was nearly eight, and his father when William was thirteen. Bishop's father died before she was one year old, an event that sent her mother into a spiraling mental illness, observed by the young Elizabeth herself, that led to her being institutionalized when Bishop was five. What must Bishop have thought of Wordsworth's secure reaction to his own mother's death: "The props of my affection were removed, / And yet the building stood, as if sustained / By its own spirit!" (2.279–281).[2] The dramatic dislocations of childhood are present throughout *The Prelude* and are echoed, in comparable scenes of chaotic disorientation and tentative accommodation, in Bishop's poetry: "[t]he questioning shrieks, the equivocal replies," to quote her Crusoe in "Crusoe in England" (*CP* 164). In their writing Wordsworth and Bishop show themselves struggling to master the fears from childhood abandonment as a means to crossing the threshold into a certain adult emotional mastery and independence. The child is the unsettling mother and father of both.

What might Bishop the lyric poet have noted and found engaging about family displacement in the autobiographical epic *The Prelude*? First, given the importance of the act of observation in Bishop's aesthetic, there is the drama of Wordsworth's eye, the way in which the dynamic interaction of sight and landscape correlates with the predicament of separation. In *The Prelude* the dramatic loci for this drama are the famous "spots of time" from "Book Twelfth," which, in this narrative of his personal growth, Wordsworth positioned to follow the disillusionment of his experience in France following the Revolution, when he left a lover and a child behind in a guilt-ridden, adult re-enactment of his own childhood loss of family. These spots of time are designed to demonstrate the restorative power of childhood experiences to fortify the grieving mind. What are the elements of Wordsworth's emotional hardiness?

The first spot of time (12.208–87), which Wordsworth positioned chronologically before the death of his father, anticipates this loss through its action, to prove that the young William had been schooled by nature to endure suffering, to master his emotions from an early age. Wordsworth describes himself with a surrogate parent, James, "[a]n ancient servant of my father's house /... my encourager and guide" (229–30), who coaches him in an adult enterprise, riding a horse: "while yet my inexperienced hand / Could scarcely hold a bridle, with proud hopes / I mounted" (226–28). William is separated from James (both a foreshadowing and a re-enactment of the death of his father, for it was when he became lost in bad weather while returning from a business trip that Wordsworth's father caught his fatal cold) and, disoriented and insecure, awkwardly stumbles while leading his horse down a rocky hill. He finds death at the bottom, a "mouldered" (237) gibbet, where a murderer had been hanged for public viewing, with the criminal's name carved in the grass kept "fresh and visible" (245). From this living death, William flees back up the hill, where a tentative accommodation with his fears is enacted. As he gazes over the landscape for James, his lost parent, he identifies images of his own grim vexation surrounding him: an exposed "naked pool" (249), a "melancholy" (265) beacon on the hill above Penrith, and a human correlative for his conflict with fear, a struggling girl with a pitcher on her head, who "seemed with difficult steps to force her way / Against the blowing wind" (252–53). One also senses that, in addition to the cold comfort of this bleak gathering of common spirits, this "visionary dreariness" (256) offers Wordsworth a certain comfort from the act of reckoning itself—visual mapping locates him and stays his emotional disorientation.

In Wordsworth's description of the death of his father (12.288–335), his eye stays grief in a similar fashion. Wordsworth shows himself in a state of restless anticipation as a boy at boarding school, waiting for his father's groom to arrive with the horses to take his brothers, Richard and John, and him home for the Christmas holiday. Attempting to gain some control over his anxiousness (mirrored in a landscape that is "[t]emptestuous, dark, and wild" [298]), William climbs a crag that allows him to survey the two highways by which his father's servant might arrive. And in this place, an eerie game of anxiety and comfort, anticipation and control, is played out in a visual conflict between the near and far, the hidden and the revealed, as the mist alternatingly blocks and reveals the vista. Willliam locates around him a similarly dislocated family: an oddly vulnerable ("a naked wall" 299), isolated ("a single sheep" 300), and ill-fated ("blasted hawthorn" 301) group of "companions" (302) to share his "[f]everish and tired, and restless" (289) mood. William finds some comfort in their shared vulnerability: he feels "half sheltered by a naked wall" (299). And such modest comfort provides him with a certain stamina after his father's death during this vacation: "these were kindred spectacles and sounds / To which I oft repaired, and thence would drink, / As at a fountain" (324–26). Bishop, as we shall see, enacts something of the same cold reckoning in "In the Waiting Room."

For the "minor female Wordsworth," the male Wordsworth offered powerfully masculine assertions of the self, an egotistical sublime, in the face of family loss. In the other famous childhood scenes in *The Prelude*, Wordsworth pictures himself re-enacting his drama of childhood mastery through a perverse inversion, when he becomes the source of death, the "fell destroyer" (1.318, 1805 version) as he snares woodcocks, steals birds trapped by others, and robs a bird's nest. Can one overcome one's grief and anger over family loss by becoming death's or destruction's agent oneself? In this scene William scuds along the hilltop like the frosty wind of wintry death that "snapped / The last autumnal crocus" (309–10), trapping his own birds, guiltily breaking with the rules of the adult world by stealing from others' traps, and violating his "better reason" (319) by giving in to youthful disorder. Something of the same hubris is present in another famous scene when he steals a shepherd's boat, empowered by new, mature mastery—in the 1805 version he rows the stolen boat "like a man who moves with stately step / Though bent on speed" (1 .387–88)—and an adult male sexual prowess: "lustily / I dipped my oars into the silent lake, / And, as I rose upon the stroke, my boat / Went heaving through the water like a swan" (373–76). There are primal resonances of the terror of independence (that is, dislocation) from the parental in both scenes: in the former, like Adam listening to the Devil in the Garden and then hearing for the first time God's footsteps, William hears "undistinguishable motion, steps / Almost as silent as the turf they trod" (324–25) following him after he robs a trap; in the latter, he loosens the umbilical tether, emerges from the womb-like cave, with its domestic quality as the boat's "usual home" (359), and his conscience projects onto Black Craig, rising suddenly in his vision above Ullswater, a striding Cyclops of his own guilt and fear that halts his odyssey down the lake. Yet the presence of an adult, however shadowy and ambiguous, has been established in both scenes. Through Crusoe, her impotent Ulysses returned from his odyssey, Bishop will finally parody this drama of masculine will.

In another scene from *The Prelude*, when the young Wordsworth hangs on the edge of a cliff, pilfering a bird's nest, his domestic drama finds its most unsettling psychological rendering in a description of the radical disorientation with which we shall see Bishop clearly identifies. "[T]he mother-bird" has built "her lodge" (327, 328) on the edge of the cliff for protection from predators—predators like Wordsworth himself, who descends the cliff to the nest. One senses from the passage that Wordsworth's description of his fear from the danger of the plundering also parallels the frightful experience of the plundered, that Wordsworth was re-experiencing his own dislocations as he perpetrated this one. What happens when one is plucked from the mother's or father's lodge, or the mother and father are taken away? One feels, as Wordsworth felt hanging from the cliff, a deep isolation in the world: "ill-sustained" (333), "[s]uspended" (334), and "alone" (336) are his terms.

Also, one's sensibilities become disassociated: one questions the world, one's place in it, and the nature of reality. And so the natural world seems different, perhaps otherworldly, to Wordsworth as he precariously hangs there: "With what strange utterance did the loud dry wind / Blow through my ear! the sky seemed not a sky / Of earth—and with what motion moved the clouds!" (337–39). Such is the thrill from having "mastered" loss through inverted re-enactment.

In "In the Waiting Room," Elizabeth Bishop describes herself encountering this disorienting yet curiously exhilarating world of the strange: "I knew that nothing stranger / had ever happened, that nothing / stranger could ever happen" (160). In effect, she slips off the Wordsworthian cliff, as she feels herself "falling, falling, / ....falling off / the round, turning world / into cold, blue-black space." Her mastery comes from a complex distancing, an orienting similar to that of Wordsworth in his childhood scenes. However, Bishop's mother left her a legacy of haunting psychological chaos, not a sustaining structure reinforced by nature's visionary dreariness.

In "In the Waiting Room," the young girl has been left in the waiting room by her parental surrogate, her James, Aunt Consuelo, "a foolish, timid woman." The room is "full of grown-up people" (159), and the six-year-old child tentatively asserts herself as a member of this modest society: "(I could read)." This reading takes her outside of this domestic gathering of "arctics and overcoats / lamps and magazines," to the larger adult world (here represented by the *National Geographic* she is reading) that is disorienting, even threatening: men and women look alike ("Osa and Martin Johnson / dressed in riding breeches"), people kill and consume one another ("A dead man slung on a pole"), children are misshapen by adults ("Babies with pointed heads / wound round and round with string"), women are strangled and distorted ("women with necks / wound round and round with wire"), and adult femininity and maternity seem ghastly ("Their breasts were horrifying"). As Elizabeth reads about this confusing world in the magazine, "Suddenly, from inside, / came an *oh!* of pain / —Aunt Consuelo's voice—" (160) and this cry precipitates Elizabeth's falling off the cliff.

In this cry of pain, Elizabeth comes upon her equivalent of the "gibbet," the living presence of death, at the bottom of the hill toward which the young Wordsworth descended when left to himself by the negligent James. Her aunt's cry echoes for Elizabeth with the demented screams of her mother before she was committed to the asylum in Dartmouth, Nova Scotia, screams recorded in Bishop's short story "In the Village" as "in memory—in the past, in the present, and those years between" (251). In the poem, the girl immediately recognizes her aunt's cry as her own: "it was *me*: / my voice in my mouth" (160). Her deepest fear in this poem is that she will become insane herself, fully disassociated from reality in a world of her own disorientation, for Elizabeth recognizes that she herself has no discernible means of control over this menacing scream: "a cry of pain that could have / got loud and worse but hadn't." The scream finds correlatives in the volcano that Elizabeth views in the *National Geographic*, welling up from within, and also the "big black wave" (161) that she feels overpowering her.

Falling into "cold, blue-back space" is the ultimate disorientation for Bishop, as it is for Wordsworth, for space without land and gravity has no north or south, no up or down, no direction. "In the Waiting Room" offers Bishop's primer in orienting herself in this indeterminate landscape. First, she locates objects to hold on to, in effect to regain the grip on the cliff or position herself on the hilltop. In spite of how alienating the people in the waiting room are, she willfully asserts that she is one of them: "But I felt: you are an *I*, / you are an *Elizabeth* / you are one of *them*." She relocates herself by reducing the people to non-threatening features: "I gave a side-long glance / —1 couldn't look any higher— / at shadowy gray knees, / trousers and skirts and boots / and different pairs of hands...." She accommodates herself to the equivocal and the strange: "Why should I be my aunt / or me, or anyone? /.... how 'unlikely'...." And she admits to a lack of control: "a cry of pain that could have / got loud and worse but hadn't" (160–61). Then a geographical positioning, Bishop's version of Wordsworth's "visionary dreariness" on the top of that stark hill, takes place:

> Then I was back in it.
> The War was on. Outside,
> in Worcester, Massachusetts,
> were night and slush and cold,
> and it was still the fifth
> of February, 1918. (161)

Here are an empirical place and a date. That there is a war going on seems cold comfort, but it is at a remove, and it suggests a distancing of the battle that has been going on within and the violences of the adult world of the *National Geographic*. And the "cold, blue-black space" has been both reduced to the cold night and isolated, distanced outside.

In these terms, Crusoe, of "Crusoe in England," is Bishop's ultimate surrogate of family displacement, an adult-child emotionally paralyzed in a world of dislocation. He has been shipwrecked, cut off from the land of his ancestors, and there is no reference to family or friends from England, for Crusoe seems to have forgotten them. He is as isolated when he returns home as he was when he inhabited his barren island—isolation is the condition of his life. In fact, Crusoe represents the family dislocation Bishop experienced when Lota de Macedo Soares, her lover and mother figure, the only adult with whom Bishop established a relationship that substantially offset her abiding sense of family loss, died in 1967. Lota appears obliquely in the poem, in Bishop's description of Friday, who has died, with its glancing references to homosexuality and youthful, uninhibited ease. Lota had put Bishop into contact with the simple, the affectionate, the unaffected, the childlike in herself: "Friday was nice. / Friday was nice, and we were friends. /.... He'd pet the baby goats sometimes, / and race with them, or carry one around." Friday was also "[p]retty to watch; he had a pretty body" (165–66).

Inserted by Bishop into this bleak landscape of Wordsworthian dreariness, Crusoe is capable of only infertile, solipsistic behavior. The opening description of a volcano forming a new island of basalt—a "black fleck" that echoes the appearance of the ghost ship in "The Rime of the Ancient Mariner" ("A speck, a mist, a shape, I wist!" [Coleridge line 153])[3]—is an image of sterile self-creation, and the "naked and leaden" volcanoes on his island suggest Crusoe's sexual impotence and frustration. No lusty robbing of nests and boats here; no Wordsworthian, masculine, assertive sublime. The only sense of home that this displaced narrator creates is from an ironic self-pity, a family of the self: "'Pity should begin at home.' So the more / pity I felt, the more I felt at home" (163). Crusoe can induce moments of self-forgetfulness with home brew "and dizzy, whoop and dance among the goats" (164), but this artificial gaiety is merely a "miserable philosophy" (an affecting statement from the perspective of Bishop's alcoholism). When he tries to transform the place itself, to create something new by dyeing a baby goat "bright red / with my red berries," he merely duplicates his own sense of alienation: "And then his mother wouldn't recognize him." In a perverse, frustrated re-enactment of childhood abandonment like that presented by Wordsworth in his scenes of trapping birds and stealing eggs), Bishop's Crusoe dreams of "slitting a baby's throat" (165).

It is fitting that in the course of this dramatic description of the paralysis of loss Bishop holds one of Wordsworth's most affirmingly solipsistic poems up to scrutiny. When a bed of snail shells reminds Crusoe of irises, which remind him of daffodils, he is unable to remember significant words from "I Wandered Lonely As a Cloud": "'They flash upon the inward eye /

which is the bliss...' The bliss of what?" (164). For Crusoe there is no bliss in solitude. There is no romantic freedom of wandering like a cloud in this island that seems "a sort of cloud dump" (162). Wordsworth's daffodils that "stretched in never-ending line / Along the margin of the bay" have mutated into Crusoe's nightmares of "infinities / of islands, islands spawning islands" (165). The task of "registering... / ...their geography," the reconnoitering and positioning of the self in these places, is an endless, exhausting, and seemingly meaningless task.

"Crusoe in England" ends with a flurry of references to Wordsworth, as if Bishop were feverishly searching for a perspective of his that might work, or, rather, were purging her poetic house of his specter. The dialogue with the world of nature—Wordsworth's "obstinate questionings / of sense and outward things" (142–43) from the "Intimations Ode"—finds its mocking echo in the monotonous, incomprehensible baas and cries of the goats and gulls: "The questioning shrieks, the equivocal replies." In those shrieks one also senses the lingering screams from Bishop's mad mother. The imaginative, synaesthetic power of the eye to see "into the life of things" (49) and to hear "the still, sad music of humanity" (91) of "Tintern Abbey" is expunged, for when Crusoe looks at his knife that "reeked of meaning, like a crucifix" from experiences on the island, he notices, "Now it won't look at me at all / The living soul has dribbled away / My eyes rest on it and pass on" (166). And, finally, the hardy, enduring primitives of Wordsworth, like the Leech-gatherer of "Resolution and Independence," present earlier in Bishop as the old fisherman in "At the Fishhouses," finds its despairing final incarnation in her Crusoe, her Ancient Mariner, who is unable to locate any consolation in the past and whose life is floating "[a]lone on a wide wide sea" (Coleridge, "Rime" 598) of emotional stasis. "How can anyone want such things?" Crusoe wonders, referring to a local museum's request for artifacts from his years on the island. The artifacts seem dead to him. And their lifelessness leads him to the numbing concluding lines of the poem: "—And Friday, my dear Friday, died of measles / seventeen years ago come March." The bracing, Wordsworthian power from recollecting endured suffering fails to console. Crusoe is left with only haunting, unabated loneliness. Such is Bishop's unequivocal, final reply to her obstinate questioning of Wordsworth's consolations for childhood loss.

There is also a curious way in which "Crusoe in England," seemingly a dramatic monologue set in the eighteenth century, is adrift on a sea of timelessness. Crusoe, of course, anachronistically quotes from Wordsworth's poem a century before it was written. Bishop's poem, which seems like an historically rooted document, thus is unmoored, as the mode of the poem playfully mirrors its thematic concern with disorientation. There is the range of other historical voices, as well. The complaints of Tennyson's Ulysses, frustrated on his home island of Ithaca after his adventures, echo in Crusoe's voice; yet Bishop does not allow her mariner another round of adventures. And as much as Wordsworth's scenes of visionary dreariness seem present in the desiccated landscape of Crusoe's island, Bishop's vision is more severe, filtered through the modernist lens of the wastelands of Eliot. So in this poem Bishop disabuses herself of a range of literary consolations: Romantic (egotistical and masculine sublimity, memory), Victorian (masculine willfulness), and modernist ("fragments...shored against...ruins" [Eliot, "The Waste Land" 431]). None of the poetic echoes in this poem can make the center hold. Dare we say, finally, that in "Crusoe in England," being an orphan becomes Bishop's metaphor for inhabiting a decentered post-modern world, *"wherever that may be?"* ("Questions of Travel").

Endnotes

1. All Bishop quotations in this study, unless otherwise noted, are from *The Complete Poems 1927–1979*. Page numbers are cited.

2. All quotations in this study from *The Prelude* are from the 1850 edition, unless otherwise noted. Line numbers are cited.

3. Quotations in this study from poems other than *The Prelude* by Wordsworth and from poems by authors other than Elizabeth Bishop are from Margaret Ferguson, et al., *The Norton Anthology of Poetry*.

Works Cited

Bishop, Elizabeth. *The Complete Poems, 1927–1979*. New York: Farrar, Straus, Giroux, 1986.

———. "In the Village." *The Collected Prose*. Ed. Robert Giroux. New York: Farrar, Straus, Giroux, 1984. 251–274.

———. *One Art: Letters*. Ed. Robert Giroux. New York: Farrar, Straus, Giroux, 1994.

Costello, Bonnie. *Elizabeth Bishop: Questions of Mastery*. Cambridge: Harvard, 1991.

Ferguson, Margaret, Mary Jo Salter, and Jon Stallworthy, eds. *The Norton Anthology of Poetry.* 4th ed. New York: Norton, 1996.

Pinsky, Robert. "The Idiom of a Self: Elizabeth Bishop and Wordsworth." *The American Poetry Review.* January/February (1980): 6–8.

Spiegelman, Willard. "Elizabeth Bishop's 'Natural Heroism.'" *Centennial Review* 22 (1978): 28–44.

———. "Landscape and Knowledge, The Poetry of Elizabeth Bishop." *Modern Poetry Studies* 6 (1975): 203–24.

Wordsworth, William. *The Prelude. 1799, 1805, 1850.* Eds. Jonathan Wordsworth, M. H. Abrams, and Stephen Gill. New York: Norton, 1979.

Elizabeth Bishop and Carlos Drummond de Andrade: "Opening of tin trunks and violent memories"

Maria Lúcia Milléo Martins
Universidade Federal de Santa Catarina

Abstract

Part of a larger study on Bishop and Drummond, this paper aims at exploring a significant portion of the "verse/universe" common to the two poets that is the recreation of memories of childhood and family. Of the seven poems by Drummond translated by Bishop, four evoke this theme. By the time Bishop was translating Drummond, in the sixties, she was not only writing about her own memories but coincidentally living in the same city as the Brazilian poet, experiencing like him a similar condition of exile from her origins. This essential exile confirms that only "in the creative time/space distance," can the violence of our memories be converted into words, becoming thus legitimately poetic memories.

The quotation in the title is taken from "Travelling in the Family," one of Elizabeth Bishop's first translations of Carlos Drummond de Andrade. As in "Infancy," "Family Portrait," and "The Table," also translated by Bishop, Drummond invites us on a fascinating trip to the past, filled with memories of childhood and family portraits. Coincidentally, the period in which Bishop translates these poems, during the sixties, is also the time for her to rethink and write about her own origins. Poets of memory, Bishop and Drummond confirm that the poetic memory not only nurtures itself from "the violence" in which things "inhabit us," but depends on an essential temporal and spatial distancing to be converted into words; this is a time when, as Costa Lima suggests, "we no longer see and from what is no longer seen we create another distinct visibility" (82). Inspired by this concept of poetic memory, this study will examine how both poets recreate memories of childhood and family and will investigate possible resonances of Bishop's reading of Drummond in her own work.

Bishop's interest in Drummond's poems about his lineage can be traced back to a strange resemblance in circumstances common to both poets' origins. Explaining the origin of Drummond's name, a crossbreeding between Scotch ancestry and *mineiro* blood, Bishop points out that "oddly enough, *mineiros*, people from the state of Minas or "the mines" are often compared to the Scots." Besides topographical similarities between the two regions, she observes that in both "life is hard, narrow, religious, and often fanatical."[1] Topography apart, one can say that "oddly enough" these same features could be found in Bishop's own origins, in the small community of Great Village, Nova Scotia, and in New England.

But of course Bishop's motivation to write about her origins cannot be attributed only to her readings of Drummond. There are previous facts to be considered as, for example, Bishop's translation of *Minha Vida de Menina* [*The Diary of "Helena Morley"*], one of the first readings recommended to her soon after her arrival in Brazil. Bishop certainly found similarities between the memories in the diary and the memory of her own past, correspondences between places that seem to resist changes and the action of time itself, and similarities in scenes and events "odd, remote, and long ago, and yet fresh, sad, funny, and eternally true" (*Diary* x). Bishop's interest in autobiography was also stimulated by Lowell's work, especially *Life Studies*. Her first childhood memoirs—"Gwendolyn" and "In the Village"— surely owe a good deal to Lowell's influence.

Out of all the circumstances that may have drawn Bishop to revisit the landscape of her childhood, one is also common to Drummond: an essential exile from this landscape. In a coincidental move to Rio—Drummond leaving his hometown, Bishop her country— the two poets join in this fantastic trip to the past, "re-collecting" their myths of family and childhood. In the case of Drummond, Affonso Romano de Sant'Anna explains that it is the poet's "non-adjustment" in the metropolis that leads him to "search for refuge in images of the past, compelling him to return emotionally to the stable world of childhood" (72–73). Adapting Sant'Anna's sentence to Bishop's case, one could say that it must have been her temporary sense of adjustment in Brazil that allowed her the necessary balance to return emotionally to the unstable world of childhood. The sense of adjustment referred to here concerns both Bishop's "golden years" in Lota de Macedo Soares' two homes and her contact with a provincial side of Brazil, resembling the Great Village of her childhood.

In "Infancy," written when the distancing is only temporal, since Drummond still lives in Minas, the poet recreates the family atmosphere, trying to recover the inner voice of the boy who "alone under the mango trees, . . . read the story of Robinson Crusoe." The poem, in Bishop's translation, begins:

My father got on his horse and went to the field.
My mother stayed sitting and sewing.
My little brother slept.
A small boy under the mango trees,
I read the story of Robinson Crusoe,
the long story that never comes to an end.

At noon, white with light, a voice that had learned
lullabies long ago in the slave-quarters—and never forgot—
called us for coffee.
Coffee blacker than the black old woman
delicious coffee
good coffee. (87)[2]

Isolated from the other family members immersed in their routine, the boy compensates for his exclusion by insulating himself in the imaginary world of reading, living Crusoe's adventures. In a Lacanian perspective, Silviano Santiago associates the boy's attitude to the way a child recognizes his/her double in the mirror, an "imaginary" recognition of him/herself in the "image" of the other (50). Thus, the vicarious experience of the book would function as a kind of mirror through which the boy discovers his own identity. Santiago also observes that, in reading texts of others, "each one of us makes of the reading one's text and inserts oneself on the margin as context" (49). In this peripheral position the boy experiences, therefore, a double exile as he is at the same time withdrawn from his own story in the family circle and living a foreign adventure that is not his. In the end of the poem, no longer the boy, but the adult exiled from his childhood, the poet ponders "[he] didn't know that [his] story / was prettier than that of Robinson Crusoe," wisely reinstating the centrality of his own story.

The child in "In the Waiting Room" experiences a similar situation of exclusion as her eyes plunge not into an imaginary world but into the fantastic realism of the February 1918 *National Geographic*. As in Drummond's poem, it is a familiar voice—"Aunt Consuelo's voice"—that brings the child back from her detachment in the world of reading to the reality of the waiting room. The child's perception of herself in relation to these two worlds is, however, far more complex than that of the boy who, despite his isolation between mango trees, lives the cozy routine of a solid family structure. For the child in the waiting room, the presence of the aunt (as the presence of the grandmother in "Sestina") is the silent substitute for the absent family structure.

Curiously, in an unpublished poem with a very similar poetic form to Drummond's "Infancy," Bishop reproduces the same sense of family unity:

> Father's in the studio
>   Painting hill and dale,
> Mother's in the sitting-room
>   Typing up a tale,
>
> Hepple's in the pasture
>   Looking at the rabbits:
> Fairies, keep them in good health
> And faithful in their habits![3]

Like the boy in "Infancy," the child here contemplates the family universe but, unlike him, she does not insert herself in this universe.

Perhaps the lack of a solid familial ground on which to stand explains in part the child's intense perception of herself in the waiting room which Lloyd Schwartz identifies as "the frightening awareness of her own individuality and equally frightening awareness of her common humanity" (137). "How 'unlikely,'" says the child, unable to conciliate the sudden consciousness of her own isolation and identity with a disturbing world of similarities and "horrifying" differences making us "all just one":

> Why should I be my aunt,
> or me, or anyone?
> What similarities—
> boots, hands, the family voice
> I felt in my throat, or even
> the *National Geographic*
> and those awful hanging breasts—
> held us all together
> or made us all just one?
> How—I didn't know any
> word for it—how "unlikely"... (*CP* 161)

Whereas in Drummond's "Infancy" both the enchantment of the voice "that had learned / lullabies long ago in the slave-quarters" and its generosity in calling for coffee restores human warmth to the boy, Aunt Consuelo's voice in Bishop's poem seems only to echo the child's contained cry of pain, a "feeling of absolute and utter desolation," as Bishop describes it in her prose memoir, "The Country Mouse."

In discussing the theme of Crusoe in Drummond's poem, Santiago curiously identifies the old black woman with the figure of Crusoe's companion, Friday. The pleasure of the woman's songs and coffee would provide the boy with a second paradisiacal space that, like the first—the paradise of the "island of reading"— would compensate for the isolation from the family. Santiago calls this space the "space of the non-familial where the company denied by [the boy's family] is offered to him by others who surround him with affection and dedication" (55). One could say that Bishop's Friday, a recognized allegory for Lota, has a similar function:

> Friday was nice.
> Friday was nice, and we were friends.
> If only he had been a woman!
> I wanted to propagate my kind,
> and so did he, I think, poor boy.
> He'd pet the baby goats sometimes,
> and race with them or carry one around.
> — Pretty to watch; he had a pretty body. (*CP* 166)

Friday surely is this other solitary fellow, a companion and also a sexual being, although unable to procreate. But Friday would sometimes "pet the baby goats... / and race with them, or carry one around." If not home in the sense of a real family, Friday could at least offer Crusoe the atmosphere of an improvised home by adoption. "—Pretty to watch; he had a pretty body," concludes the poet, unable to separate the pleasure of contemplating Friday's imitation of a family from the sensuality of his body in movement. Like the voice of the black old woman in Drummond's poem, it is this gesture of Friday that restores to Crusoe the coziness of a family atmosphere.

In the improvised home of her adult life and having the necessary distancing from the landscape of her childhood, Bishop can finally reopen the old family album. Among the photographs, Bishop also discovers old chromographs and unfinished paintings like little cousin Arthur's:

> Jack Frost had started to paint him
> the way he always painted
> the Maple Leaf (Forever).
> He had just begun on his hair,
> a few red strokes, and then
> Jack Frost had dropped the brush
> and left him white, forever.

Then, proceeds the poet, "The gracious royal couples / . . . / invited Arthur to be the smallest page at court" but

> how could Arthur go,
> clutching his tiny lily,

> with his eyes shut up so tight
> and the roads deep in snow? (*CP* 126)

In this final image of Arthur, it is as if the poet completed Jack Frost's work, giving the unfinished painting in memory the last stroke.

This last stroke, however, neither for Bishop nor Drummond redeems them from the corrosion of their memories, but perpetuates them yet more. These memories remain like that "immortal sob of life" resisting the corrosion of portraits in Drummond's poem "The Dead with Overcoats," which Bishop attempted to translate but never published:

> In the corner of the parlor there was an album of intolerable photographs,
> yards tall and infinite minutes old,
> and everyone stopped to the joy
> of ridiculing the dead in overcoats.
>
> A worm began to gnaw the indifferent overcoats
> it gnawed the pages, the dedications, and even the dust of the portraits.
> Only the immortal sob of life bursting,
> bursting, from those pages, — that it didn't gnaw.[4]

Also indifferent to the action of time, "the teakettle's small hard tears" continue "to dance like mad on the hot black stove," under the "clever almanac," in Bishop's "Sestina." Originally titled "Early Sorrow," "Sestina" privileges in its form the essence of what is perpetuated through time—the house, the figure of the old grandmother, the stove, the almanac, the tears. But the form demands repetition; what stands out in the poem is movement, as if memory refused to freeze a final image. Thus, the poem ends with the child drawing "another inscrutable house."

In this fantastic trip to the past, there is also the impulse to return to unresolved family relations, as Drummond does in "Travelling in the Family," in the long walk with "the shadow of his father" in the desert of Itabira:

> ...The shadow
> proceeded slowly on
> with that pathetic travelling
> across the lost kingdom.
> But he didn't say anything.
>
> I saw grief, misunderstanding
> and more than one old revolt
> dividing us in the dark.
> The hand I wouldn't kiss,

> the crumb that they denied me,
> refusal to ask pardon.
> Pride. Terror at night.
> But he didn't say anything. (59)

Later, at the end of the long walk, father and son finally join in a "ghostly embrace," a silent moment of mutual recognition:

> Eye-glasses, memories, portraits
> flow in the river of blood.
> Now the waters won't let me
> make out your distant face,
> distant by seventy years. . .
>
> I felt that he pardoned me
> but he didn't say anything.
>
> The waters cover his moustache,
> the family, Itabira, all.

Victoria Harrison calls attention to curious resemblances between this poem and an unpublished poem by Bishop entitled "For Grandfather." Harrison observes that whether Bishop wrote her first draft of her poem before or after she translated Drummond's, the "affinities are haunting" (177–178). Coincidences start by the idea of the imaginary trip, Drummond's father leading him through the "desert of Itabira," Bishop's grandfather taking her through the "snows of the North Pole." The "distinct silences" in both poems mingle with the anguish of the monologue and the desire to communicate with the old patriarchs. The radical difference is that, in Drummond, there is reconciliation; in Bishop, the grandfather remains out of reach:

> You'll catch your death again.
>
> If I should overtake you, kiss your cheek,
> its silver stubble would feel like hoar-frost
> and your old-fashioned, walrus moustaches
> be hung with icicles.
> Creak, creak. . . frozen thongs and creaking snow.
> These drifts are endless, I think; as far as the Pole
> they hold no shadows but their own, and ours.
> Grandfather, please, stop! I haven't been this cold in years.[5]

While in Drummond's poem the "waters" cover the father's "moustache," in Bishop's, "icicles" hang on the grandfather's. Like the embrace, the "waters" assure the presence of affection and seal the silence of mutual recognition and forgiveness. Inversely in Bishop, the "hoar-frost" or "icicles" indicate that affection is unreconcilable. The search nonetheless continues: "These drifts are endless. . . . Grandfather, please, stop! I haven't been this cold in years."

Regarding "affinities," the case of Bishop and Drummond seems to reach far beyond the domain of family and origins or the occasional play of resemblances in isolated poems. Borrowing W. S. Merwin's expression to define theories of influence, I would say that the case of Bishop and Drummond is "much more complicated than that." It involves not only the process in which Bishop assimilates Drummond in translating him and incorporating his experience into her work (the complicated play of texts), but also the two poets' coincidental task to translate a common universe—the Brazilian everyday, the landscape, and culture, or the strangely similar universe of childhood (the complicated play of texts and contexts). Still, in the field of "affinities," I would include what Drummond calls in a letter to Bishop "affinity of spirit."[6] But how to talk of things of the "soul" stepping in so secular a terrain as literary criticism? Avoiding this risk or the vain intent to unveil what Drummond had in mind, I would interpret this affinity in very earthly terms: a coincidental predestination to "be *gauche* in life." The expression is from Drummond's "Seven-Sided Poem," translated by Bishop. Originated in the tradition of the *poètes maudits, gaucherie* means in a broad sense incompatibility with the world. The term that appears again in the poem "The Table" is translated by Bishop as "awkwardness." Having its origin in the two poets' extremely shy nature, their *gaucherie* is confirmed in their relation with the world—the family world and the world at large—to ultimately become a significant trait in their art. It is worth pointing out that this *gaucherie* is a personalistic trait and, as Mikhail Bakhtin reminds us, "personalism is not psychological but semantic" (170).

Common to the two poets is also the "personalistic" perception that "we carry things," as Drummond writes,

> framework of our life,
> rigid iron fence,
> in our most anonymous cell,
> and a ground, a laugh, a voice
> incessantly resound
> in our deep walls. ("A Ilusão do Migrante" 21)[7]

But, he adds, it is only

> in the creative time / space distance,
> at the margin of pictures, documents,
> when more than we exist
> things exist violently: they inhabit us
> and look at us, they stare at us. Contemplated,
> submissive, we are their pasture,
> we are the landscape's landscape. ("Lanscape: How to Make It" 73)

Endnotes

1. This passage is from Bishop's notes for her translations of Drummond. Elizabeth Bishop Collection, Vassar College Library, Series Poetry, Box 58, Folder 12.

2. All poems by Drummond translated by Bishop cited here are gathered both in her *Complete Poems* and in *An Anthology of Twentieth-Century Brazilian Poetry* which she co-edited with Emanuel Brasil. The latter is the source for this and subsequent quotations. (Middletown, Conn.: Wesleyan UP, 1972).

3. Elizabeth Bishop Collection, Vassar College Library, Series Poetry, Box 65, Folder 20.

4. Bishop's unpublished translation of this poem is held with her notes for her translations of Drummond. Elizabeth Bishop Collection, Vassar College Library.

5. Elizabeth Bishop, "For Grandfather," Elizabeth Bishop Collection, Vassar College Library, Unpublished Poetry, Box 65, Folder 65.19.

6. Elizabeth Bishop correspondence with Carlos Drummond de Andrade, 29 April 1969, Elizabeth Bishop Collection, Vassar College Library, Correspondence, Box 1, Folder 1.5.

7. Both this and the subsequent translation are mine.

Works Cited

Andrade, Carlos Drummond de. "A Ilusão do Migrante." *Farewell.* Rio de Janeiro: Editora Record, 1996. 20–21.

———. "Landscape: How to Make It." *Metamorphoses.* 4.3 (1996): 72–73.

Bahktin, Mikhail. "Toward a Methodology for the Human Sciences." *Speech Genres and Other Late Essays.* Eds. Carolyn Emerson and Michael Holquist. Austin: U of Texas P, 1986. 159–172.

Bishop, Elizabeth. *Complete Poems, 1927–1979.* New York: Farrar, Straus, Giroux, 1983.

———. Trans. *The Diary of "Helena Morley."* New York: Farrar, Straus, Giroux, 1957.

———. Elizabeth Bishop Collection. Vassar College Library, Poughkeepsie, New York.

Harrison, Victoria. *Elizabeth Bishop's Poetics of Intimacy.* Cambridge: Cambridge UP, 1993.

Lima, Costa. "Carlos Drummond de Andrade: memória e ficção." *Carlos Drummond de Andrade and His Generation.* Eds. Frederick G. Williams and Sergio Pachá. Santa Barbara: Jorge de Sena Center for Portuguese Studies, 1986. 66–82.

Sant'Anna, Affonso de Romano. *Drummond, o gauche no tempo.* Rio de Janeiro: Lia, Editor S. A., 1972.

Santiago, Silviano. *Carlos Drummond de Andrade.* Petrópolis: Editora Vozes Ltda., 1976.

Schwartz, Lloyd. "One Art: The Poetry of Elizabeth Bishop, 1971–1976." *Elizabeth Bishop and Her Art.* Eds. Lloyd Schwartz and Sybil Estess. Ann Arbor: U of Michigan P, 1983. 133–153.

Elizabeth Bishop and George Herbert: "Self-distaste" and Self-understanding

Robert Cording
College of the Holy Cross

Abstract

For Richard Howard's 1974 anthology, *Preferences: 51 American Poets Choose Poems from Their Own Work and from the Past,* Elizabeth Bishop chose George Herbert's "Love Unknown" to juxtapose with her own poem, "In the Waiting Room." This paper looks at the way Herbert's poem and Bishop's earlier prose work, "The Country Mouse," provide the reader with a slightly different perspective from which to consider the central issue of identity in "In the Waiting Room." Simply stated: the child, like Herbert's speaker in "Love Unknown," is overly confident that she knows who she is and, perhaps more importantly, that she can know who she is (or in Herbert's poem what God wants). The past tense perspective of Bishop's "In the Waiting Room" is the perspective of the older adult who has learned, and now marks the moment of the poem as the beginning of that learning, that one must suffer the radical and sudden disorientation which the child undergoes in order to gain a new, more genuine approach (in Herbert's poem to be made "new, tender, quick") to understanding who we are. For Bishop an understanding of who we are will necessarily involve our coming to know the limits of our knowing. Like the narrator of "The Country Mouse," those who will know have to experience the bitter feeling of "self-distaste": the child will come to see she is her "foolish aunt."

"It's probably a hopeless matter, writing about favorite poems."

—Robert Hass

For Richard Howard's 1974 anthology, *Preferences: 51 American Poets Choose Poems from Their Own Work and from the Past,* Elizabeth Bishop chose a favorite George Herbert poem, "Love Unknown," to juxtapose with her then as yet uncollected new poem, "In the Waiting Room." I was then in graduate school, dividing my time between writing poems and studying them in earnest. Bishop and Herbert were my favorite poets and, as fate would have it, I was struggling in 1974 to describe, in a long overdue paper on Herbert, the tonality of many of Herbert's best known poems—that speaking voice which, say in "The Flower" or "Love 3," is utterly beguiling in its apparent simplicity and directness and yet has the power to turn the most innocuous word or phrase incandescent. When, in 1974, I first read Bishop's

"In the Waiting Room," I encountered that same power. How, I wanted to know (as both a writer and, I admit, a person with a religious temperament), did Bishop achieve such "mystery" (she'd say, "strangeness") in that series of why questions at the heart of "In the Waiting Room"? I still shiver at times over that first italicized *Why* and its tone of anxious, grave, bewilderment: "I felt: you are an *I* / you are an *Elizabeth*, / you are one of *them*. / *Why* should you be one, too?" Over twenty years later, I'm still trying to answer that question. Although I'll talk today of the connections between Herbert's "Love Unknown" and Bishop's "In the Waiting Room," and although I'll look as well at Bishop's prose piece, "The Country Mouse," my abiding and central concern is still the way Bishop's poem enacts the radical and sudden disorientation which we all must undergo as we necessarily come to know the limits of our knowing.

As Bishop's "In the Waiting Room" opens, the speaker recalls how, while waiting for her aunt, she read a *National Geographic*. In a parenthetical aside, the speaker feels the need at this particular moment in the poem to declare "I could read." For me, a whole reading of the poem lies within those parentheses. For isn't this poem about the discovery of the difference between the child's and the adult's understanding of what it means to *read*? The peculiar slant of the poem—a child's voice filtered through the past tense perspective of the adult—allows Bishop the many doublings of meaning that run throughout the poem. While the child may think reading involves only the words on the page, the older adult has learned, and now marks the moment of the poem as the beginning of that learning, that *reading* also means discovering the shock of those widening circles of unfamiliarity that the child encounters. When, at the end of the poem, the speaker comments, "Then I was back in it. / The War was on," we know and she knows that the singular "it" has a plurality of referents—the waiting room, her consciousness, the world that stretches from Worcester to Africa to "cold, blue-black space"—and that whatever order can be restored depends on mapping the various and variable constituent parts. Thirteen years before "In the Waiting Room" was published, Bishop wrote about the incident in a prose piece, "The Country Mouse" (a piece that remained unpublished until 1984 when Robert Giroux gathered Bishop's uncollected prose together). Young Elizabeth is the "country mouse" whose Nova Scotia life was disrupted when her paternal grandparents took the six-year old back to live with them in their cold, glum Worcester house. While "The Country Mouse" predominantly details the strain of young Elizabeth's divided loyalties—a Canadian child who had to memorize and daily recite, at her grandmother's feet, the verses of "The Star-Spangled Banner"—it culminates in three Wordsworthian "spots of time" in Worcester. All three moments involve a sudden eruption of painful self-consciousness. I want to concentrate on the first and third.The first moment occurs when a friend, Emma, asks about Elizabeth's parents. Bishop writes,

> I said my father was dead; I didn't even remember seeing him. What about my mother? I thought for a moment and then I said in a *sentimental* voice: "She went away and left me... She died, too." (31)

Of course, Bishop's mother is not dead; she's in a sanitarium at the time, suffering from another nervous breakdown. Looking back on this childhood incident, the older Bishop doesn't know if she lied from shame or for some "hideous craving for sympathy." But she does know that the feeling that came over her "was only too real": that feeling was "self-distaste" and Bishop was startled by the sudden discovery of her "monstrous self."

The third moment occurs in the dentist's waiting room in Worcester. The six-year-old Bishop has gone with her aunt to the dentist and, while she waits, she looks at a copy of the *National Geographic* for February 1918. Here's how Bishop describes the scene:

> It was still getting dark early, and the room had grown very dark. There was a big yellow lamp in one corner, a table with magazines, and an overhead chandelier of sorts. There were others waiting, two men and a plump middle-aged lady, all bundled up. I looked at the magazine cover—I could read most of the words— shiny, glazed, yellow and white. The black letters said: FEBRUARY 1918. A feeling of absolute and utter desolation came over me. I felt... *myself.* In a few days it would be my seventh birthday. I felt *I, I, I,* and looked at the three strangers in panic. I was *one* of them, too, inside my scabby body and wheezing lungs. "You're in for it now," something said. How had I got tricked into such a false position? I would be like that woman opposite who smiled at me so falsely every once in a while. The awful sensation passed, then it came back again. "You are you," something said. "How strange you are, inside looking out. You are not Beppo [her dog], or the chestnut tree, or Emma, you are *you* and you are going to be *you* forever." It was like coasting downhill, this thought, only much worse, and it quickly smashed into a tree. *Why* was I a human being?" (32–33)

How to translate that feeling of "coasting downhill" out of control and smashing into a tree—that is the task Bishop takes up when she turns to this material thirteen years later in "In the Waiting Room." How to capture that strange, awful (both in the sense of horrible and awe-producing, I'd say) sensation of that newly discovered "I." As Bishop puts it, *"Why* was I a human being?"

In both "The Country Mouse" and "In the Waiting Room," the discovery of selfhood is a moment, in part, of "self-distaste," a moment when the child, like so many of George Herbert's speakers, discovers her own falseness and complicity. In her 1983 essay, "The Impersonal and the Interrogative in the Poetry of Elizabeth Bishop," Bonnie Costello first makes the connection between Herbert's "Love Unkown" and Bishop's "In the Waiting Room." She writes, "Like the speaker in George Herbert's 'Love Unknown,' which Bishop has juxtaposed with ['In the Waiting Room'], the young Elizabeth is made 'new, tender, quick' through her sudden disorientation. It serves as a kind of baptism" (113). I think Costello is right; she implies, of course, that the child's original orientation to the world is wrongheaded somehow. I'd say that the child, like Herbert's speaker who thought he knew what God wanted, has only a partial knowledge of what it means to "read." Young Elizabeth thinks she knows who she is, or, to put it another way, thinks she *can* know who she is.

The past tense perspective of both the Herbert and Bishop poem is important. In "Love Unknown," Herbert employs the past tense for its usual purpose: the speaker's "long and sad" tale told to his "Deare Friend" is a cautionary tale. The speaker "well remembers all" as well he should since, though he had in mind to bring some fruit to his Lord, his attempts amounted to a series of miscalculations and mishaps. Here's the poem:

> Deare Friend, sit down, the tale is long and sad:
> And in my faintings I presume your love
> Will more complie than help. A Lord I had,
> And have, of whom some grounds, which may improve,
> I hold for two lives, and both lives in me.
> To him I brought a dish of fruit one day,
> And in the middle plac'd my heart. But he
>   (I sigh to say)
> Lookt on a servant, who did know his eye
> Better than you know me, or (which is one)
> Then I my self. The servant instantly
> Quitting the fruit, seiz'd on my heart alone,
> And threw it in a font, wherein did fall
> A stream of bloud, which issu'd from the side
> Of a great rock: I well remember all,
> And have good cause: there it was dipt and dy'd,
> And washt, and wrung: the very wringing yet
> Enforceth tears. *Your heart was foul, I fear.*

Indeed 'tis true. I did and do commit
Many a fault more then my lease will bear;
Yet still askt pardon, and was not deni'd.
But you shall heare. After my heart was well,
And clean and fair, as I one even-tide
(I sigh to tell)
Walkt by my self abroad, I saw a large
And spacious fornace flaming, and thereon
A boyling caldron, round about whose verge
Was in great letters set AFFLICTION.
The greatnesse shew'd the owner. So I went
To fetch a sacrifice out of my fold,
Thinking with that, which I did thus present,
To warm his love, which I did fear grew cold.
But as my heart did tender it, the man,
Who was to take it from me, slipt his hand,
And threw my heart into the scalding pan;
My heart, that brought it (do you understand?)
The offerers heart. *Your heart was hard, I fear.*
Indeed it's true. I found a callous matter
Began to spread and to expatiate there:
But with a richer drug then scalding water
I bath'd it often, ev'n with holy bloud,
Which at a board, while many drunk bare wine,
A friend did steal into my cup for good,
Ev'n taken inwardly, and most divine
To supple hardnesses. But at the length
Out of the caldron getting, soon I fled
Unto my house, where to repair the strength
Which I had lost, I hasted to my bed.
But when I thought to sleep out all these fault
(I sigh to speak)
I found that some had stuff'd the bed with thoughts,
I would say *thorns*. Deare, could my heart not break,
When with my pleasures ev'n my rest was gone?
Full well I understood, who had been there:
For I had giv'n the key to none, but one:
It must be he. *Your heart was dull, I fear.*
Indeed a slack and sleepie state of minde
Did oft possesse me, so that when I pray'd,
Though my lips went, my heart did stay behinde.
But all my scores were by another paid,
Who took the debt upon him. *Truly, Friend,*
For ought I heare, your Master shows to you
More favour then you wot of. Mark the end.
The Font did onely, what was old, renew:
The Caldron suppled, what was grown too hard:

> *The Thorns did quicken, what was grown too dull:*
> *All did but strive to mend, what you had marr'd.*
> *Wherefore be cheer'd, and praise him to the full*
> *Each day, each houre, each moment of the week,*
> *Who fain would have you be new, tender, quick.*

The speaker's plans—to bring his Lord a dish of fruit, a sheep, and later to rest so he might repair his strength to praise his Lord—are all frustrated. His "poor heart," with which the speaker brings his gifts, gets thrown into a bloody font and washed and wrung and later tossed into a scalding pan. When he tries to rest his heart, his bed becomes a bed of thorns. But the speaker knows why. When his friend draws the moral from each narrated part, saying, "Your heart was foul, I fear," "Your heart was hard, I fear," "Your heart was dull, I fear," the speaker quickly admits—directly on two occasions, indirectly on a third— "Indeed 'tis true." As Helen Vendler points out in her book on George Herbert, "it is characteristic of Herbert to recount his spiritual struggles in the past tense; they almost always are represented as having happened yesterday, so that the poem is giving today's view, a view tempered by knowledge of the purpose and result of each affliction"(90). Though the speaker in Herbert's poem must, in some respect, tell this "sad tale" every day since all of us are "each day, each hour, each moment," prone to do the wrong thing, and must be made "new, tender, quick" over and over again—the past tense perspective in Herbert assures us that our afflictions take place within a larger context. God's purposes, though we may not understand them from moment-to-moment, are always to mend what "we have marred," as the "Deare Friend" tells the speaker at the end of "Love Unknown."

Herbert's poems remind us, over and over, how, even when we think we are acting most righteously and meekly and humbly, our self-congratulating self is winding its way into our actions. Bishop recognizes and feels sympathy with Herbert's self-conscious understanding of what she called her "monstrous self" in "The Country Mouse." "In the Waiting Room" traces that moment when the child, who thought she was so different from the adults in the dentist's outer-office, so different even from her own "foolish aunt," must experience how, however "unlikely," she is "one of them." Yet Bishop's past tense perspective has none of the assurances of Herbert's—and therein lies part of the poem's strangeness. We expect a past tense poem to provide a comfortable distance from the narrated events; often the stance of the speaker is the one we encountered in Herbert: this or that happened but now I know why. But in the same way Bishop conflates child and adult in "In the

Waiting Room," she conflates past and present. The reader moves inside the speaker's memory as the speaker moves inside the *National Geographic* volcano so that the child's experience of sudden disorientation is also the reader's. As we read, we confront those same unanswerable whys. Or, to put it another way, we hear them again for the first time with the ears of a child.

In the epigraphs to *Geography III* that immediately precede its first poem, "In the Waiting Room," we are given a set of questions and answers from a child's primer in geography. Here's a sample:

> *What is Geography?*
> A description of the earth's surface.
> *What is the Earth?*
> The planet or body on which we live.

The answers are a child's answers, a way of beginning with a complex subject. As readers of *Geography III*, we immediately suspect that those answers are insufficient when, later, in another section, Bishop provides a verse paragraph of unanswered questions:

> *In what direction is the Volcano? The*
> *Cape? The Bay? The Lake? The Strait?*
> *The Mountains? The Isthmus?*
> *What is in the East? In the West? In the*
> *South? In the North? In the Northwest?*
> *In the Southeast? In the Northeast?*
> *In the Southwest?*

The first unanswered question, then, in *Geography III* is, "In what direction is the Volcano?" In the context of the geography primer, the answer might be simple. But in the context of "In the Waiting Room," the answers are many and complex. The volcano is both inside the *National Geographic* and inside the mouth of Aunt Consuelo when her pain spills over in a cry, a cry which, of course, Elizabeth recognizes as her own as well. The volcano is at once "black, and full of ashes" and spilling over "in rivulets of fire" just as the pictures in the *National Geographic*, at first tame and civilized (Osa and Martin Johnson in laced-up riding boots), soon spill over in "babies with pointed heads" and "black, naked women with necks / wound round and round with wire." As Brett Millier and others have pointed out, the perspective is constantly shifting at the poem's opening—Elizabeth is in Worcester, but outside in the waiting room. Once inside the *National Geographic,* Elizabeth is forced outside into "blue-black space" through the "*oh!* of pain" that comes simultaneously from inside the dentist's office (her aunt's voice) and outside in the waiting room (from inside young Elizabeth) (Millier 24–27).

Bishop's point is clear: nothing is ever one thing. The boundaries between inside and outside, between the familiar and unfamiliar, between what we call our world and other, are always artificial, self-created and often self-willed, and always, always fluid and changing, like knowledge which is "flowing and flown" in "At the Fishhouses." Still, though the point may be clear, our experience of the poem is constantly unsettling. We know the poem is a recollection, and we presume the speaker is the older Elizabeth, not the child who is nearly seven. Yet when we try to discriminate between the child's voice and the adult's there is very little to go on. Like third person fiction which immediately moves inside the protagonist's head and stays there, we have, as readers of "In the Waiting Room" no authorial perspective. And consider how the poem skips along in loose trimeter, even as it recollects those horrifying naked breasts. Even the syntax and grammar are unsettling:

> ...The waiting room
> was full of grown-up people,
> arctics and overcoats,
> lamps and magazines.

Is the waiting room full of grown-ups and boots and overcoats and lamps and magazines or are grown-ups synonomous with "arctics and overcoats, lamps and magazines" in the child's mind? Certainly one of the masterful feats of "In the Waiting Room" is Bishop's careful control of perspective. On the one hand, she keeps her poem from childishness and sentimentality by using the past tense (which maintains the distance between the speaker and child, and the reader and the child). As adults and readers of the poem, we are able to observe the child's struggles with the volcanic world of the *National Geographic* and her own female body; we see, too, how the familiar turns suddenly unfamiliar and how the child struggles to map this unfamiliar terrain by comparing, say, the exotic neck decoration of the African women to a common light bulb or by creating boundaries between herself and the magazine when she notes the cover's yellow margins and date. On the other hand, as I've noted, the poem constantly pushes us inside the child's experience, blurring the boundaries between adult speaker and child. When the "*oh!* of pain" erupts from inside the dentist's office, the reader, like the child who believed she could stand outside the event—"I wasn't at all surprised; / even then I knew she was / a foolish, timid woman"—is suddenly caught up in the confusion. At first we assign the cry of pain to Aunt Consuelo; then we're not so sure:

> ...What took me
> completely by surprise
> was that it was *me*:
> my voice, in my mouth.
> Without thinking at all
> I was my foolish aunt,
> I—we—were falling, falling....

What's happened? Has the child let out an "*oh!* of pain," horrified as she is by those "awful hanging breasts"? Have both Aunt Consuelo and the young Elizabeth cried out? Even if we're able to say in the end that the child recognizes the "family voice" in Aunt Consuelo's cry of pain, and thus her own voice as well, the momentary confusion is crucial. For suddenly, we, too, are falling—not with the child necessarily nor in the same way as the child, but falling, nevertheless, into the tumble of questions that immediately follow.

And isn't that the point? When Bishop collapses the distance between reader and child, she short-circuits our role as detached interpreter of the child's experience. The roll-call of questions, questions left unanswered because they are unanswerable, takes the reader "completely by surprise." *Why* should we be who we are? For those of us who love this poem, the effect of this *Why* is almost preternatural. Just as the child, once secure in her simple definitions—she was in Worcester, in a waiting room, it was winter, and she *could* read—is suddenly confronted by the "unlikeliness" of her likeliness to others, by the worlds-upon-worlds that she now must learn to read, we, too, (who move through the world secure in our accepted definitions of it) are confronted by those most basic questions which somehow we never really answered. Why should we be who we are? And what constitutes who we are? And, why, oh why have we come to be here?

What Bishop captures and helps us experience is the shock of being alive: isn't it amazing that there is that, and not just me. And, even more remarkably, there is something rather than nothing. The experience of the young Elizabeth is preconceptual—she is *taken* (both carried off and astonished) and "without thinking at all," she *is* her foolish aunt. (Notice the missing "like.") Like Robinson Crusoe finding footprints in the sand, the child is startled to find there are others and otherness in the world. Even more startling, perhaps, is the sense that because there is other, because there is that which is "not me," there is also me:

> ...you are an *I*,
> you are an *Elizabeth*,
> you are one of *them*.

The fact that the child has an individual identity that separates her from others, but also connects her to others, since in recognizing who she is, she recognizes others are just like her, is, as Bishop says, one of the strangest things that can happen. Though our experience as readers is not the child's, we, too, are brought to a place inside the poem where something strange happens: we hear those fundamental questions at the heart of the poem as if for the first time. We arrive with the child at this most "unlikely" place because we make, in our own ways, the same fundamental mistake as the child. We think we know how to read. We act as if we know—because we must go on functioning in the day-to-day world—what our lives mean. As in Bishop's poem, and Herbert's, it usually takes a volcanic eruption or a scalding pan to disrupt our complacency and indifference. Consider how a death of someone we love or a sudden severe illness of a friend brings us back to the starting point: for what purpose do I exist? For me, the great power of Bishop's "In the Waiting Room" is this: it enacts that moment when we experience the abyss which is always just underfoot. Haven't we all felt how, at any moment, the ground on which we stand can open and we, too, fall into that "cold, blue-black space" in which our existence becomes a question to ourselves? Think of how Bishop enacts for us the changed reality of the child. At the opening of the poem the waiting room is described matter-of-factly: lamps and boots, grownups, tables with magazines. When the child falls into the blue-black space that opens under her feet, that same commonplace scene becomes intensely focused—so much so the child can only afford a "sidelong glance." In this later scene, the child doesn't look at the objects in the waiting room; rather the objects force their reality upon the child. Elizabeth sees the same "trousers and skirts and boots" but their significance is something altogether different. Now that same waiting room forces a new reading on the child:

What similarities—

boots, hands, the family voice
I felt in my throat, or even
the *National Geographic*
and those awful hanging breasts—
held us all together
and made us all just one?

The experience the child undergoes—and we, too, as readers—involves our coming to know the limits of our knowing. For Herbert in "Love Unknown" and for Bishop in "In the Waiting Room," such an experience necessarily entails a moment when we suffer a radical and sudden disorientation: what we thought we knew is suddenly and deeply called into question. As Bishop painfully understood, such moments often involve the bitter feeling of "self-distaste": Elizabeth comes to know she is her "foolish aunt." To be made "new, tender, quick," as Herbert says we must (though, of course, that remaking takes place over and over again), we must first come to a moment when, like young Elizabeth, we become a question to ourselves. Here, in Worcester, Massachusetts, where Elizabeth Bishop lies buried, she first came to "read" the vast and multifaceted world she would travel and map in her poems.

Works Cited

Bishop, Elizabeth. *The Complete Poems, 1927–1979*. New York: Farrar, Straus, Giroux, 1983.

———. "The Country Mouse." *The Collected Prose*. Ed. Robert Giroux. New York: Farrar, Straus, Giroux, 1984.

Costello, Bonnie. *Elizabeth Bishop: Questions of Mastery*. Cambridge: Harvard UP, 1991.

———. "The Impersonal and the Interrogative in the Poetry of Elizabeth Bishop." *Elizabeth Bishop and Her Art*, Eds. Lloyd Schwartz and Sybil Estess. Ann Arbor: U of Michigan P, 1983.

Goldensohn, Lorrie. *Elizabeth Bishop: The Biography of a Poetry*. New York: Columbia UP, 1992.

Herbert, George. *The Works of George Herbert*. Ed. F.E. Hutchinson. London: Oxford UP, 1941.

Millier, Brett C. *Elizabeth Bishop: Life and the Memory of It*. Berkeley: U of California P, 1993.

Vendler, Helen. *The Poetry of George Herbert*. Cambridge: Harvard UP, 1975.

Cold War 1950: Elizabeth Bishop and Sylvia Plath

Camille Roman
Washington State University

Abstract

This paper explores Sylvia Plath's and Elizabeth Bishop's responses to the U.S. entry into the Korean War in their poems "Bitter Strawberries" and "View of the Capitol from the Library of Congress," completed in 1950. I argue—through a reading informed by cultural, feminist, and lesbian theory, historical scholarship, and archival research—that both poets construct conflicted female-grounded voices that complicate our understanding of the traditional "Penelope" role for women during this war. I further contend that their poems draw our attention to the need to more fully account for women's heterogeneously interrelated visible, quasi-(in)visible, and invisible war positionings.[1]

Both Elizabeth Bishop and Sylvia Plath responded to the U. S. entry into the Korean War, a crucial early historical "moment" in the developing 1950s Cold War culture of "containment" that saw its mission as saving the world from Communism. U. S. women during this war were expected to follow the traditional role for women in Western war that historians of gender, cultural production, and war have characterized as the role of "Penelope" (named for the classical heroine and wife of Ulysses) supporting and welcoming home the military.[2] I wish to explore how both poets complicate this female cultural representation through their constructions of conflicted female voices by reading for the first time against the Korean War context Plath's poem "Bitter Strawberries" and multiple drafts of Bishop's "View of the Capitol from the Library of Congress" (Plath 299–300; Bishop, *CP* 69).

Plath's "Bitter Strawberries" appeared initially in the U.S. newspaper *The Christian Science Monitor* on August 11, 1950, several weeks after the federal government sent military forces to Korea and near an early anniversary of the World War II bombings of Japan; Bishop completed her poem in October, enclosing it with a message to her married friends, artist Loren MacIver and poet Lloyd Frankenberg (see *Monitor* 17; *One Art* 210). Let me begin by considering Plath's representation of a conflicted female voice in her poem in order to further frame my discussion; then I will move on to both the published version of Bishop's "View of the Capitol from the Library of Congress" and several drafts located in the Bishop archives at Vassar College.[3]

In the poem "Bitter Strawberries," Plath constructs three female voices that are overheard speaking about war by strawberry pickers who retell what they heard and saw.[4] First, she presents a woman who sides with the political ideology of Cold War militarism and "containment," configuring her as "masculine" and "militant"—as a "thin commanding figure in faded dungarees" who oversees the strawberry pickers. This patriotic Penelope voice tells the others that she thinks that the Russians should be "bombed...off the map" (299). This voice is significant for it reveals that Plath did not align militarism exclusively with the public, masculine sphere as did, for example, Virginia Woolf in "Three Guineas." Instead she suggests here that women can enter into this sphere.

The second female voice is that of a "Mary" who has a "fella" of draft age. Plath does not explicitly state whether this "fella" is Mary's son, husband, boyfriend, or lover. However, "Mary" seems to function, with her concern about her "fella," in a recognizable war role related to both the Christian iconography of the Mater Dolorosa bending over the body of her dying or dead son, Christ, as well as the tradition of the sorrowful woman mourning—and thereby welcoming home—the dead, the lost, and the wounded.[5] Mary offers a statement that is difficult to interpret because it trails off after "I've got a fella / Old enough to go / If anything should happen..." (299). We are left wondering what comes next. Is she suggesting—in this unfinished verbal gesture—that she is prepared like a patriotic Penelope for her "fella" to be drafted if anything should happen? Is she expressing her anxiety about the thought "if anything should happen..." to him? Both? Her subject position in relation to Cold War militarism seems too complicated to categorize her immediately as a "Penelope." Her "slowness"—or is it reluctance?—to agree immediately with her overseer-boss and with Cold War militarism yet not to oppose openly cultural pressures offers us an important rhetorical strategy to consider. Is it a "no but yes," or is it a "yes but no"? The empty verbal space or aporia seems to signal the possibility of both resigned acceptance to her role as a "Penelope" in the national body politic as well as her desire for separation/differentiation from it. I find Mary's voice arresting because it reminds me that within a nation, if one agrees with Antonini Gramsci's cultural theory, varying "levels of consent" and/or opposition can coexist (see *Selections from Prison Notebooks*). It seems to me that Plath offers us an exploration of what the concept "varying level of consent" might have sounded like to her within the historical and cultural moment of the Cold War's "Korean War."

Plath's construction of this conflicted female voice is significant not only for its dissent with the Penelope role for women during war, but also for its complex racial and class coding. On the one hand, one can read Mary as a figure without racial or class designation. This very lack of specificity is a mark of this period's national hegemonic culture that represented its women as heterosexual, white, and middle-class married mothers and that denied, punished, and/or sought to ignore those women who did not fit into these categories (see May). On the other hand, Plath's reference to the "bronzed" young men of draft age who are hoeing in the nearby fields raises the issue of more specific social coding for "Mary." The description of "bronze" carries heterogeneous meanings here. The U.S. military began racial integration during this historical period. So "bronze" refers not only to tanned white men and to the fate of young white soldiers as "bronzed" war memorial statuary, but also to men of diverse racial cultures in military service. "Bronze" alludes to such African-American work which foregrounds the word itself as Gwendolyn Brooks's poetry on "Bronzeville." One must consider as well who might be working in such a farm setting of strawberry fields that carries with it allusions to the history of slavery in the U.S., the status of migrant farm workers (generally coded as Hispanic), and the experience of white farm laborers and college or high school students in summer jobs. These multiple codings of "Mary" complicate not only her conflict over war, but also suggest that Plath may be attempting to foreground the military and national social diversity that had been denied in previous wars, including World War II (Fussell 127–128).

The third female voice belongs to the "blond" child, Nelda, who speaks out against the bombing and the draft in a way that Mary seems unable to do and who chides the female overseer for her verbal warmongering. Nelda sounds like an adult yet possesses childlike eyes of "vague terror," reminding us of the multicultural "sacred" traditions of "wise" children who can see what adults will not or cannot see. Nelda is related not only to the dominant white middle-class U.S. culture's revered saintly female childhood figures of literature (i.e., Beth March of *Little Women*), but also to such "sacred" icons of "golden" and "haloed" children as the multi-racially coded Child Jesus and Buddha. In the context of this poem, Nelda seems to function as a Cassandra figure of prophecy and warning who is not fully socialized into Cold War culture and therefore subjugated to it. We learn from the way that the overseer snaps at her to cut off her speech, implying that there is no reason to worry, that her opposition is unacceptable. Her "worrying" is socially reprehensible. Yet we can discern as readers that Nelda's fears are well-grounded.

What brings these women's voices together is their focus on the "bronzed" young men hoeing in the nearby fields, men who literally could be drafted during this time. The very scene of harvesting points towards the fate of these men. War theorist Elaine Scarry tells us in her essay "Injury and the Structure of War" that one very common metaphor for death in war is that of "harvesting," as she goes on to describe how historians have named one day in World War I, when hundreds of thousands were slain at Tannenberg, as the "Day of Harvesting" (5). While soldiering was an exclusive U.S. male preserve during the Korean War, Plath obviously did not think that women were outside of the experience of war. For the patriotic female overseer in the poem, this war offers the opportunity for the United States as a nation to destroy its Communist enemy. For the figure Mary, the soldiers are the harvested fruits—either direct issue from their bodies as sons or the carriers of the "seeds" for planting as husbands/lovers. In either case, women in war like Mary are asked to break off and yield up their "fellas" to their national governments for "counting" and "harvesting." For Nelda, the war is a much-feared catastrophe and an end to childhood.

In the strategic juxtaposition of the militant female voice against the voices of the hesitant woman "Mary" and the protesting child "Nelda" (who also are the only figures named in the poem), Plath draws attention to the fact that it is the bronzed young men who are silent, not the women as is expected in traditional war roles. This is a war conversation ABOUT them, but not with them: they are its objects. Plath's flat portrayal of all the men as simply "bronzed" reinforces their reductively invisible and silent objectification. Intent on the work of hoeing, the men are the ones who seem to be without agency and to be endangered. Their "bronzed" bodies connote not only their virility but also their culturally symbolic deified destinations as "bronzed" statuary dedicated to slain soldiers who have died in battle for their nation or "motherland."

Although the female overseer might seem to be accorded the controlling hierarchical role in the poem because of her "commanding" power, Mary's conflicted voice is the one that grounds it. Her conflict points simultaneously to the contradictory claims of the overseer's demands for war, the child Nelda's threatened life and innocence, and the impending deaths of the young men. Almost as if they were responding directly to her conflict regarding her own "fella," the other female strawberry pickers who have listened in on the conversation indicate that when they returned to picking berries after this scene, they cupped the berries (also a metaphor for the young men) "protectively" before snapping them off for harvesting, or for their battlefield deaths. The final outcome of the conversation signaled by these pickers is consent to war. As I have contended, however, it is not the full and open consent of patriotic Penelope. It is conflicted consent, drawing our attention to the interrelationship between a visible complicity and a quasi-(in)visible dissent.

The construction of a female voice of conflict that complicates the Penelope role for women in the Korean War is equally crucial for understanding Bishop's drafting of "View of the Capitol from the Library of Congress." Although generally overlooked in published Bishop scholarship, this poem has begun to receive the kind of serious attention that it merits. Both biographer Brett Millier and critic Margaret Dickie are correct in their assessment that the published version presents Bishop's perspective on military life (Millier 223; Dickie 112–113).[6] In many respects the speaker's conflict in the poem is openly oppositional in its perspective on military life. As Dickie argues, the published poem—with its focus on the problem of hearing the music at an Air Force concert—can be read as Bishop's "sardonic commentary" on the Air Force band's "feeble" efforts to "declare its own glory or even assert its military presence" (112–113). By considering the development of multiple drafts of the poem more explicitly within its Korean War "moment," I wish to both extend and complicate this understanding of the speaker's conflict with militarism in the poem. I will begin by focusing on Bishop's denunciation of national military support for air warfare and then move into her co-equal concern about the military domination of the homefront and private citizens.

My examination of Bishop's previously uninterpreted fragments and working drafts that appear in her diary for 1950, together with her correspondence with MacIver and Frankenburg during her 1949–1950 year in Washington, D.C., support anti-militarist readings of the poem as a whole. These materials reveal that she was scrutinizing Cold War culture as she developed the conflicted and contradictory voice of the poem's speaker. From her writing desk as the Poetry Consultant at the Library of Congress, she was literally documenting the arrival of the Korean War. She described Washington, for instance, to Frankenberg several weeks after the U.S. troops arrived in Korea, as though it had been invaded and overtaken by the military. An Air Force base seems to have suddenly sprung up and obliterated Washington's spring landscape: "Washington seems composed of equal parts of airplanes, starings, electric drills, and thick, oily storm. The beautiful spring lasted exactly one week" (21 August 1950, Bishop Archives, Vassar).

One of the most caustic statements about this military "occupation" of Washington, D.C. appears in a fragment of the developing poem that was deleted. Here Bishop personifies the nation—through her depiction of the Capitol dome—in a strong, direct sexual language atypical of her as she draws attention to the fact that it is in

> (Washington airplanes always setting themselves gingerly
> poem)   down
>   Dome — also an elaborate sugar-tit — for a
> nation that likes sugar —
>
>   (box 77, folder 4, p. 3, Vassar)

While discarding this specific passage in her development of the poem, Bishop retained her political denunciation of the nation's "feeding" of the military in the published poem's lines: "Unceasingly the little flags / feed their limp stripes into the air" (*CP* 69). The red and white stripes remind one of candy canes being fed into the air—but this specific batch of candy seems repelling: "impotent," with "little" flags feeding "limp" stripes.

In addition to the conflict about air warfare that she developed through drafts of the poem, Bishop considered the vexed relationship between a militaristic government and the nation's citizens. A gendered language of masculine militarism and feminized nature appears in the first draft of her poem that we now have and indicates the kind of dissent she expresses in the published version through her negative descriptions of such patriotic symbols as the flag and the Capitol dome. Among the lines sketched in this entry are phrases that combine physical observation and political commentary as Bishop depicts the "harsh, stiff moss" of Justice on the Capitol dome, with an implied eroticized deadly masculinization of feminized nature reminding us of her letter to Frankenberg describing the military takeover of Washington, D.C.:

> Justice on the Dome   like a leaf
>   stiff
> The moss harsh stiffened, —
>
>   (box 77, folder 4, p. 3, Vassar)

In prose notes written on the same page as the "sugar-tit" passage, she noted that the "flying flags" in Washington seemed to be like "horny insects," a masculinization of the nation's flag, its most patriotic symbol. Then she added onto this fragment in prose: "The light moves from left to far left & off around the highest tier of little windows...on the Capitol dome...giving the effect of a big old wall-eyed white horse." Her depiction of the light illuminated on the Capitol dome suggests that the Capitol, the architectural symbol of the U.S. national government because it houses the Congress, seems awry. The light reminds her of a "big old wall-eyed white horse," with one eye that squints to the side rather than straight ahead. Here the problem seems to be that the Capitol light can only move "left to far left," intimating that the Capitol has limited vision. Given her earlier draft about the "harsh, stiff Justice on the Dome," one is tempted to read this as a very well-camouflaged comment upon the House Un-American Activities Committee hearings led by Senator Joseph McCarthy at this time that attacked many private citizens, especially targeting homosexuals, liberals, intellectuals, and cultural producers as a whole (see Berube and Edelman). Moreover, the "white horse" here is not the heroic horse one expects with patriotic symbolism, but a horse with abnormal vision veering off course as it fixates on the "left to far left."

It is not surprising, then, that other early drafts of the poem reveal Bishop's anxieties about the menacing qualities in the Air Force band music as it attempts to romance the nation's citizens into war support and patriotic solidarity. She sees the band's desire to coerce in terms of a "boom-boom" war-like sound and would have likely found relevant Benedict Anderson's observations about the "cultural products of nationalism": "nations inspire love, and often profoundly self-sacrificing love. The cultural products of nationalism—poetry, prose fiction, music, plastic arts—show this love very clearly in thousands of different forms and styles. This love is turned into justification for invasion of the 'other'"(41):

```
          View of the Capitol from the L of C - title
       on the steps, the military band        uniforms
       ... imagine any such thing,
                   since there is no haze
                         trees —
          Great shades ( + - the small eye on the capitol
       Big trees, big shades, edge over
       give the music room      I think the band is wanting to
                                      go more boom-boom
       to go boom-boom      I think it wants to go —
                               more boom boom boom.
                      (box 77, folder 4, p. 17, Vassar)
```

In another surviving fragment of the poem-in-progress, she indicates that the trees block and overpower the music. The reference to the fact that the music "must do" this as well as "wants to do" it ("boom: boom:" or "umpty-umpty") gives it a masculine and highly sexually charged edge, to which the feminized "trees" of the nation's citizens as well as of other nations must yield:

great shades, edge over,	let the band come through
give the music room	let the music come through
to —umpty-umpty	if that's what it wants to do
to boom – boom	to go *boom: boom:*
— if that's what it must do.	if that's what it must do
	(box 77, folder 4, p. 16, Vassar)

In the final published poem, as we have discussed, the speaker listens to impotent patriotic music that "doesn't quite come through" in spite of being played "loud and hard" by an all-male Air Force band because the military was regarded as an exclusive male domain during this time: "the Air Force Band / in uniforms of Air Force blue is playing hard and loud" (*CP* 69). Apparently the sound does not carry because the feminized landscape of "the giant trees stand in between" and "must intervene" by "catching the music in their leaves... till each big leaf sags." In contrast to the power of the trees to absorb the weight of the music, the "little flags / feed their limp stripes into the air, / and the band's efforts vanish there." Because "the gathered brasses want to go / *boom-boom*," a reference to the military commanders or "brasses" who want to go to war as well as a caustic comment on the infantilism of war in the use of "boom—boom," the speaker urges the "great shades" to "edge over" and "give the music room," which is a physical impossibility. But apparently there can be "boom-boom" or conquest if the feminized landscapes of both this nation as well as other nations yield.

Given this critique of the nation's military domination of both other nations and its own citizens, Bishop's construction of the speaker in the published version of the poem is unexpected. This speaker appears to be outwardly patriotic by sitting and listening to the Air Force concert. Indeed the poem can be read as simply a complaint from an irritated concertgoer. But doing this overlooks a vital point: the speaker's acknowledgement of her intertwined visible complicity with the militarism as well as her quasi-invisible conflict with it.

Equally surprising is the speaker's nonspecific or universal social markings, a visible compliancy with dominant Cold War culture's denial of social differentiation (see May). Yet I have referred throughout to a female speaker in the poem, drawn into the conflicted issue by conflating the speaker's gender and sexual orientation with the poet's and coding the poem's language ("one small lunette," "gold-dust," "little flags," and "great shades") as obviously feminine by following traditional mid-century views of language put forth by such linguistics scholars as Robin Lakoff who would describe this kind of language as "talking like a lady" (280–291). Outwardly compliant as well as fanciful, the speaker must be a conflicted female—or so I have reasoned. Yet if I follow out this logic, I must admit that I face yet another conflict: for the poet is lesbian, not heterosexual, in a Cold War culture that outlawed lesbians and contended that only the heterosexual female could be interpreted as truly female, truly "Penelope." Have I, then, been misreading the speaker? I wish to argue the contrary. I suggest the possibility that Bishop has intertwined her culturally-ostracized lesbianism with this publicly acceptable and visible indeterminant universal (male and female) speaker. In the words of lesbian theorist Terry Castle, Bishop relies upon "quasi-invisibility" in a Cold War culture that wants to ensure her erasure or total "invisibility" (7). It is hardly surprising, then, that the poem's speaker has difficulty hearing the patriotic music designed to "court" her loyalty or faithfulness as a citizen. Her own nation has declared her citizenship identity undesirable and her affiliation with "Penelope" unthinkable. Indeed, as the speaker says, it's "queer" that the music does not come through. Moreover, the word "queer" flanked on two sides by dashes—the only such instance in the poem—appears visually in stanza two to block the music.

So what can we learn from this opening gambit in the discussion of Plath's and Bishop's dissent with the Penelope role for women during the Korean War "moment"? At the least I hope that I have persuaded you to consider further the fact that Plath's and Bishop's constructions of conflicted female voices reveal multi-layered levels of dissent confounded with consent, indicating the need to understand women's roles in war as heterogeneously interrelated visible, quasi-(in)visible, and invisible.

Endnotes

1. I am deeply grateful to Laura Menides, Nancy MacKechnie of the Vassar Archives, Barbara Page, editor of the Elizabeth Bishop Society, and Thomas Travisano, president of the Elizabeth Bishop Society for their expert guidance, encouragement, collegiality, and advice in the development of this essay, which is related to my recently completed book manuscript discussing Bishop and the Cold War. I am indebted to the 1997

Elizabeth Bishop Conference organizing committee for giving me the opportunity to present this paper and to such conference participants in my session as David Boxwell, Rodger Martin, and Richard Flynn who responded to my paper. Earlier and related portions and versions of this piece were read at the American Literature Conference in 1996 and at the Poetry in the 1950's Conference in 1996; so I wish to thank conference organizers Susan Belasco Smith, Alfred Bendixen, and Burton Hatlen for these opportunities. In addition, I am indebted to the community of scholars cited in this essay, for they have helped to advance my thinking. This project was supported in part by grants from the Washington State University, Arts and Humanities, research travel grant program and the College of Liberal Arts dean's research grant program and by an appointment as Visiting Scholar in the department of English at Brown University, 1996–1997. I wish to thank as well Stephen Foley and Geoffery Russom, department chairs at Brown University, and Susan McLeod and Mary Wack, department chairs at Washington State University, for their support. This essay is dedicated to Chris Darwin Frigon for his continual encouragement of my work.

2. This field of scholarship is now too large to overview briefly here. I refer the reader to such standard works as Miriam Cooke's edited collection *Gendering War Talk*, Helen Cooper's edited collection *Arms and the Woman*, and Susan Schweik's *A Gulf So Deeply Cut*.

3. Excerpts from the unpublished writings of Elizabeth Bishop are used here with the permission of her estate, © 1998 by Alice Helen Methfessel, and with the permission of Special Collections at Vassar College Libraries.

4. I argue that these three female voices are related to her major poem "Three Women" in my conference paper, "Sylvia Plath: No Safe Place in the Cold War," delivered at the 1996 American Literature Assn. Conference, and in a longer piece that I am writing. In each poem, Plath explores women's complex positionings within a military-grounded Cold War culture.

5. This construction is widely discussed in scholarship about war. See Fussell, especially chapter 4; also see Cooke, Cooper, and Schweik.

6. I have benefitted greatly from both Millier's and Dickie's attention to this poem. My understanding of it also has been enriched by John Gonzales, a student in one of my graduate seminars, who included it in his seminar paper on nationalisms theory and Bishop's poetry.

Works Cited

Anderson, Benedict. *Imagined Communities: Reflections on the Origin and Spread of Nationalism.* 2nd. ed. London: Verso, 1991.

Berube, Allan. *Coming Out Under Fire: The History of Gay Men and Women in World War Two.* New York: Free Press of Macmillan, 1990.

Bishop, Elizabeth. Bishop Archive. Vassar College Library.

———. *The Complete Poems, 1927–1979.* New York: Farrar, Straus, Giroux, 1983.

———. *One Art: Letters*, Ed. Robert Giroux. New York: Farrar, Straus, Giroux, 1994.

Castle, Terry. *The Apparitional Lesbian: Female Homosexuality and Modern Culture.* New York: Columbia UP, 1993.

Cooke, Miriam and Angela Woollacott, eds. *Gendering War Talk.* Princeton: Princeton UP, 1993.

Cooper, Helen, Adrienne Auslander Munich, and Susan Merrill Squier, eds. *Arms and the Woman: War, Gender, and Literary Representation.* Chapel Hill: U of North Carolina P, 1989.

Dickie, Margaret. *Stein, Bishop, & Rich: Lyrics of Love, War, & Place.* Chapel Hill: U of North Carolina P, 1997.

Edelman, Lee. "Tearooms and Sympathy, or, The Epistemology of the Water Closet." *Nationalisms and Sexualities.* Ed. Andrew Parker et. al. New York: Routledge, 1992. 263–84.

Fussell, Paul. *The Great War & Modern Memory.* London: Oxford UP, 1975.

———. *Wartime.* London: Oxford UP, 1989.

Gramsci, Antonio. *Prison Notebooks: Selections.* Ed. & Trans. Quintin Hoare and Geoffrey Nowell Smith. New York: International, 1971.

Lakoff, Robin. "Language and Woman's Place." *The Women & Language Debate: A Sourcebook.* Ed. Camille Roman et. al. New Brunswick: Rutgers UP, 1994.

May, Elaine Tyler. *Homeward Bound: American Families in the Cold War Era.* New York: Basic Books, 1988.

Millier, Brett. *Elizabeth Bishop: Life and the Memory of It.* Berkeley: U of California P, 1993.

Plath, Sylvia. "Bitter Strawberries." *Christian Science Monitor.* 11 August 1950: 17.

———. *The Collected Poems.* New York: Harper & Row, 1981.

Scarry, Elaine. "Injury and the Structure of War." *Representations* 10 (1985): 1–51.

Schweik, Susan. *A Gulf So Deeply Cut: American Women Poets and the Second World War*. Madison: U of Wisconsin P, 1991.

Elizabeth Bishop's Embracing Gaze: Her Influence on the Poetry of Sandra McPherson, Phillis Levin, and Jorie Graham

James McCorkle
Independent Scholar

Abstract

This essay examines the influence Elizabeth Bishop has had on the poets Sandra McPherson, Phillis Levin, and Jorie Graham. The particular focus is on Bishop's apprehension of the natural world and the materiality of composition. Bishop's work, though not always an explicit source, nonetheless informs each of these poets. The essay argues against Charles Altieri's view that Bishop's poetry relies upon and is limited to description. The essay also counters William Logan's view that Bishop has exerted little or no influence. The essay argues that Bishop's use of description reveals writing as sacramental: it tests the conditions for apprehending the world, and is less a mirror to the world than it is a reflection of the processes of composition.

It is tempting to place Elizabeth Bishop in opposition to those twentieth-century poetic directions exemplified by John Ashbery and Adrienne Rich, that is, either a poetics of indeterminacy, or one of witness, informed by a struggle for identity. These two directions are positioned in opposition to more conventional lyricism, described by Charles Altieri in his *Self and Sensibility in Contemporary American Poetry* as deploying the scenic mode, with its insistence on defined and uninterrogated self and image. Altieri, in fact, cites Bishop as one of the instigators of this dominant poetic mode. Critics and literary historians have since sought recuperation of Bishop's poetry (if there was indeed need to), finding in her poems a de-centered, indeterminate conditionality, as well as a thorough meditation on issues of gender, culture, and gayness.

Bishop's work, however, remains a site of contestation. In a later essay, Altieri warns of Bishop's overwhelming appeal: "She does what she does so well that she has come to define the image of poetic intelligence most widely shared among contemporary poets. But there may be good reason to insist on the limitations of any mode that could find such diverse champions as Lowell, Merrill, Ashbery, Ostriker, and Rich, since its very generality of appeal suggests it may participate too fully in what we might call the age's richest commonplaces about what it means to be human" (232). It is revealing to note, however, that four of the five poets Altieri lists were grouped together (with Bishop as the fifth) by David Kalstone, who, in his *Five Temperaments*, found their poetics shared in considering the "possibility of writing about the self" and "how poetry can serve as autobiography" (10). Altieri's claim against Bishop loses some of its charge when Bishop is considered as sharing in critical concerns held by her contemporaries who may be more similar than Altieri allows.

In contrast to Altieri's claims about Bishop's pervasive influence, William Logan argues that Bishop "did not have–perhaps could not have had–any significant influence on the direction of American poetry in the postwar period" (122). If Logan is correct, Bishop's double orphaning–her childhood and her poetic legacy–was effected in part by the critical establishment. However, if Logan's belief that Bishop's "major gift, what might be called the stimulus to the higher and less provisional reaches of her art, was a nakedness of the observing eye, of seeing the world as if the world had never been seen before" (123), then her influence may be far greater than Logan would allow. That Bishop's descriptive abilities are stunning has been remarked upon to the point of being now a cliche. Offering what seems an unswerving description of the world has been the most readily attributable influence of Bishop's poetry, as found in the poetry of Jane Shore, Elizabeth Spires, Mark Doty, or Carol Frost–to name only four–where description typically is used to both expand the dramatic situation and define its conditions, as well as that of its narrator, in the world. Yet, this use of description is hardly unique to Bishop, and can be found working in similar ways in the work of Richard Hugo, Theodore Roethke, or David Wagoner. Such description, as Altieri argues, can be rendered too easily into a device of the scenic mode.

What makes Bishop's descriptive processes move past the scenic mode is that her descriptions are always informed by the condition of aporia: already before the condition of knowing, and hence describing, is the condition of doubt, so that even in a moment of knowing doubt exists or shadows understanding. Bishop's form of inquiry is Ignatian, where perception and apprehension begin with a composition of place, then move to analysis, and finally to the colloquy.[1] By establishing the loci—that is reading the world—one is able to converse. Yet revelation or apprehension is not attained at the point of the colloquy. Revelation is displaced into the conditions and constructions of writing. For example, the dispensation suggested in the lines "until everything / was rainbow, rainbow, rainbow! / And I let the fish go" (*CP* 44) at the conclusion of "The Fish" is not purely symbolic, nor only a didactic epiphany attained through accumulating observations. Writing is not a transparent means toward revelation; rather revelation exists in the materiality or presence of writing. The world is not so much translated into writing so as to allow us to re-enter the world anew, as does the attention shift from world to word, thus revealing the acuteness of composition. Bishop's description thus is as concerned with placing oneself in writing as it is in offering a representation of the world.

Taken with Bishop's lifelong and self-acknowledged interest in Donne, Herbert and Hopkins as well as the sedimented influence of Eliot, this consideration of writing reveals it to be sacramental.[2] To consider writing as sacramental is to understand one's obligation to writing and to find in writing the supplementary or displaced object of devotion and grace. Thus Bishop's reticence, while a personal trait, is in her writing expressive of aporia and limitation to knowledge. This is not a poetry of skepticism, which is itself a form of rigorous belief, but a poetry of difficulty. A poetry of difficulty eludes the possibilities of paraphrase and containment—the poem becomes a performance toward sacrament and presence. As George Steiner suggests in his essay "On Difficulty," the poem reveals its own ontological precariousness. The poets Sandra McPherson, Phillis Levin, and Jorie Graham, all of different poetic temperaments, draw upon Bishop's understanding of writing as sacrament. In so doing, they continue Bishop's meditations on aporia and apprehension.

In reviewing *Patron Happiness* in 1984, Jorie Graham wrote that Sandra McPherson's method is "elliptical, associative, [and] highly compressed imagistically. Lifted out of the current of history, things are made to glow in their own temporal order–insects, seeds, ash, hair, soap, string, dusty corners" (14). Of the three poets discussed here in relation to Bishop, McPherson's poetry would seem the closest to Bishop's sensibility. Bishop's moose, the hymn-loving seal, Crusoe's knife, the doily, all come to mind as objects "otherworldly" and as such having deep kinship with McPherson's universe.

Throughout McPherson's poetry there has been a sustained attention to the natural world. However, this attention is distinguished from Bishop's in that McPherson uses the natural world as a mediating mirror, whether as didactic illustrations ("Seaweeds" from *Radiation* or "The Firefly" from *Patron Happiness*) or as metaphors for human relations ("The Bittern" from *The Year of Our Birth* or "Alder, 1982" from *Streamers*). Unlike Bishop's work, which has the illusion at the very least of pure description, in McPherson's poetry the phenomenal world becomes the means of commenting upon, or elegizing, the human world. Much of the human world remains private or closeted for Bishop; in contrast, McPherson will allow her life, albeit often elliptically, to enter into poems about her birth-parents, divorce, and her daughter. Furthermore, McPherson has drawn on neglected traditions such as the blues and African-American quilt-making in her *The God of Indeterminacy* while also subtly acknowledging the boundaries she crosses in these testimonial elegies.

The presence of what seems clearly an autobiographical "I" and a potentially identifiable "you" populate McPherson's poems. The "I" in her poetry asserts that the observations are indeed authentic and originating from an individual. In contrast, Bishop avoids the "I," hence avoids localizing identity so as to maintain the possibility of identity while concurrently absenting autobiography. Identity, for Bishop, has less to do with the autobiographical than it does with the composition and construction of language. Language is identity for Bishop. The difference is crucial: McPherson seeks an exactness, which in Bishop's poems is found to be illusionary. Against Bishop's tentativeness, McPherson reiterates the presence of the individual. The poem "Fingercups," from *Streamers*, exemplifies McPherson's insistence on a natural world that can be explained, and through such description the world is found to be beautiful or wondrous or simply curious:

> Of a green so palely, recessively matched to the forest floor,
> one asks if they will turn a color
> for they could hardly fade more.
> Around them, buttercups spread witheringly bright.
>
> But there can be a deep pink sign of aging
> on a cup's curled edge.
> And when its style calves and the ovary splits,
> one drop of cucumber-scented water sprinkles the fingernail.
>
> Here I've found
> the exhausted shrew, the kissy snail
> in the green steam of a rainstorm.
> But wildflowers do the mopping up.
>
> Is it they who define the fringe?
> Or the border made by the flooding, reddened creek
> one cannot wade or swim across,
> one's joy become impassable? (66)

The gaze is precise and focused. What counts, McPherson implies, are the small and easily bypassed things of the world. One's gaze must practice looking closely to discern the world. By practicing that close scrutiny one gains self-knowledge or "degrees of bliss." As in Bishop's poems, McPherson's poems convince of an eye which has practiced this scrutiny.

McPherson's poems often revolve around a conceit or dominant metaphor established at the onset and usually through the title. In the title poem of *Streamers*, the tentacles of the cyanea or Lion's Mane, a highly toxic jellyfish, are likened to the streamers of bridal veils, hair, and conversations. The Lion's Mane finally becomes an emblem of power—beautiful, fertile, solitary, and able to navigate vast currents—for women. Like the mythological Medusa, women are transformed so that what might be "flawless Orrefors" is rendered "obnoxious, cursed" (74–5) in the male gaze. McPherson, however, does not make a final totalizing argument; issues of gender, for example, are always located in the specific and personal. By relying on particulars and always maintaining their grounding, larger claims are left implied. While not carrying out an overt or didactic political charge, "Streamers" operates subversively. To watch the other closely is to move to a position of sympathy and likeness; to fail to do so results in the continuation of agony and conflict.

The project, over the span of McPherson's poetry, is to show how to see selflessly. The self is a presence, to be sure, but not one demanding its own position or one which enforces that position. In her "Waiting for Lesser Duckweed: On a Proposal of Issa's," from her recent *Edge Effect: Trails and Portrayals*, McPherson describes hiking in December into a bird sanctuary and observing the terrain where duckweed will appear in the summer. To learn about duckweed one must also see its absence: "The way to be introduced to it / is first / to meet nothing" (39). Though unseen, the duckweed is still there, underground, "making turions." McPherson then describes with visual acuity and certainty what is not yet there but will be:

> no duckweed until the summer
> when finally where a creek
>   swims in,
>
>   there's duckweed
> barely tugging
> the moss-strandy bottom,
>
>   wheatcolored
>   seed-shrimps
>   touring in and around

the barbless roots,
hyaline drag-lines,
where a mud-smooth leech adjusts

and tows
the duckweed a bit. (40)

What is created is a temporal "edge effect" —an overlapping of present, future, and memory. The poem also provides an ethical vision of writing. Absence becomes an illusion; looking closely a neglected world reveals itself, if one relinquishes one's preconceptions.

While McPherson shares with Bishop an aesthetic founded upon descriptive processes, Phillis Levin's affinities with Bishop derive from shared metaphysical sources and sensibilities. Levin often weaves her poems together through meter and rhyme with the illuminating sureness of Bishop. In the closing verse-paragraph of the title poem, "The Afterimage," Levin writes:

As I walked
Through the dark, rainbow after rainbow
Appeared, lighting my way up the stairs.
I was so tired, I wanted to close my eyes
But I didn't want to lose the vision
And I knew it depended on my sight.
At last I lay in bed, my eyes on fire.
My body water, the flame dissolving
Through me–flakes of color drifting
Down a stream. And from that day forth,
Even when a flood brought me beyond
All land, into the deepest night, a prism
Inside of me has held the sun's plumage,
The afterimage in which I write. (20)

Here Levin's poem echoes Bishop's "At the Fishhouses" (both poems evoke the elemental and purgative effects of water and fire) and "Over 2,000 Illustrations and a Complete Concordance" (Levin's final lines recall Bishop's "the lines / the burin made. . . ignite / in watery prismatic white-and-blue"). Most apparent, however, is her extension of Bishop's "The Fish": while Bishop closes with the evocation of rainbow, Levin continues developing that vision as well as attempting to forestall its departure. The occasion of the rainbow is metaphorically evoked in Levin's poem at its climax, the visionary dark night of the soul. To write, Levin concludes, is to evoke the afterimage of vision–but also writing is always done in vision's afterimage.

As in Bishop's "One Art," loss and writing are intertwined: personal loss may occasion writing, but to write is always (and already) to be in a position of loss.

Levin's "The Afterimage," like much of Bishop's poetry, doubles time. Consider Levin's lines "flaring from shade / To shade, suspended, suspending me / Between detachment and wonder" and Bishop's conclusion to "At the Fishhouses":

> It is like what we imagine knowledge to be:
> dark, salt, clear, moving, utterly free,
> drawn from the cold hard mouth
> of the world, derived from the rocky breasts
> forever, flowing and drawn, and since
> our knowledge is historical, flowing, and flown. (66)

Levin's lines, with their central construction of anadiplosis, depend upon the echo of Bishop's famous last line with its final verb in literal transit. While Bishop has turned her gaze away from the man mending nets, the scale-glistening docks, and the comic seal to immerse herself in the oceanic and thereby lose herself–the gazing narrative eye / I is transformed into the rhetorical "you" and then finally the embracing "we"–Levin's poem maintains the quest of the self, for the narrative "I" remains solitary with her vision throughout the poem. Bishop's pronominal shifts and reticence to establish a thoroughly narrative and autobiographical "I" swerve her work away from the narcissism that Levin's poem risks in its anatomy of vision. "The Afterimage" is thus an homage to Bishop, yet it is also a rupture with Bishop's poetics. If Bishop suggests a dispersion of the self into the world– that of history and knowledge and phenomena–as a recognition of loss, effecting a mastery through submission to that loss, Levin asserts a concentration of the self, like a cauterizing flame, against loss.

At first glance Levin's work and that of Jorie Graham are distinct and oppositional. However, Levin and Graham insist on a lyric expressiveness where revelation is complete and the poem is thoroughly suffused with its own knowing. And as in McPherson's poetry, Graham's poems establish identity through an epiphanic gaze, a temperament grounded in Bishop's descriptive sensibilities. In her first volume of poems, *Hybrids of Plants and Ghosts*, Graham often composes her poems as frames through which to view a landscape or a particular object. Her poem "Still Life," whose very title indicates her interest in ekphrasis, opens with "Beyond the window frame, two withered maples overlap sufficiently / to weave a third, a tree /

all boundaries, / more opaque for the doubling" (51). Throughout this poem, definition is elided: line breaks are enjambed, but without syntactic logic, as in "a tree all boundaries." The landscape the poem depicts is a place of overlapping–trees interlock and disclose a third. Later in the poem Graham suggests distinct gender definitions: the hero leaves "home to journey over the visible" and "the heroines / [stay] behind." However, she has cast our identity in the collective "we"—we are both heroes and heroines, threaded, as the final line implies, by a "still"—a word freighted with ambiguity—spirit.

With each subsequent volume, Graham develops a more thoroughly sophisticated poetry where the observed world is increasingly textualized in ways distinct from Bishop. Bishop reserves her commentary to asides and parenthetical qualifiers; Graham draws commentary out into collages of historical accounts, philosophical discourses, and self-interrogations. Her poems try to trace the movement of thought and perception (thus her inclusion of sections of Wittgenstein's *Tractatus* in her *Materialism* serve as self-reflexive ars poetica) as it is displaced into writing. There is always, however, a degree of discrepancy for the poems still exist as mirroring interpretations of an external world or experience. "The Dream of the Unified Field," in her *Materialism*, typifies this bind. Cast as a narrative journey–"On my way to bringing you the leotard" (80)—it begins with the sense of daily and maternal duties and it accumulates observations from which an accumulation of understanding evolves: "Starting home I heard...the huge flock of starlings...heard them lift and / swim overhead through the falling snow / as though the austerity of a true, cold thing, a verity, / the black bits of their thousands of bodies" (80–1). Graham resists the pull into a poetics restricted solely to the written material; the external world of phenomena remains the material for signification and meaning.

The closing observation of Bishop's "At the Fishhouses" comes to mind again: in both poems the cold elemental world offers some verity or truth, yet beyond that perception of truth's existence, nothing more can be enunciated. As the starlings emerge from the swirl of mid-winter leaves and snow, Graham's poem follows the image of the crow as it emerges from the flock of starlings; the crow, as a "chorus of meanings," leads to a childhood memory that echoes Bishop's "In the Waiting Room" with its acute description of the gaining of identity and the concurrent shift to childhood as memory:

—regarding what?—till closer-in I saw
more suddenly
how her eyes eyed themselves: no wavering:
like a vast silver page burning: the black hole
expanding:
like a meaning coming up quick from inside that page–
coming up quick to seize the reading face–
each face wanting the other to *take* it–
but where? and *from* where?–I was eight–
I saw the different weights of things,
saw the vivid performance of the present . . . . (84–5)

The poem refuses to end here, but through this storm of recollection (ironically precipitated by the narrator's daughter's forgetfulness), to re-imagine Columbus's first contact with inhabitants of the New World. In the imagined wild snow storm, Columbus's men return with "'three very black Indian / women—one who was very young and pretty....The snow was wild. / Inside it, though, you could see / this woman was wearing a little piece of / gold on her nose, which was a sign there was / gold / on that land'" (87). The series of metamorphoses from her daughter's black leotard to the crow to her recollection of her own ballet teacher to finally these three women suggest a shared condition of identity through objectification and displacement. If the fate of the daughter is tantamount to that of the Amerindian woman, then "what should I know / to save you that I do not know" asks the mother in despair. There is a lacuna between knowledge and salvation that seems impossible to bridge.

Writing is the agency by which Graham can test the possibilities of knowing and uncover the extent of aporia, that is the impasse to knowing. In her poem "Subjectivity," also from *Materialism*, Graham examines language's capacities as closely as she examines a monarch butterfly. Again, as in Bishop's work, the poem commences with the single object as the focus of the gaze. Through the duration of the gaze, possibilities accumulate. It is through this accumulation of perception that Graham approaches knowing the thing itself. Yet, what comes to be known is "the secret blackness / of the page" (30)–both the shadow of the monarch and the writing of the poem. Nonetheless, there is an irreconcilable difference, an aporia that cannot be breached, for at the conclusion of the poem a neighbor tells the poet, "that butterfly's not dead, you know," adding "cold mornings like these they're very still" (31). What was assumed as the essential truth, that the butterfly was dead, is shown to be false. Language, particularly poetic language, is always in this state of a shimmered moment before change. Graham's anatomy lesson, that is the displacement of the butterfly into language, reveals a certain insufficiency or limitation of perception. Specular possibilities, Graham implies, cannot provide for identity or full knowledge. Indeed, the poem's importance lies not in the accuracy of the anatomy lesson—the rationalist assertions and predations upon the body that is revealed so profoundly in such pictorial traditions as Rembrandt, Eakins, and Muybridge—but in the excess or plenitude of perception which supplants the need to know. The neighbor's observation interrupts and severs this other energy of gathering value and personal authority that the poem had been accumulating. How to read this final moment is ambiguous: Does Graham submit to the aporia or does the poem recover its vision of plenitude?

An acuteness of time and transience is certainly implied throughout Graham's poetry, as well as the limitation of language and thought. As bounding frames of knowledge and perception, the sentence—as a grammatical program ensuring fullness of meaning—is found through a writing of accumulating sentences to no longer ensure understanding. The sentence is no longer capable of serving as the basis for reflection or as a repository for reflections. Graham, through accumulative description and phrasing, displaces the sentence for the poem, yet asserts the poem can never establish a fullness of knowing. This is in ironic juxtaposition to the sense of having read a poem by Graham to have had the poem reveal its own fullness, to have ventured to include all possibilities of its writing. The poem then becomes a doubled epiphany: while offering fullness, particularly through its descriptive modes, the poem is neither complete nor a final anatomy or exposure of the poetic process; the poem instead becomes part of an ongoing conversancy.

Looking back at Bishop, we find similar instances of her placing the sentence, and its particular philosophical values, under scrutiny. Indeed, this concern may be the single shared element among a wide range of otherwise disparate American poets in the twentieth century.[3] Among Bishop's poems, "The Moose" may be the best example. The poem is built by extended accumulations or insertions between what seems to be the beginning of a thought and its narrative vehicle. The sense of the opening two lines is not completed until line twenty-six, "a bus journeys west" (169); this destination in transit is reached only after a series of accumulated details often announced by the use of anaphora (the repeated "where"). The accumulative energy continues, however, not reaching the sentence's end until line thirty-six. Indeed, the period, that diacritical mark that distinguishes and separates, becomes at best ambivalent, a form of enjambment, a noted boundary but one passed over. "Goodbye" commences the next sentence, albeit a far shorter one, and a continuation of description. The sense of elegy becomes implicit as the poem seems to be a catalogue of leave-takings; this becomes apparent only after description becomes accumulative and the sentence loses its control of perception and production. While stanza breaks, semi-colons, caesuras, and brief line pauses modulate the sentence, none break the passage into controllable and signifying units. Indeed, the idea of the sentence becomes a "passage," where what is significant is its spatial and temporal ongoingness.

While in a facile sense the passage re-presents the bus's journey and seemingly supports Altieri's charge of Bishop's scenic modality, these opening stanzas pose the question of how we cognitively organize the world into writing. We need to ask here what composes a sentence; what defines a sentence; how is our Cartesian world-view informed by our view of the sentence; how is the written sentence different from the speech-event (especially as poetry is conventionally described as language turned into song). These opening stanzas to "The Moose" not only echo William Carlos Williams's famous lines from *Spring and All*, "so much depends / upon" and thereby serve as an homage, but also seem to fulfill his proposition that poetry "has to do with the crystallization of the imagination" (140). Bishop's poems reveal an investigation of language and perception through their use of description. The vision of our being-in-the-world forms poetry's sacrament. Poetry with all its contingencies both makes material and discloses the limitations of apprehending the sacramental.

Endnotes

1. I cite this brief formula, derived from Louis Martz's *The Poetry of Meditation: A Study in English Religious Literature*, in my *The Still Performance* that discusses Bishop's modes of self-reflexivity.

2. I would point out here that as Bishop draws upon English traditions she neglects the American—in the hemispheric sense—despite even her long residence in Brazil. This is a profound limitation, perhaps at the heart, though not stated, of Altieri's arguments as well as those poet-critics such as Clayton Eshleman, and arguably results in a disengaged sensibility where reticence offers both poetic and critical safety.

3. Perhaps the most important discussion on sentences in relation to their definition and place within poetry is Ron Silliman's "The New Sentence" in his *The New Sentence*.

Works Cited

Altieri, Charles. "Ann Lauterbach's 'Still' and Why Stevens Still Matters." *The Wallace Stevens Journal*. 19.2 (Fall 1995): 219–33.

———. *Self and Sensibility in Contemporary American Poetry*. Cambridge: Cambridge UP, 1984.

Bishop, Elizabeth. *The Complete Poems: 1927–1979*. New York: Farrar, Straus, Giroux, 1983.

Eshleman, Clayton. *Antiphonal Swing: Selected Prose 1962/1987*. Kingston: McPherson, 1989.

Graham, Jorie. *Hybrids of Plants and Ghosts*. Princeton: Princeton UP, 1980.

———. *Materialism*. Hopewell: Ecco, 1993.

———. "Poets Wondering Who They Are." [Review] *New York Times Book Review*. Mar. 4, 1984: 14.

Kalstone, David. *Five Temperaments*. New York: Oxford UP, 1977.

Levin, Phillis. *The Afterimage*. Providence: Copper Beech, 1995.

Logan, William. "The Unbearable Lightness of Elizabeth Bishop." *The Southwest Review*. 79.1 (Winter 1994): 120–38.

Martz, Louis. *The Poetry of Meditation: A Study in English Religious Literature*. New Haven: Yale UP, 1954.

McCorkle, James. *The Still Performance: Writing, Self, and Interconnection in Five Postmodern American Poets*. Charlottesville: Virginia UP, 1989.

McPherson, Sandra. *Edge Effect: Trails and Portrayals*. Hanover: Wesleyan UP, 1996.

———. *Streamers*. New York: Ecco, 1988.

Silliman, Ron. *The New Sentence*. New York: Roof Books, 1995.

Steiner, George. *On Difficulty and Other Essays*. New York: Oxford UP, 1978.

Williams, William Carlos. *Imaginations*. New York: New Directions, 1971.

Language's Doors:
Bishop's Translations of Poems by Octavio Paz

Lee Fontanella
Worcester Polytechnic Institute

Abstract

In the literal meaning of "January First" ["Primero de enero"] is a key to understanding the position of Elizabeth Bishop, translator of poems by Octavio Paz. There is an analogue between opening onto a new year and opening onto a translated version (by Bishop) of an existing poem (by Paz). Another analogue is the one between Paz's translation of Joseph Cornell's physical menagerie into poetry ("Objects and Apparitions" ["Objetos y apariciones"]) and Bishop's translation of Paz's poem into English. I speculate as to what for Bishop might be some of the factors of a proper translation.

Cultural and literary critic, essayist, and poet, Octavio Paz is best known for his incisive essays on the Mexican psyche, as well as for his poetry. Elizabeth Bishop, a close contemporary of Paz, translated five of his poems from the original Spanish into English: "The Key of Water" ["La llave de agua"] from the collection *Toward the Beginning* [*Hacia el comienzo*], 1964–68; "Along Galeana Street" ["Por la calle de Galeana"] from the collection *Return* [*Vuelta*], 1969–75; and "The Grove" ["La arboleda"] and "Objects & Apparitions" ["Objetos y apariciones"], both from *Return*. Then, there is "January First" ["Primero de enero"], from *A Tree Within* [*Arbol adentro*] 1976–87. The title of this paper comes from the opening lines of this poem, since they seem to me to address most broadly the poetic issue that is central to Bishop's translation activity:

> The year's doors open
> like those of language,
> toward the unknown.[1]

However, it is probably the poem "Objects & Apparitions" that has most caught critics' attention, and I personally think that there is good justification for that. Also, it is my opinion that "Objects & Apparitions" is, unfortunately, the most erroneous of these five translations.

I consider "The Key of Water" and "January First" the most accurate and, only *partly* for that reason, the most accomplished. Statements like the foregoing beg the question of what I think is involved in good translation. Surely, in some significant degree, what is involved is a good representation of what the original poet was saying, both literally and on levels above literal sense. The translator's task is somewhat—and maybe very much—like what we find at the end of the first stanza of "January First":

> Tomorrow, we shall have to invent,
> once more,
> the reality of this world.

In so saying, Paz posited, of course, the world of the year prior to one particular January the first. Bishop, in turn, posited Paz's poems as the realities that she would "have to invent, once more," in her translations. If we follow the analogy, just as the year's doors open "toward the unknown," the translator embarks on a semi-mystery that departs from a given reality, the original poem. It is this stance of Bishop's that convinces me that she, as translator, is not the completely free poet-creator, but rather the respectful poet-translator, who is out to devise a fresh product on the basis of what has been. It is as the poet says in "January First":

> tomorrow
> we shall have to think up signs,
> sketch a landscape, fabricate a plan
> on the double page
> of day and paper.

In spite of the fact that "fabricate a plan" seems to me to be a poor translation, the analogy between day (or the temporal year) and paper (on which we'll find the new design) is clear. Bishop's new design on paper is a translated poem. It would have been closer to the Spanish to say "weave a plot," instead of "fabricate a plan," thereby underscoring the idea of a story that unfolds over the temporal period of the new year. In the Spanish, "tejer una trama" means, literally, to weave a weft or woof into cloth.

It would be troublesome, if the new year were viewed as forbidding, for then if the poem is like a new year, how could the poor translator face it? Octavio Paz has the two human subjects of his new year embark on that existential venture with some reticence:

You were beside me,
still asleep.
The day had invented you
but you hadn't yet accepted
being invented by the day.
—Nor possibly my being invented, either.
You were in another day.

The elements of Bishop's new poem are like the human subjects of Paz's new year. When the translator performs her task, the elements of the new construct may remain problematically rooted in their original construct, which is the original poem. Fortunately, Paz's subjects eventually look onto the new year with hope, in spite of the year's mysteriousness:

we'll walk...
among the hours and their inventions,
. . . .
we'll bear witness to time and its conjugations.
We'll open the doors of the day,
and enter the unknown.

If again we follow the analogy—new year : translated poem—we can only infer a happy outcome for the translations—a risky and intrepid business, perhaps, but with a promising view to a Brave New World that is the translated poem.

Why were these specific poems selected for translation? I cannot respond to that, because I do not find a common thread of any sort among them. Lorrie Goldensohn makes much of "Objects & Apparitions" as it related to Elizabeth Bishop's collection *Geography III*: "If Bishop had invented the original poem herself it couldn't have fitted more neatly into [the collection] *Geography III*" (265). Maybe so, but when Goldensohn calls this a "near literal translation," she is mistaken. Of all five poems, this is the one for which we could cite most misbeats and literal errors. Sadly enough, for this is a wonderful poem of what I would call "thinginess" or substantiation—the building-up, piece by piece, of a poetic world wherein words may be observed and their interrelated sounds savored, just as in the case of Joseph Cornell's display boxes and their contents that are the subject of the poem. It was written by Paz for Joseph Cornell, who had collected and encased memorabilia connected with stars of the nineteenth century, such as the Swedish singer Jenny Lind (1820–87) and Jenny Colonne (1808–42), lover of Gérard de Nerval.

Certain aspects of the translation are strong. To be sure, cognates can be conducive to success, as occurs in the very first word, "hexahedrons." The double aspirant (H-H) in "hexahedrons" matches the Spanish "hexaedros," where there is no aspirated H, but there is a repeated E sound; to boot, the accentuation conforms. Right from the start, we want to know what is inside this glorious word that stands for the boxes in which Joseph Cornell has encased his memorabilia. Equally fortunate are the cognates "monuments to every moment" ["monumentos a cada momento"], for they not only catch the alliterated M, but also the trick of the extracted syllable—NU—in order that "monumentos" yield "momento." For this poem that sings of objects, Bishop had the wisdom to maintain the order of items mentioned and to translate them with literal precision:

> Canicas, botones, dedales, dados,
> >   [Marbles, buttons, thimbles, dice,]
> alfileres, timbres, cuentas de vidrio:
> >   [pins, stamps, and glass beads:]
> cuentos del tiempo.   [tales of the time.]

There was, probably, no way for Bishop to capture the elision from "cuentas" to "cuentos": "...cuentas de vidrio: / cuentos del tiempo." She did venture the appropriate repetition "refuse...used," in the fifth line, to match Paz's "hechos con los desechos...."

When she again attempts to respect repetitive diction in the Spanish, she fails:

> Memoria teje y destejo los ecos:
> >   [Memory weaves, unweaves the echoes....]

Paz's Spanish means "Memory weaves, and *I unweave* the echoes"— in effect, a statement on the poetic process in this poem. How could she have missed it, when time and again, the clues are there, and she captures them with linguistic accuracy, as in the examples that follow:

> But you constructed
> boxes where things hurry away from their names.

Although in this example, either "scurry from" or "shed off" might have worked better than "hurry away from," the rest of the examples that comment indirectly on the poetic process are fine translations:

Minimal, incoherent fragments:
the opposite of History, creator of ruins,
out of your ruins you have made creations.

A comb is a harp strummed by the glance
of a little girl
born dumb.

The apparitions are manifest,
their bodies weigh less than light,
lasting as long as this phrase lasts.

Joseph Cornell: inside your boxes
my words became visible for a moment.

Bishop—I must presume—understood "Objetos y apariciones." Why, then, the clumsiness of a phrase like "'One has to commit a painting,' said Degas, / 'the way one commits a crime,'" when nothing in the Spanish prompts a double use of "commit"? Why "condensation flask for conversations," when the Spanish means, literally, "vessel for the rendezvous of memories"? And her use of the idiomatic "objects putting the laws / of identity through hoops" does not satisfy the image of rolling hoops with sticks, the hoops being the laws of identity.

Often, my first impulse is to try to justify Bishop's constructions on the grounds of sonorous quality. Apart from the appeal that the poetic subjects must have had for her, Bishop is respectfully attentive to sounds in Paz's poems, as in the opening lines of "Along Galeana Street." Here the three explosive Ps, spaced one to a line, to suggest, I suppose, hammer blows, were suggested also in Paz's Spanish and recreated strategically by Bishop:

Golpean martillos allá arriba	[Hammers pound there above
voces pulverizadas	pulverized voices
Desde la punta de la tarde bajan	From the top of the afternoon
verticalmente los albañiles	the builders come straight down]

I would have said "peak," instead of "top," of the afternoon, to achieve still more explosiveness. And sometimes, Bishop does Paz one better in respect to sonorous quality. In "The Key of Water," the line "the Ganges is still green" has, almost, the potential of a movie or book title that runs around in our brain. And, in the same poem, she respects "grandes golfos de calma" through her "great gulfs of calm," but the sound of "nubes negras" ("black clouds") is, really, too hard to satisfy fully.

If I am right in thinking that translated *sound* is as important in Bishop's work as translated *sense*, then there is scarcely an achievement like "The Key of Water." Here is her translation, alongside the entire original. The exoticism of the proper nouns Rishikesh and Ganges is equal for both languages, and so is the quotation in French.

Adelante de Rishikesh	[After Rishikesh
el Ganges es todavía verde.	the Ganges is still green.
El horizonte de vidrio	The glass horizon
se rompe entre los picos.	breaks among the peaks.
Caminamos sobre cristales.	We walk upon crystals.
Arriba y abajo	Above and below
grandes golfos de calma.	great gulfs of calm.
En los espacios azules	In the blue spaces
rocas blancas, nubes negras.	white rocks, black clouds.
Dijiste:	You said:
Le pays est plein de sources.	*Le pays est plein de sources.*
Esa noche mojé mis manos en tus	That night I dipped my hands
pechos.	in your breasts.]

It is unfortunate that the ending of the translation "The Grove" is the only part of this beautiful pictorialist poem that is notably weak. I place the two versions side by side:

El patio,	[The patio
encerrado en sus cuatro muros,	enclosed in its four walls
se aísla más y más.	grows more and more secluded.
Así perfecciona su realidad.	Thus it perfects its reality.
El bote de basura	And now the trash can,
la maceta sin planta,	the empty flower pot,
ya no son,	on the blind cement
sobre el opaco cemento,	contain nothing but shadows.
sino sacos de sombras.	
Sobre sí mismo	Space closes
el espacio	over itself.
se cierra.	Little by little the names
Poco a poco se petrifican los	petrify.]
nombres.	

The English should have read "...the names grow petrified." After describing poetically a slow evolution from chaotic late afternoon, through sunset, to shadows and nighttime, the poet rests on the theme of concrete reality, wherein movement ceases and the word remains to represent the resultant scene and its meaning. And we have this, to some extent, in "Along Galeana Street." It is crucial in "Objects & Apparitions," where Bishop-translator is to Paz-poet, as Paz-poet was to Joseph Cornell—constructor and populator of "hexahedrons of wood and glass." They are, all three of them, as Paz had said, "dios solitario sobre un mundo extinto" ["God alone above an extinct world"]. Just as it was Paz's task to give life to that extinct world that Joseph Cornell had amassed, so it was Bishop's task to breathe new life into the reality that was the poem composed by Paz:

> the opposite of History, creator of ruins,
> out of your ruins you have made creations.

and

> A comb is a harp strummed by the glance
> of a little girl
> born dumb.

At the close of "Objects & Apparitions," we are back at the start, when Paz had looked onto the unknown reality of the new world that had to be invented for the new year. Bishop reinvented Paz in the form of her words that became "visible for a moment," just as Paz had reinvented Joseph Cornell's cases and, in doing so, his "words became visible for a moment." In a way, they are all three godly puppeteers with the invention of new realities as their task.

Endnote

1. I use the Eliot Weinberger edition, *The Collected Poems of Octavio Paz: 1959–1987* (New York: New Directions, 1987), this citation from p. 595. I recognize that between the Weinberger editions and the translations that appear in Elizabeth Bishop, *The Complete Poems: 1927–1979* (New York: Farrar, Straus, Giroux, 1983) there are some notable differences. I have chosen to use the former, in order to be consistent, although some translation choices in the latter may be better.

Works Cited

Bishop, Elizabeth. *The Complete Poems: 1927–1979*. New York: Farrar, Straus, Giroux, 1983.

Goldensohn, Lorrie. *Elizabeth Bishop: The Biography of a Poetry*. New York: Columbia UP, 1992.

Paz, Octavio. *The Collected Poems*. Ed. Eliot Weinberger. New York: New Directions, 1987.

"The Smallest Woman in the World": Refractions of Identity in Elizabeth Bishop's Translation of Clarice Lispector's Tale

M. Sheila McAvey

Becker College

Abstract

In the winter of 1962–63, Elizabeth Bishop translated five short stories by the Brazilian novelist Clarice Lispector, three of which are extant. I contend that using another woman's voice in a story, specifically, "The Smallest Woman in the World," enabled Bishop to explore, if not express, vicariously, some of her own conflicted views of the mother-child relationship. Lispector's blunt, sardonic humor and her unflattering perception of maternal care, of love, which are detailed in "SWW" through the character of Little Flower, as well as through the narrator's voice, make Lispector's work a natural magnet for a mind like that of Elizabeth Bishop.

During the winter of 1962–63, Elizabeth Bishop took up Robert Lowell's suggestion that she include in her translations from Portuguese writers works by the Brazilian novelist Clarice Lispector. Bishop translated five of Lispector's stories. The three that are extant, "The Smallest Woman in the World" ("SWW"), "A Hen," and "Marmosets," appeared in 1964 in *Kenyon Review*.[1] Bishop's choice of Lispector, an acquaintance and writer whose feminism was an aspect, though a significant one, of her broader concern with the isolation of the human condition, was apt. A dominant theme in Lispector's writings, as in Bishop's works, is the question of how to define oneself as a woman and as an individual being in relation to others. "The Smallest Woman in the World" is typical Lispector, with its introspective style and the humorously sardonic outlook of its narrator. Its deeper appeals for Bishop, I would argue, are the emphasis on the theme of darkness that abides in maternal care and in love itself, as well as the tale's distinctive narrating voice that is, peculiarly, both amiable and cynical. The tale's satiric portrait of the earth-mother heroine and a rogues' gallery of urban maternal characters, who reel back from or obstinately ignore any consideration of their unmaternal selves, afforded Bishop a way to delve into her own powerful ambivalence about the need to enjoy being a physical body, a body that knows love, and the self-protective dread of those very needs.

Clarice Lispector could be categorized as a moralizing, feminist writer. She was indeed concerned with issues of individual conscience and societal norms, but her feminism was inextricable from her concern with the isolation of the human condition. Her feminism has been defined as "an uncompromising, assiduously held attitude ... about the fact that ... men and women are cursed because they must ponder their lonely fate even as they live it out to its inescapable end" (Fitz, "Freedom" 58). But that perspective leaves out Lispector's wily humor, particularly as it is manifested in her unflattering characterizations of women. Comparatively, we can see in Bishop's writings a similar tenor and subject matter: the same paradoxical dread of and desire for solitude, the uncertainty of identity, and the attraction-repulsion toward the female as mother figure, which underlies a profound ambivalence about what it means to be called "woman." In "SWW," the title of which suggests much about her own self-image, Bishop found insistent echoes of harrowing memories and refractions of her own struggle to define herself. In addition, Bishop may well have encountered, in Lispector's stories, if not in Lispector's blunt philosophical realism, a way to describe her own conflicting views about women and mothering. Moreover, I would suggest that working with "SWW" provided Bishop an opportunity to take self-protective concealment behind the tapestry of another writer in order to delve into her own past.

Seeing, vision, what the "I/eye" defines as reality, is a recurrent theme in Lispector's story, "SWW," and not accidentally, in Bishop's writings, especially her post-1964 poems. One way of describing "SWW" is to say that it is a fantasy about seeing the world, and a detailed view of woman *as* the world and *in* the world. A mock fairy tale, the work concerns the discovery by a male French explorer of a 17 ¾-inch very pregnant Pygmy woman. The plot is structured by its narrating voice, which details both the explorer's response to this woman—whom "the greed of the most exquisite dream could never have imagined"—and the ambivalent reactions that a photograph of this marvel, published in a Sunday newspaper, arouses in readers, primarily female, who regard this woman-child from the safe remove of their urban world.

The tale opens with a mocking illustration of that favorite Romantic cliché, the maternal universe. The overworked vision of a lush world, animalistically alive and emphatically female, is the backdrop for the narrator's description of a delightfully humorous encounter between Marcel Pretre, "hunter and man of the world," and the story's eponymous heroine. The explorer's proud, manly bearing gets a jolt off-center when he confronts his prey, his holy grail: a child-size *woman*, not a male contender, who is obviously pregnant.

This male hunter, however rational he tries to be, is clearly flummoxed by the existence of a fecund female in a child-sized body. Reason is thrown into confusion; he is vulnerable. But, the narrator insists, M. Pretre doesn't die from shock. "Probably only because he was not insane, his soul neither wavered nor broke its bounds" (501). If the reader has not already smiled at M. Pretre's perplexed response in this confrontation with the sexual female, the narrator provides a description of the hilariously unselfconscious reaction of Little Flower to the explorer's masculine act of defining her with facts, a gesture that undermines his vaunted sense of himself:

> The explorer said timidly, and with a delicacy of feeling of which his wife would never have thought him capable: "You are Little Flower."
>
> At that moment, Little Flower scratched herself where no one scratches. The explorer—as if he were receiving the highest prize for chastity to which an idealistic man dares aspire—the explorer, experienced as he was, looked the other way. (502)

This ostensibly humorous image of the maternal, and thereby powerful, female is reconsidered more darkly at the end of this monumental encounter between *civilis* and nature. The explorer has calmed himself by methodically examining the miniature, sensual, woman standing at his feet; still, he finds himself "baffled" by the warm and bestial laughter of his prey. He assumes, as does the reader, that she is laughing at him, that, in her inarticulate awareness of the world, she has concluded that he is a prude. The narrator disabuses the reader of the idea that Little Flower has any such worldliness. The inquisitive, proud explorer cannot grasp that Little Flower, the jungle creature, is laughing delightedly because she has not been eaten by this much larger creature. The narrator reveals, to the reader, not to M. Pretre, that Little Flower's laughter arises from her animal pleasure in being still alive, in "not having been eaten yet" (505), a fate common to her tribe of Likoualas, who are customarily trapped and eaten by the carnivorous Bahundes tribe. Little Flower is feeling delighted with herself, and laughing for a very simple but self-centered reason: she is oblivious to the feelings, let alone the vanity, of the explorer.

M. Pretre remains baffled by Little Flower, but the narrator ensures that no such enchantment remains in the reader's mind. Ominously, the narrator reports, there is a darker motive for her laughter, one that provides an unexpected glimpse into the materialistic, greedily possessive soul of this maternal female. The reader is told of Little Flower's delight in the spectacle of the explorer's unusual skin color. It is sallow, white. However, the narrator warns, that delight, which might be called "profound love" in one who has no conception of love, is driven by another, less childlike motive. Little Flower, the "material girl" that the flamboyant entertainer Madonna extolled a decade ago, is in love with the novelties that she sees: M. Pretre's odd surface color, his ring, and his boots. This cynical portrait of maternity is rounded out with the narrator's bitter diatribe on the subject of love: "There is an old misunderstanding about the word love, and, if many children are born from this misunderstanding, many others have lost the unique chance of being born, only because of a susceptibility that demands that it be me! me! that is loved, and not my money" (506).

This cynical intrusion by the narrator forces the reader to confront significant, as well as sentimental, assumptions about the essence of love and of maternity embodied in the amoral Little Flower. The narrator intensifies uncertainty with a sardonic parting glimpse at the explorer and his wondrous "discovery." Little Flower, the fertile creature of nature, concludes her interview with M. Pretre by offering an unexpected "civilized" response to the explorer's mundane question about her habitat: "'Yes.' That it was very nice to have a tree of her own to live in. Because—she didn't say this but her eyes became so dark that they said it—because it is good to own, good to own, good to own" (506). Unsettled by this repeated phrase, the reader cannot avoid the disturbing truth beneath the Romantic, and sentimental, equation so dear to the heart of "civilized" minds, namely, that woman = maternal nature = pure love. So much for the narrator's initial portrait of Little Flower as Original Mother.[2]

The narrator's derisive, pessimistic evaluation of maternal care is unflinching. The description of M. Pretre's encounter with Little Flower frames a series of "portraits" of urban dwellers, primarily mothers, as they view the newspaper photograph of Little Flower that intrudes on their Sunday lives. These urban mothers, the narrator sneers, are corrupted and corrupting in their attention to their offspring, just like the jungle mother, who comes from a tribe of women incapable of protecting their young against disaster. The vignettes of urban domestic life that the narrator proceeds to describe compose a grim portrait of maternal love: self-deluded, ineffectual, and overwhelmingly self-centered.

To the narrator's eye, these civilized women enact a debilitating maternity and reveal a dreadful image of what it means to be a woman. In one vignette of domestic life, a young girl broods over the image of Little Flower, a yet-smaller female human being than herself, and comes to the distressing wisdom that no female can escape the tyrannical power of those who care for her. In another household, a young bride's untried maternal love for the "sad" Little Flower is exposed as ignorant condescension. Her mother delivers a contemptuous reprimand to her daughter regarding the great gulf that separates rational, "civilized" women from unreason of all sorts, especially emotions. This matron derides Little Flower as being, essentially, not female, not capable of human feelings such as sadness.

The narrator's mockery of sentimental definitions of maternal care is most severe in the centerpiece vignette of family love. This portrait, an exposé of the deliberate, self-centered willfulness masked under maternal love, echoes the unselfconscious but identically self-centered nature of Little Flower. The narrator details a mother's horrified reaction to her son's thoughtlessly cruel desire to acquire Little Flower as a toy. Pondering the "dangerous stranger" that her son has become, the mother considers "the cruel necessity of loving,...the malignity of our desire for happiness" (503). She senses the beast in her boy, and is even more horrified to sense the beast in her own soul, which, "more than her body, had engendered that being adept at life and happiness" (503–04). Willfully shutting out the thought of her own malign maternity, she determines—"obstinately," the narrator repeats—on a ludicrous solution: she will buy her son a new suit. The narrator makes it clear that the absurdity of this maternal gesture to obliterate the Darwinian nature of her child's hunger for love is just as futile as the mother's subsequent gesture to mask her own inner nature. The narrator mocks her efforts to smooth her features with "a refined and social smile that should put millenia between herself and "the crude face of Little Flower." Her greed to protect against realities imprisons both mother and child in blindness to that essential aspect of the self.

Such corrosive maternal love is more the order in the civilized world than the exception, the narrator implies, offering yet another exemplum of greed calling itself love. A family groups together around the newspaper illustration of Little Flower and is consumed by an identical passion to own that small person. Such human desires should be acknowledged, the narrator snidely suggests: "To tell the truth, who hasn't wanted to own a human being just for himself?"(504) But, the narrator warns, concomitant with this grasping possession is the desire to avoid such responsibilities. Possessing another, the speaker jibes, "wouldn't always be convenient; there are times at which one doesn't want to have feelings" (504).

The tale's exhausting condemnation of maternal love concludes with the narrator's humorous portrait of an elderly newspaper reader's encounter with the photograph of Little Flower. This woman, long past the naive maternal whims of a bride and the strained exertions of actual maternal care, slams her newspaper shut against the implicit suggestion that a feral, female creature has the same reproductive capacity as herself. Maternal blindness to others' natures withers, in old age, to smug self-absorption.

Both the character of Little Flower and the distancing, sardonic voice of the narrator in this tale resonate with Elizabeth Bishop's own life and writings. Little Flower, the smallest woman in the world, embodies the conflicted feelings about mothers and mothering within Elizabeth Bishop: the sense of relief Bishop must have felt in "not having been eaten" by the loneliness of her isolated childhood, her delight in the fecundity of love, as well as in the pleasure of being a woman loved by another woman. However, Bishop's life had instilled into her a wariness towards women, towards love, and reinforced her guilt-ridden sense of herself as outsider. Little Flower, the mother *in potentis*, also represents Bishop's dark perception of maternal love from a child's point of view: the dread of her neediness, her greed for love, for companionship, which manifested itself in the series of sexual relationships that exposed a persistent emotional dissatisfaction that her lovers were incapable of countering. The "great darkness" growing in Little Flower is similar to the great darkness of Bishop's view of her childhood loss, and her probably inevitable loss of faith in the sustaining nourishment that was to be had through love.

Bishop's transplant to Brazil, however badly it ended in 1967, did alter her child's-eye vision of mothering. However, it is important to remember that Bishop never lost the *perspective* of being always the outsider, "the guest in other people's houses," as David Kalstone remarked (118). The fact that Bishop had been reworking childhood stories during this period of her life, particularly "In the Village" and the translation of a young Brazilian woman's diary, later entitled the *Diary of "Helena Morley,"* suggests a need to define herself.[3] Bishop's engagement with "SWW," and specifically with the character Little Flower, enabled her to examine a female self, and the unusual narrating voice in "SWW" was another means of evoking and expressing Elizabeth Bishop's wariness about the self, women, and love. The narrator's sardonic humor and biting analyses of "civilized" maternal love suggests Bishop's own increasing pessimism regarding the human tendency to give and to withhold love. Possibly, in her eroding relationship with Lota de Macedo Soares, Bishop recognized the tale's disturbing dictum regarding "the cruel necessity of loving,...the malignity of our desire for happiness" (503).

In her close working with "SWW," Bishop might have found a means to avoid direct memories of terrible personal experiences, and, through the voice of another writer, a way to examine the profoundly painful issues of identity, love, mothers. Clarice Lispector's story gave Bishop a safe way to contend with her own demons. In addition, ironically, Bishop's engagement with this writer, and with this story, might well have fostered her own development—or return—towards a pessimistic vision of human nature. "The Smallest Woman in the World" provided her with another "I / pair of eyes" with which she could puzzle over, yet again, what it means to be a woman, and how difficult it is to seek or trust in love after a childhood of traumatizing maternal loss.

Endnotes

1. Lispector's first collection of short stories, *Some Stories [Algun Contos]*, was published in 1952, during several years' residence in Washington, DC, with her husband and infants, and three years after publication of her third novel. In 1960, these six stories were included in a collection of thirteen tales entitled *Family Ties [Lacos de Familia]*. This collection, which demonstrates Lispector's characteristic endeavor to capture the mind's stream of consciousness, is regarded as Lispector's most successful work, technically superior to her novels. Indeed, scholars and translators of her work such as Earl E. Fitz and Giovanni Pontiero note that the short-story format was Lispector's metier; in that form she best conveyed her characteristic technique: a sudden moment of epiphany, self-realization, when a character has a traumatic insight into her/his nature.

2. In naming her exotic heroine, Lispector played with the ironic connection between the creature "Little Flower" and the familiar appositive of the nineteenth-century French saint Therese Martin, the Little Flower. In largely Catholic Brazil, Lispector probably was aware of the saint's common name. Both the fictitious and the real woman are spunky in nature, but the behavioral gap between them is wide. Unlike the contentedly pregnant jungle flower, Therese Martin prided herself on her physical purity and her abstinence from daily human pleasures. Little Flower is a witty namesake to the virgin, Victorian saint. See Patricia O'Connor, *Therese of Lisieux: A Biography* (Huntington, Ind.: Our Sunday Visitor, 1983).

3. In the early years of her residence in Brazil, Bishop reworked a number of stories, that were scarcely veiled examinations of her childhood. For Bishop, prose represented a distinct way of looking back to her past, a period when her losses were multiple. The most anthologized of the stories "The Baptism" (1937), "The Farmer's Children" (begun in 1937 but published in 1947), "Gwendolyn" (1953), and "In the Village" (1953), all center on loss through death. It is clear that the dominant child's-eye view of lost maternal care in these stories held a powerful resonance for Bishop.

Works Cited

Bishop, Elizabeth. *The Collected Prose*. Ed. Robert Giroux. New York: Farrar, Straus, Giroux, 1985.

———. *The Complete Poems, 1927–1979*. New York: Farrar, Straus, Giroux, 1983.

Fitz, Earl. *Clarice Lispector*. Boston: G. K. Hall, 1985.

———. "Freedom and Self-Realization: Feminist Characterization in the Fiction of Clarice Lispector." *Modern Language Studies* 10:3 (1980): 51–56.

Goldensohn, Lorrie. *Elizabeth Bishop: The Biography of a Poetry*. New York: Columbia UP, 1992.

Jozef, Bella. "Chronology: Clarice Lispector." Trans. Elizabeth Lowe. *Review* 24 (1979): 24–26.

Kalstone, David. *Becoming a Poet: Elizabeth Bishop with Marianne Moore and Robert Lowell*. Ed. Robert Hemenway. New York: Farrar, Straus, Giroux, 1989.

Lispector, Clarice. *Family Ties*. Trans. Giovanni Pontiero. New York: New Directions, 1992.

———. *The Foreign Legion*. Trans. Giovanni Pontiero. New York: New Directions, 1992.

———. "The Smallest Woman in the World," "A Hen," and "Marmosets." Trans. Elizabeth Bishop. *Kenyon Review* 26 (1964): 501–11.

Millier, Brett C. *Elizabeth Bishop: Life and the Memory of It*. Berkeley: U of California P, 1993.

Pontiero, Giovanni. "Excerpts from *The Chronicles of the Foreign Legion*." *Review* 24 (1979): 37–43.

———. "The Drama of Existence in *Lacos de Familia*." *Studies in Short Fiction* 8:1 (Winter 1977): 246–67.

Elizabeth Bishop's Diary: Introduction to a Performance of *The Diary of "Helena Morley"*

Lloyd Schwartz
University of Massachusetts/Boston

Before Ann Marie Shea—actor, director, and Professor of Theatre at Worcester State College—gave a dramatic reading of excerpts from Elizabeth Bishop's translation (Portuguese into English) of *The Diary of "Helena Morley,"* Lloyd Schwartz offered comment and context with the following remarks.

One surprising aspect of Elizabeth Bishop's life in Brazil was that it provided her with the detachment she needed to write about her traumatic childhood in Nova Scotia without the sentimentality that invaded her earlier stories about children. This nostalgia about her childhood was also reflected in the Brazilian works she chose to translate. Her most ambitious project was *The Diary of "Helena Morley,"* which was a Brazilian classic by the time Bishop arrived there in 1951. It was the actual diary of a Brazilian teenager in the 1890s that was first published in 1942 under the title *Minha Vida de Menina* [*My Life as a Young Girl*]. Helena Morley's real name was Alice Dayrell. Her grandfather was an English doctor who came to Brazil in the 1840s. Her father was a mining engineer in the hill town of Diamantina. Her husband, Dr. Augusto Mario Caldeira Brant, twice president of the Bank of Brazil, edited the manuscript and encouraged her to publish it. Georges Bernanos, living in exile in Brazil, was one of the diary's first champions. It was among the first books Elizabeth Bishop read in Portuguese, and she was enchanted by it. She immediately wanted to translate it into English, under the title *Black Beans and Diamonds*, and she'd hoped, not so secretly, especially given the popularity of *The Diary of Anne Frank*, that it might make some money.

"The more I read the book," Bishop wrote in her nearly 30-page introduction, "the better I liked it. The scenes and events it described were odd, remote, and long ago, and yet fresh, sad, funny, and eternally true. The longer I stayed on in Brazil the more Brazilian the book seemed, yet much of it could have happened in any small provincial town or village, and at almost any period of history..." (*CPr* 82).

Diamantina, in the 1890s especially, reminded Bishop of the Nova Scotia of her childhood. In many ways the diary recaptures the happiest part of her childhood, and gives it a living reality. *"It really happened,"* Bishop wrote; "everything did take place, day by day, minute by minute, once and only once, just the way Helena says it did" (*CPr* 100). "Helena" played the same sort of pranks Bishop herself must have played, and had similar self-doubts. Translating the diary, Bishop also created for herself a new, Brazilian past. Yet she also saw that "Helena"—extroverted, spontaneous, pretty, and healthy—was an alter ego, her opposite. There's something deeply vicarious and personal about this translation. In a letter about Bishop from 1991, the poet Eleanor Ross Taylor wrote: "I was struck by her saying *It really happened*—as she did to me about The Moose—trying to excuse her genius." The diary is a fiction Bishop didn't have to invent.

These are some of the things Bishop wrote about the diary in her letters.

To Paul Brooks, editor-in-chief at Houghton Mifflin, July 28, 1953:

It is, I am certain, a real literary "find," and a "gem," etc. (and I'm rather critical) and should be known outside Brazil....and it is *funny*. (I have seen a dignified lawyer here laughing his head off, reading it.)... It is not "cute," but it gives a beautiful little picture of a way of life that has vanished, etc. The woman who wrote it is now a rich old dowager in Rio.... (*One Art* 269)

To Pearl Kazin, January 26, 1956:

I was relieved to hear that you had received the ms. safely and that you seem to go on liking it. No, *thank you* for telling me there are too many *coitados* ["poor dears"]. Take out every other one, if you want to. I'd be extremely grateful for *any* criticism about anything, honestly, so say exactly what you think. It is awfully hard to judge something one has worked over so much, as you probably know. I've tried to make it sound "natural," too, and probably sometimes I haven't.... But as you may dimly recall, Portuguese is much purer, heavier, and more formal than English, and I am getting so used to it that sometimes I'm sure I've overlooked little things like that. I'd be only too glad for any suggestions or if you want to make any changes yourself—anything as long as it sticks to the meaning.... Of course I'll be going over it again and again, anyway, here, and will probably make little changes up till the last gasp. (*One Art* 313)

To May Swenson, February 5, 1956:

"Helena Morley" and her family are from Minas, here, the mining state—and real "miners." They say here that the *mineiros* eat out of drawers, so if anyone comes in they can shut the drawers quickly and won't have to offer anything, so you get the idea. (*One Art* 316)

To Dr. Anny Baumann, May 10, 1956

The translation is really finished. The authoress's husband, aged 82, I think, is "going over it," though, word by word by word. A lot of his corrections are completely wrong, poor dear, but it is his right, and every so often he does turn up something local, or old-fashioned slang, etc., that I couldn't have got right without him. I went to Diamantina a few weeks ago for five or six days and had a wonderful time and have now finished the introduction. It's the highest town in Brazil, about 5,000 feet, very tiny, almost a ghost town, but still concentrating ferociously on finding gold, and diamonds, in every little brook. (*One Art* 317)

Houghton-Mifflin eventually turned down the manuscript, and the diary was published in 1957 by Farrar, Straus, and Giroux.

To Joseph and U.T. Summers, November 26, 1957:

Please don't expect much. It's a mess, "physically," and there are loads of corrections we just couldn't afford to make, finally. I also think now that my introduction is long-winded. However, if you "get into it" I think you'll enjoy "Helena".... I almost feel I shouldn't tell you the latest about "Helena" but then I think from her early diary you can see she was no idealist. Yesterday Lota called her up to tell her I'd got my copy—and after screaming at her to make her understand it was really *out*, "Helena"'s one comment was, "Is it giving any results?" meaning money, of course. (And she's a billionaire now.) If I ever translate again, I'll choose someone good & dead. (*One Art* 342)

To Marianne Moore, January 13, 1958:

Thank you so much for writing me again about the Introduction to "*Helena Morley*"—that cheered me up enormously; I'd about decided that it was much too long-winded and detailed. I hope by now you've had time to read Helena herself—she's much much better than any introduction.... (*One Art* 353)

To May Swenson, January 15, 1958:

I was so glad to hear you'd got the book and like the introduction—don't you honestly think it's a bit long?... I do think you'll enjoy the rest of it. It will take you back to your early family life with a bang....No, I never did manage to make Mr. Brant show me the original manuscript. I worried about it at first, but if you'd ever met the Brants you'd realize that they are incapable of *faking* anything, and probably the reasons he gave, like bad spelling and handwriting, for not showing it, were the real ones!... [T]he Brants haven't the slightest idea of why the book is good—it's like dealing with primitive painters. The only aspect that interests them at all is $$$$$. It's very interesting from the point of view of ART and its WHYS. I've kept all the old man's notes to me and think sometime

I'll do an article called something profound like "Unconscious Anti-creative Impulses in the Self-made Man." Or "The Degeneration of Taste in One Generation." (*One Art* 354–355)

To Marianne Moore, April 10, 1958:

I was so afraid that "Helena" would go unappreciated that I had a hard time in the introduction not to keep saying, "See what she says on page **," and "Isn't that a wonderful remark on page **?" and "Didn't you, dear reader, feel exactly the same way when you were thirteen, as on page ***?"... The things you quote are all my favorites too—and also didn't you like "Your father was always a good five years older than I was"? And the poor boy who thought he was a French citizen, and "The town's a regular asylum"? So many of these remarks took me right back to Nova Scotia; I'm sure I've heard most of them before.... One of the amazing things about that diary, I think, compared with other adolescent diaries, is that she sees *other* people so clearly. (*One Art* 357–358)

To Pearl Kazin, October 24, 1959:

"*Helena Morley*" is going to appear in Japanese. They are using both Portuguese and English texts, so I'll get about $100 advance for that. Did I tell you that—even after the Pritchett review—the royalty check from England was *$4.90?* That's worse than poetry. (*One Art* 376)

Works Cited

Bishop, Elizabeth. *The Collected Prose*. New York: Farrar, Straus, Giroux, 1984.

———. *One Art: Letters*. Ed. Robert Giroux. New York: Farrar, Straus, Giroux, 1994.

The Art of Naming: The Poetry of Elizabeth Bishop and the Problem of Translation

Michiru Oguchi
Iwanami Shoten, Publishers

Abstract

All verbal art is translation in the broad sense. Poetry, in particular, is the translation of experience. Bishop translated her own life, turning places and moments into words, making them communicable to others. The key to this magic lies in names, since the basis of the poet's work is naming. Bishop's use of proper and common names, and of the first person "I" reveals her philosophy as a poet, while her thoughts on poems and songs reflect her experience in different cultures. By examining the relationship between the issue of names and the problems of translation, I hope to show how Bishop's poetry can reach common readers abroad.

When I first encountered Bishop's poetry in 1989, I was strongly attracted to it and immediately began trying to translate it into Japanese. I soon got stuck on the name of a color in "The Moose." "Silted red" sounded infinitely mysterious, and I wondered what kind of red it was: pinkish? purplish? brownish? The Japanese word for "red" is only the name of a category, which has many variations. But how to convey this particular red? This was the beginning of my quest into Bishop's world, and this paper deals with the issue of names and the problem of translation.

Difference that kills: the impossibility of translating poetry

Correctness is not enough; herein lies the difficulty of translating poetry. A translator naturally wants to produce a text that will read as poetry in its own right. But there is inevitably a great distance between the original and the translation: rhyme, word order, diction, form, and writing systems do not match. This is the distance between two cultures: a different way of seeing makes a different way of saying. This difference can sometimes kill the original, betraying tone, color, or the whole atmosphere. It is not simply a matter of translating the names of things seen on the textual line. There are two phases in translation, visible and invisible, which the translator must take into consideration. Can Bishop's poetry indeed exist outside the boundaries of English? How is the translator to cope with both the invisible atmosphere and visible differences in shape? There must be a "Bishop-like approach" to words, things, and human experience. A comparison of texts in different languages is necessary, but let us begin with an examination of Bishop's own view of translation.

Bishop's eyes: translating and being translated

Literary critic Kalstone discussed Bishop's relationships with Moore and Lowell. Sociologists would call them "significant others" who helped Bishop become a poet. Both did translations which Bishop refers to in her letters. In a 1948 letter to C. Dawson, she calls Moore's translation of *Les Fables* "a great literary curiosity" (*One Art* 158), but one which, she tells Lowell, "sounds very much like her....I'm not sure how much like La Fontaine" (*One Art* 160). Lowell's treatments of Baudelaire and Rimbaud were more daring. In 1961, Bishop tried to explain her objections to his *Imitations* in a four-page letter (*One Art* 394–6) which she never sent. Her criticism of the *Imitations* shows that she valued faithfulness to the original; nevertheless, in her own translations, she was forced to make concessions. Bishop was well aware that translations often disappoint the original author, and that native readers tend to be even more severe judges. She wrote to Lowell: "You don't have to like the 'Riverman' poem. Lota hates it, and I don't approve of it myself, but once it was written I couldn't seem to get rid of it" (*One Art* 382).

Translation widened Bishop's literary ground. She translated poems, stories, and a diary, adapted legends and folk tales, and used the form of hymns, songs, samba, and haiku. Her art is a mixture of the Western tradition and acquisitions from other cultures. Bishop translated poems from French (Max Jacob; Rimbaud and others remain unpublished), Spanish (Octavio Paz), and Portuguese (Manuel Bandeira, Carlos Drummond de Andrade and other Brazilian poets); in her youth, she translated Aristophanes' *The Birds* from the Greek. "The Riverman" is an adaptation of a Brazilian folktale which she learned from Charles Wagley's *Amazon Town*. Traces of hymns, songs, and the samba can be found in the titles of her poems, while the imprint of the haiku form can be detected in "Night City."[1] But she never failed to see the limits of translation in her own work. Producing literal or formal equivalents, avoiding excessively free interpretations, is never enough. Bishop's translators must constantly ask themselves: "Would Bishop approve of this?" In other words, they must search for the method behind the "homemade" philosophy Bishop refers to in "Crusoe in England." This is where the issue of names comes in. Since the basis of the poet's work is naming, this might be the key we're looking for.

The art of naming: places, names, things

The "name" has long been a subject of debate in philosophy. In the broader sense of the term, names are divided into two classes: proper and common. At the turn of the century, philosophers such as Gottlob Frege noted that "names" have both sense (meaning) and reference. This raised new issues concerning names in linguistic philosophy, among them the distinction between proper and common names. The distinction lies in number. A proper name refers to an individual or particular place, and therefore has only one object, whereas a common name, which can mean many things of the same kind, has hundreds.

We might say that poetry and philosophy are two different but closely related methods of searching for the truth. Both focus on language and on images of ideas. But while philosophy explains in order to prove, poetry offers experience in order to reveal. The philosopher meditates on the name, but the poet wants to use it. The poet's work helps us to see things usually unseen, by wording them in unexpected ways. "Crusoe in England" shows us Bishop's awareness of her task as a poet: "A new volcano has erupted..../ They named it. But my poor old island's still / un-rediscovered, un-renamable. / None of the books has ever got it right" (*CP* 162). "I'd christened [it] *Mont d'Espoir* or *Mount Despair* / (I'd time enough to play with names)" (*CP* 165). Her Crusoe has a nightmare about "knowing that I had to live... for ages, registering their flora, / their fauna, their geography" (*CP* 165).

Indeed, names matter to Bishop on various levels: as she shows in many poems, they are her primary concern, subject matter, drama itself. At the Key West Literary Seminar in 1993, Mary Jo Salter, a former student of Bishop's, spoke of her surprise at the first line of "Florida": "The state with the prettiest name." "Why a name?" she wondered. Salter's question led me to the following thoughts. To Bishop, names are something that stick out, as is symbolically shown in "The Map": "The names of seashore towns run out to sea, / the names of cities cross the neighboring mountains" (*CP* 3). In this poem, place names such as Labrador and Norway are mentioned, and the personal name Cootchie is the title of another. But her approach is sometimes more discreet.

In "Conversation," a strained voice says: "The tumult in the heart / keeps asking questions.... / And then there is no choice, / and then there is no sense; / until a name / and all its connotation are the same" (*CP* 76). In "Poem," we hear a happier voice: "Heavens, I recognize the place, I know it! / It's behind—I can almost remember the farmer's name" (*CP* 176).

In the climax of "The Moose," old voices are overheard: "...somewhere, / back in the bus: / Grandparents' voices / uninterruptedly / talking, in Eternity: / names being mentioned, / things cleared up finally...." These voices end with a "'Yes...' that peculiar / affirmative. 'Yes...' /...that means 'Life's like that. / We know *it* (also death)'" (*CP* 171–2). No proper names are given in these examples. Is this just a coincidence, or were they dropped on purpose?

Bishop's attitude toward names is different from Lowell's. She writes to him in a 1957 letter, "I must confess...that I am green with envy...I could write...about my Uncle Artie, say—but what would be the significance? Nothing at all. He became a drunkard, fought with his wife, and spent most of his time fishing—and ignorant as sin...Whereas all you have to do is put down the names! And the fact that it seems significant, illustrative, American, etc....In some ways you're the luckiest poet I know!" (*One Art* 351). She was not actually jealous. On the contrary, she was teasing Lowell, surrounded as he was with famous names. She even seems to be gently discouraging him from writing more confessional poetry, of which she didn't approve.

A few characteristics of Bishop's own use of names are as follows: she seems to prefer common names to proper names; she tends to delete proper names where the reader expects them most; she uses some proper names as common names as in the case of "Arthur," who appears several times in her work. In "First Death in Nova Scotia," he is both an uncle and a cousin, which is rather confusing. This is also true of "Mary": we meet Aunt Mary in the Nova Scotia story, "Primer Class," but in "Sunday, 4 A.M.," we can't tell if the figure in the dream is an aunt or a friend.

Arthur stirs our curiosity because a real Arthur existed in her Nova Scotia genealogy: Uncle Artie, her mother Gertie's brother.[2] Bishop's relatives gave her the portraits of Artie and Gertie, aged 12 and 8, and looking at them, she noted that Artie resembled her (*One Art* 349). In her work he becomes her double, too. In her memoir, however, he becomes "Uncle Neddy." Confusingly enough, he shares this name with her Worcester uncle in "The Country Mouse." One proper name blends into another, rendering number, gender, and identity ambiguous.

Why this confusion? Arthur and Mary needn't be Chillingworth or Ishmael, but Bishop seems to have chosen the most conventional names possible, as if to say, "Why the big fuss? Names don't matter." In reality, names meant a lot to her, so she decided to disguise them. The title "In the Village" is better than "In Great Village," because it could be any village in Nova Scotia. By dropping the "properness" from a proper name, she can protect her privacy and be free to write. Revealing the truth by hiding facts was the best way for her to avoid writing confessional poetry or *roman à clef.* But there are proper names that one can't avoid using: one's own name and the pronoun "I."

Bishop's "I": between the ultimate name and the anonymous

Although neither proper nor common, the first person "I" is still a peculiar name with an ontological significance. In a sense "I" is more important than one's given name. It can be thought of as the ultimate name for the subject. It was in Worcester that Bishop found strangers within herself. "In the Waiting Room" records the drama of names: the discovery of two classes of "I"s and an infinite number of "Elizabeths."

The revelation of a precocious girl starts with an "*oh!*" in her aunt's voice: "it was *me*: / my voice, in my mouth, / ... / I—we—were falling, falling," (*CP* 160)—falling off to where? She tries to get rid of this strange feeling that she's never experienced before. "I said to myself: three days / and you'll be seven years old. / ... / But I felt: you are an *I*, / you are an *Elizabeth*, / you are one of *them*, / *Why* should you be one, too?." In an attempt to figure out what's happening to her, she asks herself a series of questions. "I scarcely dared to look / to see what it was I was." "Why should I be my aunt, / or me, or anyone? / What similarities— / ... / held us all together / or made us all just one? / ... / How had I come to be here"? (*CP* 161).

Sophisticated readers might call this feeling alienation, the anxiety of being, or an identity crisis. But since these modern terms were not available to the child approaching her seventh birthday, Bishop simply tells us what happened. The poet's task is not to explain emotions, but simply to render the experience.

The late poet Howard Moss has called "In the Waiting Room" Bishop's "most important poem" (*Voices and Visions*). I agree, for two reasons. First, this experience is not the girl's alone. It is a drama of self-discovery widely known in our century. Second, it is also the drama of discovery of the poet's voice, hearing others' voices in one's self. For these reasons, "In the Waiting Room" is the landmark of a poet who was encountering the mystery of names and the magic spell of "I". What, then, is Bishop's first person? Mary McCarthy once wrote that she envied Bishop's mind "hiding in her words, like an 'I' counting up to a hundred." Seamus Heaney states, "Bishop's supreme gift was to be able to ingest loss and to transmute it. She would count to a hundred by naming the things of the world, one after another...." (Heaney 165). Her "I" is no one in particular, and can therefore be anyone. The mysterious power of her first person enables her to transmute a personal story into a universal tale.

This act of naming and renaming resembles the process of translation. Losing and gaining names of people and places, a hide-and-seek of meanings: the narrator is a translator of herself, already living in a dubious world. Wasn't this sense of translation awakened by Bishop's various moves, first from country to city, and later from culture to culture? We can see this young girl's questions mature into the wisdom of "One Art."

The art of losing: counting back to the anonymous

"One Art" is undoubtedly a masterpiece of classical form. Despite its strict form and meter, however, it has a wonderful natural flow which is as lively as a musical improvisation. This villanelle, a French form, seems a product in spirit of her Brazilian years. Bishop, who had always wanted to write a villanelle, also expressed a desire to write a popular song. Although there were several attempts by others to make Bishop's poems into songs, including Ned Rorem's musical interpretation of "Visits to St. Elizabeth's" (Fountain 159), her own wish to write a popular song was never realized. In any case, the villanelle and popular song are two opposite extremes of poetry. Why should a poet of established fame be attracted to popular songs?

Actually, songs were always around her. Like many North Americans of her generation, she first encountered poetry through hymns. Although different cultures produce different songs, in any oral tradition, poets and singers were originally one and the same. Songs are poems not just for individuals to give and receive, but to share, to sing together. Poets belong to the people, and people, as singers, are also poets.

After returning to the United States from Brazil, Bishop must have kept in mind the image of Brazilian poets. She translated samba songs, and the bossa nova was becoming popular in America. Bishop admired Vinicius de Moraes, who wrote such famous songs as "The Girl from Ipanema" (1963), as well as classical sonnets, one of which—"Sonnet of Intimacy"—she translated. In *Para viver um grande amor* (1962), he says that "Being carioca is...a state of mind" (Moraes 185). According to Lloyd Schwartz, Bishop had a close personal relationship with Moraes (Fountain 328), who was one of the few people who remained friendly with her immediately after Lota's death and who seems to have represented the spirit of Brazil to her.

Yet she preferred samba songs written mostly by folk poets, from the backlands who called themselves "singers." The ideas, rhyme, and humor of their song-poems appealed to Bishop. She was as enchanted by the rhythms as Europeans had been before her. The French composer Darius Milhaud, for instance, describes these rhythms in this way: "Brazilian syncopated rhythms have an imperceptible suspension, a nonchalant respiration, and an incessant subtle jolt which are difficult to catch for ears accustomed to classical Western music" (Milhaud 180).

Although Bishop never realized her dream of writing a popular song, her interest in that genre brings us back to the issue of names. In "One Art," the singer recommends, "Then practice losing farther, losing faster: / places, and names, and where it was you meant / to travel. None of these will bring disaster." Yet everything is lost, from the most trivial to the most essential. We hear numbers: 3 houses, 2 cities, 2 rivers, 1 continent. But the final loss is "you." This is only natural, since the singer has reached zero: in the end, "I" has nothing. The poem has the rhythm and story line of a counting song, only backwards. We might call it a "counting back song" about a peculiar, tragically funny one art, of all things, to lose everything.

When he first saw "One Art," Octavio Paz "was amazed at both how wonderful and candid it was," and said to Frank Bidart, "Why, it's a confessional poem" (Fountain 333). But Bishop escapes from sounding confessional for readers who know nothing about her life. They can hear the wisdom of losing clearly enough. If Paz was right, Bishop is still successful in eluding the chase of well-informed readers who can imagine the missing names. Even for them, things are the same: what reigns in this song-poem is the ringing truth, not the facts. The "I" and "you" are anonymous, as Bishop wants them to be. Losing names is indeed not a disaster to a poet, for it is like counting herself back to an anonymous horizon. This is the paradox which will prove her a master, whose songs are as good as riddles, rhymes, proverbs, or prayers by anonymous singers, whose names we never know but whose words we never forget. This anonymity is the ultimate home, where everyone, including "I"s and "Elizabeths" and hundreds of others belong. It is when people forget the words that poets die and become only names.

What can a translator do when faced with a work like "One Art"? Just producing a formal equivalent is difficult enough. Yet both form and rhyme must be preserved in translation. Meter and the length of lines are hard to control, as syllables and intonation differ in any two languages. After comparing "One Art" in Portuguese, French, and Japanese, I have come to the conclusion that none of us translators is particularly lucky in the face of this work's contradictory nature.[3] And yet, I don't believe we should be content merely with conveying the wisdom of losing contained in the poem. Just as my quest began with the search for the name of a color, let me conclude with a curious word that can provide us with a common ground.

Differences to be bridged: a possible horizon

In Sanskrit, the word *namarupa* is made up from *naman*, for name; and *rupa*, color or shape. In other words, the one word *namarupa*, represents the world or all human phenomena. The word entered Japan from China as a Buddhist term, through its translation into two Chinese characters. Although it may be unfamiliar in the West, the discovery of this word indicates one human way of seeing: grasping the world, or human affairs through names and colors and shapes. Further examination reveals that the Sanskrit "name and color" correspond to the concepts of "form and matter," "mind and body," "the invisible and the visible" in Western thought. Thus my quest has indicated that if we keep pursuing Bishop's names and colors and shapes, her form and matter and the "Bishop-like approach," her way of seeing can be shared in many different languages beyond the boundaries of English. In this way, her poetry will surely reach common readers abroad like me.

Endnotes

1. For further discussion of the haiku form in "Night City," see Margaret Mitsutani's paper "Lost and Found in Translation" in this volume.

2. For the real names in Bishop's genealogy, see Sandra Barry, *Elizabeth Bishop: An Archival Guide to Her Life in Nova Scotia*, the Elizabeth Bishop Society of Nova Scotia, 1996.

3. For the French translation see "Un art" in Elizabeth Bishop, *Géographie III*, tr. par Alix Cleo Roubaud, Linda Orr et Claude Mouchard (Les Éditions Circé, 1993. For the Brazilian/Portuguese translation see "Uma arte" in Elizabeth Bishop, *Poemas*, Seleção, tradução e introdução; Horacio Costa (Editora Schwarcz Ltda., 1990). The Japanese is my own unpublished translation "Ichigei."

Works Cited

Barry, Sandra. *Elizabeth Bishop: An Archival Guide to Her Life in Nova Scotia*. Elizabeth Bishop Society of Nova Scotia, 1996.

Bishop, Elizabeth. *Complete Poems 1927–79*. New York: Farrar, Straus, Giroux, 1983.

—————. *One Art: Letters*. Ed. Robert Giroux. New York: Farrar, Straus, Giroux, 1994.

Fountain, Gary and Peter Brazeau. *Remembering Elizabeth Bishop*. Amherst: U of Massachusetts P, 1994.

Heaney, Seamus. *The Redress of Poetry*. London: Faber & Faber, 1995.

Kalstone, David. *Becoming a Poet*. New York: Farrar, Straus, Giroux, 1989.

McCarthy, Mary. "Symposium." *Elizabeth Bishop and Her Art*. Eds. Lloyd Schwartz and Sybil P. Estess. Ann Arbor: U of Michigan P, 1983.

Milhaud, Darius. "La Musique du Brésil." *Rio de Janeiro*. Eds. G. Schneier and A.M. Montenegro. Paris: Autrement Revue, 1990.

Moraes, Vinicius de. *Para viver um grande amor*. Rio: Livraria José Olympio Editora. S.A., 1983.

Voices and Visions. Video Series. "Elizabeth Bishop: One Art." Ed. G. Schreder. Annenberg/CPB Project, 1988.

Lost and Found in Translation:
The Poetry of Elizabeth Bishop in Japanese

Margaret Mitsutani
Kyoritsu Women's University

Abstract

I will discuss two things I have "found" through translating Elizabeth Bishop's poetry into Japanese. The first is a haiku-like stanza in "Night City." The second concerns the way that gender is revealed in the speaking voice in a poem. The existence of clearly defined "gender codes" in Japanese creates a special difficulty in translating a poem like "Crusoe in England," in which Bishop uses a male persona in order to mask private emotions. A faithful translation of simple words like "pretty" and "nice" may reveal what Bishop most wanted to keep hidden.

> Lost, is it, buried? One more missing piece?
>
> But nothing's lost. Or else: all is translation
> And every bit of us is lost in it
> (or found—I wander through the ruin of S
> Now and then, wondering at the peacefulness)
> James Merrill, "Lost in Translation"

My title was inspired both by the lines from Merrill which I've quoted above, and by the anthropologist Clifford Geertz's essay "Found in Translation," in which he proposes that these lines provide the most appropriate metaphor for the confusion and anxiety we feel when confronted by an alien culture (36–54). Following Geertz, I would like to assert that when faced with a foreign text, it is often we readers who are "lost in translation" as we seek to understand a work that upsets our notions of what poetry, or perhaps language itself, should be. Translation is much more than an "art of losing" whatever parts of the text the translator fails to reproduce in a foreign language. As both Merrill and Geertz suggest, it can lead to important discoveries, not only about the text we are translating, but about ourselves.

Elizabeth Bishop seems to have found Seattle in the 1960s alien and unsettling, not least of all because of the influence of haiku that she discovered in her students' poetry. Nevertheless, she was later to use this form in one of her most disturbing poems. The first part of this paper is devoted to an examination of Bishop's attitude toward haiku, and the "haiku-like stanza" I have found in "Night City," a poem in *Geography III*.

In the second part, I will turn my attention to specific problems that occur when Bishop's poetry is translated into Japanese, focusing on the gender of the speaking voice in "Crusoe in England." Although Bishop has intentionally kept Crusoe's gender ambiguous in the original poem, in Japanese, for reasons I will outline below, this is far more difficult to do. Is the gender of a speaking voice artificially constructed, or does it appear "naturally"? An examination of what happens to Bishop's poetry when it is translated into Japanese may provide some clues to begin answering this question.

Elizabeth Bishop and Haiku

When Elizabeth Bishop began teaching at the University of Washington in Seattle during the mid 60s, she was dismayed to discover that many of her students were writing haiku. "I've never seen so many *haikus* in my life," she told her class on January 5, 1966, adding that most were "the sort of thing one might jot down when one is feeling vaguely 'poetic'"(Wehr, in Monteiro 40). In an interview with Tom Robbins for the *Seattle Magazine* at around the same time, she again expressed her dissatisfaction with haiku: "In English, haiku are quite unsatisfactory. They make me feel as if someone has pulled a chair out from under me. Give me the limerick any day" (Robbins, in Monteiro 34). Bishop's open criticism of the form ironically seems less condescending than Robbins's description of haiku as "the little 17-syllable Japanese vignettes." Bishop found the haiku her American students were writing unacceptable not because they were "little," but because they left her feeling unsettled in a way that limericks did not. The limerick, after all, comes to a conclusion, however nonsensical, whereas her students' haiku simply stopped, leaving nothing behind but a "vaguely 'poetic'" feeling.

It is entirely possible, however, that what Bishop objected to in haiku is precisely what attracted her students to the form. At a time when much energy was being devoted to rejecting Western materialism, haiku, with the help of popular texts in Zen Buddhism, was being transplanted on American soil as an exotic, mystical poetic genre that transcended the logic of Western poetry. Unfortunately, many who embraced it failed to see that in order to construct a poem worthy of the name in such a limited space, logic is essential. Far from being "little 17-syllable Japanese vignettes," the best haiku are products of a logical system that requires the poet to juxtapose images in an unexpected way, thus startling the reader into a new understanding of them.

We might say that Bishop's students were guilty of bad translation. In translating what they perceived as haiku into their own language and culture, they were perhaps feeding their own desire for the exotic, rather than making the effort it takes to reach an understanding of the Other. If their poems were written in the naive belief that haiku don't have to, or in fact aren't supposed to "make sense," it is easy to understand Bishop's reaction to them.

This reaction, however, makes it all the more surprising to discover, imbedded in Bishop's "Night City," a stanza that very well could be a haiku[1]: "A pool of bitumen / one tycoon / wept by himself, / a blackened moon" (*CP* 167). While it is impossible to know for sure whether or not Bishop actually intended it to be a haiku, this stanza lends itself to a method of analyzing haiku suggested by Prof. Koji Kawamoto of Tokyo University. Kawamoto asserts that haiku can be divided into two parts: the "basic part" (*kihonbu*), which consists of two images juxtaposed to produce a surprising effect, and the "intrusive part," (*kanshoubu*) usually a nature image (the "seasonal word" of traditional haiku) which works upon the images presented in the "basic part," and gives the reader a hint as to how they should be interpreted (Kawamoto). In Bishop's "haiku," the two images that form the "basic part" are a "pool of bitumen" and a "tycoon," who "wept by himself," while the "intrusive part" is the "blackened moon" that overlooks the entire scene. The moon is a stock image in traditional haiku, but this one seems to have absorbed the black of the pool of liquid tar below, making it impossible for it to illuminate the "night city." Moonlight is hardly necessary, however, when the whole city is burning. After a series of images like: "A gathered lake / of aquamarine," "bright turgid blood, / ... / in clots of gold," and "green and luminous / silicate rivers," this haiku-like stanza is striking for its absence of light, and therefore, color. In a sea of lurid (psychedelic?) color, the "blackened moon" works on the two images in the "basic part," suggesting that the blackness of the "pool of bitumen" is a physical manifestation of the tycoon's loneliness and despair, the liquid tar forming a heavy, noxious counterpart to the tycoon's transparent tears. We might also note that although the remainder of the poem is written in the present tense, this tycoon, the first human presence we encounter in the poem, "wept by himself" in the past, making it clear that there is no place for human beings in this city, which "burns tears" and "burns guilt."

Whether or not this stanza was intended to be a haiku, in it Bishop has juxtaposed two seemingly unrelated images, and shown a possible relation between them through the introduction of a third, which is actually a distortion of a nature image often used in traditional haiku. The effect, although definitely unsettling, is anything but exotic. Consciously or not, Bishop seems to have grasped the logic of haiku that escaped her Seattle students.

"Crusoe in England" and the Problem of Gender

In a 1979 letter to John Frederick Nims, objecting to his proposal to annotate her poems for a student anthology, Bishop complains of a footnote to one of her poems in a Japanese anthology which explains that "Port" in "Port of Santos" means "a dark red wine" (*One Art* 638). This alone may have been enough to give her serious misgivings about the prospect of being translated into Japanese. Her irritation with this sort of misunderstanding was entirely justified; we know from her comments on teaching how much she deplored her students' failure to look up words in the dictionary, and from her criticism of Lowell's *Imitations* how highly she valued faithfulness in translation. The translator's job, like the student's, must begin with a careful reading of the original poem. And yet fundamental differences between the original language and the "receptor language" (a term I prefer to the more common "target language") can sometimes create problems of a completely different order from those that can be solved by "doing one's homework." Translation, in other words, can sometimes change the landscape of a poem, bringing to the foreground elements the poet might have preferred to have kept hidden. One such difference is the way that gender is revealed through the voice speaking in the poem.

In Bishop, the problem of gendered discourse arises most dramatically in "Crusoe in England," which is in itself a "translation" of Defoe's novel. As Frank Bidart has pointed out, although Bishop herself was horrified at the suggestion that "Crusoe in England" was "a kind of autobiographical metaphor for Brazil and Lota," that's obviously what it is (Fountain 377). Aside from the provocative line "—Pretty to watch; he had a pretty body," Bishop deliberately keeps the relationship between Crusoe and Friday ambiguous. In Japanese, however, this is more difficult to do. For although Bishop once asserted that "Men and women do not write differently" (Colonia 8), in Japanese, they do, in fact, speak differently.

Although there is a neutral register used by both men and women for public discourse in Japanese, in private conversation, male and female speech is distinguished by different pronouns for "I" and "you," different vocabulary, and different verb endings, which might be referred to as "gender codes." In translating a first-person narrative into Japanese, the translator must first choose among a number of pronouns for "I," and the decision is crucial, for it will often reveal the speaker's sex, as well as giving a rough idea of age and social status, relative to the person being addressed. For example, *watashi*, the most common first person pronoun for women, is also used by men in formal situations, when addressing someone of equal or higher social status. In written narratives, the gender of *watashi* is often distinguished by the use of the phonetic script (called *onna-de*, or "woman's hand" in classical Japanese) by women, and the Chinese character by men. *Boku* and *ore*, two exclusively masculine pronouns, are used to address people of equal or lower social status, with *ore* being the far rougher and more intimate of the two. The difficulty of retaining the ambiguity of Crusoe's gender in a language with clearly defined gender codes is further complicated by the fact that Robinson Crusoe is a very familiar figure to the Japanese reading audience.

Defoe's *Robinson Crusoe* was, in fact, the first English literary work to be translated into Japanese; a total of eight versions, not all of them complete, appeared between 1852 and 1894. Two translations are readily available in paperback today. Nineteenth century readers may have identified Crusoe with a number of Japanese fishermen who were lost at sea and picked up by foreign boats at a time when the country was still closed to the outside world. Today, they are most familiar with him as the hero of an adventure story. In other words, the expectations that Japanese readers would bring to a poem entitled "Crusoe in England" would be much the same as those of English readers, and they would be likely to find equally unsettling Bishop's translation of a familiar hero into an ambiguous figure who is intensely ambivalent both about his life on the island and his rescue from it.

The main difficulty in translating this poem comes in choosing a voice for Crusoe, and the effect that that choice will have on the depiction of the relationship between Crusoe and Friday.

The most obvious choice would be to use the formal, masculine pronoun *watashi* that has become standard in modern translations of the novel. This would make his affinity with "Elizabeth in New England" less obvious, but that would make the introduction of Friday all the more problematic. Even if it were possible to render such lines as "Friday was nice. / Friday was nice, and we were friends." and "—Pretty to watch; he had a pretty body," in masculine Japanese, the effect would be to give the impression of a sort of male camaraderie that would be utterly alien to the striking simplicity of the English, which, in the words of Anne Colwell, "communicates emotional depth without trying to" (212). The alternative would be to give Crusoe a more feminine voice, which would immediately alert readers to the dissonance between Crusoe's gender and that of the voice speaking through him in the poem. While this would make it easier to faithfully reproduce the introduction of Friday, it would also make his relationship with Crusoe (more specifically, Crusoe's feelings for him) far less ambiguous than they are in Bishop's poem, which would, in a sense, betray her intention. Here the dilemma becomes a moral one as well as an artistic one: is the translator justified in exposing what the poet wanted to keep hidden?

Paradoxically, words that might seem most difficult to capture in translation are often fairly simple. For instance, the two names that Crusoe gives to his mountain, "Mont d'Espoir or Mount Despair," can be rendered as *kibou* and *zetsubou*, the Japanese words for "hope" and "despair," which have one Chinese character in common (*bou*), giving them a visual link similar to the one between the two names in the original. Furthermore, since Japanese, unlike Chinese, has a phonetic alphabet, the pronunciations of the original words can be reproduced alongside the Chinese characters without disrupting the text. This dual use of Chinese characters and phonetic readings is a technique translators commonly employ when they want to preserve the original word while at the same time giving an equivalent in Chinese characters, and can also be used with key words in a poem, such as "Continent, city, country, society" at the end of "Questions of Travel." In "Crusoe in England," however, it is simple words like "nice" (undoubtedly one of the blandest words in the English language) and "pretty" that most clearly reveal the ambiguity of Crusoe's gender, and are therefore most problematic for the translator. From the translator's point of view, they are the key words which will determine the tone of the entire translated poem, as well as its success or failure.

As we have seen in "Crusoe in England," the necessity for defining the gender of the speaking subject through the use of clearly defined gender codes can create problems for the translator when the speaking subject is, in fact, a mask which the poet is using to conceal private emotion. Although the existence of clearly defined gender codes gives the illusion that gender is merely an artificial construct, however, this is not necessarily the case. Translations of novels in which dialogue is central, such as those of Hemingway, sometimes fall flat because despite the proper use of gender codes, a male translator has failed to convey the female characters' speech effectively, or vice versa. While gender codes can be consciously chosen, gender in speech is also revealed in other, more subtle ways.

In comparing two translations of "In the Waiting Room,"[2] I noticed that a number of passages, such as "I knew that nothing stranger / had ever happened, that nothing stranger / could ever happen" were identical. Two women translators, working independently, had captured the almost seven-year-old girl's voice in the same way; the gendered voice seemed to arise naturally, and to be in some way in harmony with Bishop's own. While each translator had solved other problems in her own way, the simplest words, which posed such a problem for the translator of "Crusoe in England," were in this poem indeed the simplest to translate effectively. While two translations are not enough to base a conclusion on, I think this discovery presents some interesting possibilities for an exploration into the question of how gender is revealed in literary style. This line of inquiry may lead us to something important, waiting to be "found" in translation.

Endnotes

1. This was first pointed out to me by both Michiru Oguchi, whose paper also appears in this volume, and Nana Naruto, my colleague at Kyoritsu Women's University, a distinguished haiku poet and recipient of the Modern Haiku Association Award for 1997.

2. The unpublished translation of Michiru Oguchi and Yasuko Ikeuchi's translation, published in *Kotoba o nusumu onna tachi* (translation of A. Ostriker, *Stealing the Language*. Tokyo: Doyobijutsusha, 1990.)

Works Cited

Bishop, Elizabeth. *The Complete Poems, 1927–1979*. New York: Farrar, Straus, Giroux, 1983.

———. *One Art: Letters*. Ed. Robert Giroux. New York: Farrar, Straus, Giroux, 1994.

Colonia, Regina. "Poetry as a way of life." *Journal do Brasil* (Rio de Janeiro) (6 June 1970): 8. Rpt. George Monteiro. *Conversations with Elizabeth Bishop*. Jackson: UP of Mississippi, 1966, 50–53.

Colwell, Anne. *Inscrutable Houses: Metaphors of the Body in the Poems of Elizabeth Bishop*. Tuscaloosa: U of Alabama P, 1997.

Fountain, Gary and Peter Brazeau. *Remembering Elizabeth Bishop*. Amherst: U of Massachusetts P, 1994.

Geertz, Clifford. "Found in Translation: On the Social History of the Moral Imagination." *Local Knowledge: Further Esssays in Interpretive Anthropology*. Basic Books, 1983, 36–54.

Kawamoto, Koji. *Nihon shiika no dentou: shichi to go no shigaku* [*The Tradition of Japanese Poetry: The Poetics of Sevens and Fives*]. Toyko: Iwanami Shoten Publishers, 1991.

Merrill, James. "Lost in Translation." *Selected Poems*. Manchester: Carcanet Press, 1966, 103–108.

Robbins, Tom. "Now Playing: A Touch of the Poetess." *Seattle Magazine* (April 1966): 8–12. Rpt. George Monteiro. *Conversations with Elizabeth Bishop*. Jackson: UP of Mississippi, 1966, 33–37.

Wehr, Wesley. "Elizabeth Bishop: Conversations and Class Notes." *Antioch Review* 39:3 (Summer 1981): 319–28. Rpt. George Monteiro. *Conversations with Elizabeth Bishop*. Jackson: UP of Mississippi, 1996, 38–45.

Bishop and *National Geographic*: Questions of Travel and Imperialism

Carol E. Miller
Benedictine University

Abstract

The questions of travel Bishop poses in her work critique and attempt to subvert the imperialist impulse of Europeans/Euramericans travelling or living abroad, even as they acknowledge Bishop's struggle against that impulse in herself. Later in her life, Bishop traced her awareness of this problem to her first encounter with "othering," which occurred during that visit to the dentist's office she memorialized in "In the Waiting Room." The role *National Geographic* plays in reinforcing an imperialist sense of access/entitlement to the world will inform my reading of Bishop's work as it addresses marginalization, the construction of identity, and the privilege of mobility.

The poem "Questions of Travel," like much of her work, problematizes Elizabeth Bishop's relationship to the places and often contested spaces she occupied during the course of her transient life. Echoed or implied in the poems "Arrival at Santos," "Brazil, January 1, 1502," "Santarem," and many others are Bishop's questions: "Should we have stayed at home and thought of here?" "Is it right to be watching strangers in a play / in this strangest of theatres?" "Oh, must we dream our dreams / and have them, too?" "*Is it lack of imagination that makes us come / to imagined places?*" Such questions inform Bishop's critique of the imperialist impulse to penetrate, to appropriate, to consume, to explain, to catalog. Bishop objects to the fact that the history of travel is also the history of conquest, written "in the weak calligraphy of songbirds' cages." At the same time, however, she acknowledges that "surely it would have been a pity" not to have seen, heard, consumed, or pondered those things that only travel to the "strangest of theatres" makes possible. Bishop is acutely aware of the power of her own fascination with the "imagined places" she—and "we"—are not content to imagine from afar. What troubles Bishop is that we lack the imagination to see those places any differently when we are in them, that we lack the ability to see them as they are rather than as we dream or construct them to be.

David Kalstone writes that the first three poems in *Questions of Travel* are "explicitly poems of method, shucking off habitual notions of culture and history. It is for this reason that Bishop reprints 'Arrival at Santos' from her previous volume and follows it with a poem ["Brazil, January 1, 1502"] that suggests tropical reproof for conventional European notions of conquest and possession." "Questions of Travel," the third poem, "falls back on minute discriminations, the anthropologist's technique, the awakening to a world question by question" that undermines habit (214). But even as she questions and critiques conventional notions of conquest and possession—especially as those resurface in tourism—Bishop also acknowledges her own complicity, as a traveler, in the European history of conquest and possession. Bishop depicts herself as the tourist who, in the final line of "Arrival at Santos," finds herself "driving into the interior," and who, in "Brazil, January 1, 1502," becomes conflated with the 16th century "Christians, hard as nails" who "ripped away into the hanging fabric" of that interior in their drive to possess Brazil. Clearly, Bishop is not simply indicting the imperialist impulse of *other* Europeans or Euramericans traveling or living abroad; she is examining that impulse in herself as well. She is inviting her reader to ask the same questions of travel she has had to ask. Chief among these is whether it is possible to travel or live in the "strangest" of places *unconventionally*—whether it is possible to divest oneself of the habit of imperialism born of a limited imagination, and a limited ability to imagine the world and one's place in it.

Bishop was possessed of a "sense of responsibility toward a world to be lived in and not conquered," Thom Gunn writes (84). That responsibility ran contrary, in large part, to what her culture expected of her, and what it taught her to expect from others. The poem "In the Waiting Room" depicts what Bishop came to realize, in retrospect, was one of her first lessons about her relationship to the other and to the other world "out there." Much has been written about the ways in which this poem describes a child's coming to self-consciousness—"the simultaneous realization of selfhood and the awful otherness of the inevitable world," as Brett Millier puts it— and how it creates "a self-other paradigm" through "shifting inside/outside" perspectives (Millier 23, 24). Several critics have also commented on Bishop's invention or intentional misremembering of the contents of the February 1918 issue of *National Geographic* that sparks the series of realizations the poem reveals. This invented *National Geographic* is significant and deserves further attention, as does the larger role the National Geographic ideology played in Bishop's identity formation. *National Geographic* taught Bishop how to see the world and her position in it, and that created conflict for her—questions of travel—as she made her way through "imagined places." Although Bishop seems to have learned to question *National Geographic's* insistent representation of the Western and non-Western worlds as opposites, although she seems eager, at times, to reject its basic proposition that an unbridgable chasm of difference exists between the two, and that this "natural" difference creates a "natural" hierarchy of First and Third worlds, she remained "haunted," in her words (Millier 394), by the *National Geographic* vision throughout her life, and was not always willing or able to envision things differently.

In their study, *Reading National Geographic*, Catherine Lutz and Jane Collins make it clear that the National Geographic Society has not altered its ideological mission since its inception. In the late 19th century, the newly-formed Society positioned itself as an important contributor to the development of a national awareness of "new global responsibilities." The Society "published articles on the geographic and commercial possibilities of America's new possessions, discussed the benefits of colonialism, and assigned itself a role of arbitrator in determining the proper spellings of parts of the world, hitherto unknown or ignored, and now brought into view by colonialism" (18). The Society advanced a social-evolutionist doctrine that focused on what it believed to be the "evolutionary guarantee" of progress "through the increasing triumph of rationality over instinct." It used its magazine to reinforce "America's vision of its newly ascendant place in the world by showing 'how far we've come'" in relation to more "primitive" peoples and cultures. The magazine's "underlying story was always the evolutionary chronicle, with its contrastive work, its encoding of hierarchy and power relations" (19). Indeed, juxtaposition of the Western and non-Western worlds formed the magazine's fundamental editorial principle, as placing "articles on the United States side by side with articles on the non-Western world often helped depict progress and cultural evolution" (26). And although the Society adopted, in 1915, as one of its seven editorial principles, the policy that only "what is of a kindly nature is printed about any country or people," this allowed the magazine to depict the formerly colonized or "primitive" peoples of the world as lower on the evolutionary ladder, while cloaking its claims of Western superiority in the rhetoric of good taste and good sportsmanship (26–27).

The National Geographic Society also sought, from its inception, to "combine scholarship and entertainment . . . to be a potent force in exploration and scientific research" while winning the attention of a mass audience (Lutz and Collins 24). That it has succeeded in this endeavor is hardly debatable. *National Geographic* magazine currently enjoys the third largest circulation in the United States (only *Reader's Digest* and *TV Guide* outsell it); it is widely used in schools, widely subscribed to by middle-class parents as an educational tool for their children, and is rarely thrown away (2). Because it has been successfully positioned as educational and scientific, the magazine speaks with an authority other mass-marketed publications do not. From the outset, then, *National Geographic* could claim to "present 'true facts' in a judicious manner," giving its images a scholarly veneer (24). Because readers believed in the "scientific truth" of the magazine's representations of the world—because they *wanted* to believe in such a "truth"—the editors "were free to construct their own particular vision [of] 'the West' and 'the rest'" (25, 26). They relied heavily on photographic images to do so, and did nothing to quell the popular belief that the magazine's photographs were spontaneous, candid, objective, and truthful—that they were all part of a growing body of scientific evidence (28). However, as Lutz and Collins note, the *National Geographic* photographer "has always been and predominantly remains, both literally and symbolically, a white man. And not just any white man, but the whitest and most masculine version possible: the great hunter/adventurer...free to roam the globe in search of visual treasure" (184–85). What this means for the *National Geographic* reader is that the great majority of the photographic images in the magazine not only frame the world he or she is "reading" from a white, masculine perspective, they also encourage him or her to occupy the seat of power and privilege that perspective claims as its own. They depict the world as open territory to be plundered or explored. They imagine no impediment whatever to the white man's access to or mobility in the world. They allow readers to possess what is in their sight, to assert a possessive gaze.

That possessive gaze is only reinforced by the advertisements in *National Geographic*. In his study of the more than one thousand ads that appeared in the twelve issues of the magazine in 1929, William M. O'Barr found that those depicting "tourists interacting with native peoples" consistently illustrated the "nonegalitarian nature of their relationship" (58). One of the most pervasive themes of travel advertisements appearing in *National Geographic* in 1929 was that "visitors can look at but do not have to mingle with, touch, or become involved with the natives" (63). For example, an ad sponsored by the Hawaii tourist bureau claims: "The torches of native fishermen will sparkle to you from a distant coral reef as you sit chatting with old chance-met acquaintants of the Riviera" (O'Barr 67). After all, why interact with the culture when you can *survey* it from a safe distance? The world is also presented, in these ads, as "a curio shop where the astute tourist can collect mementos and gifts at bargain prices." They assure tourists: "The world is yours....Native hawkers sell India's treasures for a song," and urge them to buy "brass bowls by the pound" and "[b]ring back the world—in your trunk, your picture album, and your heart." In other words, O'Barr writes, "the world, its peoples, and their artifacts are objects that are there to be possessed either literally or in photographs" (63). As is the case with most magazine advertising, these ads functioned primarily to support the editorial content of the magazine. As Lutz and Collins write: "In its articles on the non-Western world, the *National Geographic* has frequently included photographs that show a Western traveler in the local setting covered in the piece" (203). In all of these instances, the possessive gaze of the traveler serves to reinforce that of the reader. One such photo that includes two white women positions them at the top of a slight incline. They smile bemusedly and patronizingly down on an Ituri forest man in central Africa, who looks at the ground in front of him (204). "In its lack of reciprocity, this gaze is distinctly colonial. The Westerners do not seek a relationship but are content, even pleased, to view the other as an ethnic object" (204). The photo is deliberately composed to "[promote] distancing rather than immersion," and to repeat and justify the viewer's possessive gaze (205).

Clearly, Bishop became aware, at some point in her life, of the ways in which Western culture had trained her to see the world through the eyes of a conqueror, as a hunter/adventurer/consumer free to roam the globe at leisure. She could not have posed her questions of travel had she not understood that her culture had prepared her to both "master" and hold herself apart from the "less evolved" peoples and places of the world, even when she found herself in those places, among those people. Her implicit critique of *National Geographic* in "In the Waiting Room" suggests that she was also aware that the magazine was one of the tools her culture used to educate her about the entitlements that come with "progress" and cultural superiority. However, although she seems conscious of the fact that she had been trained to see the world through the lens of a *National Geographic* photographer's camera, Bishop was unable to resist looking through that lens from time to time. The invented issue of *National Geographic* that appears in "In the Waiting Room" and Bishop's explanation of that invention suggest that she did not—and perhaps could not—fully examine her own complicity in the construction of a fixed and essentially different, essentially exotic other—the other as ethnic object. While she was willing, and able, to acknowledge her own complex relationship to the world she lived and traveled in—especially the non-Western world—while she was able to articulate her complicity in the history of conquest, her work reveals that she remained in many ways "a creature divided," as the late poem "Sonnet" suggests, by a desire to bridge the chasm of difference and a cultural mandate to hold herself apart from—and even to define herself in opposition to—the imagined other.

In a letter to Frank Bidart dated July 27, 1971, Bishop writes of the recently published poem, "In the Waiting Room":

> Well, it is almost a true story—I've combined a later thought or two, I think—and—because you might like this kind of information—I did go to the library in N.Y. and look up that issue of the *National Geographic*. Actually—and this is really weird, I think—I had remembered it perfectly, and it was all about Alaska, called "The Valley of Ten Thousand Smokes." I tried using that a bit but my mind kept going back to another issue of the *National Geographic* that had made what seemed like a more relevant impression on me, so used it instead. (*One Art* 545–46)

Bishop did not, in fact, do what she claims to have done in this letter—she did not go back to another issue of *National Geographic* that contained the images of Africa she felt were more relevant. As Kalstone writes, "the African material mentioned in her poem [is not] to be found in another issue of the magazine which she cited when the disparity was pointed out to her" (246). He argues that that does not "matter in our reading of the poem," because the magazine's physical presence is what's important: "Its subject matter prompts and contributes to her vertigo, but the physical print, the mere literalness of the magazine with its date and familiar yellow and black are an anchor, as definite, and reductive, as her own name" (246). I would argue, however, that Bishop's invention of an imaginary issue of *National Geographic* does matter a great deal precisely because of its subject matter—the "African material" she attributes to it. Why was Bishop's impulse, when searching for a serviceable and "relevant" representation of the other, to turn to stock images of a primitive, savage Africa? Why cannibals? Why detached Western explorers bearing witness to the scene? Why naked African women with "awful hanging breasts"? Did she invent an issue of *National Geographic* in order to expose *National Geographic* as an invention, a fiction, a construct? Or did she recall an imagined *National Geographic* to reinscribe an imaginary notion of the other? Is it possible for the poem to do both, to critique the ideology of Western superiority inscribed in the imperialist narrative of "progress" even as it endorses, on some level, that narrative's objectification of the other?

In 1918, Osa and Martin Johnson had not yet become famous (Millier 445). It was not, in fact, until the mid-1920s that Martin Johnson became "every American's introduction to Africa, New Guinea, and Borneo," as Millier points out (80). We can hardly find fault with Bishop's falsification of their presence in the February 1918 *National Geographic*, as there were certainly other Western explorers and anthropologists presented in the magazine. This element of the fictional edition of the magazine only proves that Bishop knew its pattern of inserting Westerners into "native" scenes well, and knew that her reader would not question their presence. However, the image of cannibals preparing a feast of human flesh—euphemistically labeled "Long Pig"—poses a more significant problem. Given the National Geographic Society's publication of its seven principles in March of 1915, which dictated that "[n]othing of a partisan or controversial character" and "[o]nly what is of a kindly nature...about any country or people" could be printed in the magazine (Lutz and Collins 27), it seems unlikely—though not impossible—that Bishop saw such images in *National Geographic*. I am not prepared to argue that the magazine never printed such images, nor that Bishop never saw such images. It is revealing, however, that Bishop chose to "remember" images of cannibalism for this poem, since the cannibal triggers an immediate response in the reader and sets up an irreconcilable opposition. Peter Hulme writes that "cannibalism" has come to mean "'the image of ferocious consumption of human flesh frequently used to mark the boundary between one community and its others', a term that has gained its entire meaning from within the discourse of European colonialism" (86). Indeed, the image of cannibals functions in exactly this way in Bishop's poem, erecting a distinct boundary between the emerging self (Elizabeth) and the other, between the "civilized" and the "savage." The mere suggestion of cannibalism insures that no rapprochement between self and other, subject and object is possible.

Bishop uses the poem's images of "black naked women" with "awful hanging breasts" in a similar way. Her inclusion of black, bare-breasted women in the invented edition of *National Geographic* is hardly suspect; on the contrary, it suggests once again that Bishop knew the magazine's formula well. "The 'nude' woman sits, stands, or lounges at the salient center of *National Geographic* photography of the non-Western world," Lutz and Collins argue, pointing out that "[u]ntil the phenomenal growth of mass circulation pornography in the 1960s, the magazine was known as the only mass culture venue where Americans could see women's breasts" (172). What is curious, however, is Bishop's depiction of the breasts as "hanging."

In his study of the National Geographic Society's first two decades (1888–1918), Philip Pauly writes that the "principle of absolute accuracy dictated printing photos of bare-breasted native maidens...but the demand of artistry and the uncontroversial meant that these native subjects were young, well-proportioned and often draped like classical nudes" (528). Lutz and Collins concur, having found that, prior to the 1970s, *National Geographic* tended to use light and shadow to at least partially conceal women's breasts. Since that time, the magazine has begun to foreground breasts more and more. However, in accordance with cultural taboos on "sagging or dimpled breasts," *National Geographic* continues to honor the "demand of artistry" by featuring primarily the breasts of very young women. While it has included photographs of older women's breasts, the magazine "bows to cultural pressures by almost invariably printing them in smaller or dimly lit formats" (Lutz and Collins 175).

I don't wish to suggest that Bishop never actually saw images of "hanging breasts" in *National Geographic*. It is more instructive to consider why she chose to "remember" the atypical (for *National Geographic*) and much less appealing or culturally acceptable representation of women's breasts—*awful* breasts—in her poem. Many critics have interpreted Bishop's inclusion of these "awful hanging breasts" as an indictment of restrictive social and cultural attitudes toward women, and the "*oh!* of pain" in the poem as young Bishop's painful realization of the fact that, as a woman, she will suffer a similar fate. Millier, for example, asserts that Elizabeth "is shocked to perceive her future as a woman—self-mutilator, sexual object, vain creature" in the African women, and that her identification, in the poem, "is with womanly pain, the impossibly conflicted life a self-aware woman must lead, the prospect of a startling and inexplicable acquisition of 'awful hanging breasts'" (26, 27). However, while Bishop does use breasts as a possible point of identification with the other—or at least to consider such an identification—she can ultimately only find it "unlikely" that the "awful, hanging breasts" of "black naked women" have anything to do with the identity Elizabeth is learning to claim. What critics like Millier fail to acknowledge is that in presenting her reader with these images of "black, naked women," Bishop's poem reinforces myths of black women's sexuality perpetuated by *National Geographic* and other vehicles of mass culture—myths that only serve to reinscribe the essentialist opposition between white and black women. Lutz and Collins write:

The racial distribution of female nudity in the magazine conforms, in pernicious ways, to Euramerican myths about black women's sexuality. Lack of modesty in dress places black women closer to nature. Given the pervasive tendency to interpret skin color as a marker of evolutionary progress, it is assumed that white women have acquired modesty along with other characteristics of civilization. Black women remain backward on this scale, not conscious of the embarrassment they should feel at their nakedness....Their very ease unclothed stigmatizes them. (172)

This white/black, civilized/savage split is only exacerbated by popular representations of black women as excessively and exuberantly sexual creatures. According to this stereotype, rooted in the pseudo-science the National Geographic Society endorses, black women "densely code sex, animal, dark, dangerous, fecund, pathological," Donna Haraway writes (154). Bishop's representation of African women in the poem's invented issue of *National Geographic* does little to contest that stereotype. Instead, Bishop creates an image of (dark, primitive) African women that is not only impossible for (white, civilized) Elizabeth to identify with, but that also emphasizes the *awfulness* of both their blackness and their sexuality, manifest in their decidedly unappealing, even frightening nakedness. These are not the standard "well-proportioned native maidens" so often pictured in *National Geographic*. On the contrary, these are mature—even "over-ripe"—women with grossly exaggerated sexual features. Their "awful" breasts—markers of their frank and awful sex—*hang* there for all to see, testifying to their monstrous fecundity. "Their breasts were horrifying," Elizabeth tells us in the poem, and it is not unreasonable to conclude that what she finds horrifying is the inevitability of her own emerging sexual identity, especially if Bishop is making oblique reference to the "horror" of her own lesbianism. However, that Elizabeth comes to this realization when confronted with stereotypical images of savage Africans possessed of unseemly appetites— whether cannibalistic or sexual—cannot be ignored. Nor can we ignore that these images come largely from (or are enlarged by) Bishop's imagination. Elizabeth may sympathize with the "black, naked women," as Millier suggests, but she cannot *empathize* or *identify* with them because they do not represent "real" women any more than the men carrying the "Long Pig" represent "real" men. Both are inventions, fictions, constructs in opposition to which Elizabeth is left to assert her own "real" identity. She turns away from these images, from the reductive myths of the non-Western other they represent, "to look/ to see what it was I was" "back in" the waiting room. While the poem does play with an insider/outsider dichotomy, when Elizabeth strays "outside" of herself to the imaginary realms the invented *Na-*

tional Geographic opens to her, she finds nothing usable (like boots, trousers, skirts are usable), familiar (like the family voice is familiar), or even "likely" there, and so returns "inside," where the poem ends.

The image of the other Bishop constructs in "In the Waiting Room" ultimately works to reinforce the civilized/savage binary that not only reinscribes the oppositional nature of the relationship between "the West" and "the rest," with its implicit hierarchy, but also casts the other as impossibly and unreachably different. Whether Bishop did so deliberately or unconsciously is not clear. Nor is it clear whether she did so to parody or subvert the *National Geographic* narrative of progress, because so much of the issue's content is invented. That Bishop felt it necessary to explain the liberties she took in the poem suggests she was less concerned with subversion than she was with finding "relevant" images to use in this work. On the other hand, one could argue that Elizabeth is, in effect, like the anachronistic figures of Osa and Martin Johnson that Bishop inserts into the invented issue: she's taken "outside" of her place and time, deposited on the scene in Africa, and is asked to bear detached witness to the "strange theatre" of the place, to adopt the colonial gaze but not to participate. Interpreting the poem this way makes Bishop's indictment of the National Geographic Society's imperialist project more visible, but it does not resolve the problem of her representation of Africans as ethnic objects. Rather than suggesting that they might have some agency, some ability to assert their *own* identities, Bishop depicts them simply as static figures that fulfill Western fantasies of essential difference, backwardness, and inferiority.

In "The Eye of the Outsider," one of the first critical works to give serious consideration to the political stance Bishop takes in her work, Adrienne Rich writes that she is interested in "how the outsider's eye enables Bishop to perceive other kinds of outsiders and to identify, or try to identify, with them" (127). What Rich values in Bishop's work is "her attempt to acknowledge other outsiders, lives marginal in ways that hers is not" (131). Rich recognizes, however, that Bishop's attempts to identify with or speak to or for the marginalized and powerless are not always successful:

> The personae we adopt, the degree to which we use lives already ripped off and violated by our own culture, the problem of racist stereotyping in every white head, the issue of the writer's power, right, obligation to speak for others denied a voice, or the writer's duty to shut up at times or at least to make room for those who can speak with more immediate authority—these are crucial questions for our time, and questions that are relevant to much of Bishop's work. (131)

However, Rich concludes that, despite the fact that Bishop's attempts to identify with the outsider or the other are not always "fully realized or satis- fying," it is important that, "through most of her life, Bishop was critically and consciously trying to explore marginality, power and powerlessness, often in poetry of great beauty and sensuousness"(135). That is clearly the case, even in a poem like "In the Waiting Room," which lapses too easily into stereotyping and objectification of the non-Western other. It is also clear that Bishop was very aware of her own conflicted feelings toward the outsiders she encountered during her life.

The late poem "Santarem" perhaps best expresses that conflict, her awareness of it, and the sense it produced in her of being "a creature di- vided." Bishop begins "Santarem" with a tentativeness—and a qualifica- tion—that we don't find in "In the Waiting Room": "Of course I may be remembering it all wrong / after, after—how many years?" The same could certainly be said of "In the Waiting Room," but Bishop only seems to ac- knowledge that in the later poem of the two. As is the case with "In the Waiting Room," what is particularly significant in "Santarem" is what Bishop remembers, or thinks she remembers: "I liked the place; I liked the idea of the place," with its two rivers "coming together" rather than diverging. The *idea* of the place so appeals to her because rather than maintaining the op- positional nature of "life/death, right/wrong, male/female," it resolves op- position, contains it, dissolving contradiction "in that watery, dazzling dia- lectic." Feeling the divisions, the contradictions and conflicts in herself at last in a place where they might be allowed to coexist, she writes: "That golden evening I really wanted to go no farther; / more than anything else I wanted to stay awhile / in that conflux of two great rivers." Appealing as that idea is to Bishop, however, she does not create a naive or idealized scene in the poem. She notes the abundant evidence of colonization in ev- erything from oars (instead of paddles) to nuns "off to their mission" to English names (and "Cathedral" rather than "church") to the occasional pair of blue eyes in brown faces. But even some of these bespeak "the idea of the place," as the dissolution of Western/non-Western "opposites" winks subversively in those blue eyes. Of course, in the end of the poem, "the idea of the place"—the alternative way of thinking about and being in the world it represents—that Bishop "liked" (instead of finding it "unlikely") collides with the idea of the place Mr. Swann has. Swann clearly represents the ideological stance Bishop was critiquing in the questions of travel she posed, a stance that she realized she had been taught to assume but sought to resist. It is certainly "lack of imagination" that brings Swann to this "imagined" place, just as it is lack of imagination that prompts him to ask, "What's that ugly thing?" of the tiny piece of the place Bishop brings back on board the ship. Swann "wanted to see the Amazon before he died," but to *see* it in what way? From the deck of a ship, surveyed from a safe distance. The poem implies that Swann's desire is to turn his imperializing gaze on the Amazon and to confirm his expectations of the place: it is dark, backward, ugly—the opposite of Europe's light, progress, beauty—just as he suspected. He can't—or won't—see "the idea of the place" Bishop sees, not only because, unlike her, he refuses to make contact with it, but also because he doesn't have to see it. Nothing in his culture has ever demanded of him that he see any differently, nor that he question the certainty of his own superiority, his own position as an "insider." On the contrary, his culture has rewarded him for claiming that position unquestioningly. Bishop did question, even when the answers eluded her, or implicated her, or exposed her, or revealed her deep-seated prejudices. And she did try, sometimes successfully, to imagine new ways of seeing the world and its people.

Works Cited

Bishop, Elizabeth. *The Complete Poems 1927–1979*. New York: Farrar, Straus, Giroux, 1983.

————. *One Art: Letters*. Ed. Robert Giroux. New York: Farrar, Straus, Giroux, 1994.

Gunn, Thom. "Out of the box: Elizabeth Bishop." *Shelf Life*. Ann Arbor: U of Michigan P, 1993. 77–86.

Haraway, Donna. *Primate Visions: Gender, Race, and Nature in the World of Modern Science*. New York: Routledge, 1989.

Hulme, Peter. *Colonial Encounters*. London and New York: Routledge, 1992.

Kalstone, David. *Becoming a Poet: Elizabeth Bishop with Marianne Moore and Robert Lowell*. Ed. Robert Hemenway. New York: Farrar, Straus, Giroux, 1989.

Lutz, Catherine A. and Jane L. Collins. *Reading National Geographic*. Chicago: U of Chicago P, 1993.

Millier, Brett C. *Elizabeth Bishop: Life and the Memory of It*. Berkeley: U of California P, 1993.

O'Barr, William M. *Culture and the Ad*. Boulder: Westview Press, 1994.

Pauly, Philip. "The World and All That Is in It: The National Geographic Society, 1888–1918." *American Quarterly* 31 (1979): 517–32.

Rich, Adrienne. "The Eye of the Outsider: Elizabeth Bishop's *Complete Poems, 1927–1979*." *Blood, Bread, and Poetry*. New York: Norton, 1986. 124–35.

Poetic Identity/Identity Politics: A Geography of the Self

Eden Osucha
University of California, Davis

Abstract

Elizabeth Bishop's poetry bears little trace of the poetic trends that influenced her contemporaries. While other poets thrilled in the liberatory puissance of "confessional" verse, Bishop wrote her "self" into the margins of her poetry, suppressing what poetic fashion would have her confess: herself as woman and as lesbian. Instead, the sexually ambiguous voice of her writing eschews easy association with the work of other "woman" poets. Does this elision of a sexualized, gendered identity express ambivalence or even hostility toward feminism? I argue the converse point. Bishop's poetry has profoundly feminist implications *because* of its inexplicitness on the twinned issues of gender and sex. Bishop's aversion to poetic self-revelation recognizes the "confessional" as closely bound to dangerous (for women and, especially, for lesbians) ideas of "sins" and "liars"—that which is confessed, and those who do not confess. Her poetry inverts marginalization—traditionally a position of entrenched disempowerment for women and homosexuals—into a vantage point from which Bishop can write autobiographically without installing herself as autobiographical author/subject.[1]

> ...Even if one were tempted
> to literary interpretations
> such as: life/death, right/wrong, male/female
> —such notions would have resolved, dissolved, straight off
> in that watery, dazzling dialectic.
> —from "Santarém"

Elizabeth Bishop's late poem, "Santarém," resolves the most vexing of the poet's "questions of travel": the itinerant's pleasures in mutability and transience, versus a desire for permanence—both spatial (home) and conceptual (meaning). This tension frames "Santarém," though it is in these lines that it also finds its release. Bishop's narrator may recall that "that golden evening I really wanted to go no farther," but, ultimately, she[2] is not dissuaded from answering the ship's whistle. ("I knew I couldn't stay.") She brings aboard the ship a significant, powerfully oracular souvenir: "an empty wasps' nest...small, exquisite, clean matte white, / and hard as stucco." This gesture transcends the double-edged ideal of travel as a constancy of both fulfillment and denial; the empty wasps' nest—simultaneously a literal home and a simulacrum—makes an ironic souvenir of journeys past and a hopeful omen of those to come.

My paper is not about travel, nor even about geography as we conventionally know it. Yet as the point of departure for my critical project, "Santarém" is ideal. Within a poem that resolves questions of geography, Bishop presages the questions of biography that have come to problematize "straight" readings of her poetry. "Santarém" provides a suggestive metaphor for posthumous criticism of Bishop's work: the attempt to locate her poetic identity via an assembled fulcrum of oppositional binaries—male/female, truth/inauthenticity, homosexual/heterosexual, confessional/anti-confessional, feminist/not-feminist—despite the "watery, dazzling dialectic" of poetry that dissolves such "literary interpretations."

The insights of queer theory suggest that these "epistemologically charged pairings" are among "the most crucial sites for the contestation of meaning" in our culture (Sedgwick 72). They have also become the key signifiers of Bishop's poetic identity. Thus the contestation of Bishop's poetic identity is located within extant discourses of identity politics, though this discursive framework is mostly unacknowledged in interpretations of the poems' latent political content. For this reason, I will focus on the politics of such readings.

The least stable of these elements are the questions of Bishop's relationship to poetic "confession" and to feminism. The identity politics of Bishop criticism present the two questions as inexorably linked, so much so that it has become impossible to address one without addressing the other. Critics who interpret Bishop's poetry as a rejection of the confessional mode cite "the lack of a direct, explicit presentation of gender issues and...the absence of a strong, central, explicitly female voice in her poetry"; this "decentered, sexually ambiguous [poetic] voice" is also interpreted as evincing Bishop's ambivalent or even hostile attitudes toward feminism (Brogan 60). The link is reinforced by revisionists' readings of Bishop as a self-consciously feminist poet. These critics' strategy of de-coding the semiotically dense poems requires an essentialized notion of Bishop's "self" as a poetic identity that remains constant in the poems even as it is imbricated in their symbols. In this way, feminist approaches to Bishop are suggesting that her poems "confess" what is ostensibly suppressed: the poet's gender and her homosexuality.

The twinning of feminism and confession is a byproduct of mainstream feminism's frenetic obsession with authenticity. Yet the requirement of "authenticity" is antithetical to feminist aims; it can only be met through confession, an intensively regulatory practice that shrouds itself in expressed goals of emancipation. In *Autobiographics: A Feminist Theory of Women's Self-Representation*, Leigh Gilmore observes that "having to identify yourself— as a feminist, for example—in order not to be identified falsely by others is an ongoing pressure...that members of the unmarked, dominant culture rarely face...in the same way as those whose identities require authorization" (227). Gilmore suggests that "feminist confessions or lesbian and gay coming-out stories are naively invested in the authentic," an argument that is germane to the discourse of identity politics in Bishop scholarship. For although Gilmore observes that "many claims to authenticity are on the verge of becoming passé" due to, among other developments in Women's, and Gay and Lesbian Studies, the emergence of queer theory, such "claims to authenticity" are *still* dominant concerns in feminist scholarship on Bishop.

Bishop's apparent aversion to poetic self-revelation is deeply political. The "confession," she recognized, is closely bound to dangerous (for women and especially for lesbians) ideas of "sins" and "liars"—that which is confessed, and those who do not confess.[3] Bishop's writing expresses feminist values because of, and not in spite of, its inexplicitness on gender and sexuality.

I propose that Bishop's poetic identity is best read as a feminist strategy of self-representation in which the poet's "self" is *not* hidden or "closeted," but is liminally situated, a profound distinction. The former model adumbrates the inevitable presentation of the truth; in Bishop's liminal approach to poetic self-representation, "truth" (as readers have come to expect it) doesn't and need not exist. The poems thus present a strategy that codifies the critical insights of Gilmore's feminist theory of women's self-representation, proposed in her major work, *Autobiographics*.

Autobiographics, in Gilmore's theory, refers to "those elements [of self representation] that...mark a location in a text where self-invention, self-discovery, and self-representation emerge within the technologies of autobiography....Autobiographics, as a description of self-representation and as a reading practice, is concerned with interruptions and eruptions, with resistance and contradiction as strategies of self-representation" (42). As a theoretical framework, "autobiographics" enables a feminist reading of Bishop's work that stakes its critical claims in the poet's evasiveness on questions of identity, rather than compensating for such evasions via a critical strategy of de-coding the text.[4]

Approaching Bishop through the critical praxis of Gilmore's theory also enables reading a lesbian perspective in Bishop's poetics that does not contradict the poet's own discretion. Gilmore warns against "a critical narrative that suggests that lesbian and gay writers are more 'out,' more visible, when they write in traditional forms, that experimentation is a developmental phase that gives way to more 'straightforward' writing practices" (207). She shows how such writing experiments "[offer] a way to make a lesbian subject position visible and not to disguise it," praising Gertrude Stein's writing for its liminal presentation of "a lesbian subject position."

The self-representational affect for which Gilmore lauds Stein is also achieved in Bishop's writing. "Crusoe in England," especially, evinces Bishop's bold experiments with autobiographical subjectivity. Bishop's transposition of the autobiographical "I" for the fictitious hero Robinson Crusoe is as clever and compelling a self-representational palimpsest as Stein's *Autobiography of Alice B. Toklas* (1933). Gilmore posits Stein as the matrilineal precursor to such contemporary experimentalists as Jeanette Winterson, Sandra Cisneros, Maxine Hong Kingston, and Jamaica Kincaid. Bishop, herself an admirer of Stein's work during her life (*One Art* 47, 584; Kalstone 31, 77), should not be overlooked in plotting such a literary heritage.

Lee Edelman notes that "poetry, in Elizabeth Bishop's master-trope, takes place beneath the aegis of geography" (91). I am suggesting that poetic identity is similarly formulated. The alluring though problematic desire to read autobiography in Bishop's poems poses familiar "questions of travel" about the possibilities of location, the mutability of place, and the pleasures of travel and transcendence. The late poems, in particular, invite such interpretations. In them, the trope of geography is consistently inverted, with the effect that "inside is continually permeated and shaped by outside" (Costello 117).

My project takes place beneath the aegis of a "geography of the self." I use this phrase to distinguish between geography as a directly presented theme and geography as a representation of indirectly treated themes (or, rather, these themes' indirect treatment). Importantly, this phrase denotes the specific concerns of feminist literary criticism: its practitioners have had to become expert cartographers of the interior (for an early argument concerning the specific concerns of feminist critical theorists, see Showalter 39). I also propose a geography of the self as a means of locating identity politics in reading Bishop. "Geography" introduces a second figurative trope: landscape, as simultaneously "site" (location) and "sight" (perception), as a figure of epistemological inquiry. The question of confession in Bishop's poetic practice is such a discursive landscape.

Literary confession is a device employed in an ideology and a critical practice of feminism that privileges an "authentic" or "true" self. This claim is grounded in Michel Foucault's analysis of the power relations/positions embedded in the confession: "The confession is a ritual of discourse in which the speaking subject is also the subject of the statement; it is also a ritual that unfolds within a power relationship, for one does not confess without the presence...of a partner who requires the confession...and intervenes in order to judge, punish, forgive, console and reconcile...." (Foucault, qtd in Glimore 61). The confession thus tightly tethers agency to truth-telling, and "authenticity" to authorization:

> Telling the truth may be a form of punishment, as well as an effort to stave it off. In order to stand as an authoritative producer of "truth," then, one must success-fully position oneself as a confessing subject whose account adequately fulfills enough of the requirements of confession. (Gilmore 107–108)

In other words, one is authorized to confess only *in* one's confession; truth is performed rather than revealed. And "truth," the confessional subject, is not the author's *own* in any meaningful sense (i.e., such that implies actual agency), but only that which she is authorized to claim.

For women, confession is further problematized by the gendered nature of truth. Women have frequently been branded "liars," a legacy codified in our language's "old wives' tales," "witch trials," and "False Memory Syndrome." Gilmore describes a gendered truth as foundational to the operations of confession. "Truth," she writes, "is marked as a cultural production entwined with our notions of gender so completely that even the structural underpinnings of truth production are masculinist...from the formation of rules in confession to the installation of a man as judge" (109–110).

This deconstruction of confession as an Orwellian coercive device for "truth production" clashes with contemporary readers' expectations that confession in poetry—especially in women's writing—is a mode of liberation and unbridled self-expression. Confession, in Gilmore's model, can produce only the most bridled sort of self-expression. Yet the myth of confession's liberatory puissance is entrenched in the dominant feminist rhetoric.

Gilmore shows how reading and writing autobiography and quasi-autobiographical verse are both inextricably bound up "in the cultural practices of policing and resistance" (108) that comprise the confession. Her feminist deconstruction of the practice provides a critical lens through which to read Bishop's own reticence about confession in her writing.

❖   ❖   ❖

"I *hate* confessional poetry," Bishop is reputed to have told Wesley Wehr (45). Bishop, in her few public pronouncements on the subject, was unequivocal in her criticism of confession as faddish, bad art and a plague to her poetry students' writing. Bishop's poetry, however, conveys a more complex, politicized, and nuanced critique of confessional poetry. The poet's bold experimentations with the autobiographical "I," her ambiguous, ambivalent presentation of routine confessional clues, and her manipulation of confessional form itself, all indicate what could be articulated as Bishop's concerns with the way in which access to self-authorization is regulated by the very genre that claims to make self-authorization possible. The poetry supersedes the bounds of the confession, and frustrates critical attempts to locate it within the either/or parameters of confessional/anti-confessional assessments. Bishop's poetry both presents and represses confessional elements, a feminist strategy that rejects the requirements of confessional authenticity and insists on a self whose possibilities for expression are as proliferate as the map-maker's colors she acclaims in her first collection of poetry.

Bishop's general objection to confessional poetry was partly aesthetic. Marilyn May Lombardi, for example, cites letters to Lowell written in the early 1960's that convey Bishop's criticism of how confessional authors "boasted about their private catastrophes so shamelessly and congratulated themselves so continually on their candor" (30). Later in Bishop's life, though, this high poetic reproach became only a minor tenant of her critique, one she herself breached with the publication of the villanelle, "One Art," an eloquent, brilliant record of her own "private catastrophes."

Lombardi acknowledges that Bishop objected "to the way confessional art transformed the poet into a diarist and the reader into a confidant or confessor" (31); however Lombardi does so without fully probing the political implications of what she observes. Yet this point is a crucial one, linking Bishop's poetic project to Gilmore's critique of women's autobiography. Like Gilmore, Bishop was disturbed by confession's transposition of confessee/confessor over the paradigmatic figure of writer/reader. She recognized that confessional poetics enforces a false binary out of truth and untruth, a distinction that is conventionally taken for granted as being self-evident but is ultimately normalized by the process of confessing. Bishop's poetry defends itself against such reductions with metaphors of irreducibility and contradiction: among them, "that watery, dazzling dialectic" of

"Santarém"; "The World is a mist. And then the world is / minute and vast and clear..." from "Sandpiper"; "Yesterday brought to today so lightly! / (A yesterday I find almost impossible to lift.)," the closing lines from "Five Flights Up"; "that world inverted" of "Insomnia"; the half-mirror "Gentleman of Shalott" who's "...in doubt / as to which side's in or out"; and "The Man-Moth" who feels the moon's "queer light" to be "...neither warm nor cold, / of a temperature impossible to record in thermometers." Contrastingly, Bishop's descriptions of the external world are precise and unerring; these lines seem self-reflective, conveying an inner world that is ambiguous and ineffable. They express the poet's paradoxical desire to be read as "impossible to record." What is recorded here is a poetic self that "denies certain antitheses, confounds certain pairings" (Goldensohn 285).

In another conversation with Wehr, Bishop commented on confessional art vis à vis a complaint about her poetry students:

> They keep telling me that they want to convey the "truth" in their poems. The fact is that we always tell the truth about ourselves despite ourselves....If my students would concentrate more on all the difficulties of writing a good poem, all the complexities of language and form, I think they would find that the truth will come through quite by itself. (38)

What seems a straightforward aesthetic critique of her students' writing also presents an ironic comment on the role of "truth" in Bishop's own work. These comments posit "truth" as somehow independent from truth's teller (in this instance, the aspiring poet). The writer concentrates on mastering her craft ("on all the difficulties of writing a good poem, all the complexities of language and form") and somehow "the truth," implacable and eternal, "emerges"— seemingly of its own volition. However, considering Bishop's reputation as an exacting perfectionist, capable of taking decades to get a poem "right," it's unlikely that, "by itself," "the truth" could emerge "despite" *her*self. Too, Bishop's experimentations with self-representation, notable as a poetic perspective that manipulates the assumed boundaries of the geography of the autobiographical self, present "truth" as being constitutionally *not* immutable, or even singular, both of which Bishop's comments imply.

The mutability of "truth"—manifest variously as biographical truth (i.e., gender, sexuality) and the truth of narrative detail—is a critical aspect of Bishop's poetic project. Yet truth's role, its poetic presentation, persists as a controversial area in reading Bishop. Some contemporary scholars have framed the issue as a question of straight literality, using instances of anachronism and detail-fudging in poems conventionally read as anecdotal, to belie the poet's claim that she "always tells the truth in [her] poetry."[5] But this probative approach to the poetry is a troubling trend in scholarship. It demands that the reader become the "confidant or confessor" that Bishop intended her work to discourage. I concur with Bonnie Costello's response to such arguments: "...we can respect Bishop's insistence on the factual basis of these poems without becoming naive literalists. The details of her poems are 'true' as absorbed and transformed by the beholder's mind and again by memory and poetic invention" (253 n.18). To contest Bishop's authenticity as the truth-teller of her own poems is to enact the technologies of confession.

Bishop often wrote the "truth" about herself into her poetry. Costello maintains that "readers familiar with the facts of Bishop's biography...easily make connections between the life and the writing" (175). She includes among these biographical facts "[Bishop's] mother's madness," "the poet's own illness," and "romantic crises and confusions," a litany of laments that seems borrowed from the poetic milieu of Robert Lowell.

Yet, when "confessional elements" make their appearance in Bishop's poetry, they often do so under the guise of universality, which shifts the onus of the particular. Reading poetic confession is, conventionally, reading the poet (who is, after all, the alleged subject of poetic confession); Bishop's liminal self-representation distracts such an attentive gaze. In the tradition of her early modernist forbearers, Bishop presents her self as most "knowable," most easily recognizable in her poems by the works' own formalist grace, descriptive acuity, and word play that is at all times both precise and evocative. Though scenes from her life constitute the "thematic center" of her poetry, Bishop, herself, is not present in these scenes. This is a tenuous balance nearly challenged by the last book, *Geography III*, whose best poems frame Bishop's attempts to navigate the currents of her personal life without compromising the sanctity of what she considered "the useable self."

For instance, "The Moose" (a poem from *Geography III*) is, in James Merrill's words, a striking example of Bishop's way "with Lowell's kind of subject matter" (260). In the poem's "haunting slow movement," a period that occurs after the sweep of a gloriously detailed opening passage and before the encounter with the numinous creature of the poem's title, voices from "back in the bus" begin telling their "painful—or once painful—tales":

> deaths, deaths and sicknesses;
> the year he remarried;

the year (something) happened.
She died in childbirth.
That was the son lost
when the schooner foundered.

He took to drink. Yes.
She went to the bad.
When Amos began to pray
even in the store and
finally the family had to put him away.

Merrill reads the poem's allusions to "death, remarriage, alcoholism, manic spells, the asylum" as confessional elements that obliquely disclose narrative events culled from "in and between the lines of Robert Lowell's and Elizabeth Bishop's own lives. The themes which in 'The Moose' seem so general are in fact achingly particular. Yet Bishop, even as she introduces these 'confessional' elements into the poem, consigns them ('not concerning us') to the back of the bus" (259–260).

❖ ❖ ❖

Bishop's reputation as an anti-confessional poet has become synonymous with her reputation as a "closeted" lesbian poet. The link between these two identities is not a coincidence; the figure of the closet both literally and figuratively resembles a confessional. It, too, is a domain within and from which truth is "performed" rather than merely "spoken." The closet embodies the technology of confession. In the discourse of truth particular to the closet, the act of confessing is "coming out."

Fountain and Brazeau's oral biography of Bishop quotes Frank Bidart, who says that Bishop once told him that she "believed in closets, closets, and more closets" (327). Elsewhere, Bidart elaborates: "The skepticism she felt about the gay rights movement was based on her sense that straight society would never truly accept homosexuality, that sooner or later it would punish writers for 'coming out'" (Bidart 7). Bidart explains Bishop's reticence about "coming out" via the cultural politics of her lifetime.[6] But this affinity for closets—like her mistrust of confession—expresses more than fear of homophobia; it rejects the simplistic model of gay liberation in which "the closet" is an archetype of repression from which lesbians and gays must "come out," a critique produced today in the vanguard of "queer" studies. Scholar Judith Butler articulates this position with pointed questions: "...so we are out of the closet, but into what? What new unbounded spatiality? The room, the den, the attic, the basement, the house, the bar, the university...?" (16)

Butler's point is that spatiality cannot possibly be unbounded; on the "out" side of the closet are only more rooms whose doors, "like Kafka's door, [produce] the expectation of a fresh air and a light of illumination that never arrives" (Butler 16). In *Epistemology of the Closet*, Eve Kosofsky Sedgwick draws a similar conclusion: "The image of coming out regularly interfaces the image of the closet" (71). Rather than abandon "the closet," the subject who "comes out" reifies the dominance of this tautology. *Being* "out" then necessitates a continual performance of the initial act of *coming* "out"; the "out" subject is perpetually becoming that which she professes to already being. Aptly, Sedgwick characterizes coming out as a performance that never ends. The closet is reproduced in the identity politics of Bishop scholarship as that discourse's secret de-coder ring. Applied to Bishop, the critical strategy of de-coding a poem's hidden ur-text is, effectually, "outing" the poet as a "closeted" lesbian. The paradoxical effect, of course, is that this reinforces the poem's (and the poet's) "closetedness."

In *Stein, Bishop, and Rich: Lyrics of Love, War, and Peace*, Margaret Dickie attempts to read Bishop as a "lesbian love poet" who finds expression in poems in which desire is "[projected] onto the landscape or onto distant literary figures" (84). Even "Roosters" gets treated as a "buried aubade" (85). To support de-coded readings, Dickie cites "evidence" gathered in books by Marilyn May Lombardi (1995) and by Lorrie Goldensohn (1992), both Bishop scholars who use unpublished drafts of "sexually explicit" poems and their own pointed de-codings of published ones to suggest that "had Bishop lived in a later era, she might have become a love poet of startling power" (Lombardi 84). The danger of reading Bishop's poetry for its "confessional" content is that it straps the poet herself into a tautological comparison with self-consciously confessional poets—such as Adrienne Rich, in the case of Dickie's book—in which Bishop's unique voice is subsumed and undervalued. Indeed, this teleological undercurrent becomes evident at the very end of Dickie's book, when she praises Rich's "out" writing as more evolved than the cryptic (read: "closeted") work of Stein and Bishop: "At last, a lesbian poet can create a lyric that will accommodate such revelations of feeling as Rich makes here....Writing in the line of women poets from Stein through Bishop who have gone to great extremes to speak their intimate feelings, Rich has expanded the range of a lesbian public lyric voice by returning it to this more modest resonance" (210).

Bishop's poetic self-marginalization affects a lyric ambiguity that shrouds the poetic self. In this way, the allusive aesthetics of her poetry can be read as the emblems of such a strategy. Wayne Koestenbaum observes that Bishop's poems "were written from a vantage point of isolation, and their discretion is a consequence of her wish to navigate, through art, the contradictions of her difficult life. What moves me in her poems is the way they subtly speak about that isolation; I am moved, in other words, by her uncertainty" (86).

The poetry inverts marginalization into a vantage point from which to write beyond the strictures of "either/or" identifications. This form of liminal self-representation, exemplified in Bishop's writing, reveals the essential constructiveness of identity and the innate limitations of feminist confession; as Gilmore make clear, both insights are powerful tools in a feminist practice of self-representation. The troping of marginalization also subverts the divisions between similarly disadvantaged identities, an achievement in Bishop's poetry eloquently described by Adrienne Rich as the mark of the "the outsider's eye." "Her experience of outsiderhood...enables Bishop to perceive other kinds of outsiders and to identify, or try to identify, with them" (Rich 127). This identification with "other kinds of outsiders" is notable in "Songs for a Colored Singer" and "Faustina, or Rock Roses" from Bishop's first two books, and in the Brazilian-era poems "Manuelzinho," "Squatter's Children," "The Burglar of Babylon," and, especially, "Pink Dog."[7] In other poems, Bishop pushes the category of "outsider" beyond logical extremes; her otherworldly "Man-Moth," for example, is a compelling portrait of human alienation. Throughout the body of her work, Bishop's complex representations of alienated subjectivity resists the forces of sociopolitical marginalization.

Liminality, in this geography of the self, expands the possibilities of self-representation so that Bishop's representations encompass a multitude of selves. Perhaps her wildest conceptualization of "outsiderhood" went unwritten: years after a car accident in which her college friend Margaret Miller's arm was severed below the elbow, Bishop told Frank Bidart that she'd "always wanted to write a poem spoken by the arm, but couldn't" (Bidart 7).

Endnotes

1. I dedicate this paper to the teachers who have encouraged and inspired me. I am especially indebted to William Cain, Julie Donnelly, Leigh Gilmore, and my parents, Barbara Osucha and Ted Osucha.

2. For the sake of convenience, I've chosen to en-gender the poem's narrator as female, a nod to "Santarém"'s semblance as memorial tableau. I am noting this choice as deliberate (rather than as axiomatic or the unconscious reification of received interpretation) so as to *not* undermine my account—which I intend as an intervention in the production and circulation of reductive autobio-*graftings* of Bishop's work—before it's even begun.

3. Bishop's skeptical attitude toward poetic confessions is evident in her response to Adrienne Rich's 1973 collection *Diving into the Wreck*. Around the time of its publications, a friend of Bishop's remembers the poet's unequivocal response: "*My God*, I've been a feminist since *way* back. I don't feel that you have to write about sex that way....I could never use [sexuality] as a subject or write about things as baldly as Rich does" (Fountain 329).

4. While Gilmore's critique of the feminist reading strategies of de-coding specifies Gertrude Stein as a subject of such readings, her analysis is applicable to recent scholarship on Bishop that employs similar tactics.

5. Lee Edelman reads "In the Waiting Room" as a poem that manipulates literal facts while simultaneously presenting itself as meticulously factual. He asks "toward what end does Bishop attempt to appropriate a literal grounding for her poem if that poem insists on fracturing the literality on which it positions itself?" (95–96) Edelman's answer is that the poem uses the appearance of literality to remain allusive and that the "literal" here functions as a trope which marks "the poem's insistence on confusion."

6. "One must remember that for the vast majority of [Bishop's] life, in both social and literary terms, *not* to be in the closet was to be ghettoized; people might know or suspect that one was gay, but to talk about it openly in straight society was generally considered out-of-control or stupid" (Bidart 7; Fountain 333).

7. However, my praise for this achievement of Bishop's poetry is tempered

by my concern with the politics of such a choice in subject: a white woman's attempts to assume the voices of black characters could arguably be read as the poetic equivalent of black-face. I concur with Adrienne Rich's mixed response to this problem in reading Bishop's "Songs for a Colored Singer": "A risky undertaking, and it betrays the failures and clumsiness of such a position…. What I value is her attempt to acknowledge other outsiders, lives marginal in ways that hers is not, long before the Civil Rights movement made such awareness temporarily fashionable for some white writers" (131).

Works Cited

Bidart, Frank. "Elizabeth Bishop." *Threepenny Review* 58.2 (Summer 1994): 6–7.

Bishop, Elizabeth. *The Complete Poems: 1927–1979*. New York: Noonday, 1994.

———. *One Art: Letters*. Ed. Robert Giroux. New York: Farrar, Straus, Giroux, 1994.

Brogan, Kathleen. "Lyric Voice and Sexual Difference in Elizabeth Bishop." *Writing the Woman Artist*. Ed. Suzanne W. Jones. Philadelphia: U of Pennsylvania P, 1991. 60–76.

Butler, Judith. "Imitation and Gender Insubordination." *Inside/Out: Lesbian Theories, Gay Theories*. Ed. Diana Fuss. New York: Routledge, 1991. 13–31.

Costello, Bonnie. *Elizabeth Bishop: Questions of Mastery*. Cambridge: Harvard UP, 1991.

Dickie, Margaret. *Stein, Bishop, and Rich: Lyrics of Love, War, and Place*. Chapel Hill: U of North Carolina P, 1997.

Edelman, Lee. "The Geography of Gender: Elizabeth Bishop's 'In the Waiting Room.'" *Elizabeth Bishop: The Geography of Gender*. Ed. Marilyn May Lombardi. Charlottesville: UP of Virginia, 1993. 91–107.

Fountain, Gary, and Peter Brazeau, eds. *Remembering Elizabeth Bishop: An Oral Biography*. Amherst: U of Massachusetts P, 1994.

Gilmore, Leigh. *Autobiographics: A Feminist Theory of Women's Self-Representation*. Ithaca: Cornell UP, 1994.

Goldensohn, Lorrie. *Elizabeth Bishop: The Biography of a Poetry*. New York: Columbia UP, 1992.

Halliday, Caroline. "'The Naked Majesty of God:' Contemporary Lesbian Erotic Poetry." *Lesbian and Gay Writing: An Anthology of Critical Essays.* Ed. Mark Lilly. Philadelphia, Temple UP, 1990. 76–108.

Kalstone, David. *Becoming a Poet: Elizabeth Bishop with Marianne Moore and Robert Lowell.* Ed. Robert Hemenway. New York: Noonday, 1989.

Koestenbaum, Wayne. "The Stripper and the Swan: A Poet's New Voice Emerges in a New Collection." *The New Yorker.* 1 May 1995: 85–86.

Lombardi, Marilyn May. *The Body and the Song: Elizabeth Bishop's Poetics.* Carbondale: Southern Illinois UP, 1995.

Merrill, James. Afterword. *Becoming a Poet: Elizabeth Bishop with Marianne Moore and Robert Lowell.* By David Kalstone. New York: Noonday, 1989. 251–262.

Rich, Adrienne. *Blood, Bread, and Poetry: Selected Prose 1979–1985.* New York: Norton, 1986.

Sedgwick, Eve Kosofsky. *Epistemology of the Closet.* Berkeley: U of California P, 1990.

Showalter, Elaine. "Towards a Feminist Poetics." *Women Writing and Writing About Women.* Ed. Mary Jacobus. New York: Harper, 1979.

Wehr, Wesley. "Elizabeth Bishop: Conversations and Class Notes." *Conversations with Elizabeth Bishop.* Ed. George Monteiro. Jackson: UP of Mississippi, 1996. 38–46.

Elizabeth Bishop: At Home with Whiteness

Renee R. Curry
California State University/San Marcos

Abstract

In "The Imaginary Iceberg," Elizabeth Bishop prepares her readers for the power of the white peaks. In the first stanza, she whitens the terrain by way of multiple similes and metaphors: "like cloudy rock," the sea like "moving marble," and the "breathing plain of snow." This terrain prepares us for the dazzling display of the "white peaks" themselves: "The wits of these white peaks / spar with the sun." Although Bishop will not always present whiteness as related to peaks, mountaintops, dominance, and power, such displays do occur repeatedly. Their repetition suggests an imaginative, if not an ideological, regard for the hierarchical nature of that which is white.

Elizabeth Bishop writes whiteness into one of her earliest poems, included in her earliest book, *North & South*. The whiteness in "The Imaginary Iceberg" intrigues especially because it has been overlooked by literary scholars. Strictly speaking, I want to discuss the meaning of the line in the second stanza that reads, "The wits of these white peaks / spar with the sun," but a fuller discussion of the entire poem as well as its critical reception is necessary. Many scholars have discussed this poem; some have discussed this exact line; and, some have discussed the "wit" in the line, but no one has analyzed the whiteness of the peak itself.

Jeredith Merrin points out the poem's religiosity and moralism (59, 114). James McCorkle sees in the poem attempts at "provisional moments" of communion with others (12). C. K. Doreski explores this poem's suggestion that imagination is more powerful than eyesight (6). Anne Stevenson cannot see "how to read this poem in any light other than Transcendentalist" (708); and Margaret Dickie reads the iceberg as an allegory of lesbian love's secret attraction. Each of these readings displays knowledge and integrity, but the scholarship of Betsy Erkkila, Marilyn May Lombardi, Anne Colwell, and Susan McCabe paves a more direct path toward an understanding of white authorship. These four readings address the relationship of "The Imaginary Iceberg" to female subjectivity, home, and the authorial body, readings that enable us to discern what it means for a woman poet in a white body to write white, and, therefore, to write about an indisputable, yet invisible, dominance. Although these scholars address the female body as an intricate part of the writing process and product, none of them focuses specifically on the whiteness of Bishop's body. Erkkila, Lombardi, Colwell and McCabe permit me to suggest meanings in Bishop's poetry that tend to "gurgle up" rather than to stem only from consciously determined and poetically manipulated language.

Betsy Erkkila writes an expansive and meticulous article about Bishop's political affiliations during the time that she worked on "The Imaginary Iceberg." Bishop was a "New York radical" who dutifully read her Russian Marxist criticism daily; however, Bishop balked at doctrinaire pronouncements, idealism, and utopianism. Erkkila points out that "In the mid '30s, however, she herself began to move toward an increasingly self-conscious attempt to give her work more social weight and significance" (290). More importantly during this time, Bishop was moving away from the art world's Eurocentric focus on high modernism and making moves—literal and figurative—toward the geography bordering North and South America (291). Elizabeth Bishop was not apolitical; she was simply not doctrinaire. Because Bishop's politics are only subtly portrayed or invisibly foundational in the poetry, her work provides an important template through which to read the subtleties of racial whiteness. Erkkila's work supports the presumption that at the time of "The Imaginary Iceberg," Bishop was politically aware and was already reflecting upon Key West and South America as geographical and imaginative places of difference. In fact, Erkkila's work makes it clear that Bishop's texts invite readings of racial markings (although relatively few have been done), especially as they connote difference and otherness in relationship to a white standard of being.

As Margaret Dickie points out, until Adrienne Rich tells us differently, it is quite typical to discuss Bishop as apolitical. Rich and Dickie, however, make sturdy claims for Bishop as a poet who often writes "about multiracial Brazil, about the poor and the tenant... lives marginal in ways that hers is not" (7). Dickie and Rich praise Bishop's "acknowledgment" of "other outsiders" (7) without questioning the value of mere acknowledgment, especially when the acknowledgment of others in art equates with cultural (and financial) gain for the acknowledging artist. What do the acknowledged others gain?

Dickie recognizes that Bishop had the "leisure for the 'perfectly useless concentration' that such art requires" and that Bishop chose her art and "devoted herself to the discipline of 'heroic observations'" (14), but Dickie does not name this particular leisure as white, privileged, woman's leisure.

Anne Colwell sees more than mere acknowledgment in Bishop's writings about otherness, but she suggests that Bishop may only be able to "connect" with otherness by "taking it into herself" (122). Further on in Colwell's book, she writes that for Bishop, "connection occurs not because the body moves beyond its boundaries into another body but because the body expands its boundaries to take something into itself" (146). This movement of accommodation is indeed more than acknowledgment, but it is a possessive attempt at co-optation or erasure. Colwell proposes Bishop as a poet fully aware that acknowledgment and accommodation fall short as gestures toward connection with otherness; Colwell claims Bishop understands that "we cannot know what we experience because of our subjective walls, because of our flawed human senses, our tendency to imagine our own bodies everywhere" (122). However, even the "our" in Colwell's proposal suggests a privileged, white, position in the tendency to imagine "our own bodies everywhere." In Toni Morrison's *The Bluest Eye*, for instance, the African-American child cannot imagine her body anywhere. She wants to imagine her body as another body, a white one, and to see with other eyes, blue ones. She would not be included in the "our" of Colwell's proposal.

Rather than looking at Bishop's images and representations as those that express her acknowledgment and concern for others, I want to look at such poems as "The Imaginary Iceberg," which opens with the bold declaration, "We'd rather have the iceberg," as racially marked texts that connote what it means to "have" and to prefer whiteness.

Lombardi's research on the origins of "The Imaginary Iceberg" describes R. H. Dana's *Two Years Before the Mast* as the "scaffolding on which Bishop builds her vision of the iceberg" (88–89). In this mariner's tale, Dana describes an iceberg sighting. Lombardi notes that the "enmity between the ice mountain and the heavens" particularly appealed to Bishop (90). This animosity becomes a type of hostility that can be handled by "wit" in Bishop's poem, especially the wit of whiteness as it faces off with its only comparable warrior, the heavens. Bishop's addition of whiteness to the peaks adds an element of purity, strength and excellence to their already named wit. Whiteness dominates the peak in this poem, and not with grace, but with flailing limbs raised in attack. Bishop's pure and intelligent whiteness quickly fades to gracelessness as the ridiculous sparring occurs—the white peaks cannot win against the heavens. The racial markings of this poem suggest that whiteness, although glorious in its attainment of the peak, might have gone too far in its increasing enmity toward the heavens, and in its insistent hierarchical journey.

Susan McCabe concentrates a portion of her analysis on the exact lines regarding the white peaks. In discussing them, she notes the "allegorical genius and courage" of the line (51). McCabe does not discuss the whiteness of the peaks, but I would add to her analysis that the allegorical genius and courage of the line stem matter-of-factly from the established whiteness of the peaks. The word "white" in English is emblematic of excellence (Dyer 70–71). At the sound level of the line, Bishop plays with the way in which absenting the silent letters in the word "white" would give us "wit." "Wit" exists in "white." "White" does not exist without "wit." Better yet, wit is white (with a few minor, humble, additions). Although a white writer might write "white," she is assuming and including an embedded wit. McCabe reminds us that, "Everything of this poem reveals as it conceals" (52). In looking at "white" as a racial marker of an automatically assumed "wit"— an intelligence, sagacity, perception, cleverness, or shrewdness—McCabe's claim about "The Imaginary Iceberg" could not be more accurate.

Anne Colwell's argument about the poem provides the most illuminating reading of Bishop's white-peaked iceberg: "It remains both ineffable and the mirror of human understanding" (39). Bishop's iceberg, as Colwell sees it, "does not search out its own reflection, cannot move, change, or be changed by the adornment of the perceiver's gaze" (42). The iceberg, remember, is witty. Due to its size, its hierarchical imperative, it stares down at others. It is white. It is powerful. Like powerful white people, the iceberg has no cause to change.

Elizabeth Bishop prepares her readers for the power of the white peaks throughout the first stanza of the poem. In this stanza, she has already whitened the terrain by way of multiple similes and metaphors: "like cloudy rock," the sea like "moving marble," and the "breathing plain of snow." This terrain prepares us for the dazzling display of the "white peaks" themselves: "The wits of these white peaks / spar with the sun." In this poem, to be covered in whiteness (as is the iceberg) is a peak experience, only to be topped by witnessing whiteness (as do the sailors/people on the witnessing boat). Although Bishop will not always present whiteness as related to peaks, mountaintops, dominance, and power, such displays do occur repeatedly. Their repetition suggests an imaginative, if not an ideological, pattern. Interestingly, Colwell points out that Bishop developed a pattern of living atop mountains and that she was fond of observing landscapes from above: "Everywhere she worked—her apartment in Rio de Janeiro overlooking the beach, her study above the waterfall in Petropolis, her mountain house in Ouro Preto, her Lewis Wharf condo above Boston Harbor—had a magnificent view" (1).

In a discussion of H. G. Wells's use of whiteness, David J. Lake also notes the importance of mountaintop and peak whiteness:

> ...whiteness seems to be shifting its meaning, or at least its emotional tone, from negative to positive, as it becomes associated with high mountains and, in general, elevation, both literal and metaphorical. The link between whiteness and height is provided by *ice* or *snow*, which are found on mountains. (16)

An ideological link may also be drawn between the literal elevation of a white mountain peak, or an iceberg peak, and the hierarchical nature that we associate with whiteness and the power of white people. Richard Dyer argues that both the Aryan and the Caucasian models of white supremacy share "a notion of origins in mountains" and that these mountainous origins endow the white race with a particular power:

> Such places [mountains] had a number of virtues: the clarity and cleanliness of the air, the vigour demanded by the cold, the enterprise required by the harshness of the terrain and climate, the sublime, soul-elevating beauty of mountain vistas, even the greater nearness to God above and the presence of the whitest things on earth, snow. All these virtues could be seen to have formed the white character, its energy, enterprise, discipline and spiritual elevation, and even the white body, its hardness and tautness (born of the battle with the elements, and often unfavorably compared with the slack bodies of non-whites), its uprightness (aspiring to the heights), its affinity with (snowy) whiteness. (21)

White peaks in poetry signify for Bishop an ideological regard for the hierarchical nature of that which is white.

Other authors have written a patterned whiteness into their texts. Writing about whiteness in Edgar Allan Poe, Mary F. Sisney notes that whiteness does not always pose a fixed meaning for the white writer (88). Arnold G. Bartini finds that whiteness can correlate with particular authorial fears such as Robert Frost's "inner fear" of an indifferent, "morally neutral" nature (353). Bishop's use of whiteness as descriptor in her poetic work is not fixed, nor particular to an inner concern of the poet, but rather, it is a crucial signifier of culturally embedded, and unquestioned, beliefs about the inherent strength, courage, power and goodness of that which is white, and those who are white.

At this point in our discussion of whiteness, it seems fair to ask, but when is a white peak simply a description of an actual mountaintop or an iceberg with snow on it? How can we make the leap from snow-capped structures to white racial representation? Marilyn Lombardi turns to Frank Kermode's *The Genesis of Secrecy* for revelations that relate to Bishop's poetics. Kermode and Lombardi encourage readings that enable our "divinatory powers" to grow, readings that compel us beyond the most obvious images and toward deeper understandings (Lombardi 45–46). In other words, a white peak in poetry, by virtue of being written into poetry, is never simply a literal, snow-capped iceberg. It is a prophetic image that asks for our openness to its foresight. I divine this image as a blatant display of white racial dominance. By blatant, however, I do not mean that Bishop is in control of the iceberg's revelations about whiteness.

Many Bishop scholars argue that the poet deliberately incorporates multiple layers and uncertainties of meaning for well-designed and well-controlled interrogative purposes. Although these arguments for control do persuade to a certain point, and although I have the highest regard for Bishop's intellectual capabilities, and although I am convinced that she felt deep concern for racial and social injustice, the whiteness that manifests in her poetry is not the result of her own managed incorporations. Bishop knows that the language of her poetry must be more well-mannered than that of her letters (in which she freely uses derogatory racial language in referring to "savage" Latins and West Indians [*One Art* 192, 243]), and she does exert enough control to make the poetry acceptable, even impeccable at times. However, the letters, the pervasive racial unrest in the world, and the connotative burden placed on the word "white" all contribute to unraveling Bishop's usual decorum. These factors manifest a white positionality undetermined by the poet. Bishop is at home with whiteness, with its comforts and discomforts.

The repetition of words as well as modes of imaginative display in her poetry provide keys as to the poet's ideological make-up. Jeredith Merrin similarly claims that Bishop's poetry works through "figures and tropes" that "are actually ingrained habits of mind, powerful psychological gestalts" (in Lombardi 48). Lombardi suggests that Bishop's habits of reiteration reveal her determination to "see a thing clearly" (97). Bishop's reiterations of whiteness are an attempt for her to reach further and further toward an understanding of something, but I argue that Bishop does not understand racial whiteness as that "thing" for which she searches. Anne Colwell stresses that Bishop does understand the struggles that being embodied generates and that Bishop, therefore, "translates her ambivalence about embodiment in flesh into ambivalence about embodiment in poetic form, and her evasions, her richly ambiguous phrases, words, and structures, all preserve that ambivalence and, by saying two things in one utterance, express her uncertainty, her struggle, and her openness to multiplicity" (202). Colwell herself does not mention that the authorial body under discussion is white. Colwell's argument works up to the point of naming the color of the flesh. She does not name the flesh, as Bishop does not, because whiteness is invisible. To say flesh is to assume white flesh. I suggest that some of the multiple layers and meanings in Bishop's poems are as invisible to her as is her own whiteness.

Knowledge about whiteness is like knowledge about writing for Bishop in that, as McCabe points out, "Bishop is, almost above all, an epistemological poet who reminds us at every turn that we cannot know anything fully or absolutely, and that the activity of writing cannot save us with its 'magical powers,' but reveals our 'grave difficulties'" (xiv). Recognition of whiteness has been a grave difficulty, not only for Bishop, but for many of us who are white. Bishop's poetic language reveals the magnitude of this lack.

Works Cited

Bartini, Arnold G. "Whiteness in Robert Frost's Poetry." *The Massachusetts Review* 26 (Summer/Autumn 1985): 351–56.

Bishop, Elizabeth. *The Complete Poems 1927–1979*. New York: Farrar, Straus, Giroux, 1983.

———. *One Art: Letters*. Ed. Robert Giroux. New York: Farrar, Straus, Giroux, 1994.

Colwell, Anne. *Inscrutable Houses: Metaphors of the Body in the Poems of Elizabeth Bishop*. Tuscaloosa: U of Alabama P, 1997.

Dickie, Margaret. *Stein, Bishop, & Rich: Lyrics of Love, War, & Place*. Chapel Hill: U of North Carolina P, 1997.

Doreski, C. K. *Elizabeth Bishop: The Restraints of Language*. New York: Oxford UP, 1993.

Dyer, Richard. *White*. New York: Routledge, 1997.

Erkkila, Betsy. *The Wicked Sisters: Women Poets, Literary History and Discord*. New York: Oxford UP, 1992.

Lake, David J. "The Whiteness of Griffin and H. G. Wells's Images of Death, 1897–1914." *Science Fiction Studies* 8.1 (March 1981): 12–18.

Lombardi, Marilyn May. *The Body and the Song: Elizabeth Bishop's Poetics*. Carbondale: Southern Illinois UP, 1995.

————, ed. *Elizabeth Bishop: The Geography of Gender*. Charlottesville: UP of Virginia, 1993.

McCabe, Susan. *Elizabeth Bishop: Her Poetics of Loss*. University Park: Pennsylvania State UP, 1994.

McCorkle, James. *The Still Performance: Writing, Self, and Interconnection in Five Postmodern American Poets*. Charlottesville: UP of Virginia, 1989.

Merrin, Jeredith. *An Enabling Humility: Marianne Moore, Elizabeth Bishop, and the Uses of Tradition*. New Brunswick: Rutgers UP, 1990.

Sisney, Mary F. "The Power and Horror of Whiteness: Wright and Ellison Respond to Poe." *CLA Journal* 29 (September 1985): 82–90.

Was Elizabeth Bishop a Racist?

Steven Gould Axelrod
University of California, Riverside

Abstract

This essay analyzes racial messages embedded in Elizabeth Bishop's writing. It examines tropes of Africanness as well as other material pertaining to race and class. The essay focuses attention on two poems from Bishop's early career ("Cootchie" and "Songs for a Colored Singer") and a story and a poem from her later career ("Memories of Uncle Neddy" and "In the Waiting Room").

We rightly prize Elizabeth Bishop for her ability to figure a fluid universe of shifting particulars and multiple identities.[1] Her texts construct a world of "infant sight" where everything is "only connected by 'and' and 'and,'" a site of alternating "angles" and "transvestite twist[s]," a locus of "questions" (*CP* 59, 58, 23, 200, 93). A verbal space of such freedom would seem inhospitable to the fixed, dead monochrome of racial stereotype or class hierarchy. Yet within Bishop's rhetoric of free play, one can sometimes spy that other logic, rocklike and caked with custom. The question before us, then, is the relation of Bishop's work to the racial and racist messages that were part of her cultural system. Do Bishop's texts problematize and subvert essentialized racial categories, or do they reproduce them intact? I would like to initiate a dialogue on this difficult yet significant topic by focusing on four Bishop texts that include tropes of Africanness: "Cootchie" and "Songs for a Colored Singer" from her early career, and "Memories of Uncle Neddy" and "In the Waiting Room" from her later work. Although I do not intend to single Bishop out for blame, I also intend not to ignore racist discourses and thereby implicitly participate in them.

On May 5, 1938, Bishop wrote to Marianne Moore praising William Carlos Williams' representation of Negroes in *In the American Grain*, adding: "I want very much to attempt something about them myself—those I have anything to do with here are all so *good*. Their cheerfulness is amazing—as Cootchie, the maid here, said to me the other morning, 'That [is] why I like colored folks—they never commit suicide'" (*One Art* 74). Less than two years later, however, Cootchie herself was dead—whether by her own hand or from natural causes, I don't know. Bishop's promised poem about her had become an elegy, which Moore found upsettingly gloomy (*One Art* 88–89, 110–11). Bishop's would-be signifier of "cheerfulness" (74) had morphed to one of "gloom" (110). In later years, she had to fend off reviewers' complaints about the poem—not so much that "Cootchie" was gloomy as that it was "condescending" (479). What might strike a reader today, especially in the first stanza, is the amount of mileage the poem attempts to make from freighted contrasts of black and white:

> Cootchie, Miss Lula's servant, lies in marl,
> black into white she went
>   below the surface of the coral-reef.
>
> . . . .
> The skies were egg white for the funeral
>   and the faces sable. (*CP* 46)

This kind of play on color seems to me to indicate a subjectivity unused to variations of skin tone—not hostile to skin tones different from her own but attentive to them, noting them as aberrant or marked, made anxious by them. This is the naive discourse of a subject enfolded within a cultural cocoon of whiteness but peeking out, registering exotic beauty in "the faces sable," yet also taking comfort in a fantasized erasure of difference, a wish-fulfillment restoration of the norm, a final obliteration of "black into white." It is important to note, however, that this code of anxiety about races other than white co-exists with another code of compassion: for the low-caste Cootchie who ate "her dinner off the kitchen sink / while Lula ate hers off the kitchen table"; for the African-American mourners; for the deaf, aged, and dependent Miss Lula who cannot quite comprehend her accelerating "losses"; and for all human beings in their ultimate aloneness, dismissed as "trivial" by the larger social organization when no longer of use, waved goodbye by a "desperate" sea whose consoling gesture goes unnoticed (46). Bishop's racial anxiety, then, imbricated in what Brett Millier calls her "esthetic appreciation of poor people" (273), subsists alongside a more sophisticated and empathic set of responses.

Bishop's other early text figuring Africanness, "Songs for a Colored Singer," which first appeared in 1944, was written, according to Bishop, "for Billie Holiday, but very *vaguely*" (*One Art* 478). Modeled on the blues but never set to music, the sequence displays the same contradictory layering of naiveté and sophistication, empathy and distance as does "Cootchie." Compared to Langston Hughes's "The Weary Blues," "Song for Billie Holiday," and "The Backlash Blues" (50, 360, 552), or for that matter Frank

O'Hara's "The Day Lady Died" (325), the first two of Bishop's "Songs" seem stereotypical. The first "Song" merely reproduces a black woman's complaints about her kind and faithful but restless and spendthrift husband:

> I say, "Le Roy, just how much are we owing?
> Something I can't comprehend,
> the more we got the more we spend...." (*CP* 47)

Whereas blues-based poems by African Americans generally recognize white racism as a fact of life, Bishop's text erases that motif. The problem, instead, is black male profligacy. "Le Roy" answers his wife with a frown, "Darling, when I earns I spends" (47). Bishop's poem posits neither white racism nor black poverty as central problems but rather a failure of black men to settle down and save their money. The poem's refrain nervously insists that whatever this couple's problems may be, the lack of an adequate income is not one of them: "Le Roy, you're earning too much money now." It is not a great surprise that Bishop never actually attempted to have this text put to music and sung by Billie Holiday. This is a poem putatively for and about African Americans written by a person who has not known such individuals on a basis of equality and who holds herself apart from them. Bishop had no black friends to give the poem to, and if she had, she might have received a jolting response. The poem surely intends a sympathetic attitude to blacks: the woman speaker understandably complains about lacking material possessions and an enduring home, and even her problematical spouse is granted a faithful, kind, and inquiring nature. But at the same time, the poet seems motivated by a desire to evade guilt for inequities of race and class. The social dilemma, as the poem poses it, is not that the black breadwinner earns too little for his labor but that he's "earning too much," a fantasy that may temporarily diminish anxiety but only by misrepresenting social realities. The poem is ultimately disconcerting for the power of its need to distance and deny.

In the second "Song," the speaker determines to leave her philandering, high-spending husband. Again, the problem of the poem has nothing to do with a white supremacist social structure or economic exploitation but only with the failings of the black male. The solution in this "Song" is for the black woman to go her "own way" (*CP* 48). The third "Song" adds little that is new. The fourth and final "Song," however, is by far the most resonant text, the one most identifiable with Bishop's best work. Its grieving, frightened speaker is haunted by a vision of something shining in the leaves, which slowly achieves definition as a tearful black face and then as a multitude of such faces:

> Like an army in a dream
> the faces seem,
> darker, darker, like a dream.
> They're too real to be a dream. (51)

Perhaps it is not fanciful to suppose that this passage is a moment in which the text reflects on itself, and specifically on the consequences of its strategy of distorting its awareness of the suffering of others. The text reveals itself as haunted by those faces it has distanced and denied but which return resolutely to consciousness, "too real to be a dream." I imagine that the subject position represented here belongs not only, or even primarily, to a woman of color but to a white woman who has unsuccessfully attempted to appropriate an African American voice, and who now experiences the weight of her failure, an anguished sense of her inability to escape racist paradigms, and perhaps even a guilty fear of retribution.

In part Bishop's problematic representations of working-class African-Americans (and of working-class Brazilians, too, in a poem like "Manuelzinho" [*CP* 96–99]) may be understood as an unfortunately uncritical transmission of the race and class hierarchies absorbed from the discourse of her time and place. Her mediation amounts to what Christopher Newfield calls, in reference to Emerson, "a liberal form of racist thinking" (17). Although the stereotypes in her texts may be infrequent, muted, and relatively innocuous, they are nonetheless present, and they are harmless only in comparison to more hostile formations. In fact, the blandness of Bishop's representation of social otherness (except in the revealing fourth "Song") may testify to the comfort author and reader presumably feel with such stereotypes; it may also reflect their wish not to perceive a social threat posed by those they assume to be kept in their place by innate qualities rather than systems of oppression. Bishop's representational schema, then, despite its conscious good will, perpetuates what Jody David Armour calls "ubiquitous unconscious bias" (130).

In addition to an uncritical transmission of cultural bias, Bishop's reproduction of stereotypes stems from a second, more personal cause: the unending, ambivalent mourning she felt as a result of losing both parents by the age of five. A functional orphan, living in gloomy homes where her status seemed to her similar to that of the family canine ("Country Mouse," *CPr* 21, 23), she was prepared, late in her career, to project herself into an image of a hairless "Pink Dog" on an avenue in Rio (*CP* 190–91). Self-conceived as injured, unloved, strange, and ugly—a beggar living by her wits—she needed a category of individuals who would simultaneously provide comfort and reinforce a sense of her own superior value. These comfort providers must also remain emotionally distanced, functionally interchangeable, able to be hired, fired, and controlled. Substitutes for the absent parents, they must never be allowed to repeat the injury the actual parents had inflicted through death and abandonment. Like the little boy in Freud's *Beyond the Pleasure Principle* who invented the game of *fort/da* as a way of mimicking and mastering the feared absences of his mother ("Beyond" 14–17), Bishop obsessively hired and fired domestic workers throughout her adult life, memorializing them in poems of loss and abandonment such as "Cootchie" and "Songs for a Colored Singer." A woman deprived of her parents, Bishop wrote poems about domestic workers that seemed, almost against her will, to turn into elegies and laments. The attachment disorder and separation anxiety that plagued Bishop's adult life, that resulted in alcohol abuse and a string of troubled intimate relationships, were sublimated in the narratives of race and class that her culture provided to her. She established relations with domestic workers, and she created textual figures of social others, in an attempt to give and receive affection while retaining distance and control, and to assuage her never-ending grief. She felt two mutually exclusive desires: to remain superior to poor people of color and to identify herself with them. She wanted both to deny and to claim a connection.

Bishop produced African images twice in her later work. Both occur in elegiac contexts, again attesting to the basis such images had for her in loss. Moreover, both occur in the contexts of visual representation: a framed portrait and a magazine photo. She thus figured art as a space where issues of separation, loss, and impaired autonomy might be safely worked through—and perhaps suggesting the pervasive Africanist presence in American art (as Toni Morrison, Sterling Stuckey, Eric Sundquist, and others have recently argued). Both texts reveal the cathexis that underlies Bishop's earlier, too-comfortable discourse of Africanness.

"Memories of Uncle Neddy," drafted in 1958–62 but not published until 1977, works backward in time through layers of memory to something like a primal scene. As the story's narrator plunges into her childhood memories, she reveals herself compulsively attracted to blackness: "I love the black shadow, like the finest soot, that suddenly shows up, slyly, on white bread, or white walls" (*CPr* 228). The sooty shadow suggests to her "death and dying" (228)—and undoubtedly, therefore, the dead. More specifically, blackness has become explicitly associated with Uncle Neddy himself. The narrator states: "I realize only now that he represented 'the devil' for me, not a violent, active Devil, but a gentle black one, a devil of weakness, acquiescence, tentatively black, like the sooty mildew" (228). We observe in this sentence an uncritical transmission of a casually yet powerfully bigoted metonymic chain that begins with the seventeenth-century devil residing in the American forest and ends with dark-skinned peoples of the nineteenth and twentieth centuries. Indeed, we can witness the dynamic movement of this association within the narrator's very reverie as it progresses from the image of the "violent, active Devil" of the Puritan imaginary to the "gentle," acquiescent servant-figure of the Euro-American colonial imaginary. These polar images of the Devil are the bad and good guises of the racial other, just as Freud thought that the Devil and God reflected the bad and good guises of the father ("Seventeenth-Century" 86). Imaged as either a violent or a gentle African, Uncle Neddy has taken the place of the author-narrator's unremembered dead father, loved for the kindness and care he might have provided, and hated for the violence of his rupture. This ambivalence inevitably recalls the binarism of Sylvia Plath's "Daddy." Like Plath's eponymous character, who is both "a devil. . . the black man" and "a bag full of God" (Plath 223, 222), the image of Neddy reminds his elegist of "the devil" but also seems "godly" (*CPr* 228, 230).

Moreover, Neddy has taken the place of the barely remembered and forcefully repressed mother as well. Bishop's story based on her mother's removal, "In the Village," is studiously unemotive (*CPr* 251–74). In 1934 Bishop reported her mother's death to an acquaintance in a tone of chilling and evasive approval: "I guess I should tell you that Mother died a week ago today. After eighteen years, of course, it is the happiest thing that could have happened" (*One Art* 24). Because Bishop suppresses her anger and sadness at her mother's disappearance, forced institutionalization, and death, those feelings tend to leak metonymically into associated affectional objects such as domestic workers and the mother's brother. Uncle Neddy's portrait "looks rather more like his sisters than like Uncle Neddy," whereas a portrait of his sister, the narrator's mother, "looks almost more like a boy" than does the one of Neddy (*CPr* 230, 233). In another of Bishop's transvestite twists, uncle and mother seem to have exchanged hats in the story's psychic economy. The narrator's unrecognized and contradictory feelings toward her mother and father hold her tight in their grip. She is "very fond of" and even "loves" her uncle, the "black shadow" that occupies their space and screens their memory; yet he also represents "the devil" to her—the cause of all her woe

(228).

The African motif culminates in the narrative's climax: a traumatic "black Christmas" that screens primal scenes of paternal and maternal abandonment and that prefigures abandonments to come (*CPr* 243–44).

> ...Laid out under the tree, even by flickering candlelight, everything looked shapeless and sad, and I wanted to cry. And then Santa Claus came in, an ordinary brown potato sack over his shoulder, with the other presents sagging in it. He was terrifying. *He couldn't have been dressed in black, but that was my impression, and I did start to cry.* He had artificial snow sprinkled on his shoulders, and a pointed red cap, but the beard! It wasn't white and woolly at all, it was made of rope, a mass of frayed-out rope. This dreadful figure cavorted around the room, making jokes in a loud, deep, false voice. *The face that showed above the rope beard looked, to me, like a Negro's. I shrieked. Then this Santa from the depths of a coal mine put down his sack that could have been filled with coal, and hugged and kissed me.* Through my sobs, I recognized, by touch and smell and his suddenly everyday voice, that it was only Uncle Neddy. (244, emphasis mine)

In this scene the child's dread is insistently associated with a trope of Africanness. It is not surprising that an unsophisticated family in rural, early twentieth-century Nova Scotia might concoct a fantasy figure of an African as an uncanny and terrifying image. If a black man was, for them, merely a character produced by written and oral discourse, a figural "boogey man," the child might easily access that stock image in her moment of estrangement and fright.[2] What *is* surprising is that the sophisticated narrator-author should put no space between her past and present subject positions. She recuperates the child's racist epistemology without a trace of irony. Bishop cannot provide an ironic perspective because she has achieved no distance from the contradictory and deep-seated feelings the story evokes. Her narrative cannot reconcile the vocabulary of fear underpinning this scene with the vocabulary of affection that elsewhere in the story associates blackness with gentleness, kindness, and creativity. For example, Neddy is a man who was "kind to us, to any children,...always" (248). Moreover, he is a tinsmith who works "like a black snail" (238), providing his niece with an image of the sort of painstaking artist she herself would become.

The mixed feelings Bishop evinces toward Black images—fear and comfort, alienation and love—reflect not only the bias of her culture but also, passing through that bias, her mixed feelings toward her parents and toward herself in so far as she has absorbed those ambivalently loved objects into her subject. Perhaps she would not have had to involve images of racial and class others in her psychological drama if she could have confronted her feelings more directly, if she could have adequately mourned her losses. But Bishop was a person who, as Frank Bidart tells us, believed in "closets" (Fountain 327). She spoke by indirection, even, or especially, to herself. As the narrator states toward the end of "Memories of Uncle Neddy": "Although there are more, these are all the memories I want to keep on remembering" (*CPr* 249). Bishop can tolerate such "memories" only because they are shaped by her strategies—useful to her in the short run but ultimately problematic—of deflecting grief onto others, transforming it with humor, and associating it with people of color.

Bishop employed the African trope one last time, in her great poem of 1970, "In the Waiting Room." Here Bishop attempts to close the gap between her narrator's subject position and that of the Africans (and Latin Americans) who so frequently bore the burden of her fantasies. The poem's protagonist, "Elizabeth," who both is and is not the young Bishop herself, waits for her aunt in a dentist's waiting room and undergoes a momentary psychic osmosis not only with her (fictional) "Aunt Consuelo" but also with images of African women seen in a (fabricated) issue of *National Geographic*. The passage is about as famous as any in late twentieth-century American poetry:

> My aunt was inside
> what seemed like a long time
> and while I waited I read
> the *National Geographic*
> (I could read) and carefully
> studied the photographs:
> the inside of a volcano,
> black, and full of ashes;
> then it was spilling over
> in rivulets of fire.
> Osa and Martin Johnson
> dressed in riding breeches,
> laced boots, and pith helmets.
> A dead man slung on a pole
> —"Long Pig," the caption said.
> Babies with pointed heads
> wound round and round with string;
> black, naked women with necks
> wound round and round with wire
> like the necks of light bulbs.
> Their breasts were horrifying.
> I read it right straight through.

I was too shy to stop.
And then I looked at the cover:
the yellow margins, the date.

Suddenly, from inside,
came an *oh!* of pain
—Aunt Consuelo's voice—
not very loud or long.
I wasn't at all surprised;
even then I knew she was
a foolish, timid woman.
I might have been embarrassed,
but wasn't. What took me
completely by surprise
was that it was *me*:
my voice, in my mouth.
Without thinking at all
I was my foolish aunt,
I—we—were falling, falling.... (*CP* 159–60)

This is an order of racial representation far more complex than that in "Cootchie" or "Songs for a Colored Singer." The Latin American woman (predictably named "Consuelo" or "Comfort" but unexpectedly identified as an aunt rather than a servant) and the nameless African women are not simply recuperated as stereotypes but involved with the self, whose ego boundaries have dissolved. Stephen Greenblatt, a notably astute reader, has cited the verses about the African women as a convincing representation of human commonality (120). According to this reading, the narrator recognizes herself, across racial lines, in the Africans; she recognizes a bond with them as women in patriarchal societies and as human beings in an often horrific world. Yet we must consider that this recognition is at the same time a *méconnaissance*. A white, middle-class girl in Worcester, Massachusetts, she remains radically unlike them. The ideology of universalism disguises a world of difference—in history, geography, customs, wealth, social organization, opportunities, and values. Erasing distinctions, universalism keeps inequities of race, class, and nation hidden from sight, and therefore exempted from change. As Roland Barthes once wrote, critiquing the *Family of Man* photographic exhibit, the myth of human community holds us at the surface of identity, "prevented by sentimentality" from penetrating into the "ulterior zone of human behavior where historical alienation introduces some 'differences' which we shall here quite simply call 'injustices'" (101). Moreover, the perspective of Bishop's narrator seems coincident with that of the magazine she is reading. Just as the *National Geographic* frames the foreign other as exotic and erotic, an image to be consumed, a spectacle for the North American gaze, so "Elizabeth" finds the photographed women to be fascinatingly grotesque: "naked women" with necks like those of "light bulbs" (*CP* 159). At the same time, they are objects ready to fall into the subject, fodder for the viewer's contemplation of that most favored of North American topics, the self. The look at Africanness becomes a study of self-objects. "Elizabeth" tells herself "you are one of *them*" (160)—referring to the women in the *National Geographic* as well as to her Latina aunt and the people in the waiting room. The narrator's need to see herself, her aunt, the African women, and the dentist's patients as "all just one" (161) may be shaped by the object relations that haunt her past, a triad just barely discernible in the photos from Africa: a dead man slung on a pole, a mother with horrifying breasts, and between them a child with a pointed head and a difficult future. "In the Waiting Room" concludes its hallucinatory vision of merged selves by returning to the world of boundary and historicity. Now "Elizabeth" exists once again as simply a lonely "I," the longed-for and feared oneness replaced by the familiar world of places and times, distinct subjects, and nations at war.

Was Bishop a racist? Probably no more so, and perhaps even less so, than most white-identified Europeans and North Americans of her time. Her early racial representations characteristically combined stereotype and distance with identification. I believe that though Bishop was insufficiently self-critical, she *meant* to display tolerance and kindness. I also believe that her representations of racial alterity reflected the personal suffering that never left her. She tried to make her pain manageable by associating her lost parents, the most crucial others in her life, with racial, class, and national others. Unable to mourn openly, she mourned her losses indirectly in "Cootchie" and "Songs for a Colored Singer." She then constructed more resonant figures of sorrow and fright in the African (and Latin American) figures who improbably inhabit the childhood recollections of "Memories of Uncle Neddy" and "In the Waiting Room." These late figures of social otherness, akin to her depilated "Pink Dog," evoke a powerful complex of psychological and cultural recognitions: desire and dread, marginality and oppression, gentleness and creativity. Moreover, "In the Waiting Room," completed in the last decade of her life, envisions a new sort of closeness or empathy. The poem at least attempts to extricate its author and readers from ubiquitous cultural bias. If, to achieve that end, it tends to universalize (and thereby to essentialize and immobilize), it also exhibits a countervailing desire to historicize and particularize. As Bishop's narrator asks at the end of her meditation: "How had I come to be here, / like them...?" (*CP* 161).

Endnotes

1. I am grateful to Rise B. Axelrod, Jennifer Brody, and Laura J. Menides for helpfully critiquing drafts of this essay.

2. Bishop once said in the embarrassed presence of Gwendolyn Brooks that as a child she had smeared burnt cork or coal on her own face and played in blackface (Fountain and Brazeau 315). In a similar vein, the narrator of "Memories of Uncle Neddy" tells of enjoying a record entitled "Cohen on the Telephone": "I . . . laughed, although I hadn't any idea who or what a Cohen was or what I was laughing at" (*CPr* 246). Stereotypes of African and Jew were constructed for her by the ideological matrix of the dominant culture without the noise produced by actual experience.

Works Cited

Armour, Jody David. *Negrophobia and Reasonable Racism: The Hidden Costs of Being Black in America*. New York: New York UP, 1997.

Barthes, Roland. *Mythologies*. 1957. Trans. Annette Lavers. New York: Hill and Wang, 1972.

Bishop, Elizabeth. *The Collected Prose*. Ed. Robert Giroux. New York: Farrar, Straus, Giroux, 1984.

———. *The Complete Poems 1927–1979*. New York: Farrar, Straus, Giroux, 1983.

———. *One Art: Letters*. Ed. Robert Giroux. New York: Farrar, Straus, Giroux, 1994.

Fountain, Gary and Peter Brazeau. *Elizabeth Bishop: An Oral Biography*. Amherst: U Massachusetts P, 1994.

Freud, Sigmund. "Beyond the Pleasure Principle." 1920. Trans. James Strachey. *Standard Edition*. Vol. 18. London: Hogarth, 1955. 7–64.

———. "A Seventeenth-Century Demonological Neurosis." 1923. Trans. James Strachey. *Standard Edition*. Vol. 19. London: Hogarth, 1961. 72–105.

Greenblatt, Stephen. "Kindly Visions." *The New Yorker* 69.33 (Oct. 11, 1993): 112–120.

Hughes, Langston. *The Collected Poems*. Ed. Arnold Rampersad and David Roessel. New York: Knopf, 1995.

Millier, Brett C. *Elizabeth Bishop: Life and the Memory of It*. Berkeley: U California P, 1993.

Morrison, Toni. *Playing in the Dark: Whiteness and the Literary Imagination*. Cambridge: Harvard UP, 1992.

Newfield, Christopher. *The Emerson Effect: Individualism and Submission in America*. Chicago: U Chicago P, 1996.

O' Hara, Frank. *The Collected Poems*. Ed. Donald Allen. Berkeley: U California P, 1995.

Plath, Sylvia. *The Collected Poems*. Ed. Ted Hughes. New York: Harper & Row, 1981.

Stuckey, Sterling. *Going Through the Storm: The Influence of African American Art in History*. New York: Oxford UP, 1994.

Sundquist, Eric. J. *To Wake the Nations: Race in the Making of American Literature*. Cambridge: Harvard UP, 1993.

Contributors

DON ADAMS is Assistant Professor of English at Florida Atlantic University. His monograph, *James Merrill's Poetic Quest*, was published in 1997 by Greenwood Press.

STEVEN GOULD AXELROD is Professor of English at the University of California/ Riverside. He is the author of *Robert Lowell: Life and Art* (Princeton 1979) and *Sylvia Plath: The Wound and the Cure of Words* (Johns Hopkins 1990), both of which discuss Elizabeth Bishop. His current scholarship focuses on "the poetics of domesticity."

CRYSTAL BACON is an Associate Professor of Communication at Gloucester County College in New Jersey. Her scholarship on Bishop began during her studies for the MFA at the Warren Wilson Program for Writers. Her poems have appeared in a number of publications, and she was awarded a New Jersey Council for the Arts Fellowship for 1998.

SANDRA BARRY, an independent scholar and poet, lives in Halifax, Nova Scotia. Her book, *Elizabeth Bishop: An Archival Guide to Elizabeth Bishop's Life in Nova Scotia,* was published in 1996.

NEIL BESNER is Chair of the English Department at the University of Winnipeg. His major research interests are in Canadian literature and Latin American fiction. He is especially interested in Bishop's Brazilian work. His review of Carmen Oliveira's biography of Lota de Macedo Soares and Bishop appeared in *The Elizabeth Bishop Bulletin* (Summer 1997).

JOELLE BIELE is a Fulbright Senior Scholar, teaching American Literature at the University of Oldenburg, Germany. She received her Ph.D. from the University of Maryland/ College Park.

BARBARA COMINS, Assistant Professor of English at City University of New York, was formerly a professional cellist. In addition to a B.A. and M.A. in Music, she holds two M.A.s plus a doctorate in English, which was funded by a CUNY Graduate Center superfellowship and an NEH award. She has published articles in *The Wallace Stevens Journal, The Poetry Calendar,* and *The Edith Wharton Review.*

HARRIET Y. COOPER has taught at New York University, where she received her Ph.D. (1993), and at the New School for Social Research. Earlier, she worked in public relations at the Metropolitan Museum of Art and in research for LOOK magazine. She is writing a book on D. H. Lawrence and Italy.

ROBERT CORDING is Professor of English and Poet-in-Residence at the College of the Holy Cross. In 1992, he was Poet-in-Residence at The Frost Place in Franconia, NH. In addition to articles about and reviews of contemporary poetry, he has published three collections of poems: *Life-list,* which won the Ohio State UP/Journal Award (1987); *What Binds Us To This World* (1991); and *Heavy Grace* (1996).

RENEE R. CURRY is Program Director of the Literature and Writing Program at California State University/San Marcos. She has been writing about Elizabeth Bishop since 1984, and her most recent book, *White Women Writing White: H.D., Elizabeth Bishop, and Sylvia Plath*, is forthcoming from Greenwood Press.

GAIL H. DAYTON is a Doctor of Arts student and a teacher at Middle Tennessee State University. She has published in *The Distillery: Artistic Spirits of the South* and was awarded the William R. Wolfe Graduate Writing Award in 1996 and 1998. Her research on Bishop's literary application of time and memory elements is the primary focus of her dissertation.

JOAN L. FIELDS is in the Department of English/Humanities at the University of Southwestern Louisiana. She has presented and published papers on Renaissance literature, Modernist and Post-Modernist Poetics, ESOL, and composition theory. Her encounters with a mix of African-American, Cajun, and international students promoted her analysis of tonalities in printed text. Elizabeth Bishop's poems and prose offer fascinating illustrations of aural imagery as figurative communication.

LEE FONTANELLA is Head of the Humanities and Arts Department at WPI. He is trained in Hispanic literature and for most of his career taught in, then chaired, the Spanish and Portuguese Department at the University of Texas/Austin. He has written a number of books in the fields of Hispanic and comparative literature and in the history of photography, and has curated museum shows for the Spanish government.

GARY FOUNTAIN teaches at Ithaca College. He is the author of *Remembering Elizabeth Bishop: An Oral Biography* and is currently completing a biography of the writer, cultural critic, and authority on Haiti, Selden Rodman.

LORRIE GOLDENSOHN, poet and critic, teaches at Vassar. She is the author of *Elizabeth Bishop: The Biography of a Poetry,* which was nominated for a Pulitzer Prize in 1992. She has completed a collection of poems entitled *Seven Bullets* and is working on a book about twentieth century war literature.

AUDREY E. HOOKER teaches American and British literature at the Mercersburg Academy in Mercersburg, PA. Her interest in Elizabeth Bishop began during her graduate work at Wake Forest University. She has pursued research into Bishop's published and unpublished correspondence and its relevance to her poetry.

KIRSTEN HOTELLING is an Assistant Professor of Modern Poetry and Poetics at Illinois State University. She has published articles on Marianne Moore and May Swenson, and is completing a book on the feminist poetics of Moore, Swenson, and Bishop.

MARIA LÚCIA MILLÉO MARTINS is Professor of English at Universidade Federal de Santa Catarina, Brazil. She wrote her M.A. thesis on Elizabeth Bishop and is currently finishing her doctoral dissertation on Elizabeth Bishop and Carlos Drummond de Andrade at the University of Massachusetts. As translator, she published in Brazil *Antologia de Poesia Norte Americana Contemporanea.* She was twice awarded Fulbright Scholarships.

M. SHEILA MCAVEY is Professor of English at Becker College. Her research interests encompass the reflection of women's lives in literature from medieval to contemporary periods. The study of Elizabeth Bishop's life and work is part of that larger endeavor.

JAMES MCCORKLE is a poet whose work is included in several editions of *The Best American Poetry* and who has received fellowships in poetry from the Ingram Merrill Foundation and the National Endowment for the Arts. He is also the author of a study of recent American poetry, *The Still Performance,* and the editor of *Conversant Essays: Contemporary Poets on Poetry.*

HELEN MCNEIL teaches at the University of East Anglia, England. She is the author of *Emily Dickinson* (Virago and Pantheon 1986) and of "Elizabeth Bishop" in *Voices and Visions: The Poet in America*, Helen Vendler, ed. (Random House 1987).

CAROL E. MILLER is Visiting Assistant Professor of English Language and Literature at Benedictine University She was awarded the Tinsley Helton dissertation fellowship at the University of Wisconsin/Milwaukee, and her critical work on Bishop includes "Toward an Alternative Formal Tradition," forthcoming in *After New Formalism* (Story Line Press).

MARGARET MITSUTANI has translated the works of Kyoko Hayashi, Kenzaburo Oe, and Yoko Tawada into English and has published an article in Japanese on Bishop's prose poems. She has a B.A. from the College of Wooster (Ohio) and a Master's in Comparative Literature from Tokyo University.

GEORGE MONTEIRO is Professor of English and of Portuguese and Brazilian Studies at Brown University. His recent publications include *The Presence of Camoes* (UP of Kentucky 1996), *Conversations With Elizabeth Bishop* (UP of Mississippi 1996), and *The Presence of Pessoa* (UP of Kentucky 1998). *The Blue Badge of Stephen Crane* is forthcoming from Louisiana State UP.

MICHIRU OGUCHI is an editor at Iwanami Shoten Publishers, Tokyo, where she is working on a Dictionary of Philosophy. She calls herself "a common reader abroad," pursuing Bishop's poems and places since 1989. Her travel letters on Great Village appeared in the *Elizabeth Bishop Society of Nova Scotia Newsletter* (Fall 1995). She was an AFS student in Vermont and has an M.A. in French Literature from Tokyo University.

CARMEN L. OLIVEIRA is a Brazilian writer and scholar. She is the author of *Flores Raras e Banalissimas [Rare and Commonplace Flowers]* (1995), a biographical account of Elizabeth Bishop's life with Lota de Macedo Soares in Brazil.

EDEN OSUCHA is a graduate student at the University of California/Davis. In addition to Elizabeth Bishop and her contemporaries, Osucha's interests include Modernism, queer theoretical praxis, Roland Barthes, narratives of AIDS and other illnesses, and representations of the body. She has also been politically and professionally active in the movement to end sexual violence.

BARBARA PAGE is Professor of English and Associate Dean of the Faculty at Vassar College. Her essays about Bishop include: "Shifting Islands: Elizabeth Bishop's Manuscripts" (*Shenandoah*); "Nature, History, and Art in Elizabeth Bishop's 'Brazil, January 1, 1502'" (*Perspectives on Contemporary Literature 14*); "Off-Beat Claves, Oblique Realities: The Key West Notebooks of Elizabeth Bishop" (in *Elizabeth Bishop: The Geography of Gender*), and "Elizabeth Bishop and Postmodernism" (*The Wallace Stevens Journal*).

MARIA CLARA BONETTI PARO is Assistant Professor of American Literature and Chair of the Department of Modern Languages at the Universidade Estadual Paulista/Araraquara Campus, Sao Paulo. She has conducted an exhaustive study of Walt Whitman's reception in Brazil and has published numerous essays on Brazilian and American literature. At this time, she is doing research on Bishop's portrayal of Brazil.

CAMILLE ROMAN is an Assistant Professor at Washington State University and a visiting scholar at Brown University for the year 1998-1999. She is a member of the Advisory Board of the Elizabeth Bishop Society and has written reviews for *The Elizabeth Bishop Bulletin*. Her essay is part of a completed book manuscript entitled *Elizabeth Bishop and the Cold War.*

LLOYD SCHWARTZ teaches at the University of Massachusetts/Boston. He is the award-winning classical music editor of *The Boston Phoenix* and a regular commentator on NPR's *Fresh Air*, as well as co-editor, with Sybil P. Estess, of *Elizabeth Bishop and Her Art.* His latest book of poetry is *Goodnight, Gracie.*

STANLEY SULTAN is Professor of English at Clark University. An author of fiction as well as a critic, he has published short stories, a novel, and essays about Renaissance drama. Most of his work, however, has been on Modernism, major modernist writers, and literary theory, including theory of literary history. His most recent book is *Eliot, Joyce and Company* (1987). *Joyce's Becoming*, a philological biography, is nearing completion.

DAVID THOREEN teaches creative writing and literature at Assumption College. His work has appeared in *American Literary Review, Mid-American Review, Pynchon Notes, Hemingway Review,* and *Worcester Review.* Related essays on Thomas Pynchon are forthcoming from the *Oklahoma City University Law Review* and *ANQ.*

THOMAS TRAVISANO is Professor of English at Hartwick College, president of the Elizabeth Bishop Society, and former editor of *The Elizabeth Bishop Bulletin.* He is the author of *Elizabeth Bishop: Her Artistic Development* (1988) and co-editor of *Gendered Modernisms: American Women Poets and Their Readers* (1996). His *Exploring Lost Worlds: Lowell, Jarrell, Bishop, Berryman* is forthcoming.

Menides and Dorenkamp at Elizabeth Bishop's gravesite, Hope Cemetery, Worcester, Massachusetts.
WPI photo by Neil Norum.

Laura Jehn Menides, Associate Professor of English at Worcester Polytechnic Institute, writes poetry, fiction, and opera lyrics, as well as literary criticism on Elizabeth Bishop and other contemporary authors. Her work on Bishop includes "Elizabeth Bishop's Worcester Connections" in *The Worcester Review* (1997) and the forthcoming *Elizabeth Bishop Revisited.*

Angela G. Dorenkamp, Professor Emerita of English and Women's Studies at Assumption College, worked with an interdisciplinary team under an NEH grant to produce *Images of Women in American Popular Culture,* now in its second edition. She has also served as national President of the College English Association and as Chair of the Massachusetts Foundation for Humanities.

Menides and Dorenkamp were Co-chairs of the 1997 Elizabeth Bishop Conference held in Worcester at Worcester Polytechnic Institute.

WPI Studies

WPI Studies is sponsored by Worcester Polytechnic Institute, the nation's third oldest independent technological university. WPI Studies aims to publish monographs, edited collections of essays, and research tools and texts of interest to scholarly audiences. WPI Studies accepts manuscripts in all languages, and is especially interested in reviewing potential publications on interdisciplinary topics relating science, technology, and culture. WPI Studies is edited by a board of WPI faculty from many disciplines. The board is chaired by Lance Schachterle, Assistant Provost and Professor of English, to whom potential authors should direct their inquiries (WPI, Worcester, MA 01609).

To order other books in this series, please contact our Customer Service Department at:

800-770-LANG (within the U.S.)
212-647-7706 (outside the U.S.)
212-647-7707 FAX

or browse online by series at:

www.peterlang.com